ALL THE NEWS

Writing and Reporting for Convergent Media

Thom Lieb

Towson University

PEARSON

Boston • New York • San Francisco

Mexico City • Montreal • Toronto • London • Madrid • Munich • Paris

Hong Kong • Singapore • Tokyo • Cape Town • Sydney

Acquisitions Editor: Jeanne Zalesky	*Composition Buyer:* Linda Cox
Associate Editor: Jennifer DeMambro	*Manufacturing Buyer:* JoAnne Sweeney
Editorial Assistant: Brian Michelson	*Electronic Composition:* NK Graphics
Marketing Manager: Suzan Czajkowski	*Interior Design:* Carol Somberg
Production Editor: Pat Torelli	*Cover Administrator:* Linda Knowles
Editorial Production Service: NK Graphics/Black Dot Group	*Cover Designer:* Kristina Mose-Libon

For related titles and support materials, visit our online catalog at www.ablongman.com

Copyright © 2009 Pearson Education, Inc.

Between the time Web site information is gathered and then published, it is not unusual for some sites to have closed. Also, the transcription of URLs can result in typographical errors. The publisher would appreciate notification where these errors occur so that they may be corrected in subsequent editions.

ISBN-13: 978-0-13-134505-8   ISBN-10: 0-13-134505-2

Library of Congress Cataloging-in-Publication Data

Lieb, Thom.
  All the news : writing and reporting for convergent media / Thom Lieb. — 1st ed.
    p. cm.
  Includes index.
  ISBN 0-13-134505-2
  1. Journalism — Authorship. I Title.
  PN4775.L455 2008
  808'.06607 — dc22

                                                              2008001812

Printed in the United States of America
10 9 8 7 6 5 4 3 2 1   12 11 10 09 08

Credits appear on page 338, which constitutes an extension of the copyright page.

Contents

Chapter **9**

Writing the Advanced Audio Story 161

Chapter **10**

Writing the Basic Video Story 179

Chapter **14**

Journalistic Principles 251

Chapter **15**

Legal Issues and Journalistic Ethics 267

Chapter **16**

Writing in a Diverse Environment 293

Appendix **A**

Print and Online Writing Style 308

Appendix **B**

Broadcast News Style 322

Appendix **C**

Associated Press Style 327

Preface

As the field of journalism continues to change at an unprecedented pace, those preparing to enter the profession must be able handle a wide range of challenges:

- Writing for a variety of media.
- Mastering the mechanics of precise communication.
- Working in an environment in which audience members function as reporters and news commentators.
- Being able to find and focus story ideas for a specific audience.
- Conducting effective research.
- Understanding the principles of responsible journalism.
- Confronting pressures that lead to ethical lapses.
- Covering an increasingly diverse population.

These challenges are initially and most critically confronted in the first media writing course. Many textbooks have tried to address some of these issues but rarely in a cohesive, integrated manner. "All the News: Writing and Reporting for Convergent Media" is the first text to take a fresh look at news writing in the age of convergence and offer the tools the instructor and journalism student need to succeed in this new environment.

Writing for a Variety of Media

At its core, "All the News" focuses on the most important aspect of the basic journalism course: **writing**. This text is designed to prepare students to write for all the major media: print, online, radio and television. Gil Thelen, president and publisher of the "Tampa Tribune" — one of the players in the multimedia Tampa News Center — stresses the importance of convergence training for journalism students: "Journalism schools must produce graduates who are willing and able to acquire new skills in the workplace. A thorough grounding in the differences in writing for print, online and broadcast would be a good start in school."[1]

In nine chapters (Chapters 4 through 12), students learn how to tell stories with text, audio, video and online elements. "All the News" provides the depth of traditional print-focused textbooks, but it adds the breadth of broadcast journalism and online journalism texts, too.

The book's structure makes it compatible with a wide range of curricula:

- One basic media writing course.
- Beginning and advanced media writing courses.
- Separate print/online and broadcast courses offered concurrently or consecutively.

Students write from the start. Each chapter includes several **Assignment Desk** exercises, most of which allow students to apply the principles of the chapter in a variety of writing exercises. Rather than hiding the exercises at the end of each chapter, they will be placed within each chapter to engage students as they are reading.

Mastering the Mechanics of Precise Communication

To help students get up to speed quickly, "All the News" offers an appendix focusing on print and online writing style, another that focuses on broadcast writing style, and a third that covers the basics of Associated Press style.

● **Working in an Environment in Which Audience Members Function as Reporters and News Commentators**

"All the News" makes it clear that news has become a conversation with the audience. This point is discussed at appropriate places throughout the book, and students are trained in writing for new formats, such as blogs, which engage audience members.

● **Being Able to Find and Focus Story Ideas for a Specific Audience**

Many beginning journalism students struggle to develop even a single good story idea of their own. Chapter 2 opens a conversation about finding story ideas with a focus on determining what's news. Chapter 3 continues the discussion by offering suggestions for developing ideas. To help students see the matters in practical terms, that chapter includes a sidebar on finding ideas at every turn of daily life.

● **Conducting Effective Research**

Chapter 3 discusses the pros and cons of using Google and other search engines and leads students to other sources of information. The focus of the chapter is primarily on gathering information through interviews, with sections offering advice on conducting interviews in person and via phone, e-mail and instant messaging.

● **Understanding the Principles of Responsible Journalism**

Chapters 14 and 15 offer a fresh approach to the topic of responsible journalism. Chapter 14 begins the discussion with a look at the widespread public and industry dissatisfaction with traditional objective journalism and proposes a new model of producing high-quality journalism that serves the public. Chapter 15 addresses major principles of relevant media law.

● **Confronting Pressures That Lead to Ethical Lapses**

As part of the discussion in Chapter 15, major ethical issues are addressed. The emphasis is on problems that crop up repeatedly in journalism: fabrication and plagiarism, conflicts of interest, advertiser pressure, and so on.

● **Covering an Increasingly Diverse Population**

The importance of this issue is emphasized by making it the topic of the final chapter. Chapter 16 includes not only a discussion of diversity issues in the news but also provides pointers to help students find nontraditional sources.

ANCILLARY MATERIALS: THE BLOG

A companion blog at http://21stcenturynews.blogspot.com/ will offer regular updates to the text, links to news stories of interest to news writing instructors and students, and more.

NOTES

1. Gil Thelen, "Debate: Convergence," Journalism Studies, vol. 4, no. 4, 2003, p. 515.

Acknowledgments

The old saying is wrong: Writing is decidedly *not* a solitary pursuit. Especially on a project of the magnitude of this one, it's far more a communal effort.

Any attempt to thank all those who helped me with this book would take many pages and doubtlessly omit some key people. So I'll start with a heartfelt thanks to everyone who made even a tiny contribution to the effort.

Before I get to thanking individuals, I'd like to collectively offer my gratitude to the many professionals who took the time to write the "Why Choose Journalism?" pieces. I have found them all entertaining and inspiring, and I trust my readers will, too.

In addition, I'd like to thank all those who granted permission to use text passages, scripts, screenshots and other items. Your materials have gone a long way in helping me show my readers the many dimensions of good journalism in the age of convergence.

My colleagues at Towson University deserve a special thanks. Freelance television journalist and lecturer Jenny Atwater has helped in many, many ways, reviewing chapters, sharing exercises, writing scripts and answering far too many times my "one last question." In working with me on developing our new curriculum, Beth Haller was invaluable in creating sample syllabi for use with this text. Kim Lauffer, Sandy Nichols and John Turner also all provided great assistance in reviewing materials, helping me locate resources and much more.

Other academic colleagues also are due big thanks. Elliot King of Loyola College in Maryland provided the initial impetus for the book. Dana Chinn of the USC Annenberg School of Journalism spent a good deal of time educating me about convergence and how it can be structured in the curriculum. Rebecca Leung of SUNY New Paltz and Danna L. Walker of American University provided feedback on chapters and answered lots of pesky questions. Mindy McAdams of the University of Florida helped me find the right people to grant clearances for the use of several examples in the book. Finally, Tom Petner of Temple University proved to be a great resource for tracking down just the right person on many occasions.

A wide range of professionals also helped immensely. I'll start with four who were once my students. Katie Arcieri of the Annapolis Capital was invaluable in helping me round up examples of a variety of stories. Freelance writer and editor Yvonne Simmeth Feeley offered great feedback on several chapters. Freelance writer Beth Gavaghan recorded a range of newscasts from our hometown. And Maria Stuart of the Livingston County (Mich.) Daily Press & Argus provided invaluable advice on several chapters and also supplied recordings of newscasts.

A group of great people from the Hearst Corp. helped me track down material for the book. They include Fred Young, senior vice president for news of Hearst-Argyle Television Inc.; Michael Gay, executive producer of digital content; Mark Miller, news director of WBAL Radio; and Jonathan Killian, creative services director of WBAL-TV.

Robin Mazyck of the Christian Broadcast Network provided many sample scripts and offered invaluable feedback on several chapters.

As he has been in the past, Vince Rinehart, editorial copy desk chief of the Washington Post, proved to be a great friend and an invaluable resource. Vince reviewed several chapters, offering great feedback, put me in touch with countless journalists and did a host of other favors large and small. In one way or another, his imprint is on nearly every chapter of this book.

Two longtime friends, Meg Bothwell and Suzanne Bourdess, assisted in compiling video recordings of news from various locations. Another friend of many years, Doug Miller, provided help with graphics.

Mark Sullivan proved an invaluable aide in reviewing the manuscript to help select graphics, in the process catching many typos and style errors and raising many good questions.

Maureen O'Brien is perhaps due the biggest thanks for offering love, support and understanding over the nearly four years this project has taken.

On the publishing side, I would like to offer my thanks to all those who offered their services as reviewers for the book: Emmanuel C. Alozie, Governors State University; Jodi Amatulli, Quinnipiac University; Elizabeth Bookser Barkley, College of Mount St. Joseph; Susan Brockus, California State University – Chico; Barbara Bullington, East Carolina University; Richard A. D'Enrico, University of Albany; Maria B. Marron, Central Michigan University; Ellen B. Meacham, University of Mississippi; Michael L. Mercer, University of the Incarnate Word; Gary Mielo, Sussex County Community College; Kenneth D. Nordin, Benedictine University; Donna Pazdera, University of Texas – Pan American; Sonny Rhodes, University of the Incarnate Word; Julia Ruengert, Pensacola Junior College; Barbara Schlichtman, University of Hawaii at Hilo; Linda Steiner, University of Maryland, College Park; Linda Thorsen Bond, Stephen F. Austin State University; Samuel W. Whyte, Montgomery County Community College.

My initial editor, Deirdre Anderson, deserves thanks for believing that the time was right for a book such as this. Karon Bowers did a great job of picking up the project in midstream and seeing it through to completion. Jeanne Zalesky, acquisitions editor, and Jenny Lupica, my development editor, helped keep things moving in the race to deadline, offering quick responses to many queries. Robert Tonner, copyright and permissions manager, and Annie Pickert, visual researcher, also merit special thanks.

Chapter 1

News in the Age of Convergence

When Katherine Smith joined the staff of the Tampa Tribune, she had no idea what she was getting into.

"All I knew was print," she recalls. But within a few years, she found herself providing sports coverage to TBO.com, the Tribune's online arm, writing breaking news e-mail alerts, blogging and sitting in front of the cameras of sister television station News Channel 8.

"It took some getting used to being in front of a camera," Smith recalls. "I'm sure we could have some big 'blooper reels.'"

Even with those bloopers, after a decade of dealing with the challenges of working in one of the most convergent news environments around, Smith wouldn't trade her experience.

"This is the way things are going," she says. "Our job is to get the news out, and we reach such a mass audience in this way. It's impressive to know that you are the main source of news for so many people."

Although the Tampa Tribune/TBO.com/News Channel 8 experiment was one of the first to cross media boundaries, it is far from the only one. The changes there reflect a major shift in how journalists work. While smaller news operations made the first steps in that shift, now even the largest media companies have followed their examples:

- CBS News has expanded CBSNews.com into "a 24-hour, multi-platform digital news network" designed to bypass cable. Among the site's features are broadcasts of "CBS Evening News"; countless streaming videos, including raw feeds of events, such as presidential speeches; and a dozen regularly updated audio programs that users can download onto their computers or MP3 players.[1]
- The New York Times, USA Today, The Wall Street Journal and the Los Angeles Times have merged the news staffs of their print and online newsrooms.[2] The editor of the Los Angeles Times announced that the paper's Web site would become the primary focus for breaking and presenting news.[3] Arthur Sulzberger,

chairman of The New York Times, told those attending a conference in 2007: "I really don't know whether we'll be printing the Times in five years, and you know what? I don't care, either."[4]

- Gannett, the parent company of USA Today, began converting the newsrooms of its 89 other U.S. daily newspapers into "Information Centers." In a memo to employees, the chief executive officer of the company explained that the focus of these centers was to be "gathering the information our readers and viewers want using words, images and video and distributing it across multiple platforms: the daily newspaper, online, mobile, non-daily publications and any other media possible to meet our readers' needs." In addition, the CEO noted, "We are also embracing community interactivity in our sites with increased involvement."[5]

- The Wilmington (Del.) News Journal began producing twice-daily news broadcasts, offering Wilmington residents their own newscasts for the first time ever. The News Journal further blurred the lines by offering the programs solely on its Web site.[6]

- The Washington Post's online division—washingtonpost.com—won the first Emmy award ever given for "outstanding achievement in content for non-traditional delivery platforms." (Along with The New York Times Online, washingtonpost.com managed to grab five of the seven nominees for the video award).[7]

- Hearst-Argyle signed an agreement with YouTube to distribute local television news, weather and entertainment produced by its local television stations.[8]

- ESPN started to offer sports fans news, scores, stats, headlines and video coverage of the day's most exciting highlights and their favorite ESPN shows—all delivered via cell phone.

In short, the traditional lines separating newspapers, broadcast stations and Web sites are blurring at a rapid pace, and content increasingly is showing up on new delivery platforms. Media **convergence**—the blending of the media—has become a fact of life in the 21st century, and journalism will never be the same.

What's Driving Convergence?

Although the rise of convergent journalism strikes most people as a new phenomenon, it grows out of trends that in some cases date back decades. First and foremost is a shift in news consumption habits. Not long ago, people had limited choices of where they got their news: usually one or two daily newspapers, a handful of local radio stations, and two or three national networks. When cable came along—and with it the 24-hour news networks—the audience began moving away from the traditional outlets. The rise of the World Wide Web accelerated that change. Today, newspapers and network news programs draw only a fraction of the audiences they once did.

Along with this shift in media usage has come a shift in the public's expectation about news access. Weaned on 24/7 cable news and always-on Internet—and driven in no small part by the uncertainty of the world after the events of Sept. 11, 2001—more people feel the need to stay connected to the news and to be alerted to important stories as soon as they occur. Now even the newer news media have to pay attention: It's no longer enough for an online news site to be updated once a day or a cable news network to offer a fresh newscast every half hour. The audience of the 21st century expects immediate access to the news, anytime, anywhere. They want the latest e-mail alerts, Weblog posts, and audio and video feeds, all delivered automatically to their wireless laptops, cell phones, iPods and other devices.

Gil Thelen, president and publisher of the Tampa Tribune, acknowledges that these changes drove the Tampa convergence project:

> We had to catch up with our customers who are using multiple information sources throughout the day. They often wake up to a clock radio, scan a paper, listen to a morning TV show as they dress for work, tune to news radio in their cars, go online when they reach the workplace, listen to more radio on the way home, watch evening news, finish the paper, then read a magazine before bed.
>
> The implication for news organizations is inescapable. To dominate its marketplace, a company must supply news and information whenever, however and wherever customers desire.[9]

Key people at other news organizations around the globe have delivered much the same message. Tom Curley, president and CEO of The Associated Press, made a similar point in a speech to the Online News Association:

> [O]ur audience is clearly shifting—and changing.
>
> All those readers and viewers we've been losing to other media are being engaged as never before in this new media world.
>
> But there's a big difference now. The users are deciding what the point of their engagement will be—what application, what device, what time, what place.[10]

Dolph C. Simons Jr., editor and publisher of the Lawrence (Kan.) Journal-World, told The New York Times: "I don't think of us as being in the newspaper business. Information is our business and we're trying to provide information, in one form or another, however the consumer wants it and wherever the consumer wants it, in the most complete and useful way possible."[11]

NBC News president Steve Capus had much the same take on the changing environment. "We've been a TV business that dabbles in digital," he told the Washington Post. "Now, we're positioning as a news content-production center going forward that happens to do television."[12]

An additional factor behind the trend toward convergence is media consolidation. Media companies have become increasingly voracious in their appetite to buy media properties, often in the same market. Pressures to cut costs have led many companies to search for ways to use the same content across several platforms. In some cases, that has led to a push for reporters to gather content and produce stories for a variety of media. In other cases, partnerships between different media companies have created synergistic opportunities, with reporters regularly crossing from one media platform to another.

Another driving force behind convergence has been the spread of broadband Internet access, which has rapidly increased the use of multimedia. Web site visitors used to have to endure long waits to access online audio, video and slide shows. Today, widespread cable and DSL connections have made access to such content instantaneous. Now that they don't have to wait for multimedia, people want it. FoxNews.com, for example, saw the number of people who visited the broadband section of its Web site more than double in just three months after it added substantial video content.[13]

Audience Participation Marks Another Major Shift

Moving in tandem with the spread of convergence has been another major shift in the field of journalism: the rise of audience participation. Until recently, journalists gathered and presented the news, and for the most part the audience just read, listened and watched. With the availability of free or low-cost tools that allow virtually anyone to create and distribute multimedia reports, however, the audience has begun to expect that they should have a say in all news stories. As journalist and new media expert Dan Gillmor has put it, journalism has begun moving from a lecture to a conversation. After spending time studying three major newspapers' efforts to incorporate online news into their operations, sociologist Pablo J. Boczkowski found a marked change in how the audience factored in news decisions:

> Instead of being primarily journalist-centered, the news online appears increasingly to be also user-centered. In the online environment, users have a much greater direct effect on the news. . . .
>
> The news as conversation may be partly due to journalists' increased awareness of their audience's viewpoints. It may also be partly the result of the growing authorship of new media content by members of the public, housed both within traditional news sources such as online papers and nontraditional ones such as personal Weblogs.
>
> Whether or not some of this conversational content is considered "news" by currently working journalists, my research provides enough grounds to suggest that it may be becoming increasingly newsworthy to the audience of new-media news.[14]

Matt Drudge was one of the first people from outside the traditional journalistic establishment to attract serious attention, when his Drudge Report (www.drudgereport.com/) broke several major political stories, including the news of the relationship between President Bill Clinton and White House intern Monica Lewinsky. Drudge had no previous journalistic training or credentials—his prior work consisted mostly of odd jobs in the retail and food industries—but he quickly became widely read and highly paid.[15]

Following in his wake, a multitude of others also made names for themselves with online reporting and commentary on their **Weblogs**—or **blogs**—which allow anyone to instantly publish thoughts, reactions and other musings on an infinite range of topics,

FIGURE 1.1

Internet writer Matt Drudge speaks to the press outside the federal court in Washington after a hearing on a defamation suit against him by White House aide Sidney Blumenthal. *Source:* **Brian K. Diggs/AP Images**

events or Web sites. For example, Andrew Sullivan's blog "The Daily Dish" (www.andrewsullivan.com/), one of the most widely read and influential blogs, provides its readers with a unique perspective on politics, religion and other topics. Sullivan, who came to blogging after having served as editor of the New Republic, an influential magazine of political opinion, says blogs offer journalists—and anyone else who is interested—a new way to reach wide audiences while promoting audience interaction and debate.

Blogs first gained widespread public attention at the end of 2002, when bloggers of varying political leanings reacted to what they felt was a major story overlooked by the mainstream media: Sen. Trent Lott apparently longing for the days of segregation in a speech he gave at the 100th birthday celebration of Sen. Strom Thurmond. Startled by the inattention to the story—of all the major media outlets, only ABC News even mentioned it—the bloggers began a conversation that the mainstream media eventually joined in. In the end, the coverage led to pressure from the Republican Party for Lott to step down as Senate majority leader—the first person in his position ever to do so.[16]

Bloggers are but one component of what is often referred to as **citizen journalism** or **user-generated content**. That concept encompasses a wide range of people and purposes including:

- Members of the military and citizens of Iraq—including an Iraqi dentist who published Healing Iraq (http://healingiraq.blogspot.com/)—who have posted their accounts of life in post-Saddam Iraq;
- Residents of Santa Rosa, Calif., who have been asked to provide programming for local television station KFTY, which laid off most of its professional newsgathering staff;[17] and
- Contributors who supply photos and video footage—and full stories—to You Witness News (http://news.yahoo.com/you-witness-news), a collaboration between Yahoo and the Reuters News Pictures Service, and the competing NowPublic.com, a collaboration with the AP.

The work of bloggers and other citizen journalists has led to some notable successes. For example:

- Bloggers took a critical look at documents that Dan Rather of CBS News used to raise new questions about President George W. Bush's National Guard service. The public scrutiny prompted Rather and CBS to step back from their defense of the documents and ultimately led Rather to resign from CBS.
- Local residents helped the Fort Myers (Fla.) News-Press conduct research that led to the resignation of a local official and lower utility bills for local citizens.[18]
- Average citizens used cell phones to shoot still photos and video clips that provided some of the most compelling images from the London subway bombings, Hurricane Katrina and the Virginia Tech shootings—under conditions in which traditional journalists had limited access.

- Residents of and visitors to Southeast Asia posted reports and photos during the 2004 tsunami and set up sites such as The South-East Asia Earthquake and Tsunami Blog (http://tsunamihelp.blogspot.com/) to offer support for people trying to find missing friends and relatives and to list offers of help for the victims.

Not everyone is a fan of these new forms of journalism. "Content that is factual, reported, verified, placed in context and therefore credible is a sometime thing," notes Poynter Institute Media Business Analyst Rick Edmonds.[19] As but one example, the same Matt Drudge who broke the Clinton-Lewinsky story was later instrumental in spreading an unfounded rumor that presidential candidate John Kerry had had a two-year affair with a young journalist.[20] In another case, the Web site Truthout.org posted a baseless rumor that White House Deputy Chief of Staff Carl Rove had been indicted in a case involving the leak of a CIA operative's identity.[21]

Further, many observers haven't been won over by citizen journalism sites. Edmonds, for instance, believes that many citizen journalism sites barely qualify as journalism, with their combination of such lightweight fare as family vacation photos and stories bearing headlines such as "Another Pet Missing, Perhaps Stolen" and "New 'Harry Potter' Is Magnificent."[22] Nicholas Lemann of The New Yorker adds:

> The best original Internet journalism happens more often by accident, when smart and curious people with access to means of communication are at the scene of a sudden disaster. Any time that big news happens unexpectedly, or in remote and dangerous places, there is more raw information available right away on the Internet than through established news organizations. . . .
>
> Eyewitness accounts and information-sharing during sudden disasters are welcome, even if they don't provide a complete report of what is going on in a particular situation. And that is what citizen journalism is supposed to do: keep up with public affairs, especially locally, year in and year out, even when there's no disaster. . . . But when one reads it, after having been exposed to the buildup, it is nearly impossible not to think, This is what all the fuss is about?[23]

Nevertheless, there is concrete evidence that the public and media insiders agree that audience participation represents an important trend that is here to stay. A survey in early 2007, for example, found that a majority of Americans believed bloggers would be important to the future of journalism, and nearly three-fourths of those surveyed believed that citizen journalists also would play an important role.[24] And in a survey of newspaper editors, three-fourths of those responding "think that this evolving relationship with readers and users would be positive for journalistic quality."[25]

What These Changes Mean to the Journalist

In one sense, the spread of convergence and the rise of audience participation make no difference to the practice of professional journalism. The journalist's central job remains as always, "to provide citizens with accurate and reliable information they need to function in a free society."[26] Doing so is vital to helping the public make decisions on how to vote, what reforms to support, how best to preserve natural resources, how to be prepared for emergencies, how to understand others who are different from themselves, and much more.

In addition, journalism in a free society serves as a check on those in power. Journalism in the United States sometimes is referred to as "the fourth branch of government" or "the Fourth Estate." What these phrases mean is that when properly practiced, journalism can have as much impact on public policy as can the legislative, judicial and executive branches of government. Journalists don't wield this power directly but instead provide information to the public so they can lobby, petition, run for office, and so on.

The founders of the United States felt this role of journalists was so important that they provided protection for freedom of the press in the Constitution. In a short but powerful passage, the **First Amendment** to the Constitution forbids Congress from passing laws placing limits on freedom of the press:

> Congress shall make no law respecting an establishment of religion, or prohibiting the free exercise thereof; or abridging the freedom of speech, or of the press; or the right of the people peaceably to assemble, and to petition the Government for a redress of grievances.

Although many laws have been passed that curtail press freedoms—laws prohibit publishing libelous statements, for instance—they have largely been created to ensure that journalists live up to their responsibilities and don't unnecessarily harm innocent people.

Even though the fundamental role of today's journalist has changed little, much of the practice of journalism has changed and will continue to change. To start, today's journalist needs to be able to write well across several media. Even though printed materials such as newspapers and magazines are falling out of favor, most news stories begin life as words tapped out on a keyboard. Changes in delivery make it critical that journalists can write clearly and simply and get to the point promptly. Further, it's not enough for a journalist to be able to write news for a single platform; today's journalist needs to be able to write stories for text, audio, video and online delivery.

The 21st century journalist also needs to be able to conceptualize story packages that use a wide range of elements. That requires not only asking the right questions of the right people but also asking:

- What pertinent databases, original documents and other resources are available that I can share with my audience?
- What photos would best complement my story and make it easier to envision?
- How would audio, video and animated graphics help my audience understand and relate to this story?
- How can I use audience contributions to strengthen my story?

In addition, today's journalist also needs to be comfortable with continuous deadlines. While the journalist of past generations had hours or even days to write a story, today's journalist might begin filing stories almost as soon as he or she begins gathering information. Starting even as events unfold, the journalist may create an e-mail or cell phone alert, a blog post, or a radio or television bulletin. As more information comes in, a short text story might follow. Next might come a longer piece for a daily newspaper, and finally a thorough interactive multimedia package for the Web.

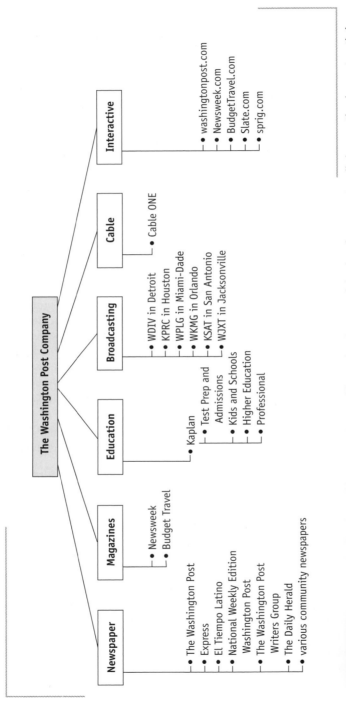

The Washington Post Company

Newspaper
- The Washington Post
- Express
- El Tiempo Latino
- National Weekly Edition Washington Post
- The Washington Post Writers Group
- The Daily Herald
- various community newspapers

Magazines
- Newsweek
- Budget Travel

Education
- Kaplan
  - Test Prep and Admissions
  - Kids and Schools
  - Higher Education
  - Professional

Broadcasting
- WDIV in Detroit
- KPRC in Houston
- WPLG in Miami-Dade
- WKMG in Orlando
- KSAT in San Antonio
- WJXT in Jacksonville

Cable
- Cable ONE

Interactive
- washingtonpost.com
- Newsweek.com
- BudgetTravel.com
- Slate.com
- sprig.com

FIGURE 1.2 Companies like the Washington Post Co. are able to take advantage of the rise of convergent media because they have set up their infrastructure to work with this new trend. They are able to share information between their magazines, cable television stations, Web sites, and more. Source: http://www.washpostco.com/business.htm

8

At the same time, the 21st century journalist needs to pay more attention than ever to being accurate and ethical. In an age of constant deadlines, it's tempting to lower the standards of what's acceptable. Doing so risks losing the vital respect and support of the public.

Today's journalist also needs to keep tabs on what bloggers and citizen journalists are discussing. The professional journalist is no longer the only source of information, and because of that he or she needs to know what other conversations are taking place. As Kelly McBride of the Poynter Institute has written: "We should monitor the blogosphere the way we monitor other subcultures we might have ignored in the past—by looking and listening. We should recognize that, like cable television and tabloid newspapers, the Internet is a force that will change the way we cover the news."[27] The New York Times is one of many news organizations that incorporate the comments and critiques of bloggers into news stories to try to present a full sense of public thought. Many news organizations use blogs and online community discussions to find story ideas that merit a closer look. Many citizen journalists take pride when their work calls attention to problems initially overlooked by traditional media outlets.

Beyond monitoring the conversations of the public, today's journalist needs to look for opportunities to harness the power of the masses. Through e-mail, online chats and other tools, audience members need to be brought into the conversations on the issues of the day. Editors at Scientific American magazine, for example, have posted story proposals and asked for audience feedback to "help guide us in writing, editing and illustrating the article."[28] Journalists at the technology site CNET.com "are expected to answer every question that comes in through the blogs and reader comments, and get involved in every debate that has legs."[29]

Finally, today's journalist needs to be comfortable with a wide range of technology. A journalist should have at least a base level of competence in taking pictures, recording audio and updating a blog. As technologies evolve, every journalist will need to stay abreast of the changes, committing to a process of ongoing education. Some journalists will become virtual "one-man bands," expected to gather all sorts of multimedia content. That's already happened at a number of news organizations:

- Preston Mendenhall of MSNBC took photos and gathered audio and video during a two-week visit to Afghanistan in early 2001. His special report "Pariah Nation: A journey through Afghanistan" (www.msnbc.com/news/afghan_front.asp) is just one of many examples of what an individual journalist can accomplish—work that ordinarily would have required a team of four or more reporters and production people.
- Kevins Sites covered wars in Somalia, Iran, Lebanon, Uganda, Congo, Sudan and elsewhere for Yahoo's Hot Zone. Working on his own, Sites produced packages including audio, video, photos and text to help his audience understand the human toll of armed conflict. Three team members back in Los Angeles helped edit and choose material for his reports, but Sites did all the newsgathering and writing by himself.[30]
- Naka Nathaniel travels the globe to produce multimedia features for The New York Times on the Web. Like Sites, he gathers photos, audio and video. In addition he creates animated Flash elements. In many cases, Nathaniel does his own final editing back home in Paris, but sometimes the Times multimedia staff pitches in with editing.[31]

All of those demands add up to a big challenge—but that challenge is what makes this one of the most exciting times ever to work as a journalist.

ASSIGNMENT
DESK **1.1**

Think back to a recent event on campus. Close your eyes and try to recapture the sights, sounds and smells. Then think about what you told people about the event. You might have sent off a quick instant message to a classmate, a longer e-mail to a closer friend, then had a lengthy phone conversation or face-to-face talk with someone else. In this sense, the way you "reported" on the event was similar to how a journalist working across the media handles the same story. For this first Assignment Desk, type up the following accounts of the event:

A capsule report of no more than 50 words (two to three sentences);
A longer version of about 200 words (one page double spaced); and
A fuller version of about 500 words.

How do these accounts differ? Why did you make the choices you did in determining what to include and what to leave out of each version?

How Changes in Journalism Can Strengthen Public Trust

Today, many people—including many journalists—hold the news business in low esteem. A Gallup Poll taken in fall 2004 found that only 44 percent of Americans have confidence in the news media to report stories fairly and accurately.[32] In addition, the audience believes that journalists fail to serve the public in a number of ways:

- They don't try to make important stories interesting or understandable;
- They inject their personal biases into their reporting;
- They don't check their facts or they make up stories; and
- They don't care what the public thinks.

With a virtually bottomless toolbox, the journalist of the 21st century can address each of these concerns by using appropriate technologies to help engage readers, presenting original documents so the public can draw their own conclusions, and offering myriad chances for the audience to enter discussions about important topics.

A few examples might help to illustrate how a journalist can accomplish those objectives:

- Stories about state budget crises have become so routine that they barely capture public attention. But a handful of enterprising journalists have created online budget balancing simulators that let people try their hands at getting out of the financial muck, making an abstract story concrete. Combining the resources of its newspaper and Web site, the Sacramento (Calif.) Bee went one step further, giving its readers the tools to not just devise a budget but also to e-mail their plans to state leaders (www.sacbee.com/cgi-bin/sacbee/surveys/opinion/budget.cgi).

- The Patriot Act, which was passed by the U.S. Congress to give law enforcement officials more tools to fight terrorism, has been praised by some but criticized by those who say those tools come at too much cost to personal freedom. Two student journalists at the University of Alaska at Fairbanks tried to find the truth by interviewing local community members about the act's effects on them. The resulting award-winning online project (www.uaf.edu/journal/extreme/) gave many people their first understanding of the act and its consequences.

Case Study: One Story Across the Media

In the rest of this book, we will cover the basics—and then some—of writing news for all the major media platforms. Before we start that process, though, let's take time to look at how one story was covered across the media. Doing so will allow us to identify the strengths and weaknesses of various media and offer general guidelines for writing across the media.

A Former President Undergoes Heart Surgery

A few years after leaving office, former U.S. President Bill Clinton was hospitalized with chest pains. Doctors found serious blockage of the arteries connected to his heart and scheduled quadruple bypass surgery. The surgery occurred on a Monday. By Wednesday, he had been released from intensive care and was moving around.

There was no question that the follow-up to his surgery was newsworthy. As a former—and fairly recent—president, Clinton was a prominent figure. With the death of former President Ronald Reagan a few months earlier, Clinton was one of only four living ex-presidents. His surgery, while routine, was risky: It required doctors to stop his heart for an hour or more. The timing of the surgery added to the newsworthiness of the story: It took place in early fall, not long after Clinton had begun campaigning for presidential candidate John Kerry. Clinton's recovery would force him to step aside from the political arena through the November elections.

At the same time, the story was not a major one. Clinton came through surgery well, and his prognosis was good. The story faced competition for space and time from other, more serious stories: a hurricane in Florida, proposed changes in national security agencies, questions about President George W. Bush's military service, and follow-up stories on the tragic deaths at a Russian grade school. In addition, there were few photo, audio or video opportunities.

As a result, coverage was brief and to the point. Let's start with a CNN screen crawl:

Out of Intensive Care Ex-Pres Clinton recovers after bypass surgery; sat up, walked with assistance today

That doesn't look like much, but in just 17 words, it identifies a newsmaker and presents four key facts about him. Notice the use of a present-tense verb (*recovers*). That's done to give the writing immediacy.

Now let's look at a radio dispatch from AP Network News:

> Former President Clinton is out of intensive care and resting in a New York hospital room now, two days after his quadruple heart bypass surgery. His office says Clinton walked with assistance, sat up in bed and sat in a chair. He'll still be mending at home for a couple of months after getting out of the hospital.

This account manages to add a location to the information in the screen crawl. In addition, it reminds the audience how long it has been since his surgery and adds a sentence about what happens next. The radio report also makes an attempt at **attribution**—that is, letting listeners know who was making the claims. Once again, notice the use of present tense in the first sentence.

The CNN Headline News report on Clinton's recovery does not veer far from AP's radio report:

> Former President Clinton is out of intensive care and could be home from the hospital this weekend.
>
> Doctors think it will be as many as three months, though, before he will fully recuperate from his quadruple bypass surgery.
>
> They say Clinton had significant artery blockage and he could have suffered a heart attack if he didn't have the surgery.

Both the radio and television reports ran 17 seconds, with the television report differing from the radio report in several ways. For starters, it reveals why Clinton needed the surgery. CNN's report skips the details about Clinton's activities and instead substitutes information about when Clinton was expected to be released and what could have happened if he had not undergone the surgery.

The information in the CNN report is sourced to doctors. Notice that no names are given; unfamiliar names eat up precious time, are hard for listeners and viewers to grasp, and add nothing to the story. Finally, notice that once again the report starts with a present-tense verb.

Because television cameras are not welcome in hospital recovery rooms, the CNN report could not use live footage of Clinton. Instead, the report was read over top of archival video footage of Clinton apparently delivering a commencement address. No indication was given as to when or where the footage came from; inattentive viewers might mistake it as a testament to Clinton's amazing and instantaneous recuperative powers.

The Washington Post's brief account of Clinton's recovery did not run until the following day. The report, sourced to "Staff Reports and News Services," ran in a roundup of items under the banner "Nation in Brief":

> Former president Bill Clinton moved out of the intensive-care unit at a New York hospital yesterday afternoon and walked short distances with assistance, according to officials at his charitable foundation.
>
> His surgeon at New York-Presbyterian Hospital/Columbia University Medical Center, Craig R. Smith, said Clinton was having "an average amount of post-op pain."
>
> Clinton, 58, is expected to stay in the hospital several more days after he underwent quadruple bypass surgery on Monday. He experienced chest pain and shortness of breath last Friday. The operation required cutting his sternum, or breastbone, lengthwise and stopping his heart for 61 minutes.

Even though this account runs less than 100 words, it manages to include a wealth of information the other reports lack: the name of the hospital, the name of the surgeon, his pain level, Clinton's age, what led to the operation, and what the operation entailed. Two sources are cited for attribution (although the first, *hospital officials*, is vague — the name or names probably were withheld for space reasons). Note that this is the first account that gives Clinton's first name and the first to use past tense to begin the story.

Articles from other large print media, such as The New York Times and USA Today, tended to be longer and packed with more detail about his health background and the steps on the road to recovery. Otherwise, they did not differ substantially from the Post article.

Most online reports of the event were simply dropped onto the Web from a print source or from the AP wire feed. One of the few online accounts that actually took advantage of the strengths of the medium ran a day earlier, on the Web site of Monterey/Salinas/Santa Cruz, Calif., television station KSBW. The centerpiece was a longer AP story:

President Bill Clinton is reportedly talking and taking liquids a day after undergoing a quadruple heart bypass surgery at a New York hospital.

A source told The Associated Press that Clinton remains in fine spirits as he continues to recover in the intensive care unit at New York Presbyterian Hospital/Columbia.

Clinton's heart surgery came in the nick of time.

Doctors said "something was going to happen" in the next couple of weeks had Clinton not had the quadruple bypass operation. They say the heart disease they repaired was extensive and blockage in several arteries exceeded 90 percent.

Doctors said his arteries were so severely clogged that they posed an imminent danger of a major heart attack.

Doctors said Clinton's heart problem was not as sudden as had been portrayed. He had suffered shortness of breath and tightness in his chest for several months, blaming them on an inconsistent exercise routine and acid reflux.

Clinton also has high blood pressure and might not have been adequately treated for high cholesterol.

A member of Clinton's surgery team said everything is going "very well."

The former president underwent the four-hour procedure Monday at New York Presbyterian Hospital/Columbia.

Clinton went to the hospital late last week, but doctors had to delay surgery until Monday because he was on a blood-thinning medication, and they wanted to decrease the chance of excessive bleeding.

It's up to the doctors to decide when he can be moved to a more comfortable section of the hospital, where patients are treated to a piano player at a daily complementary high tea. Other perks include meals prepared by a gourmet chef and concierge service.

Clinton is expected to leave the hospital in four or five days, but the hospital's chief of cardiology said Clinton's return to full health will take weeks.

It looks like Clinton won't be doing any campaigning for Sen. John Kerry — or anyone else — in the coming weeks.

He'd been planning to campaign for Kerry. But a Clinton spokesman said he won't be in "traveling shape" for the next few weeks — and he won't be fully recovered for two to three months.

The spokesman said it's "too soon to know" just what Clinton will be able to do.

Former U.S. President Bill Clinton speaks with host Jon Stewart on Comedy Central's "The Daily Show" a month before Clinton had major heart surgery.
Source: **Peter Kramer/Getty Images**

Although that story is good, solid journalism, it's the complementary pieces that bring this package to life:

- A CNN video clip featuring Clinton's doctors
- A message from the Clinton family
- A biography of Clinton
- A slide show of Clinton through his years as president
- An article discussing details of the surgery
- A video clip of a doctor discussing the type of surgery Clinton underwent
- A Flash animation tour of the virtual heart
- A Flash animation heart risk test
- A link to send Clinton a personal message
- Links to three recent articles leading up to Clinton's surgery

Not everything in this package was produced by KSBW. Instead, the KSBW journalists' most important contribution was in anticipating questions their audience might have and in gathering a range of resources to answer those questions. Particularly useful are the tools offered to let a site visitor determine if he or she might be facing a similar problem and the ability to send a get-well wish to Clinton.

ASSIGNMENT DESK 1.2

For our second assignment, return to the event you wrote about in the previous assignment desk exercise. Although your longest written account probably offered a good glimpse of what the event was like, now you're going to think about including multimedia to help engage your audience at an even deeper level.

Make a list of photos, audio, video and printed materials that could help bring the event to life for someone who wasn't there. Include everything you can think of—what media people call *assets*—and what each element would add to your account. Be as creative as possible.

Why Choose Journalism?

It's a new day! Welcome to a world where ingenious ways of gathering and presenting news have been embraced.

If you don't have a cell phone, Internet access, some sort of MP3 player, a computer and cable TV, get one of each.

The changes occurring in the field of journalism have made a camera phone a necessity and Web savvy a must. Gone are the staid rules on how a journalist does his or her job. Gone, too, are the archaic ways people watch their news.

So, why choose journalism? Because it's fun. Seriously!

Nothing beats the adrenaline rush of meeting a deadline as you sift through mounds of raw information, video, sound bites, quotes—all in an effort to tell a compelling story.

A career as a journalist can be extremely challenging. But at the end of the day, it can be rewarding as long as you stay true to your core beliefs.

I wish you nothing but the best.

ROBIN MAZYCK
Internet producer
Christian Broadcasting
CBNNews.com

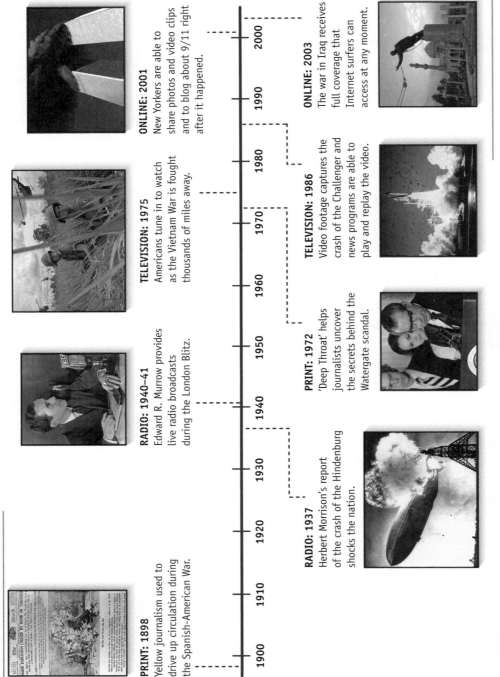

PRINT: 1898
Yellow journalism used to drive up circulation during the Spanish-American War.

RADIO: 1937
Herbert Morrison's report of the crash of the Hindenburg shocks the nation.

RADIO: 1940–41
Edward R. Murrow provides live radio broadcasts during the London Blitz.

PRINT: 1972
'Deep Throat' helps journalists uncover the secrets behind the Watergate scandal.

TELEVISION: 1975
Americans tune in to watch as the Vietnam War is fought thousands of miles away.

TELEVISION: 1986
Video footage captures the crash of the Challenger and news programs are able to play and replay the video.

ONLINE: 2001
New Yorkers are able to share photos and video clips and to blog about 9/11 right after it happened.

ONLINE: 2003
The war in Iraq receives full coverage that Internet surfers can access at any moment.

1900   1910   1920   1930   1940   1950   1960   1970   1980   1990   2000

FIGURE 1.4

Timeline of Defining Moments in News Media
Source (in chronological order): Corbis/Bettmann; AP Images; AP Images; Mike Lien/The New York Times/Redux Pictures; AP Images; NASA/AP Images; Richard Cohen/Corbis; Jerome Delay/AP Images.

Conclusion

As the case study shows, news reports today come in a wide range of shapes and sizes. By the time you finish this book, you will be able to create all of them and to take your place in this new, multiplatform world of journalism. In upcoming chapters, you will learn how to:

- Find the news;
- Conduct research and interviews;
- Write basic and advanced news stories using text, audio, video and online elements;
- Report on common types of news events;
- Work with the legal and ethical rules that govern journalists; and
- Incorporate diverse voices into the news.

Once you master this wide range of knowledge and skills, you will take your place as one of the best-prepared journalists ever, producing work that educates the public and addresses public concerns about journalistic quality.

KEY TERMS

attribution, 12   First Amendment, 7
citizen journalism, 5   user-generated content, 5
convergence, 2   Weblog/blog, 4

DISCUSSION QUESTIONS

1. Where do you turn for news? Do you use different sources for different types of information? Why do you use the sources you do? Do you use multiple outlets of the same type (for example, Web sites, magazines, TV networks)?
2. When an important story occurs, how often do you check for updates on it? Does this depend on the media that are available to you?
3. Do you use blogs? If so, for entertainment, news or opinion? Have you ever created or contributed to a blog?
4. How does your interest in a story relate to the number and type of sources you use to learn about it? The time you spend learning about it?
5. When you're reading or watching news, how long does it take you to reach your limit with a given story and move on to another? What's the longest you would spend on a given story? Is there such a thing as "too much news" in a report?

NOTES

1. "CBS News Unveils Web Strategy," CBSNews.com, 12 July 2005, **www.cbsnews.com/stories/2005/ 07/12/entertainment/main708433.shtml**; Andy Fixmer and Leon Lazaroff. "Web Firms to Distribute CBS Shows on Internet," the Washington Post, 13 April 2007, p. D3.

2. Justin Gillis, "New York Times Merges Staffs," the Washington Post, 3 August 2005, p. D3; Steve Klein, "A New Day for USA Today," Poynter Online, 13 December 2005, **www.poynter.org/ column. asp?id=31&aid= 93536&**; "Dow Jones Announces Reorganization," CBSNews.com, 22 February 2006, **www.cbsnews.com/stories/ 2006/02/22/ap/business/ mainD8FUDIIO8.shtml**.

3. "'LAT' Editor: Web Will Be 'Primary Vehicle' for New Delivery," Editor and Publisher, 24 January 2007, **www.editorandpublisher.com/eandp/search/article_ display.jsp?vnu_content_id=1003536826**.

4. Eytan Avriel, "NY Times Publisher: Our goal is to manage the transition from print to internet," Haaretz.com, 8 February 2007, **www.haaretz.com/ hasen/spages/822775.html**.

5. "Gannett Introduces the Newsroom of the Future," Poynter.org, 3 November 2006, **http://poynter.org/ forum/?id=32365**.

6. Ken Sands, "Newspaper Provides Online Newscasts," Poynter Online, 19 October 2004, **www.poynter.org/ column.asp?id=56&aid=73016**.

7. "Washingtonpost.com Wins National Emmy Award," 26 September 2006, **www.washingtonpost.com/wp-dyn/ content/article/2006/09/26/AR2006092600458.html**.

8. "Hearst-Argyle Posts Local News Content on YouTube," Media Life, 4 June 2007, **www.medialifemagazine. com/ml/ac/ws060507.asp**.

9. "Debate: Convergence," Journalism Studies, 4, no. 4 (2003): pp. 513–514.

10. Remarks by Tom Curley, president and chief executive officer, The Associated Press, to the Online News Association Conference, 12 November, 2004, **http://journalist. org/2004conference/archives/000079.php**.

11. Timothy O'Brien, "The Newspaper of the Future," The New York Times, 26 June 2005, section 3, p. 1.

12. Frank Ahrens, "NBC Taking Big Step Back from Television," the Washington Post, 20 October 2006, **www.washingtonpost.com/wp-dyn/content/ article/2006/10/19/AR2006101900205.html**.

13. Matt Stump, "FoxNews.com Usage Rises With Video Content," Multichannel News, 3 May 2004, **http://www.multichannel.com/index.asp?layout=article Print&articleID=CA413950**.

14. "Redefining the News Online," Online Journalism Review, February 2004, **www.ojr.org/ojr/workplace/ 1075928349.php**.

15. Kate Lorenz, "Success Without a College Degree? Seven Hotshots Who Made It," AOL Find a Job, 2006, **http://jobs.aol.com/article/_a/success-without-a-college-degree/20061019144909990004**.

16. Esther Scott, "'Big Media' Meets the 'Bloggers': Coverage of Trent Lott's remarks at Strom Thurmond's birthday party," J.F. Kennedy School of Government, Harvard University, 2004, **www.ksg.harvard.edu/presspol/ Research_Publications/Case_Studies/ 1731_0.pdf**.

17. Joe Garofoli, "Tonight at 11, News by Neighbors," SFGate.com, 11 February 2007, **www.sfgate.com/ cgi-bin/article.cgi?file=/c/a/2007/02/11/ MNGDEO2QOA1.DTL**.

18. Lisa Snedeker, "A Most Noble Idea, Citizen Journalism," Media Life Magazine, 22 November 2006, **www. medialifemagazine.com/artman/publish/article_8701.asp**.

19. Rick Edmonds, "As Blogs and Citizen Journalism Grow, Where's the News?" Poynter Online, 14 November 2005, **www.poynter.org/content/content_view.asp? id=91391**.

20. Jake Easton, "John Kerry Rocked by Affair Claim," PoliticalStar.com, 12 February 2004, **www.politicalstar. com/john-kerry.html**.

21. Anne Marie Squeo, "Rove's Camp Takes Center of Web Storm," The Wall Street Journal Online, 16 May 2006, **http://online.wsj.com/public/article/SB114774060320 053665-yW4EYDFzYadmGaqpnXr0ZlqmEF0_ 20070515.html?mod=blogs**.

22. Edmonds.

23. Nicholas Lemann, "Amateur Hour," The New Yorker, 7 August 2006, p. 48.

24. Institute for Connected Society, "We Media-Zogbt Poll: Most Americans Say Bloggers and Citizen Journalists Will Play a Vital Role in Journalism's Future," 15 February 2007, **ifocos.org/2007/02/15/we-media-%e2%80%93zogby-poll-most-americans-say-bloggers-and-citizen-reporters-will-play-a-vital-role-in-journalisms-future/**.

25. "Trends in Newsrooms: The annual report of the World Editors Forum," World Association of Newspapers, 2007, **www.editorsweblog.org/analysis/2007/03/2_how_ editors_view_emerging_forms_of_jou.php**.

26. "Principles of Journalism," Project for Excellence in Journalism, **www.journalism.org/resources/principles**.

27. Kelly McBride, "Journalism in the Age of Blogs," Poynter.org, 20 September 2004, **www.poynter. org/column.asp?id=53&aid=71447**.

28. See for example "Interactive Publishing: A simpler origin for life," Scientific American.com, 12 February 2007, **http://blog.sciam.com/index.php?title=a_simpler_ origin_for_life&more=1&c=1&tb=1&pb=1**.

29. Jemima Kiss, "CNET, Journalists and the Whole Social Net Thing," 17 January 2007, **http://blogs.guardian. co.uk/organgrinder/2007/01/cnet_journalists_and_the_ whole.html**.

30. Bobbie Johnson, "A Year of Living Dangerously," Guardian Unlimited, 20 February 2006, **http://technology.guardian.co.uk/news/story/0,,1713754, 00.html**.

31. Steve Outing, "Nathaniel's Global Multimedia Road Show," Poynter Online, 1 June 2004, **http://www.poynter.org/column.asp?id=31&aid=66437**.

32. "Stunner: Americans Don't Trust the Press," Media Life Magazine, 24 September 2004, **http://www.medialifemagazine.com/news2004/sep04/ Sept20/5_fri/news1friday.html**.

Deciding What's News

Before you can write news, you have to understand what news is. On one hand, that should seem easy to do, because we're all awash in news most of our waking moments. But on the other hand, just as watching hundreds of movies is no guarantee you'll be a successful filmmaker, the mere act of reading, watching and listening to news is not enough to make you a great news writer. To become one, you have to go a step beyond and *study* the news.

The best way to start that process is by following the news every day. A good diet of news consists of a variety of radio, television, print and online sources. That will let you see how different media define news, let you watch how stories develop over time, and familiarize you with news writing styles used across the media.

Studying the news also helps you get a sense of what's going on around you. More than ever, we live in a connected world. What people do and how they live in any part of the world affects other people who live thousands of miles away. Similarly, breakthroughs in science, medicine and technology often have consequences far beyond their immediate spheres.

Keeping up with the news, therefore, will help you find connections and ask questions that can lead to good stories. It also will help you build a core of knowledge about the way the world works that will keep you from being duped: Knowledgeable people are not easily fooled or manipulated.

Finally, staying current on the news lets you determine if something really is news. If you don't know what's happened before, there's no way you can judge the importance of an event or utterance. If you have no idea of what's going on in the world right now, you can't possibly determine where anything new fits into the scheme of things—and therefore you can't be a good journalist. Remember, your key role as a journalist is to inform the public and help them make decisions. You can do that only if you are informed yourself.

As you begin to pay more attention to the news, you'll notice that some types of stories appear over and over again, but others show up in a more hit-or-miss fashion. What that shows is that some stories are fairly

FIGURE 2.1

Google News is the first stop for many of those looking for news online. Its automated system compiles stories from thousands of news sources around the world. *Source:* http://news.google.com

universally recognized as news, whereas others are not. These decisions come down in large part to four factors: audience, medium, competition and editorial judgment.

Getting to Know Your Audience

News is, at its simplest, a report of something new. But that's far from a working definition: There is *always* something new happening. What you need to be able to do is to sift through all of that information and find what's *truly* important for your audience.

The need to know your audience has become increasingly important as what was once a mass audience has splintered off to become consumers of more specialized media. Where once families gathered together to watch the same television programs and share the Sunday newspaper, today people are abandoning media traditionally thought of as offering something for everyone—including general-interest newspapers and broadcast television news programs—and seeking out specialized media.

That's not to say that there are no stories that interest almost everyone. News of natural disasters, the deaths of well-known figures and the results of major sporting events attract a wide audience. But beyond those sorts of big stories, people today tend to seek out stories that are targeted to their specific interests. That shift began with the widespread adoption of cable television and accelerated with the birth of the World Wide Web. Now, when most people have ready access to hundreds of television channels and thousands of online news sources, every news outlet needs to find a niche that sets it apart from the competition. Even media that were once thought of as "general interest"—daily newspapers, for instance—today are more forthcoming about targeting a specific audience: generally upscale and well educated.

Succeeding in this environment requires understanding what matters to your audience. Doing so requires time and commitment. You can't go off and sit quietly and wait for enlightenment; neither can you assume that your audience is just like you (except not quite as bright and insightful). That may sound obvious, but one common criticism of journalists is that they miss or underplay stories of great concern to their audiences—and devote far too much time, space and energy on stories of little interest or importance.

So how do you determine who makes up your audience? Fortunately, if you're working for an established media outlet, some of the work is already done. Most media outlets collect extensive data on their audiences and use that data to attract advertisers. Just by looking at the data—or even at the ads that the data have been used to attract—you can get a basic understanding of your audience.

The key word, though, is *basic*. Although research can reveal general demographic information—sex, age, race, income, and so on—to gain a deeper understanding requires that you spend time with audience members. That can be as simple as watching and listening to what people are doing and talking about and attending meetings and events. Some media outlets offer more formal chances to do the same thing. Virtual or face-to-face town meetings, for instance, let members of the public sit down with writers and editors to discuss what's on their minds. Some news organizations go a step further and create editorial advisory boards made up of members of the public. Online chat sessions and blogs that encourage reader feedback offer journalists additional opportunities to take the pulse of their audiences.

ASSIGNMENT DESK 2.1

How much do you know about the makeup of your campus? Based on your observations, indicate how the college population is broken down by the following categories:

- Gender.
- Age.
- Race/Ethnicity.
- Geographical origin.
- Major area of study.

Now do some research and find out what the actual breakdown is. How close did you come?

The Medium's Impact on Your Message

The second major factor in deciding if something is news is the medium in which it will appear. Several things come into play here. First is the nature of the medium. For instance, as you spend more time analyzing the news, you'll notice that some stories that get good television coverage are barely mentioned in other media. Often, that's because an otherwise weak story is accompanied by video footage that's sure to grab the audience. Because television is primarily a visual medium, that footage can raise the value of a story that might otherwise be passed over. Similarly, radio news favors stories with strong sound bites and natural sound, and online news is perfect for stories with a variety of media and interactivity.

Frequency of deadlines is also critical in determining what gets covered. In many cases, stories are passed over because they don't coincide with publishing or broadcast cycles. For instance, if the last radio newscast of the day takes place at 6 p.m., a story that breaks minutes later might never be aired. By the time of the first newscast the following day, it may be regarded as old news.

The availability of time and space also helps determine what gets covered. In a medium in which most stories run under 60 seconds, television news is not the best choice for covering complex topics. With the exception of a few public radio networks (such as National Public Radio), radio is even worse. Many stories get no more than a one-sentence summary. Only newspapers, newsmagazines and online news sites can offer in-depth coverage that is more likely to enlighten than to confuse.

Obviously, a journalist who works across the media has to weigh all this in determining how to present a given story. The same story may be handled differently for different media, with some reports merely a statement of the news and other reports more thoughtful and detailed.

ASSIGNMENT DESK 2.2

Attend a school-sponsored event featuring an outside guest. It might be a speaker, an artist, a musician or someone else. Your assignment is to write brief accounts of it for at least two of the following audiences: your current best friend, a high school friend, your parents, a professor or an employer.

What did you include and leave out of each account? How did your tone and language differ from one account to another? Are there some stories that you would report exactly the same to each of these audiences?

The Role of Competition

Determining what's news also depends partly on knowing if and how a given story has been covered in other media. Journalists always prefer to be first with the news, especially when they beat their direct competition. Although the **scoop** mentality is not without perils, breaking a story is one of the most exciting things a journalist can do. "The drive to be first with the basic facts of a newsworthy development remains embedded in the culture of newsrooms and in the minds of reporters," New York Times Public Editor Byron Calame has written.[1]

In the vast majority of cases, however, you will not be the first to break a story. When a competitor beats you to a story, you have to make sure that your story offers additional value: updated information, more explanation, a different perspective—something that sets your account apart from the others.

It's most important to see how stories are being handled by news media that directly compete for your audience's time and interest. But it's also a good idea to pay attention to what the **agenda-setting media** are up to. That elite group is composed primarily of the following:

- Major national newspapers (and their Web sites): The New York Times, the Washington Post, The Wall Street Journal, the Los Angeles Times and USA Today.
- Major newsmagazines: Time, Newsweek, and U.S. News and World Report.
- Major broadcast news networks: ABC, CBS, NBC, CNN, Fox News and MSNBC.
- A variety of "insider" newsletters and specialized broadcast programs, Web sites and blogs.

Whenever one of those news sources reports a story that has consequences for your audience, you can count on many members of your audience being aware of the story and expecting you to provide a unique follow-up to it.

That's not to say that you need to be concerned with every story that appears in the agenda-setting media. Although most journalists take a deep interest in every story on the

Why Choose Journalism?

Regardless of how the delivery method changes over time, skilled information-gatherers and storytellers will never go out of style. Democracy is not possible without journalists who can obtain, analyze and give the public an accurate accounting of their government at work. And our sense of humanity is elevated when we are made—through thorough reporting and deft writing, editing, camera work and creative packaging—to understand the experiences of people who are not like ourselves. Sure, anyone can post information online in the form of a blog. But journalists help sift through the volumes of information out there, give it a sense of order and make judgments about whether the information is reliable and how important it is to the people in their communities.

AMANDA JANES
formerly of the Washington Post, the Arizona Republic and
The Record of Bergen County, N.J.

front page of The New York Times, many members of the public do not. The most important thing you can do is give your audience the news it cannot get anywhere else.

Editorial Judgment

With an understanding of your audience, medium and competition, you're ready to assess a given event or announcement to determine its newsworthiness. Over time, this step becomes second nature for journalists. Initially, however, it helps to walk through a checklist of traditional **news values**. Most news stories include several of the following news values.

Impact

The primary measure of the value of any information is its effect on the audience. If a bill pending in the state legislation would double the cost of tuition, that information is obviously important to readers of a campus newspaper. The price increase has a direct **impact**. Most journalists believe that direct impact is the paramount measure of newsworthiness.

Also important are indirect and potential impact. A hurricane or flood will have a direct impact only on the people who live in the area or have family or other connections there. However, if the tragedy damages crops or requires federal government support, it could indirectly affect many more people, in the form of higher food prices and taxes.

Potential impact refers to things that might happen as a consequence of an event. For example, shortly after Democrats gained control of the U.S. Senate by a margin of 51 to 49 in the fall 2006 elections, Democratic Sen. Tim Johnson of South Dakota was hospitalized with a brain hemorrhage. While the story would be regarded as news under any circumstances, it took on special importance because of its potential impact. If Johnson had died or for any other reason not been able to resume his duties, the governor of South Dakota would have had the authority to appoint a replacement. Because the governor was a Republican, such a move almost certainly would have shifted the balance of the Senate back to Republican control.

Prominence

Simply put, names make news. From local government officials to international sports stars and celebrities, even the minor actions of well-known people can draw intense attention. In some cases, that attention is well deserved: The actions of a president or the head of a large company can have an impact on many people. But in other cases, too much focus on **prominence** can lead to overblown coverage of the inconsequential actions of minor celebrities.

Unusualness

News stories tend to focus on things that are out of the ordinary. A million cars driving along a highway without incident isn't news, but one bad driver causing a crash is. Unfortunately, like prominence, **unusualness** also can lead journalists to ignore important stories and focus instead on insubstantial ones: A local gardener who grows a tomato in the shape of George Washington's head is more likely to get coverage than a story about the many people who go to bed hungry every night in the same community. Journalists need to be careful that this news value does not blind them to important stories that are found in day-to-day happenings.

Currency

News is one of the oldest examples of recycling. Topics that are popular today will disappear, then reappear months or years from now. This cycle is fueled largely by the focus on unusual events: When something unusual and dramatic occurs, it attracts attention to similar events and underlying conditions. For example, when a national study finds that the percentage of high school graduates who are functionally illiterate has reached record levels, writers will ask why, and they will also pay more attention to related stories. Those subsequent reports have **currency**: a direct tie to stories already in the news. Over time, another topic will take center stage and the cycle will start over.

Conflict

In a sense, every news story is an exercise in storytelling. Most interesting stories are based on some sort of **conflict**: people battling nature, other people, themselves, disease, the system, and so on. A profile of a person born into a wealthy family and given the family's huge corporation to run is not interesting; a profile of a person who was born into poverty and created a successful business is much more interesting because that person had to overcome great odds. Journalists need to be careful, however, that they don't overemphasize minor conflicts to try to make a story more appealing.

Timeliness

Timeliness refers to how recently an event happened. All else being equal, an event that occurred more recently is more newsworthy than a similar event. At news outlets that have infrequent deadlines (once a day or less), timeliness becomes more important in weeding out stories. For instance, if two serious traffic accidents occur during a one-week period, and the weekly community newspaper has room for only one story, the more recent one would run.

Proximity

Proximity refers to physical nearness: If all factors are equal in two events, the one that has occurred closest to your audience is more newsworthy. Although well-written stories about unfamiliar people in distant places can be fascinating, most Americans can find out everything they need to know about the world from CNN and MSNBC, with BBC News (http://news.bbc.co.uk/) and Reuters (http://today.reuters.com/news/ home.aspx) thrown in for additional perspectives. Generally, people are most interested in news about people and events in their own communities. So the most useful thing that most news organizations can do is provide the local news that no one else is covering. Many news organizations have shifted to make local news their centerpiece, offering space to reports on virtually everything that occurs in the local community: softball game scores, school lunch menus, times and locations of fund-raisers, and much more.

The change is most pronounced at newspapers. As Lisa Snedeker wrote in Media Life magazine:

> After decades in which local news was supplanted by national and international stories, newspapers all across America are returning to their more humble roots, covering school board meetings and rotary lunches and high school swim meets.
>
> In terms of news coverage, it's the biggest thing to sweep through newsrooms in decades, and it's part of a fundamental reevaluation of the newspaper's role in the community.[2]

An executive of the Fort Myers (Fla.) News-Press, which became a pioneer for Gannett's neighborhood online publishing model, adds:

> Reporters have to be willing to redefine news. Many of these stories would never make it into the general-interest daily newspaper but are important to a neighborhood. We have to be willing—eager, even—to write about someone's cat in a tree. The cat-in-a-tree story

FIGURE 2.2 The BonitaNews.com's Bonitial Living section is a classic example of hyperlocal journalism, with stories focusing on virtually every aspect of life in the Florida community.

doesn't replace traditional coverage of community issues. It supplements the coverage with an extra layer of ultra-local community news.[3]

Affinity

People are interested in other people who share characteristics or have an **affinity** with them (religion, nationality, race, and so on). For example, stories involving the pope would be considered more newsworthy in an area with a significant Roman Catholic population than in an area primarily populated by Mormons or Baptists.

Human Interest

Stories that have strong emotional content are said to have human interest. Some—like a story of a half-blind kangaroo saving the life of a farmer who had raised her—make the audience feel good and help offset heavy and often downbeat news. Others—such as a story about a man who was fired from his job for taking time off to be with his dying wife—might bring tears to their eyes. Like some of the other values discussed previously, this one often is valued too highly, leading to important stories being pushed out of the news by emotional stories of little consequence.

Being able to evaluate potential stories using these news values is the first step toward deciding what stories to pursue and report.

ASSIGNMENT DESK 2.3

Using the front page of the print or online version of today's local newspaper, list all the stories you find there. Then read all the stories, making a note of which news values you find in each. What trends do you detect?

Next, skim through the same newspaper and pick another six to 10 stories. Do the same analysis. Comparing the two sets of stories, can you reach any conclusions about why the stories on the front page were selected for that special treatment?

Taking the Lead

Although good journalism demands alertness to public needs and wishes, it also requires that journalists sometimes take the lead. Ultimately, it is the journalist's job to help people understand the world and function better in it. As Tom Rosenstiel and Bill Kovach have written of the profession of journalism:

> It should do more than gather an audience or catalogue the important. For its own survival, it must balance what readers know they want with what they cannot anticipate but need. In short, it must strive to make the significant interesting and relevant. The effectiveness of a piece of journalism is measured both by how much a work engages its audience and enlightens it. This means journalists must continually ask what information has most value to citizens and in what form. While journalism should reach beyond such

topics as government and public safety, a journalism overwhelmed by trivia and false significance ultimately engenders a trivial society.[4]

Doing the job well can be difficult, however, as journalists face a host of pressures. Some of those pressures are detailed in the next section.

Audience Fascination with Celebrity and Trivia

For as long as there have been celebrities, people have been fascinated with them. People spend countless hours trying to learn everything they can about their favorite stars—their successes, their failures, their love lives, their toys. There's nothing wrong with using celebrity news as mindless entertainment, just as there is nothing wrong with reporting it as part of a balanced news diet. But this fascination sometimes encourages journalists to ignore important stories, thereby distracting the public from stories they should care about.

Jim Chisholm of the World Association of Newspapers brings this point home with a story about an occasion when he hosted foreign news workers:

> During a recent trip to the United States, my European colleagues were, without exception, staggered that while the European news media were concerned with the problems in Iraq, U.S. media were wall to wall with that ultimate determinant of the future of the world, Michael Jackson.
>
> One has to ask whether the notion of importance has already flown out of the window and whether the people behind the decision to lead on Jackson's misfortunes have in fact disqualified themselves already from any debate on the declining interest in media.[5]

Ratings Pressures

Journalists sometimes feel pressured to cover sensational but relatively unimportant stories to draw a large audience. The presumption behind such actions is that presenting serious news will drive off the audience—and in turn, the advertisers. But good journalists have shown time and time again that people will pay attention to well-reported, well-written serious stories. In the long run, such stories are always better for a news outlet's bottom line—and its reputation.

Bias Toward the Status Quo

Although the most common criticism of the news media is that they are liberal and progressive, the true story is that the media overall are most biased toward keeping things as they are, especially if the public seems satisfied with the status quo. But doing so can cause the news media to abdicate their most important responsibility. The Lexington (Ky.) Herald-Leader owned up to one such failure 40 years after the fact when it published this "clarification" on July 4, 2004:

> It has come to the editor's attention that the Herald-Leader neglected to cover the civil rights movement. We regret the omission.

The clarification was accompanied by a package of stories titled "Front-page news, back-page coverage." It recounted how editors kept news of the civil rights movement out of the paper, which was one of many that ignored the major national movement. A former NAACP leader was quoted in the report as saying the decision to omit coverage at the time was intended to retain readers. "They catered to the white citizenry, and the white community just prayed that rumors and reports would be swept under the rug and just go away," he said.[6]

Advertiser Pressures

Virtually every news outlet relies on advertisers to finance most of the costs of reporting and publishing. Because of that, many media executives are timid when it comes to reporting anything that might offend an advertiser. All too many journalists steer clear of packages like the Orlando Sentinel/WESH NewsChannel 2's joint project "Building Homes, Building Problems," a yearlong investigation of home construction that found many new homes riddled with problems. The series (http://extra.orlandosentinel.com/buildingproblems/default.aspx) cost the media outlets greatly in lost real estate advertising revenue—but it helped countless readers and viewers make sure they were not being sold shoddy homes. That's a nobler goal than avoiding offense to advertisers.

Ownership Pressures

Few news outlets have managed to remain independent in recent years. News operations of all sorts have been bought at a rapid clip by companies that regard them more as good investments than as public services. Those parent companies often press for increased profits, even when their properties are returning 20 percent a year, a much better rate of return than just about any other business generates. That drive for higher profits can lead to layoffs and buyouts, greatly reducing the time and resources available for the remaining journalists to do their jobs. Like some of the other pressures, this one can in turn result in a reliance on easily reported, shallow news stories, at the expense of more vital stories that can take time to pull together. Ownership pressures are particularly problematic in the age of convergence. As Rick Weiss, a union representative for the Washington Post, put it when the paper's owners announced plans to cut at least 80 newsroom jobs: "The more time I spend blogging, doing radio shows and TV spots, the less time I have to generate the news that everyone wants. They are counting on reporters, editors and columnists to fill a lot of airtime."[7]

Newsmaker Pressures

Politicians, lobbyists and business leaders (and the public relations agencies that represent them) possess a great deal of skill in manipulating the news media to see that stories they want out get out—and the stories they don't want out stay unreported.

Conclusion

Determining what's news is a complex process that depends on journalists remaining engaged, interested and informed. While they constantly monitor what their audiences are interested in, good journalists also stand ready to point audiences into directions that might not be comfortable or familiar. At the same time, they resist internal and external pressures to abandon their own notions of news judgment in favor of powerful interests and quick profits. Rising to those tasks is not always easy, but that's what makes them *good* journalists.

KEY TERMS

affinity, 29

agenda-setting media, 25

conflict, 27

currency, 27

impact, 26

news values, 26

prominence, 26

proximity, 27

scoop, 24

timeliness, 27

unusualness, 26

DISCUSSION QUESTIONS

1. Newspaper executives increasingly note a loss of college-age readers. Are newspapers and other traditional news media relevant to 18- to 24-year-olds? If not, what would it take to make them relevant?
2. With the public having so many choices of print, broadcast and online news sources, what are the implications for determining what's news?
3. More and more Americans are picking their news outlets to reflect their viewpoints. Is this a good thing or a bad thing? What's gained and what's lost when we no longer have a shared national news?

NOTES

1. Byron Calame, "Scoops, Impact or Glory: What motivates reporters?" The New York Times, 3 December 2006, www.nytimes.com/2006/12/03/opinion/03pubed.html?ex=1172898000&en=d4ede4db2242844e&ei=5070.
2. Lisa Snedeker, "Putting Local Back Into the Local Paper," Media Life Magazine, 19 October 2006, www.medialifemagazine.com/cgi-bin/artman/exec/ view.cgi?archive=501&num=7987.
3. Kate Marymont, "How They Did It: Fort Myers' 'mojo' journalists search out news at the neighborhood level, identify community contributors," Gannett News Watch, February 2006, www.gannett.com/go/newswatch/2006/february/nw0210-2.htm.
4. Project for Excellence in Journalism, "Principles of Journalism," http://www.journalism.org/resources/principles.
5. Jim Chisholm, "Question of News Value Driving Papers," Newspapers and Technology, February 2004, www.newsandtech.com/issues/2004/02–04/wan/02–04_chisholm.htm.
6. "Paper Apologizes for Civil Rights Coverage," the Washington Post, 5 July 2004, p. C3.
7. Joe Strupp, "Guild Leader Criticizes Plan for 'Washington Post' Job Cuts," Editor and Publisher, 10 March 2006, www.editorandpublisher.com/eandp/news/article_display.jsp?vnu_content_id=1002156960.

Chapter 3

Research and Interviewing

Once you understand what qualifies as news, the next step is to learn how to gather news. The process consists of two main parts: doing research to come up with story ideas and prepare for interviews; and conducting interviews. This chapter will guide you through those steps.

Developing Story Ideas

As a news consumer, it seems that there is no limit to the number and type of news stories available to you. Even in the course of a single day, you can find thousands of stories covering every imaginable topic.

As a beginning news writer, however, you might feel just the opposite: that there is little for you to write about. Rest assured that is a mistaken impression. Once you understand how reporters work, your challenge will become picking the most interesting and important stories to focus on, not merely finding ideas.

To begin, let's back up. When you were younger, there was a time when you had little idea what was happening in the world outside your home, beyond the stories that your family members brought into the home. As time went by and you became more interested in the outside world, you began seeking out information on sports, fashion, a hobby or popular culture. Later your interests likely expanded to include some aspects of politics and national or international news.

As your interests expanded, so did your range of sources of information. Initially, you might have gotten most of your news secondhand from friends. Over time, you turned to the media: the Internet, radio, television, magazines and newspapers. You also developed the skills needed to reach beyond your regular sources, using Google and other search engines to scour the world for news of interest. By now, you likely have developed a deep pool of knowledge about one or more topics; in fact, your friends might turn to you when they want the latest news on that topic.

How did that transformation occur? You worked at it. Little by little, you found new sources of information, built a knowledge base, and learned which sources were the most trustworthy and which got information first. All that took years to accomplish.

Considering that process of becoming an informed news consumer, it shouldn't come as a surprise that becoming a producer of news also takes time and effort. And yet many new journalists have trouble grasping that, complaining that there is nothing to write about, when in reality there are an unlimited number of stories waiting to be written.

So how do you go about finding all those stories? That's what we'll look at in this chapter. By the end of it, you should understand how journalists develop good story ideas, day after day after day.

Finding Story Ideas Online

First, an important warning: You cannot create good journalism by doing a Web search and rehashing the results. If you can find something on the Web, so can your audience. Your job is to find something *new*.

If you keep that in mind, you will find that the Google search engine is a fantastic tool. In only a few years after its initial release in the late 1990s, Google changed the way people around the world searched for information. In recent years, the majority of all searches on the World Wide Web have been conducted using Google—a practice so pervasive that *google* has entered our vocabulary as a verb meaning "to conduct a Web search" (as in "Have you *googled* the new athletic director?").

Google was not the first search engine and was far from the only one at the time of its public debut. But it offered a new perspective on how a search engine should work: The links from other relevant Web pages are used to determine the most relevant pages for a searcher. Google also does a good job at checking the spelling of search terms and offering correct spellings when you have misspelled them.

Most important, Google searches deliver results with depth and precision that its competitors cannot match. For instance, a search on the phrase "myocardial infarction" (the medical term for heart attack—the quote marks are used to indicate that Google should look for the exact phrase, not just one word or the other) returns more than 5 million results. Although that number is staggering, the first entry offers all the information most searchers would be looking for. (If you want to see just how good Google is, click the "I'm Feeling Lucky!" button rather than the "Google Search" button next time you use it. You'll get the single Web page Google chooses as most relevant for you. In many cases, it's exactly what you need.)

Evaluating Search Results. Not all information on the Web is created equal. In looking through search results, you need to assess the value of them. When you find something that looks useful, ask yourself:

- Who created this information? What are their credentials?
- What is the purpose of this information? Is it to inform or persuade? Is it based on facts or does it have an obvious bias?
- How current is this information? Has it been recently posted or updated, or might it be out of date?

Tapping into the Power of Google

Many regular Google users have spent years using the popular search engine to track down all sorts of information without ever realizing how powerful it really is. Even if you have played with the tabs (Web, Images, Video, News and Maps) on the Google home page, you have no idea what Google is capable of until you take a look under the hood.

To get there, click the "Advanced Search" link on the Google home page (see Figure 2.1). Doing so will let you fine-tune your search in a wide variety of ways:

- Including and excluding words and phrases: Searchers can specify words and phrases to *include* or *exclude* from results.
- Searching for specific types of files: If you are looking for a spreadsheet, PowerPoint presentation, PDF or other specific type of file, you can limit your search results to just that file type.

- Searching for recent pages: If you are looking for only the most recent information, you can use this filter to limit results to the past three, six or 12 months.
- Searching only specified domains: You can limit your search results to one specific Web site, such as that of a university, a business or an organization.
- Searching for links to a URL: Checking out other sites that link to a Web site can offer insights into the credibility of a site and provide further discussion of topics on it.
- Searching for synonyms: Adding a tilde sign (~) in front of a search term will cause Google to look for other similar words, too.

In addition, Google lets you search books and scholarly papers, with advanced search capabilities for each.

Google Advanced Search

Find results	with **all** of the words	television hearing	20 results	Google Search
	with the **exact phrase**			
	with **at least one** of the words	indecency obscenity		
	without the words			
Language	Return pages written in	English		
File Format	Only return results of the file format	Adobe Acrobat PDF (.pdf)		
Date	Return web pages first seen in the	past 6 months		
Numeric Range	Return web pages containing numbers between ___ and ___			
Occurrences	Return results where my terms occur	in the text of the page		
Domain	Only return results from the site or domain	.gov e.g. google.com, .org More info		
Usage Rights	Return results that are	not filtered by license More info		
SafeSearch	⦿ No filtering ○ Filter using SafeSearch			

Page-Specific Search

Similar	Find pages similar to the page	e.g. www.google.com/help.html	Search
Links	Find pages that link to the page		Search

Topic-Specific Searches

Google Book Search - Search the full text of books
New! Google Code Search - Search public source code
Google Scholar - Search scholarly papers
Google News archive search - Search historical news

Apple Macintosh - Search for all things Mac
BSD Unix - Search web pages about the BSD operating system
Linux - Search all penguin-friendly pages
Microsoft - Search Microsoft-related pages

U.S. Government - Search all U.S. federal, state and local government sites
Universities - Search a specific school's website

©2007 Google

FIGURE 3.1 While most people are content to use Google's simple search box, journalists know that they can get much better results using the Advanced Search.
Source: http://www.google.com/advanced_search

The Best Way to Find Information Online

News Pointers

The best way to find a fact might be to look instead for a source. That's the advice of Meg Smith of the News Research department at the Washington Post. Because the Web is so full of outdated and erroneous information, Smith says looking for facts isn't the best idea. Instead, she recommends that journalists concentrate on finding the best source for the information they need. That typically means using primary documents rather than secondary ones.

For instance, for biographical information, Smith advises tracking down personal Web pages, resumés, and company or government biographies. Less trustworthy but often acceptable are edited biographical sources (such as Who's Who), interviews and memoirs.

For research and statistics, the best bet usually is to head directly to the agency, institution or organization that created the data. Next best are experts, scientific articles that cite the data in their literature reviews, and news releases by the researchers or others who have gathered the data.

Smith advises steering clear of fan sites, blogs, Wikipedia (a collaborative online encyclopedia that anyone can edit—and intentionally add misinformation to) and "ANYTHING sent to you by e-mail."

Perhaps the most valuable tool for research as far as Smith is concerned is LexisNexis. The subscription service—typically offered free by universities to students and employees—indexes more than 4 billion documents, including news, public records, corporate documents, legislative information and more. The scope of its contents wouldn't mean much without LexisNexis' powerful search features. For instance:

- theat! searches for words beginning with theat (including theater, theatre, theatrical).
- gr*y searches for any four-letter word beginning with *gr* and ending with *y*.
- Michael w/2 Brown finds all instances in which Brown shows up within two words of Michael (allowing for things like middle names and initials).
- (dog or canine)—with the parentheses—finds references to either word.

The main problem with using LexisNexis is that if a searcher is not specific, the results can be overwhelming. Fortunately, using the News Search feature allows the same kind of customization as Google's Advanced Search offers (see Figure 3.1).

One caution on using LexisNexis: Unlike Google, if a searcher misspells a word, LexisNexis looks only for the misspelled word, returning only indexed documents that contain similarly misspelled words.[1]

The best information will help you gain a fuller understanding of the topic, define key terms for you, and help you prepare questions to be used to gather original information through interviews.

For example, suppose your local government announces a new department charged with preparing the area for a terrorist attack. Do a Google search on "terrorism preparedness" and you'll find a wealth of background information, including tips from the federal government, other cities' preparedness plans, and much more. Choose the most promising results and carefully sift through them, and you'll have a range of angles to pursue in your story. (Too many results? Click "Search within results" at the bottom of the page and add more search terms to refine the results.)

While a Google search can turn up helpful results, you often can find better information, in less time, by taking a different route. For example, when Honda announced its first consumer hydrogen-powered car, many journalists and other people seeking information

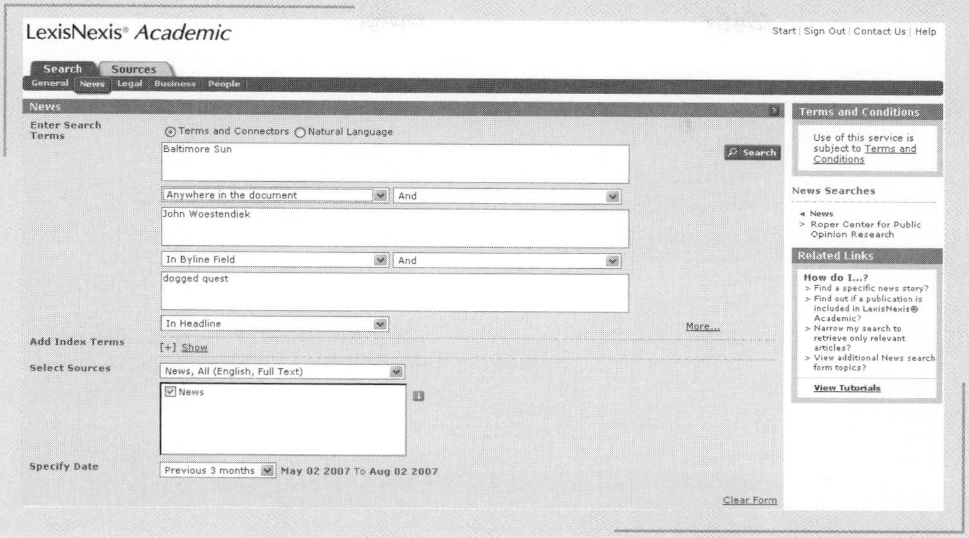

FIGURE 3.2 The LexisNexis search engine lets a reporter fine-tune the information quest. In this example, the reporter is searching for a specific story published in the Baltimore Sun. Adding the author's byline and the article's headline help ensure the best results.

went to Google, where a search on "Honda hydrogen" returned more than 1.2 million results. Although it's likely that those results included everything imaginable about the vehicle, they also included lots of speculation and less-than-accurate information. A more direct route would have been starting not at Google but instead at Honda's official Web site, where one more click would have taken the searcher directly to an extensive section devoted to the vehicle. For basic information, it's hard to imagine a more authoritative source than the manufacturer itself. Similarly, if you need to check which films were made by a specific director, you can probably do so much more quickly by visiting the Internet Movie Database (www.imdb.com) than by doing a Google search, and you'll have less chance of getting bad information from fan sites or other less professional offerings. (Keep in mind that if your story focuses on a controversy, then visiting only the authoritative source would not be sufficient to produce a balanced story.)

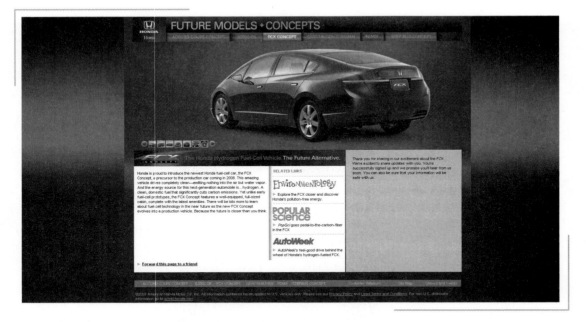

FIGURE 3.3

Reporters who were curious about Honda's announcement of a hydrogen-powered car could get most of the basics about it directly from the Honda Web site.

ASSIGNMENT DESK 3.1

In the past few years, the problem of excessive drinking on college campuses has attracted a great deal of attention. Make a list of search terms you would use on Google to find out as much as you can about this topic. If you have access to the Web, work with those terms to see what results you get. What other online sources would you use to fill in background information?

Unlike Honda.com and imdb.com, countless other places on the Internet that might have just what you are looking for have closed off content to search engines—making it part of the **Invisible Web**. That phrase refers to the countless databases maintained by government, business, universities and other sources. The archives either are not directly searchable (in most cases, because they require a user to enter text into a search box before they return results from the database) or are otherwise hidden from search engines. For instance, Citizen ICAM (http://12.17.79.6/ctznicam/ctznicam.asp) offers access to information on crimes reported within the previous three months in the Chicago area. The results, presented in simple graphical format, can help a writer get a sense of trends in crimes around the area. Although the information is freely available to the public, it will not turn up in a Google search. Fortunately, you can get to the gateway for that information by Googling "Chicago crime database." As a general rule, it's always a good strategy to add the word *database* to search topics, just to see what sources turn up.

You won't be so lucky with many other resources from the *Invisible Web*. Even if you know they exist, the only way to get to them is by knowing their URLs or starting with a good portal, such as Invisible Web (www.invisible-web.net/), DirectSearch (www.freepint.com/gary/direct.htm), Profusion (www.profusion.com/ index.htm) or CompletePlanet (www.completeplanet.com/). More information on using those sites and exploring other ways to search the Invisible Web can be found at Robert Lackie's Web site, "Those Dark Hiding Places" (http://library.rider.edu/scholarly/rlackie/ Invisible/Inv_Web.html) and "Depth Reporting" (www.depthreporting.com).

Among the "invisible" items of particular importance to journalists are the millions of news stories that are hidden in news site archives. Although some news stories will show up in a LexisNexis or Google search (when using Google, be sure to choose the

Depth Reporting

Friday, May 4, 2007
3D graphics with GE-Graph

The free GE-Graph plots data graphically on Google Earth. Here's an example: I took 2000 Census data on median home price household income by ZIP code for our circulation area, used Microsoft Access to combine it with a file that gave the latitude and longitude for each ZIP code, and cut and pasted it into GE-Graph. GE-Graph can also import data from a file or you can type it in, and it has various options for choosing colors, labels and transforming the data. You then click "Run" and it exports the data as KML, Google's mapping format. This was the result:

About Me

MARK SCHAVER
LOUISVILLE, KENTUCKY, UNITED
STATES

Depth Reporting originates as a semi-irregular email I send to the staff of The Courier-Journal, where I'm the computer-assisted reporting director. I share pointers to useful Web sites, examples of computer-assisted and investigative reporting, and whatever else strikes me as interesting, funny or worthwhile. I welcome comments or suggestions, and can be reached at mschaver (at) courier-journal.com.

View my complete profile

Subscribe To My Feed By Clicking This Icon

FIGURE 3.4 DepthReporting.com offers reporters tips on getting to the invaluable information in the Invisible Web.

"news" option, and then select "archives" for information more than a few weeks old), finding other stories requires that the searcher go directly to the online news site and use its search feature.

ASSIGNMENT DESK 3.2

Using the Invisible Web tools discussed in this chapter, see what you can find about the following:

- Recent crime reports in your town or the nearest large city.
- Recent patent applications and approvals.
- Information on toxic waste sites within 50 miles of your school.
- The latest filings of the Securities and Exchange Commission.

Citing Sources. Journalists need to be extremely careful when conducting online research so that they do not steal others' work and use it as their own. Even longtime journalists have fallen into the trap of inadvertently pasting someone else's words into a news story or column without citing the source. In many cases, the offenders have been fired as soon as the transgression came to light, even if they had worked for decades without incident.

The warning made earlier in this chapter bears repeating: Online research should be used *only* to provide background information and story ideas. On the rare occasions when you might want to incorporate previously published information (whether from online or print sources or from wire services your organization subscribes to), you *must* include the source of the material, even if you are paraphrasing it. Unlike scholarly papers, however, the style of citation is less formal, and footnotes are not used. Here's an example, in which a writer refers to a fact from an Associated Press story:

> Earlier this week, The Associated Press reported Judge Monroe had promised she would answer the legislators' questions.

It would have been wrong to write that sentence without the phrase "the Associated Press reported."

When you are citing an online source and your own work will be published online, you should add a link to the original source:

> Earlier this week, The Associated Press reported Judge Monroe had promised she would answer the legislators' questions.

One category of information you should never reuse, even with a citation, is quoted material. If you haven't heard the words spoken yourself—and that does not count hearing them on radio, TV or online newscasts—do not include a quote. Doing so is considered plagiarism.

Using Blogs for Research and Story Ideas

Blogs are becoming a more important resource for journalists. Recent surveys show between a one-fourth and one-half of all working journalists use blogs regularly for research. In an interview with BulldogReporter.com, Wall Street Journal reporter Nick Wingfield said that blogs are particularly important for reporters covering technology. "There are a lot of superb blogs out there and many [of us] are cherry picking out interesting stories there," he said.

Wingfield identified three primary ways journalists use blogs:

- **To find story tips**. Blogs sometimes break news, often by leaking information. Journalists can use those stories to do further research for their own stories.
- **To get a sense of what people think**. Many blogs serve as sounding boards for people to debate issues. As Wingfield explained, blogs allow a reporter to take the pulse of the public. Both pro and con comments can give a sense of public opinion.
- **To alert them to stories they otherwise might miss**. By subscribing to a tightly focused blog, a journalist will often learn about stories that would otherwise have fallen through the cracks.[2]

Using News Releases for Story Ideas

Journalists have long had a love-hate relationship with public relations practitioners. The hate part is based on the primary job of PR people: that is, managing the news and controlling what information reaches the public and what doesn't. Journalists often feel frustrated by PR practitioners who keep them from getting answers to important questions.

On the other hand, journalists often feel the love for PR practitioners because they also provide ideas for stories by way of the news releases they issue. In fact, a large percentage of news and feature story ideas grow out of news releases. That's a time-honored tradition in journalism. A PR practitioner brings a topic or event to a journalist's attention, and the journalist follows up by writing a story on it. Mission accomplished for both parties: getting the word out for the PR person's client, and coming up with interesting ideas for the journalist's publications.

For this to work, however, a journalist cannot just rewrite a news release (or, worst of all, add a byline and pass it off as his or her own work). A news release should be regarded as a story *idea*. It needs to be checked further. Sources mentioned in the release should be contacted for additional information, and other sources should be asked for their reactions. For broadcast or online stories, the reporter should gather or create additional sound bites, video clips and interactive elements.

After those steps, a journalist might end up with quite a different story from the one in the news release. For example, let's say that a new supermarket chain is moving into town. The chain's PR firm will likely send out a news release announcing the opening of the store, providing information about the size of the store, its gourmet selections, and so on. Rather than reprint the news release as a story, a good journalist will examine the consequences of an event. How will it affect the existing supermarkets and small food stores? Do shoppers plan to change their habits? Could it spur a price war on food? Those are the sorts of questions that need to be asked to come up with a story that does more for the audience than merely rehash the store owner's official story.

ASSIGNMENT DESK 3.3

Visit the online press room of the National Geographic Society (http://press.national geographic.com/pressroom/index.jsp?siteID=1), the FBI (www.fbi.gov/pressroom.htm) or the American Red Cross (www.redcross.org/press/0,1079,0_314_,00.html). Read one of the news releases.

Make a list of sources in the release, with at least three questions for each source.

Next, do some local research to find other sources and create additional questions.

Finding Story Ideas in Nonlocal Stories

Some observers have commented that journalism is the oldest form of recycling, and in a sense, that's true: There are few truly new ideas. Instead, journalists often look to put twists on existing stories. One of the most common ways of doing this is by localizing a nonlocal story; that is, by looking at a story that originates elsewhere and asking, "How does that relate to what's going on locally?" or "Is there something like that happening around here?"

Today's culture of instantaneous news publishing makes this process fairly easy. A journalist begins by looking at stories created by news organizations in other locations. Google News offers ready access to more than 4,500 news sources. Although many of these sources run identical stories about major events (typically sourced from AP or Reuters), they also feature homegrown stories. Those are the ones worth paying attention to.

For example, when San Francisco media reported on a plan to cover the city with affordable, high-speed Internet access, an attentive journalist would ask, "Is anything like that in the works around here?" When 20 people died after a tour boat flipped over on a lake in upstate New York, the logical question for any journalist who works in a town near water became, "Do we have any safeguards to prevent this sort of thing from happening here?"

Even wire service stories that report on matters of national concern can spur great ideas for local stories. For instance, when a study was released claiming that 90 percent of U.S. men and 70 percent of U.S. women over the age of 60 are overweight, an enterprising journalist would have looked for a local angle: "Are local residents better or worse than that? What resources are available to help overweight older residents of the area slim down?"

ASSIGNMENT DESK 3.4

Using Google News or the state reports in USA Today, pick five nonlocal stories and come up with ideas for localizing them. Do whatever research is necessary to find local background information on the topics and develop a list of potential sources.

Finding Story Ideas in Older Stories

One common complaint about journalists is their "attention deficit disorder": They quickly abandon a story when a new one comes along and forget about following up on the first story. The public often is left with lots of unanswered questions.

To address that problem, some journalists make it a habit to follow up on stories they have covered in the past, and some news organizations have institutionalized these kinds of stories with regular follow-up features. (One indication of the interest in such stories is the popularity of entertainment programs such as VH-1's "Where Are They Now?") For instance, if months ago, a story reported that a promising young athlete was involved in a severe accident, many people would be interested in knowing how his or her recovery has gone and what his or her plans are. If a storm caused major damage to a local neighborhood last year, people would be interested in how rebuilding efforts have progressed and how those displaced by the storm have coped.

Using Databases for Story Ideas

Given the time, a journalist often can find story ideas in piles of data collected by government agencies. The data covers a wide range of topics and includes airplane service difficulty reports, storm events, FBI crime data, highway fatalities, problems with medical devices and federal contracts awarded to private companies. (A great list of databases of public records is available at journalism.berkeley.edu/resources/car/publicrecords.html. Investigative Reporters and Editors Inc. maintains a list of several dozen databases available for sale to journalists at http://www.ire.org/datalibrary/databases/.)

Generally speaking, a computer-assisted story starts not with the data but with a question. For instance, after several states began using red-light cameras to ticket motorists who

News Pointers

Tools for Following the News

FEED READERS

A wide range of news sites, blogs and other online sites offer RSS feeds that allow people to subscribe. Doing so guarantees that the subscriber will always be informed of the latest news from the site. When a person signs up for an RSS feed, every new item will be sent to him or her as soon as it becomes available.

To read RSS feeds, the subscriber needs a feed reader. Some Web browsers, such as Firefox and Internet Explorer include built-in feed readers. Item titles are displayed in a sidebar next to the main browser window; clicking on a title opens the full story or post in the browser. In addition, a number of dedicated desktop feed reader programs are available (mostly for free), as are a range of online feed readers, such as NewsGator. A current list of

feed readers is available at http://hebig.org/blogs/archives/main/ 000877.php.

As an alternative, offerings like MyYahoo and Google News allow users to create personalized home pages, each featuring a unique blend of news.

E-MAIL ALERTS

E-mail alerts are another way to stay on top of news. Many news organizations (CNN and The New York Times, for instance) and non-news organizations and companies that are often in the news (for example, the American Medical Association) provide the chance for interested parties to sign up to receive alerts of new information via e-mail. In addition, Google allows users to customize news alerts on any topic (www.google.com/alerts).

did not stop at traffic lights, many drivers wondered whether the cameras were helping to prevent accidents or were merely helping local jurisdictions raise money. In Washington, D.C., the use of cameras resulted in more than $32 million in fines during their first six years of operation. That led two reporters for the Washington Post to obtain a database of accident reports filed by Washington police. Their study of the data revealed that the cameras had not helped lower accident rates. The number of accidents at intersections with cameras actually had *doubled* during that time.[3]

In another example, reporters at The News and Observer in North Carolina were interested to know if North Carolina State basketball players had sold any of the tickets they had been given to their games. Doing so is a violation of NCAA rules. Finding the answer was a challenge because the team's guest records were not computerized. So The News & Observer staff created its own database and checked players' guest lists for regular season games against their guest lists for the highly sought after tournament tickets. Many of the tournament "guests" did not show up on the regular season guest lists, and

News Pointers

10 Great Public Records

Authors Jeff Taylor and Alison Young created this list for the Detroit Free Press Jobs Page in the early days of the Internet. Many of these types of records are now available online, but Young warns that "reporters shouldn't become lazy about assuming that everything is online because much of the best stuff is still on paper and you have to use some shoe leather to go get it."

1. **Court documents:** Court records include criminal case files and files of civil lawsuits. These files are useful for backgrounding companies and individuals. A quick check of court records can reveal many things: Has a person been charged with/convicted of crimes in the past? Is a company or individual being sued by creditors? Are consumers suing a company for allegedly fraudulent business practices? Divorce records can be a gold mine, with some case files revealing all sorts of usually private financial information. Depositions are particularly useful. Occasionally they'll be a part of a court file. Often you can get access to them through attorneys. Other courts also have useful records: district courts, federal courts, bankruptcy courts.

2. **Property records:** Property records can give clues to the wealth, assets and debts of individuals. They also will let you know if the person has tax problems: Both the Internal Revenue Service and the state taxation department will attach tax liens to the property of individuals who owe them money.

3. **Police reports:** Police reports about crimes are public information, as are booking mug shots of people who are arrested. Also public are search warrants, which are usually filed by the police at their local district court.

4. **Inspection reports:** These can involve a variety of records—all available to the public: fire safety inspection reports, food safety inspection reports (for restaurants, school cafeterias, supermarkets, meat processors), building safety inspections, elevator/escalator inspections, nursing home inspections, etc.

5. **Licensing records:** Many stories involve people or services that require state or federal licenses. Some examples: doctors, nurses, beauticians, limo companies, daycare centers, foster homes, insurance agents, etc. If they have licenses, an agency keeps a licensing file on the person or business that may have complaints/disciplinary action reports and other interesting information. For example: a doctor's licensing file may include information about

when players were confronted with the discrepancy, some admitted to selling the tournament tickets.[4]

Computer-assisted reporting does not necessarily require lots of time, but it does require a commitment from a news organization and its staff to go after unique stories of interest to the audience. The topic is covered in depth in many books and Web sites; two good starting points are DepthReporting.com and Statistics Every Writer Should Know (www.robertniles.com/stats/). In addition, PowerReporting.com offers quick access to many documents and databases.

Finding Story Ideas on a Beat

Many story ideas arise in the course of a writer covering a **beat**. A beat can be either a specific geographical location, such as a suburb or neighborhood, or it can be topical, such as education, local government or high school sports. For both types of beats, journalists need to check in regularly to find news of interest to their audiences.

where he or she went to medical school, did his or her residency, where he or she has previously lived and whether he or she is licensed to practice in other states.

6. Corporate records: Both for-profit and not-for-profit companies must file incorporation papers and annual reports in the states where they do business. These records can give you the names and addresses of the people who started the company and the names and addresses of current officers — important information if you're looking for people to interview. Large, publicly traded corporations have to file extensive financial records with the Securities and Exchange Commission.

7. Not-for-profit tax returns: All charities (except church charities) must file a tax return called an IRS Form 990 — which is available for public review. This is an extremely useful document that gives a breakdown of the group's finances, where the money comes from and how it was spent, and it discloses the salaries of the CEO and highest paid employees and outside contractors. Keep in mind that tax-exempt organizations are not just traditional charities, like the United Way or the local soup kitchen. They also include: universities, hospitals, the National Football League, some museums, unions and the folks that put on the Academy Awards.

8. Drivers licenses and auto/boat registrations: Drivers' records include a person's address, date of birth, height, weight, eye color and driving violation history. Auto and boat registration records give a clue about a person's wealth. Privacy legislation has restricted access to both types of records in recent years.

9. Campaign finance records: Candidates for local, state and national office must file reports disclosing who contributed to their campaigns. This information — available for each candidate — typically includes the names of contributors, their company or occupation, the amount given and the date. Most local records are still kept on paper.

10. Computerized records and the Internet: Huge databases are increasingly available through government agencies and on the Internet. The Internet can provide access to many government records 24 hours a day. This is particularly useful for stories that break at night. For instance, if a plane goes down, at www.faa.gov there is a wealth of information about previous incidents/accidents.

Having a beat offers a journalist the chance to develop sources and contacts over time. That is a huge advantage that general assignment reporters do not have. Instead, they get sent from one story to another, covering a wide geographical range and a wide range of topics. Although that type of work can be exciting, it also means that the writer has to start from scratch almost every day.

Beats vary from one news organization to another. Large general-interest newspapers might have 100 or more beats, with a reporter assigned to each one. Smaller print, online and broadcast organizations might have only one or two beats, or none; all writers might be general assignment reporters, whose area of coverage can change day to day or even hour to hour.

Typical beats include:

- Business and economics.
- Consumer information.
- Education.
- Health.
- Medicine.
- Police and courts.
- Religion.
- Science and the environment.
- Transportation.

For more specialized news outlets, beats would be much more focused. For instance, reporters for a business publication would typically cover specialized beats such as entrepreneurship, sales, finance, franchises, employment, and so on.

If you are assigned to a beat, the most important task is to establish good sources. Without good sources, you will have no stories. Fortunately, there are a number of ways to build a source list quickly:

- Ask the reporter who formerly worked the beat to pass along his or her list of contacts.
- Check previous stories from the beat to identify key players.
- Try to track down "Mr. or Ms. Right," that is, the person who knows everyone important on the beat.
- Encourage sources to share their good experiences with other potential sources.
- Look for general experts at the local and national levels to provide background information. LexisNexis and expert directories offer plenty of leads.

As you build your list of sources, it's important to evaluate your contacts. You need to assess each source's level of expertise and potential biases. And you need to make sure every source is willing to talk on the record: that is, the information he or she provides can be published or broadcast with the person providing the information cited as the source.

It's also vital to keep your information organized. Don't just throw a bunch of business cards and sticky notes into a drawer. The best way to store information so you can quickly retrieve what you need is to enter it into a spreadsheet or an e-mail program's address book. Try to get the following information for each source:

- Full name.
- Title.
- Work, home and mobile phone numbers.
- Pager number.
- Vacation home phone number.
- E-mail address.
- Names of spouse, children, secretaries and administrative assistants.
- Any other personal information that might be useful later (e.g., alma mater, former jobs, etc.).[5]

Having a great range of sources gets you on the way to doing a great job. The next step is knowing how to work with your sources. The following tips can help you get the best results:

- Be available: "Let people on your beat know you're interested in hearing tips, suggestions, complaints, whatever," advises Steve Buttry of the American Press Institute. "Make sure they have your phone number and e-mail. If it's appropriate, give them home, cell and pager numbers, too. Make rounds frequently in person and by telephone."
- Listen to tips and show interest: "Sources may want to bend your ear about a matter other than what you want to talk about," says Buttry. "Listen. You may get a good news tip. Even if the source thinks it's a story and you don't, show interest. However boring or annoying a source may be, however uninteresting you find this alleged tip, you don't know when a little bit of knowledge might be helpful. Even if the information is completely useless, the source will appreciate your interest and may someday tell you something that is important or interesting."
- Tell sources what you're doing: "Tell good sources about stories you're working on, even the ones that may not involve them directly," Buttry says. "You may know that a source isn't directly involved with an issue, but if you tell him about the stories you're working on, he may steer you toward other sources who might be helpful, or he may tell you something helpful that he's heard around the office."[6]
- Let sources know you're interested: Larry Welborn of The Orange County (Calif.) Register says that "you have to teach (sources) to give you a call. Tell them how to do it. 'You know, I am looking for that slice-of-life story, that unusual, happy ending, maybe one of those Horatio Alger deals. Give me a call when you get something.' If they say, 'I never hear anything,' tell them, 'Sooner or later, you will . . . and when you do, call me.' That lets people know that you think they are players. Flattery works."[7]
- Be professional: To get respect, you have to look and act as though you deserve it. Dress professionally, show up on time, and be painstakingly careful with names and facts. Do your homework on the organization or topic, and learn the terminology used by insiders.

- Be relentless: "New reporters should salt their beat with business cards," advises the Poynter Institute's NewsU faculty. "Take would-be sources to lunch if your organization's budget and your expense account will allow it. Find out when potential sources are going to be appearing in court and seek them out in the hallway during recesses. Look for them in the coffee shop or local bar that cops frequent and strike up conversations. Be relentless but friendly and open. Your determination may impress and win over potential sources, and even if it doesn't, they may decide it isn't worth the effort to avoid talking to you."[8]
- Ask for help: Don't try to bluff your way through things. Let your sources know when you need their assistance. "People like to be asked for help," Welborn says. "It makes them feel useful. I often ask, 'Can you help me find out X, Y and Z?' And I'm amazed how many times people break their backs trying to help. Or I ask them to explain something. People want to be of service. Let them."[9] L. Kelly of The Wichita (Kan.) Eagle adds: "Don't be afraid to let people know that you're new to this and you might have a stupid question. Don't assume that if someone is speaking jargon to you, that you'll be able to figure it out later. . . . When news breaks, it's going to be life-changing for [many]."[10]

ASSIGNMENT
DESK **3.5**

Choose a topic on campus that interests you: student government, athletics, residence life, Greek life, the arts, and so on. Using sources such as your school's Web site and back issues of the student newspaper, draw up a list of at least 10 people who would be valuable sources for a beat covering that topic. Make sure your list reflects a range of positions and a diversity of sources.

Once you have assembled a good collection of sources, you will have what researcher Gaye Tuchman referred to as a **news net**.[11] A news net is constructed from contacts who over time prove to be reliable sources of information. By routinely checking in with those sources, writers gain a degree of confidence that they will always get the important stories. In a sense, the news net is like a fishing net, woven so that the "big fish" don't get away. The sources for a given news net tend to be people at the top; depending on the beat, sources might include executives, political leaders, church leaders, school board members or other high-level figures.

Although regular access to such high-level sources guarantees that few major stories are missed, it's still possible that many "little fish" will fall through, and some of those will prove to be important in the long run. For instance, trends typically occur when a wide range of people begin acting or thinking differently. Often, these ripples go undetected by the elites in society who might have little direct contact with the majority of the public. So it's important not only to keep your eyes on your net, but also to look beyond it.

Another problem that sometimes occurs from focusing on high-level sources is that doing so can lead journalists to merely repeat sources' assessments, without checking to see if things are really as they say. Media critics have referred to this tendency of many journalists to function as no more than "stenographers with amnesia": That is, they simply report what the leaders say and don't remember the many cases in which those assessments and pronouncements have been proven wrong.

This disconnect was brought home emphatically for journalists who covered the massive devastation of Hurricane Katrina in 2005. While officials at all levels of government trumpeted their success in dealing with the disaster, journalists on the scene in places like New Orleans found anything but success: people without food, water and shelter for days on end, dead bodies floating down the streets, and many other tragic scenes. For many journalists, the gap between official pronouncements and the reality of the situation was so great that they appeared stunned, and some had a hard time remaining objective.

The lesson here is *not* that beat journalists should work without a "net," but rather that the net should be enlarged to include not only high-level sources, but also people who are affected by their decisions.

Conducting Interviews

No matter where a story idea comes from, most of the information for the actual story will be gathered in interviews. Interviews vary in length and format, and the information gathered in them appear in a range of different types of stories:

- **News interviews** are done in connection with news events and can consist of as little as two or three questions asked in a minute or two. These interviews primarily serve to gather immediate reactions about events in the news or to add pertinent facts. For example, when a study was published that reported a link between light smoking and highly elevated risks of dying of heart disease or lung cancer, some journalists turned to the authors of the study for comments, and other writers sought out additional researchers and public health experts for their reactions. The results of this type of interview typically appear in news stories.
- **Depth interviews** also often grow out of news events, but they run longer than news interviews and provide more opportunity to explore a topic with the subject. For instance, if the president of a local university announces a new direction for the school, a depth interview will allow a writer to explore the consequences: what the news means for students, faculty and others. The information from that interview would likely appear in a news analysis.
- **Profile interviews** are focused on a person. Whenever a person—whether politician, entertainer, athlete, inventor or something else—appears on the public's radar screen, people are eager to know more about him or her. Profile interviews can run from an hour to several days or more. They offer a journalist the opportunity to learn all about the person. The information gleaned from a profile interview typically appears in a personality profile (discussed in Chapter 6).

Preparing for an Interview

Depending on the circumstances behind an interview and the time available beforehand, your preparation might be minimal or extensive. If you are working on a news story about a tornado that's just hit town, you don't have the luxury of spending days researching tornadoes before you interview the mayor. On the other hand, a profile interview that is planned weeks ahead of time allows you plenty of time to prepare. In preparation for an interview you might:

- Get basic background information on a topic, using anything from reference works to government documents. If the topic is new to you and time permits, you might squeeze in a book or two on the topic. For instance, if you are assigned a story on two local residents who have started a vineyard but you don't know anything about winemaking, you might want to read a book on the topic.
- Check for related news articles. This is obvious when dealing with a news-related event. For instance, thinking back to the university president's announcement: Have other local schools made such changes? Other national schools? You might find yourself consulting a range of sources from general-interest local newspapers to special-interest publications (in this case, the Chronicle of Higher Education would be an obvious choice).
- Find sources who represent a range of views and perspectives. Experts—whether government officials, business executives, researchers or others—are always good to talk to (and the PowerReporting.com Web site can help you find many experts quickly). But they don't always have the most interesting things to say, and they can't give a full perspective on a story. Ask yourself who will be affected by an event or announcement, and make sure you talk with them as well as with the experts.
- Read interviews, Q and A's and profiles featuring the person you will be interviewing. Remember that your job is to find something new for your audience. The more you know about what a person has said and what's been written about him or her, the better your chances of asking original questions and coming away with unique information.

Once you've done your research—even if it consists of only skimming a recent news story or two—you should put together a list of questions. Start with as many as you can think of. The only restriction is that your questions should stick to a clear central theme. For instance, if you're interviewing the university president about his announcement, avoid questions about the school's football team, unless the elimination of athletics is part of the new direction.

Your list should combine both **closed-ended** and **open-ended questions**. The former are questions that solicit a short, pointed answer, often "yes" or "no." They work well at obtaining and verifying factual information (for example, "I understand that you formerly worked for the state of Idaho. Is that correct?"). Open-ended questions solicit longer, less definitive answers. They are appropriate when you are trying to gather more in-depth information ("What would you say are the top priorities for your committee?") or find how someone feels about a subject or event ("How would you have handled the situation differently?").

One of the most important functions of open-ended questions is drawing out **anecdotes**. An anecdote is a short, pointed story. Anecdotes bring stories to life by offering specifics in place of generalizations. Some interview subjects will toss out anecdotes with

Why Choose Journalism?

Journalism is the one job in which you're paid to be nosy and persistent. It is a job that values understanding, whether it's figuring out the politics of the defense budget or the defensive strategy of a political campaign. If I want to delve further into foreign policy or football or mutual funds, I can ask the experts and they usually answer my questions. If I'm skeptical or uncertain, I can continue asking questions—and they will continue to answer. Journalism is rarely predictable. I go to work knowing today will bear no resemblance to yesterday, and tomorrow will be completely different.

DONNA CASSATA
The Associated Press

no prompting, but many need encouragement; in some cases, they might not even understand what an anecdote is. The best way to fish for anecdotes is by offering one to the interviewee:

> **INTERVIEWER:** Times must have been tough when you lived in that neighborhood.
>
> **SUBJECT:** Oh, they were!
>
> **INTERVIEWER** *(trying again)*: How bad were they?
>
> **SUBJECT:** Believe me, plenty bad.
>
> **INTERVIEWER** *(trying another tactic)*: A friend of mine lived in an apartment there, and he woke up one night to the sound of his door being broken down, only to find a bunch of police pointing guns in his face. They were supposed to be raiding the apartment downstairs but got his number by mistake.
>
> **SUBJECT:** Oh, that's nothing . . . (proceeds with brilliant anecdote).

In all cases, make sure your questions are simple. If you ever watch presidential news conferences, you'll notice that some journalists try to sneak three or four questions into one because it might be their only chance to get the floor. However, trying to pack several questions into one typically results in an incoherent mess that no one could possibly answer. For best results, keep your questions short and stick to one point each.

Also, make sure your questions are answerable. If you're interviewing someone who has worked a job for 25 years, don't ask, "What was the most memorable moment of your career?" That question requires the subject to try to conjure up memories from a quarter of a century, then weigh them all against each other. Instead, try something like this: "You must have met a number of interesting people in that job. Who were some of the more memorable?"

Once you have your list, order your questions in terms of importance. Most people have strict limits on their time and may not have time to answer all your questions.

You don't want to have them leave before you get to your most important questions. Even if you've been promised unlimited time for your interview, something might happen that causes the interview to be cut short, so make sure you start out with your best questions.

It's always a good idea to close an interview with a variation of the question, "Is there anything else I should know?" A source will often surprise you with details or further information that you had not thought of. In addition, that type of question can help you come up with more article ideas. Livingston (Mich.) Press & Argus Managing Editor Maria Stuart says nothing can be more important than the final question you ask:

> One of the biggest mistakes reporters I've worked with over the years have made is not asking a final, "So, is there anything else going on?" Or, "Have you heard anything else I should know?" Or even, "Is there anyone else I should talk to?" Sure, they're working on the story at hand, but that story's going to be done in a couple of hours. People always know things beyond the interview at hand, so why not ask?

ASSIGNMENT DESK 3.6

Using the beat and list of sources you developed in Assignment Desk 3.5, come up with a story idea for the campus newspaper. Choose someone from your source list to be your primary interviewee, and create a list of at least 10 interview questions. Make sure your questions address all aspects of your story topic and include a mix of open-ended and closed-ended questions. At least two of your questions should be designed to draw out anecdotes.

Interview Formats

Most journalists agree that a face-to-face interview is the best way to gather information. Unfortunately, time and schedules do not always allow for face-to-face interviews. When you can't arrange to meet with an interviewee in person, you will have to opt for interviewing by telephone, e-mail or instant messaging.

Face-to-Face Interviews

Talking with someone in person provides the most direct and intimate form of communication. It also lets the interviewer take note of the subject's body language and gather physical descriptions of the subject and his or her surroundings, when appropriate to the story. As Howard Kurtz of the Washington Post has written in comparing face-to-face interviews with e-mail interviews: "When you see someone's expressions or listen to someone's voice, you get a sense of the person that words on a screen lack. A back-and-forth in real time often leads to illuminating moments. And, of course, typed answers can be rather bloodless—and they make it impossible for me to write, *he said with a smile*:)."[12]

Journalists differ on their preferred methods of taking notes during a face-to-face interview. Some journalists who write exclusively for print or online publication prefer the tried-and-true method of taking notes on a notepad (or a laptop computer, but a laptop can create a virtual wall between the interviewer and the interviewee). If you decide to take notes this way, *don't* try to write down every word the interviewee says. Instead, focus on three things:

1. Major points.
2. Good quotes.
3. Specific facts (names with verified spellings; dates; places).

Once the interview ends, head for a computer as soon as possible and type up your notes. If you transcribe your notes quickly, you'll be surprised at how much information you retain that you did not write down. If you let your notes grow cold, however, they might not even make sense to you.

The other alternative—mandatory for broadcasters and favored by many print and online writers—is to use an audio recorder. This method gives you a reliable record of everything that the interviewee said. If any questions arise about quotes or facts, you have the original record to support you. And obviously, you have your sound bites ready to roll.

The risks of relying on a recorder are numerous, however:

- The interviewee might be intimidated by the recorder.
- Background noise might make your interviewee unintelligible.
- The tape might run out or the memory might fill without your noticing.
- Batteries might die.

Even if everything goes well, you'll be forced to wade through a long recording every time you want to locate a fact or quote. To eliminate that problem, some journalists take a recorder and a notepad, jotting down the times or counter readings at critical moments in the interview:

01:12   "The purpose of this project . . ."

03:27   Joanne Kern, vice president from 1998 to 2004

07:19   "No one could have foreseen . . ."

Perhaps the most important advice for successful interviewing is to remember that you are there to *listen*. Keep your own comments and opinions to a minimum. Don't rush to fill every pause in the conversation. Instead, give your sources time to think and respond, and you'll get the best material.

If an interviewee says something you don't understand, don't hesitate to ask him or her to repeat it or explain it to you. Ultimately, you'll be responsible for your story, and if your audience cannot figure out something, they'll blame *you*, not your source.

Telephone Interviews

When time or distance prevent a face-to-face interview, a telephone interview is the best alternative. On the phone, you can hear the interviewee's voice, sense his or her comfort or discomfort, and pick up on inflections in tone.

Phone interviews can pose logistical problems, though. If you take notes, you might end up with long silences while you write. While those pauses are a minor nuisance in person, where the interviewee can see you writing, they can be deadly on the phone.

Another option is to use an inexpensive adaptor to record a phone interview directly to an audio recorder. In addition, several software packages allow recording telephone conversations directly to a computer, where they can be accessed and edited easily. In either case, you need to make sure that you follow the laws of your state on recording phone calls. Most permit recording of calls as long as one party (in this case, the journalist) is aware of the recording. Several others, however, require that all parties be notified that the conversation is going to be recorded and given the chance to refuse. These "two-party states" are listed in Table 3.1.

E-mail Interviews

E-mail interviews offer more convenience than face-to-face or telephone interviews, but they offer less chance to interact or capture nuances. Some journalists use e-mail interviews only to set up face-to-face or phone interviews, gather basic factual information, or ask a follow-up question or two after a conventional interview. Others, though, find e-mail a valuable tool that offers several benefits over traditional interviewing methods. In 1997, for instance, Seattle Times reporter Deborah Nelson won a Pulitzer Prize for investigative reporting for a story on corruption in a federal Indian housing program. Nelson found e-mail provided a perfect way to interact with the top official involved. "He was very busy and difficult to catch by phone," she told American Journalism Review, "so the e-mails allowed us to maintain a running dialogue. When I wanted a database of HUD grants to tribes, I didn't have to wait years for a (Freedom of Information Act) response; he had it e-mailed to me as an attachment."[13]

Like Nelson, many other journalists also find a lot to like about e-mail interviews:

- They offer non-native speakers a chance to polish their responses.
- They allow more time for thought and reflection.
- They overcome the challenges posed when dealing with sources who live far away and in greatly different time zones.

TABLE 3.1

States That Require All Parties to Consent to Having Telephone Conversations Recorded

California	Michigan
Connecticut	Montana
Delaware	New Hampshire
Florida	Pennsylvania
Maryland	Washington
Massachusetts	

Source: United States Telephone Recording Laws (www.callcorder.com/phone-recording-law-america.htm).

- Some subjects, especially those who might be involved in activities society frowns on, do not like to talk on the phone or give out phone numbers.
- They can be productive for conducting follow-up interviews over time, saving you the time normally taken up by chit-chat on the phone.
- One e-mail can reach dozens or even hundreds of sources in the time it would take to make a single phone call.
- The widespread adoption of wireless e-mail devices makes it easier to reach many people by e-mail than by phone.
- Time savings resulting from cutting down on travel to and from interviews and playing phone tag allows more time to work on more stories.
- They provide a record of the conversation.
- They may be the best way to communicate with people with hearing impairments.[14]

Not everyone is upbeat about e-mail interviews, though. For many journalists, several problems limit their usefulness:

- Interview subjects who are pressed for time may provide only the most cursory answers, robbing stories of the richness that comes from the give-and-take that takes place between two people meeting in person. As New York Times Magazine contributing writer Michael Sokolove told Quill: "Getting out in the world informs you. . . . You're supposed to be a witness, the journalist. The antithesis of that seems to be sitting somewhere e-mailing."
- It's easier to fall victim to someone who's pretending to be someone else, or to buy into a hoax when the only contact is via e-mail. In one example, a reporter for ComputerWorld based a story about cyberterrorism on an e-mail he had received from someone claiming to be a terrorist. In reality, the "terrorist" was another journalist looking for a good story himself.[15]
- Journalists will likely miss many good stories if they spend most of their interview time in the office at a computer rather than out interacting with people.
- Business executives, politicians and other people who are frequently interviewed may provide only rehearsed or evasive responses.
- Relying on e-mail for interviews limits access to many people who don't have computers or Internet service — in some cases, the people most affected by laws, natural disasters, and so on.
- E-mail interviews lack the candor and spontaneity that comes from face-to-face conversations.

If you decide that e-mail is the best choice for a given interview, you should follow a few ground rules in your initial e-mail:

- Identify yourself and your affiliation, and make it clear that the comments you are seeking might be published.
- Provide your phone number and offer to talk via phone if your source is more comfortable doing that.
- Provide an idea of how lengthy the interview will be, offering an estimate of the number of questions you plan to ask.
- Give the source an idea of how quickly you need to get the information. If you don't do this, your e-mail might be set aside even though you are on a tight deadline.

- Request that your source confirm his or her name and title, and ask for a contact phone number.
- Use your e-mail program's spell checker. If it does not have one, write your message in a word processing program, use its spell checker, then paste the text into the body of the e-mail.

Wait to hear back from your source for at least a few days before sending a follow-up note. If you send a follow-up, make it clear that you were concerned that your initial e-mail did not arrive, which is a real possibility in these days of spam filters and computer viruses.

In some newsrooms, journalists must indicate in their stories when information has been gathered via e-mail. For example:

"The film is about family, but it is also about Israel. Great hopes and innocence break into pieces," Zvi-Riklis says in an e-mail interview from her home in Israel.

In addition, USA Today requires reporters to talk with a source to verify that he or she wrote an e-mail. Adell Crowe, standards and development editor at USA Today, told American Journalism Review—in an e-mail—that "There is no limit on e-mails in a story, but because we have to identify communication by e-mail as such, one doesn't want to do it too often. . . . If there are repeated e-mail references, then we had better be sure we explain to the reader why we can't reach this person."[16]

ASSIGNMENT DESK 3.7

Working with the material you developed in Assignment Desks 3.5 and 3.6, create an e-mail interview request for your selected interviewee. Make sure that you include all the information noted in the text discussion. Also create a follow-up e-mail to be sent after waiting several days without receiving a response.

Instant Messaging as an Interviewing Tool

With the widespread use of instant messaging in the business world, it was inevitable it would become another journalistic interviewing tool. Although it doesn't offer the depth even of e-mail interviews, instant messaging does offer an instantaneous way of confirming facts and gathering information and opinions. Journalist and consultant Paul Conley writes of his addiction to instant messaging: "I can't report without it. I can't edit without it. I'm not even sure I can live without it." Conley is primarily sold on instant messaging for its ability to let him reach hard-to-get people and the speed with which he can get results. Because instant messaging sessions are even less formal than e-mails, however, it's even more important that you let your sources know if you intend to publish any content from an instant messaging session.[17]

Washington Post reporter Ylan Mui uses instant messaging to communicate with students in the school district she covers. "Just in the course of a conversation I came up with different story ideas," she told American Journalism Review. "It helps because it's so much more casual that you can pick up on things without having to do a full-blown interview."[18]

FIGURE 3.5

Leann Frola of the Poynter Institute used instant messaging to interview TVNewser blogger Brian Stelter when he was offered a job with The New York Times immediately upon graduating from college.

lfrola (12:53:10 PM): what exactly are you going to be doing at the times?

lfrola (12:53:20 PM): and how will it be diff from what you're doing now?

thebump (12:57:47 PM): I'll be helping shape the Times' media coverage on the web

thebump (12:58:24 PM): The Times is doing a number of intriguing things online -- I'm a regular reader of their blogs

thebump (12:58:48 PM): Hopefully I'll add to their already impressive stable of online content

lfrola (12:59:26 PM): when you say media coverage -- do you mean their coverage of news about the news?

lfrola (12:59:36 PM): in the way that you do now?

thebump (12:59:53 PM): Yes. On TVNewser, I found myself frequently linking to the media reporting by The Times

thebump (1:01:51 PM): Their reporting is already second to none, and I'll be bringing my web sensibility to help integrate what they do

lfrola (1:02:29 PM): are you going to be keeping up your blog as well?

thebump (1:02:45 PM): No, I'll be leaving TVNewser on July 20

thebump (1:02:53 PM): mediabistro will be hiring a new editor for it

lfrola (1:03:10 PM): oh ok. do you have any idea who will be taking it over?

thebump (1:03:17 PM): No

lfrola (1:04:15 PM): can you tell me a little more about what you'll be doing at the times when you say shaping coverage -- will you still be aggregating, or will you be sort of an editor that shapes coverage or a reporter...

lfrola (1:04:36 PM): or maybe it doesn't fit neatly into one of those thigns, but just a bit more specific?

thebump (1:04:43 PM): I really can't say yet, because that's something we're going to figure out later this summer

thebump (1:05:40 PM): (sorry!)

lfrola (1:06:35 PM): it's ok! i understand

lfrola (1:07:33 PM): what are some of the things you'd like to do?

Following Up

Whatever type of interview format you use, it's always good to ask "Do you mind if I get in touch with you again if I find I have any more questions as I'm wrapping up my article?" Unless you have upset your interview subject, the answer is invariably "No problem." Sure, you could call or write again without asking that question, but asking in advance leaves the door open a little and makes your subject more receptive to follow-up questions.

Conclusion

Although your initial impression may be that finding a story idea is hard work, after a while your biggest challenge likely will be limiting your ideas to those you can reasonably handle. You have a wide range of options for finding story ideas and conducting background research: Online searches, blogs, news releases, nonlocal news stories, older stories and online databases can all spur ideas for interesting news and feature stories. Interviews will let you build on your initial research and provide the raw material for a wide range of stories.

KEY TERMS

Invisible Web, 39
anecdotes, 50
beat, 45
closed-ended questions, 50
depth interviews, 49

news interviews, 49
news net, 48
open-ended questions, 50
profile interviews, 49

DISCUSSION QUESTIONS

1. Read the stories on the front page of the print or online edition of today's local newspaper or watch a local TV newscast. Where do you think those stories originated? What trends do you detect in the sources of story ideas?
2. For the same set of stories you used in the previous question, make a list of sources cited and their titles or job descriptions. Does any particular type of source appear to be favored over other types?
3. Again working with your set of stories, make a list of additional sources who could be used to expand the depth and breadth of each story.
4. Using Google News (http://news.google.com), search for "transcript" to find the full transcript of a recent interview with a newsmaker. Then find at least one story based on that interview. Did the writer include everything of importance from the interview? If not, what was omitted?

NOTES

1. Much of the information in this sidebar is based on a training session held by Meg Smith of the Washington Post: "Just the Facts: Recognizing Trustworthy Information Online," 21 July 2005.
2. Brian Pittman, "Wall Street Journal Tech Scribe Reveals How Journalists Use Blogs in Reporting—and What PR Practitioners Should Do About It," Bulldog Reporter, 27 July 2005, **www.bulldogreporter.com/profile/archives/ jso/1546.html.**
3. Del Quentin Wilder and Derek Willis, "D.C. Red-Light Cameras Fail to Curb Accidents," the Washington Post, 4 October 2005, p. A1.
4. Pat Stith, A Guide to Computer Assisted Reporting, Poynter Online, 7 June 2005, **www.poynter.org/content/content_view.asp?id=83144.**
5. Steve Buttry, "Developing and Cultivating Sources," American Copy Editors Society, February 2001, **www.copydesk.org/words/ sources.htm.**
6. Buttry.
7. Larry Welborn, "Courting Sources: How to get good people to tell you stuff," Poynter.org, **www.poynter.org/content/content_view.asp?id=95300.**
8. "On the Beat: Covering Cops and Crime," Poynter's NewsU, **www.newsu.org/.**
9. Welborn.
10. Meg Martin, "Leaving Fingerprints: Inside the police beat," Poynter.org, 22 November 2005, **www.poynter.org/content/content_view.asp?id=92447.**
11. Gaye Tuchman, "Making News: A Study in the Construction of Reality" (New York: Free Press, 1978).
12. Howard Kurtz, "Interviews, Going the Way of Linotype?" the Washington Post, 21 May 2007, **www.washingtonpost.com/wp-dyn/content/article/2007/05/20/AR2007052001549_pf.html.**
13. Kim Hart, "Inbox Journalism," American Journalism Review, December 2005/January 2006, **www.ajr.org/Article.asp?id4005.**
14. Many of the points in this list and in the list of cons are based on Bonnie Bressers, "Mixed Message: Experts debate use of e-mail as interviewing tool," Quill, March 2005, pp. 10–14.
15. Dan Verton, "Journalist Perpetrates Online Terror Hoax," ComputerWorld, 6 February 2003, **www.computerworld.com/securitytopics/security/cybercrime/story/0,10801,78238,00.html.**
16. Hart.
17. Paul Conley, "Instant Messaging as a Reporting Tool," Paul Conley blog, 29 July 2005, **http://paulconley.blogspot.com/2005/07/instant-messaging-as-reporting-tool.html.**
18. Hart.

Chapter 4

Writing Short News Reports and Leads

Once you understand the process of deciding what news is, you are ready to move to the next step: extracting the heart of a news story from what often resembles a jumble of facts. In this chapter, we will look at the process of finding the heart of the news, and then we will look at various techniques for presenting that information. We will learn how to write short news reports—bulletins, screen crawls, alerts and briefs—and then we will see how to use the same strategies to create compelling introductions for longer news stories. Learning how to write short reports first will help you when you move on to writing leads for longer stories because there is nowhere to hide when you're writing a short report: You either nail the news, or it's painfully obvious that you've missed the mark.

Finding the Heart of the Story

A news story typically is based on one of the following situations:

- Someone does or says something of interest or importance.
- Something important happens to a person, place or thing.

Let's look at an example. These stories appeared on the home page of one day's online version of The New York Times:

1. Bush Bluntly Defends Iraq Strategy, but Admits Problems
2. Election in Belarus Did Not Meet Standards, Observers Say
3. Plight Deepens for Black Men, Studies Warn
4. Rumor, Fear and Fatigue Hinder Final Push to End Polio
5. Israel Briefly Reopens Crossing
6. $200 Million Gift to Finance New Science Center at Columbia
7. Dell to Double Workforce in India
8. NFL Commissioner to Retire[1]

Of those eight stories, numbers 1, 2 and 3 report on *someone saying something of importance* (in the third example, the source of the statement is "studies," as opposed to a person or people). Number 4 is an example of *something important happening to a thing* (in this case, several problems hurting efforts to eradicate polio). Numbers 5 through 8 report on *someone doing something of importance* (in number 5, the "someone" is the country of Israel; in number 6 it is the unmentioned donor of the money).

The stories attached to those headlines varied greatly in length and complexity. Some, such as the NFL commissioner's retirement, were short (550 words) and relatively simple. It should be obvious that getting to the heart of such a story requires little effort: The announcement of the resignation is, by definition, news. Many other stories are just as straightforward: Someone is charged with or convicted of a crime; someone is injured or dies; someone wins a sporting competition. In a sense, those stories almost write themselves.

Other stories, though, such as The New York Times story about polio, are much longer (3,865 words—the equivalent of a 15-page double-spaced paper) and complex (several multimedia enhancements were added to the text). Such stories are based on a broad range of sources and information and require a writer to work much harder to get to the heart of the news.

Extracting the Essential Facts

No matter how simple or complex a story, your goal is the same: to isolate the heart of the news and present it simply and clearly to your audience. To many beginning news writers, this seems like a mysterious process, but it's actually what we do in conversation every day of our lives: Filter out unimportant events and details and cut to the chase. You're looking for the *most* important or interesting aspect of the news.

A good first step in cutting to the chase is to examine your facts for answers to the **5 W's and an H**:

- *Who* made the statement, performed the action or was the object of the action?
- *What* happened or was said?
- *When* did the event or announcement take place?
- *Where* did the event or announcement occur?
- *Why* did the event or announcement happen?
- *How* did the event or announcement happen?

Answering these questions will help you focus the story and shine a spotlight on the most newsworthy aspect. You don't need to be able to answer every question; many times, you will not know the answer to one or both of the last two questions (but digging for those answers often leads to the most compelling stories).

Let's try an example. The following notes are based on an actual story:

A group of four local residents went out to share a celebration dinner last night at a restaurant in the Uptown area close to campus. The area is popular with many college students. The people were William Washington, 22, a recent college graduate who just received his first job offer; his sister, Monica, 22; their mother, Vanessa, 48; and a female friend, Jennifer Mason, 23.

They left the restaurant just before 10 p.m. On the way to their car parked a few blocks away, they were confronted by two men in dark hooded sweatshirts. The men approached them at the corner of Main and Park streets and told Washington's mother to hand over her purse. She told police that she did so without resisting.

The men took the purse, then fired a single shot into the head of William Washington. The three women reported that he had not tried to interfere in the robbery and had said nothing to the robbers.

The men fled on foot, but one witness said he saw at least one of them get into a white car and speed away.

William Washington was admitted to a nearby hospital. He is in critical condition this morning.

Police inspector Natasha Arnon called the shooting unprovoked. "What we know is there was not a struggle," she said. Police are asking for the public's help in identifying the attackers.

Even for a short and relatively uncomplicated story, this one requires work to find the best news angle. Let's examine the questions one by one:

Who: The notes refer to several people: William Washington, Vanessa Washington, Monica Washington, Jennifer Mason, a witness, two robbers, Natasha Arnon and "police" (one or more representatives of the police department). Which of those is the best "who"? You could argue for a few different answers to that question, but if you think about the requirement to focus on the most important aspect of the news, one answer seems to be the best: **William Washington**. He was the person to whom the most important action happened. There's a problem, however: Most people will have no idea who William Washington is. So instead it's better to identify him in a way that's more meaningful. One example would be **a 22-year-old local man**; another would be **a recent college graduate**.

What: Now that we have selected a "who," we turn to "what." Again, there are several potential answers: He got a job offer; he went to a restaurant to celebrate; he was shot in the head; he is in critical condition. The first two can quickly be ruled out. They are not newsworthy in and of themselves. If all that had happened was that he got a job offer and went out to celebrate, you wouldn't be writing a story. Of the other two possibilities, the shooting is the better choice, simply because you can't mention his being in critical condition without having a reason for it. So the "what" is **was shot in the head**.

When: This one seems easy at first. As the notes indicate, the shooting occurred **last night**. That's a basic time element, which is necessary to every story. But there is more to it than that: He was shot **while walking to his car after dining out**. That information provides a setting for the crime.

Where: Finally, what seems to be an easy one: The notes say the shooting occurred **at the corner of Main and Park streets**. If that area is well-known, that will be sufficient.

If not, however, you might want to substitute **in the Uptown area** or, if most people in your audience would not be familiar with that area, use **in an area popular with local college students.**

Why: The information you have does not explain why the shooting occurred. If anything, it would seem to indicate that the shooting occurred **for no apparent reason.**

How: In answering this question, you can ignore the obvious answer (**with a gun**) and instead think about "how" referring to the circumstances of the shooting. One good answer to that question would be **by two men who stole his mother's purse.**

ASSIGNMENT DESK **4.1**

Now it's your turn to try to find the essential facts of a story. Here is the rundown:

The City Council met last night to consider an ordinance.

The ordinance would ban smoking in all city parks. That would make this the first city in the area to do so.

Council members reached unanimous agreement on passing the ordinance. It will come back for a formal vote in coming weeks.

Under the ordinance, people caught smoking in a city park would be fined $100, starting with the first offense.

Councilman Gary Wenders said there has not been that much opposition to the ban.

"People are beginning to demand that when they step outside for a breath of fresh air, they should not find themselves choking on a smokers' fumes," he said. "We all agree that people enjoying the city's parks should be entitled to a smoke-free, healthy environment."

Answer as many of the 5 W's and an H as you can.

Presenting the Story

Once you have extracted the essential facts, the next step is to present them in an easily understood manner. Let's start by stringing together all the facts from the shooting story:

> A 22-year-old local man walking to his car after dining out last night in the Uptown area was shot in the head for no apparent reason by two men who stole his mother's purse, according to police and witnesses.

That sentence does a good job in presenting all the major details of the story. A person could read or hear that single sentence and come away with a good idea of what happened.

Attribution

When it's obvious where information has been obtained, you don't have to provide a source. For instance, if a store has burned to the ground, anyone can see that, so it's sufficient to write "Fire has destroyed one of the city's oldest department stores." When the source of information is not so obvious, you have to include the source of information. That process is called providing **attribution**.

For print and Web writing, attribution typically comes after a statement because the news is more important than who's saying it. This example comes from USA Today:

> Farm-raised salmon—widely thought to be among the most healthful foods on the

American diet—sometimes contain dangerous levels of toxic chemicals, says a landmark study out today.

For broadcast, writers must inform listeners or viewers of the source of the information right away to prepare them to evaluate the information that follows. Here's an example from National Public Radio:

> A leading advocate of California's central valley says proposed cuts in Governor Arnold Schwarzenegger's budget will force some people to move.

Without attribution at the beginning, this could sound like a statement of fact.

Lead Structure

Notice that the shooting example takes the form of a simple declarative sentence. In the vast majority of cases, that structure is the best for presenting news.

Declarative sentences typically contain three parts: a **subject** followed by a *verb* and an <u>object</u>. In writing news, the object is not limited to a simple word or phrase like a traditional direct object, but it instead refers to the information needed to complete the thought. These three examples feature different types of objects:

> **Gunmen in two cars** *attacked* <u>a minibus heading to Baghdad from a Shiite town north of the capital</u> Monday, killing seven passengers, including a child, police said. (AP)

> **Senator Arlen Specter, the senior Republican on the Judiciary Committee,** *said* Sunday that <u>Attorney General Alberto R. Gonzales might resign rather than face a potential no-confidence vote in the Senate</u>. (The New York Times)

> **Genetic testing** *confirms* <u>that the cow diagnosed with the first U.S. case of mad cow disease was born in Canada,</u> agriculture officials said Tuesday. (AP)

ASSIGNMENT DESK **4.2**

Take the answers to the 5 W's and an H that you arrived at in Assignment Desk 4.1. Write at least three sentences presenting the key information, each with a different subject.

Next, look at the sentences you've written and choose your favorite. Why does that one appeal to you more than the others?

Short Reports

So what role does a summary sentence like the one we just wrote play in getting the news out? Well, it depends. In some situations, the lack of time, space or information may mean that that single sentence—possibly aided by one or two others—can serve as an entire story. These types of short reports come in a wide variety of guises:

- Broadcast and Web bulletins: **Bulletins**, typically running only one or two sentences, can be used in broadcast and online news to get information to the public quickly. As the name implies, a bulletin carries a sense of urgency. In creating one, the writer in effect says, "We don't know much yet, but this seems important for you to know." Broadcast bulletins sometimes are superimposed over regular programming, but on major stories, programming might be interrupted as someone reads the bulletin. Here's an example of a typical broadcast bulletin:

  > The space shuttle Columbia has broken up during re-entry, with all seven crewmembers presumed dead.

- E-mail alerts: Some news operations transmit news bulletins by e-mail for those who are more likely to have access to e-mail than to a radio or television. An example sent by CNN:

  > Anna Nicole Smith died of an accidental drug overdose, according to Charlie Tiger, Seminole Police Chief.

- Crawlers: The shortest reports that can pass for stories, these usually are seen sliding across the bottom of the screen on news and sports channels. **Crawlers** offer viewers summaries of stories that are not important enough to make the newscast that day.

Pearl Widow Sues Pakistan Bank Over Murder of Husband   Bloomberg

CALIFORNIA MOTHER ACCUSED OF BEATING HER TWO CHILDREN   Fox 45

A WEST POINT GRADUATE SERVING IN IRAQ IS SUING THE AR   CNN

N IMPORT SAFETY PANEL TO REPORT TO PRES BUSH IN 60 DAYS   CNBC

FIGURE 4.1 Screen crawls have become a staple of television newscasts, presenting brief story summaries and updates.

Some examples:

> Wounded humpback whales apparently back in Pacific Ocean
>
> Apple debuts DRM-free iTunes Plus
>
> Ernst & Young partners hit with tax fraud charges.

- Newspaper briefs: The print equivalent of crawlers, newspaper briefs bring readers summaries of interesting stories that don't merit full coverage. Briefs generally contain from one to three sentences. In some cases, a writer is asked to create a brief for a story he or she is working on; in other cases, an editor prepares the brief. Here's an example of a brief:

> A fire destroyed a Midtown pizzeria yesterday morning, sending five firefighters and one civilian to the hospital with minor injuries, the Fire Department said. The fire was reported at 11:29 a.m. in a building housing Abitino's Pizzeria, on First Avenue near 52nd Street. When firefighters arrived, the first three floors of the five-story building were ablaze, and it took them about an hour to put out the fire, Deputy Chief Thomas McKavanagh said. Dominick Abitino, one of three brothers who opened the restaurant in 1992 along with their father, said, "It's a family business, and we're all sad here." (The New York Times)

Style Guidelines for Short Reports

The style used for short reports differs from one news organization to the next and is determined to some extent by the medium. Some guidelines call for action verbs in all cases, some don't. Some have strict limits of one sentence, whereas others permit items to be as long as three sentences.

The tense used in short reports also varies. Present tense is often used to give a sense of immediacy:

> State Supreme Court *allows* use of marijuana for medicinal purposes.

Another way to accomplish the same thing is by writing in the past perfect tense. This makes more sense in examples such as this one:

> Music legend James Brown, "the Godfather of Soul," *has died* of congestive heart failure.

"Dies of congestive heart failure" would have been clumsy in that sentence.

Notice that no time element typically appears in a short report because it is assumed the action or announcement has just taken place.

When a short report spotlights something that has not yet happened, you can use future tense or an infinitive:

> China *will shut down* factory that made tainted food.

> Software update *to add* new features to PlayStation 3.

ASSIGNMENT
DESK 4.3

Take 30 minutes and see how many examples of short reports you can find in the media. Use any media you have access to: television, newspapers, online news sites, newsletters, and so on. Your school library should be able to provide many good sources for this exercise. Once you've found your examples, read through them and select two or three that best tell a story quickly. What makes them effective?

Moving on to Longer Stories

By this point, you've probably noticed that the short reports we've been looking at resemble the opening sentences of many print, online and broadcast news stories. There's a good reason for that: Like short reports, the opening sentence or two of most news stories is designed to summarize the story quickly. For that reason, the opening of a print or online news story is called a **summary lead**.

The typical summary lead used on print and online stories differs from a short report in two minor ways: It is written in past tense and includes a time element. Here's an example:

> The Supreme Court gave its conditional approval today to "informational checkpoints" on the nation's streets, ruling that police may briefly stop traffic in order to inform vehicle occupants of a recent crime and ask if they have any information about it. (the Washington Post)

Making the Most of Short Reports and Summary Leads

If you follow the steps we've gone through so far in this chapter, you'll find it is not hard to write a good short report or summary lead. It does take more effort, though, to write a great one. Four tips can help you accomplish that:

1. Be as specific as possible.
2. Avoid backing in.
3. Be concise.
4. Use active voice.

Be as Specific as Possible

No matter what medium you're writing for, you will be fighting for your audience's attention. To win the battle, you need to make sure that your short report or summary lead showcases the most interesting or important aspect of the story. This example, typical of campus newspapers, illustrates what happens when a writer misses the news:

> In an open forum on the topic of strategic initiatives, Provost Margaret O'Keefe discussed the university's role as a "Metropolitan University" Monday afternoon.

This is a generic lead: Change a few specifics and it could be used on a thousand different stories. Aside from the provost, who would read any further? The lead contains a bunch of nonessential information and fails to provide the faintest hint that anything mildly interesting or important occurred. Further, it's too vague: Readers are not given a clue as to what the strategic initiatives are or, for that matter, what a "Metropolitan University" is.

The main problem here is that the writer answered the question "What happened?" in the easiest way possible. What the writer did not do is answer the question "What was the most important or interesting thing that was said or done?" Doing that takes more work, but it's the only way to make sure readers get what they should from a story.

In this case, the writer should have looked at what the provost said during the meeting. For instance, suppose she had said that the university planned to use enrollment growth to leverage the state to provide more funding. To the audience of a campus newspaper, that's big news. At a minimum, it means the campus will see notable growth in enrollment. At its worst, such a plan could backfire, leaving the campus with many more students but no more resources.

The writer would have done much better to focus on that statement in the summary lead:

> Admitting more students to the university is the key to gaining more resources, Provost Margaret O'Keefe said Monday in a forum on the university's role as a "Metropolitan University."

Notice that the provost's quote was paraphrased. Rarely are someone's exact words used in a lead. The writer can usually do a better job of summarizing a quote by paraphrasing. Notice also that the phrase "to use enrollment growth to improve its financial situation" has been discarded for a simpler phrase. Chances are that the original phrase reflected the provost's own words, and the writer—being lazy once again—just recycled them. But the original phrase doesn't reflect the way most people talk and therefore is more difficult for readers to comprehend. Finally, notice that "Monday" was moved to a more appropriate position.

Avoid Backing In

The original lead in the previous example also suffered from the flaw of backing in; that is, placing an introductory clause or phrase before the subject. Here's another example:

> In the latest attempt to exert pressure on Sudan over the killing in the Darfur region, a group of conservative to moderate Republicans in Congress demanded

Why Choose Journalism?

Journalism is many things:

It is a social leveler, because it gives you license to walk up to important people and ask them uncomfortable questions.

It is an ego boost, because you get to see your work—and maybe your name—every day on the page or on the screen.

It is great fun, because you get to know what's going on before anyone else, and you get the inside dirt on a lot of stuff very few are privy to.

But mainly, it is a public service. This is because everyday Americans deserve one clean shot at the unvarnished facts before advocates and spin-meisters try to influence their decisions. This will warm your heart quicker than Scotch.

ALEX JOHNSON
MSNBC.com

Thursday that President Bush impose sanctions against the government for its failure to rein in the violence. (The New York Times)

Turn the sentence around, and it's much stronger:

A group of conservative to moderate Republicans in Congress demanded Thursday that President Bush impose sanctions against Sudan's government for its failure to rein in the violence, in the latest attempt to exert pressure on the country over the killing in the Darfur region.

Be Concise

Another common flaw is trying to cram too much information into a short report or lead. Two good rules of thumb are that sentences should contain only essential information and should run no more than 30 words. In most cases, that means sentences should focus on one point (in Chapter 5, we'll look at how to handle things when there are two or three major points). Yet leads like this appear all too commonly:

The White House has ordered the new CIA director, Porter J. Goss, to purge the agency of officers believed to have been disloyal to President Bush or of leaking damaging information to the media about the conduct of the Iraq war and the hunt for Osama Bin Laden, according to knowledgeable sources. (Newsday)

At 52 words, that lead runs almost twice as long as the recommendation (and unfortunately it doesn't set any records—you can find 80- and 90-word leads without looking too hard). Unlike many long leads, this one doesn't run long because the writer couldn't figure out what the news was; he clearly knows what it is and wants to give the reader as much as possible right at the start. But it's just too much for a reader to digest at once (and it packs a grammatical problem as well: *officers believed to have been . . . or of leaking* is not parallel). Let's try streamlining the lead to its essentials:

> The White House reportedly has ordered the new CIA director to purge the agency of officers believed to have been disloyal to President Bush or to have leaked damaging information.

The new version runs 30 words. Granted, we had to set aside a number of details for the moment, but the news is still the same: The CIA is cleaning house. The omitted details can be placed in subsequent paragraphs, so no information needs to be cut from the story.

The next example runs 61 words:

> The number of U.S. convicts imprisoned with death sentences dropped in 2003 to its lowest level in 30 years, helping to provoke the third straight annual decline in the nation's death row population and signaling the continuation of a slow trend away from state- and federally ordered executions, according to data released yesterday by the Justice Department's Bureau of Justice Statistics. (the Washington Post)

In this case, there are just too many ideas vying for the reader's attention:

- The number of U.S. convicts imprisoned with death sentences dropped in 2003 to its lowest level in 30 years.
- That was the third straight annual decline in the nation's death row population.
- The decline marks the continuation of a slow trend away from state- and federally ordered executions.
- The information came from the Justice Department's Bureau of Justice Statistics.

When you break the lead down like this, you can see easily that the first point is the heart of the story. Tacking on the attribution in the final point gives us a lead like this, which counts only 28 words long:

> The number of U.S. convicts imprisoned with death sentences dropped in 2003 to its lowest level in 30 years, according to data released yesterday by the Justice Department.

Again, the other information can be moved into the body of the story, so nothing important will be lost.

Let's look at one final example:

> Many American youngsters participating in federally funded abstinence-only programs have been taught over the past three years that abortion can lead to sterility and suicide, that half the gay male teenagers in the United States have tested positive for the AIDS virus, and that touching a person's genitals "can result in pregnancy," a congressional staff analysis has found. (the Washington Post)

At 58 words, this lead carries a lot of information—probably too much for the average reader. A better lead can be gleaned from the paragraph that followed, which notes that those examples are among a great deal of "false, misleading or distorted information" persented in the program.

Pull together parts of each and you end up with something like this:

> Many American youngsters participating in federally funded abstinence-only programs over the past three years have been provided "false, misleading, or distorted information," a congressional staff analysis has found.

Using fewer than half the words of the original lead, this version conveys the same idea, possibly with more impact because of its directness.

That lead is similar to the lead that The Associated Press ran on the story:

> Some federally funded sex education programs that teach an abstinence-only approach have factual errors and are ineffective, a congressional report says.

Note that the AP lead is even shorter (21 words versus 28).

Use Active Voice

The AP lead we just looked at also used active rather than passive voice. A short report or lead represents your only chance to catch the attention of audience members. Using active voice increases the odds that you will grab readers' attention. In a sentence written in active voice, the subject undertakes an action, creating a sense of movement that can help sweep readers in. In a sentence written in passive voice, the subject is acted on, so the sentence appears more static. Let's look at some examples:

> At least 2,000 county students were unable to get to school on time yesterday after the tires of 44 school buses were deflated by vandals.

> At least 2,000 county students showed up late for school yesterday after vandals deflated the tires of 44 school buses.

Both leads provide essentially the same information. But in the first, passive voice saps the power of the sentence. In the second, active voice makes both the students and vandals participants in the action, which does a much better job of moving things along.

Conclusion

Although the task of finding the news in a mass of facts might seem intimidating, it's not hard to do if you break the process down into three steps: finding the heart of the story, extracting the essential facts, and presenting the story. In some situations, the story might run only 10 or 20 words; in others, a summary of that length is used to introduce a much longer story. In the next chapter, we'll begin our exploration of how longer news stories are structured, focusing initially on print stories.

KEY TERMS

5 W's and an H, 60
attribution, 63
bulletins, 64

crawlers, 64
summary lead, 66

DISCUSSION QUESTIONS

1. Which media do you regularly use to keep you up to date on the news? Does the medium vary with the type of news?
2. When you hear a news bulletin or see some other type of short news report, what factors determine whether you seek additional information on the story?
3. Look through the main news section of your local newspaper's print or online edition. What percentage of stories is about a person doing or saying something of interest or importance? What percentage is about something happening to a person, place or thing?
4. Again looking through the main news section of your local newspaper's print or online edition, how good a job do the leads do in answering the 5 W's and an H?

NOTES

1. The eight stories cited appeared in the lead position on The New York Times Web site (**www.nytimes. com/**) **midday March 20, 2006.**

Writing the Basic Text Story

Chapter **5**

The main lesson of the previous chapter—that a writer needs to get to the heart of the story and tell it quickly and clearly—remains at center stage as we move into writing complete stories. Journalists sometimes forget that lesson or, even worse, ignore it. Unfortunately, readers are often skimmers; that is, people are pressed for time and do not have the luxury of digging through extraneous material. Writing that fails to get to the point will lead many readers to move to another story.

The **inverted pyramid,** which is the dominant format for text stories, offers a good starting place for creating text stories that will attract readers (see Figure 5.1).

The Inverted Pyramid

A traditional children's story is structured like a pyramid: Beginning with "Once upon a time," the author gradually spins out a tale that culminates in a big ending. Characters are introduced, and suspense is built along the way to keep things interesting. That format works for children's stories because the reader (or listener) is in no hurry and wants to be entertained. As we'll see in Chapter 6, the same format also can work for newspaper and magazine stories that are more entertaining than important. But the bulk of stories that get printed in newspapers are **hard news** stories, which report on events that have great impact on the audience. Their primary job is to convey important information quickly. To accomplish that, the inverted pyramid format turns things upside down.

The inverted pyramid format does away with notions of building suspense and carefully parceling out information. Everything gets placed on the table right at the top. As the article continues, the writer includes information of lesser importance, with the least important information appearing at the end.

Many beginning news writers fail to see the point of writing a story this way. If you have 250 words in which to tell your story, they protest, why give it away in the first 25 or 50? Again, it all goes back to the reader. For every person who reads a full article, there are many others who will have only enough time or interest to

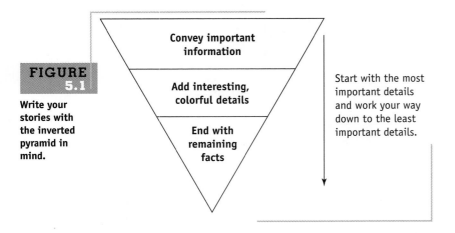

**FIGURE
5.1**

**Write your
stories with
the inverted
pyramid in
mind.**

read part of it. Those readers will become frustrated if they can't find what they're looking for right away.

Such reader behavior might strike new writers as odd, but it's a simple necessity. A major newspaper, for example, contains as much text as a novel, and virtually no one has the time to read that much every day. Stories written in the inverted pyramid format let readers dart from one story to another, gaining at least a basic idea of what's going on in the world just by reading the leads. When they come across a story that's particularly relevant or interesting to them, readers can slow down and read the full article.

Some beginning news writers find the inverted pyramid format alien, having had most of their writing experience with the traditional pyramid form taught in English composition classes. But in truth, we use the inverted pyramid form all the time without thinking about it—even in our daily conversations.

For example: Let's say you need to find an apartment near campus for yourself and a friend, and your budget is limited to $600 a month. You spot a classified ad that reads "University area, 2BR, $595/mo."

Your next step would probably be calling to learn more: the location of the apartment, whether pets are allowed, what type of building the apartment is in, whether you're allowed to paint, how much security deposit is required, and so on. If the answers to these questions satisfy you, you would check out the apartment in person, examining the condition, cleanliness, noisiness and other matters. At this stage, you're still gathering essential information: If the apartment fails the test in any of these areas, you'll likely forget about it.

But as you gather essential information on the phone and in person, you'll likely also find that you're picking up some less important bits of data, too: The color of the living room carpet, the size of the refrigerator, and so on.

When you call your friend to report back on the apartment, you'll probably use the inverted pyramid form: Starting with the most important details, you'll work your way to the less important ones and likely will not even mention some of the smaller details. Without realizing it, you've used the inverted pyramid format.

Why Choose Journalism?

There are so many romantic and less-than-romantic reasons to choose journalism—the chance to see and experience the world the way few people do, to be a witness to history, to meet people from the humble to the high and mighty, to earn your own fame and fortune. But for me, there's one powerful draw: a belief that newspapers are, really, the owner's manual to our society and our democracy, and that our role in ensuring the newspaper's accuracy, credibility, fairness, precision and sheer liveliness has a lot to do with whether we really fulfill this crucial role in the world. And besides, it's just fun.

VINCE RINEHART
the Washington Post

Starting the Story

Most inverted pyramid stories begin with summary leads, which as we saw in Chapter 4, quickly report the key idea of the story. Summary leads are the workhorses of print reporting and begin the majority of news articles.

Some stories, however, call for a lead with more style. Good candidates for more creative leads include:

- Stories that are more interesting and unusual than important.
- Stories that most readers already will have heard about before seeing a newspaper (for example, sporting events and major political events such as elections).
- Stories in which the writer can best make his or her point by beginning with a comparison or contrast.

Sometimes, summary leads can be dressed up a little to do this work. These summary leads, for example, are written with flair:

Spider-Man has apparently met his match in Shrek, as "Shrek the Third" unseated "Spider-Man 3" from the top box office spot last weekend, in the process setting a record for opening weekend revenues for an animated film.

Media consolidation remains the rage, and the financial news world firms up a bit today as MarketWatch agreed to be acquired by Wall Street Journal publisher Dow Jones for $518 million, or $18 per share. (Motley Fool)

First, there was "American Chopper," the series. Now there's American Chopper, the boxer shorts. (Washington Post)

WARNING: Smoking may be hazardous to your movie rating. (The New York Times)

Each of these quickly summarizes the news, but the writers have put a little more effort into the lead than simply writing a "who did what" version.

Writers often go a step further and use **delayed leads**—also known as *feature* or *soft leads*. Such leads do not flash the major facts of a story to the reader but instead try to catch the reader's attention in a more creative manner. Delayed leads work best when writing about information that's more interesting or unusual than important. Delayed leads generally run between two and four paragraphs, depending in part on the length of the article: A 10-paragraph story should not have a four-paragraph lead.

Rather than beginning with a summary of the story, delayed leads tempt the reader into the story. Unlike summary leads, delayed leads do not follow a single formula. The only rule is they must be well written and interesting. Two common techniques writers use in creating delayed leads for news stories are contrast and mystery:

CONTRAST

Always the innovators, Radiohead has done it again. This time, however, it's not so much the music that is challenging conventions—it's the groundbreaking system of delivering the music. (Seattle Post-Intelligencer)

MYSTERY

It's been one week, 5 days, 8 hours, 23 minutes, and 32 seconds. A total of $61.75 unspent. More than 1 day, 1 hour and 40 minutes of life saved. A whopping 308 cigarettes that Paul Kenney hasn't smoked.

"That's the one that gets me," said Paul Kenney, 43, of Blue Point, who had yet to enter the numbers into his online journal. (Newsday)

Several other types of delayed leads typically are used on long news and feature articles. We'll look at those in Chapter 6.

Delayed leads always should be used with caution. They have to be compelling enough to keep the reader involved for several paragraphs. Many delayed leads fail to meet that goal.

ASSIGNMENT DESK 5.1

Based on the story summaries provided, write a lead for each one. Determine whether a summary lead or a delayed lead is best for each. Be prepared to explain which you like best for each example and why.

1. NASA launched another space shuttle this morning. The launch was postponed for two days because of stormy weather. Because of problems occurring during previous shuttle launches, the crew was planning to begin a detailed inspection of the shuttle today. They will be using a camera and sensors mounted at the end of a 50-foot robotic arm.
2. Two blood drives are being held in the area during the next 10 days. They are being held because the blood supply in the state is a critically low level. For many blood types, less than one day's supply is available at many hospitals.

Continued

Assignment
Desk **5.1**
Continues •

3. The annual Nathan's Famous Hot Dog Eating Contest in Coney Island, N.Y., was held yesterday. The winner managed to eat just under 54 hot dogs and buns in 12 minutes. The winner was Takeru Kobayashi. It was his sixth consecutive win.

4. A local man has been in a coma since suffering severe head injuries in a car crash 19 years ago. He suddenly began speaking a few weeks ago. As time has gone on, he has begun to talk more and even begun to move his limbs.

Moving Beyond the Lead

All delayed leads and many summary leads are followed by a short paragraph that helps the reader understand the importance of the news. This **nut graf** (*graf* is short for *paragraph*) provides an opportunity to add more pertinent information than the lead can comfortably hold, while simultaneously aiming to help the reader understand what makes this news important.

A nut graf essentially tells the reader, "This is what the story is all about." It helps the reader understand why the story matters and helps the writer get a clear focus on the story.

Jacqui Banaszynski of The Seattle Times says that good nut grafs "place a story in context":

> That context can be about timing (why is the story important now?), history (what change does this event signal?), politics (what issue or battle does this address or arise from?), or any other underpinning that gives significance to the raw information. At its simplest, a nut graf is a segue between the [lead] and the body of the story; it summarizes the significance, background and projected impact of the news.[1]

Let's look at a number of leads and nut grafs to see how they are constructed. The first example comes from a story that reports on a straightforward event:

> A 16-year-old Palestinian laden with explosives blew himself up Monday in a crowded outdoor market in Tel Aviv, killing three Israelis, wounding 32 and scattering body parts and blood-spattered vegetables on the ground.
>
> The attack tested Israel's promise to show restraint during the absence of the ailing Yasser Arafat. Palestinian leaders—including Arafat—immediately condemned the attack, the first since a Sept. 22 bombing in Jerusalem. (AP)

The summary lead of this report follows the basic format of subject-verb-object: *suicide bomber–blew up–himself and others.* The writer does a good job of including the basics in the lead:

WHO: A 16-year-old Palestinian. Few readers would recognize the bomber by name, so he is instead identified by nationality and age. The age is significant because most other suicide bombers had been older.

WHAT: Blew himself up.

WHEN: Monday.

WHERE: In a crowded outdoor market in Tel Aviv.

WHY: Not stated.

HOW: Laden with explosives.

If the lead has a problem, it's that it runs long at 36 words. The writer could have cut 10 words by eliminating the final phrase, which adds little and is unnecessarily graphic, and ending the lead with "killing three Israelis and wounding 32."

Although the lead does not answer "Why," the nut graf does a good job with that task. It informs the reader that the action took place during a politically precarious time, when the de facto Palestinian leader was absent, and Israel had promised to show restraint. If you read no more than these two paragraphs, you would have a good idea of what's happened.

The second sample lead and nut graf come from The Associated Press story reporting on an action undertaken by a government agency:

> Foods containing olive oil can carry labels saying they may reduce the risk of coronary heart disease, the government says, citing limited evidence from a dozen scientific studies about the benefits of monounsaturated fats.
>
> As long as people don't increase the number of calories they consume daily, the Food and Drug Administration confirmed a reduction in the risk of coronary heart disease when people replace foods high in saturated fat with the monounsaturated fat in olive oil. That means a change as simple as sautéing food in two tablespoons of olive oil instead of butter may be healthier for your heart.

News Pointers

Where Does the *When* Go?

Almost every summary lead answers the question "when." But placing the time element correctly can take some care. For example:

> The Group of Eight called Saturday for more aid, increased debt relief and responsible lending to Africa, vowing that the world's wealthy nations would not forget their pledges to the poverty-stricken continent. (AP)

A writer who was not careful might try one of these two approaches to adding the time element:

> The Group of Eight Saturday called for more aid, increased debt relief and responsible lending to Africa, vowing that the world's wealthy nations would not forget their pledges to the poverty-stricken continent.

> The Group of Eight called for more aid, increased debt relief and responsible lending to Africa, vowing that the world's wealthy nations would not forget their pledges to the poverty-stricken continent Saturday.

In the first case, it looks as though Saturday is part of the organization's name. In the second one, it seems as though the Group of Eight member nations had just made their pledges Saturday.

Starting the lead "On Saturday..." is no better, because it delays the important information. So the only workable approach is the one taken by the AP. Although it is not as conversational as the best news writing, this version nonetheless solves the problem of having the time element possibly confuse readers.

This lead also relies on subject-verb-object but turns things around from the straightforward *the government–says–food containing olive oil can carry labels touting its health benefits.* Can you guess why the writer chose to structure the lead this way? Starting with *"The government says. . . ."* is not likely to draw readers in: The government (its agencies and representatives, actually) says things every day. What's interesting is that a federal agency has become convinced enough that olive oil benefits those who consume it that producers of foods containing the oil can now legally make that claim.

The 34-word lead sentence does not pack as much basic information as the previous example:

WHO: The government.

WHAT: Approved labels citing health benefits of products made with olive oil.

WHEN: Today (implied)

WHERE: In Washington, D.C. (implied)

HOW: Not stated.

WHY: Citing limited evidence from a dozen scientific studies about the benefits of monounsaturated fats.

Nevertheless, for its purposes this lead does a good job of conveying the main point. The lead does not run excessively long, but cutting the final clause or moving it to a separate sentence would make it even easier to comprehend.

The nut graf does a lot of the heavy lifting for this story. First, it identifies what government agency took the action. Second, it alerts readers that they can't just start eating more foods with olive oil in them: They must replace other foods in their diets. Third, it gives a specific example of how this news translates to the reader's daily life.

In both cases, the writers have managed to do a good job of conveying the essence of the stories to readers. A writer can do that only when he or she fully understands what has happened and can answer a number of vital questions that go beyond the basic 5 W's and an H:

What does this action or statement mean?

What are likely consequences?

How can my readers use this information?

For our third example, let's look at a delayed lead and see how the nut graf aids it. This excerpt comes from an article written by Richard G. Jones and John Holl of The New York Times:

Cecil Brooks III was puffing away in West Orange on Wednesday night, celebrating the cigar and savoring one of the final opportunities to smoke in bars and restaurants in New Jersey.

"We want to pay homage because it's the last time we'll be able to enjoy everything at the same time: smoke, drink, eat and listen to great music," said Brooks, the owner of Cecil's Jazz Club, where about two dozen people gathered to mark the end of public indoor smoking in New Jersey. "We want to send the smokes off in style."

At 12:01 a.m. tomorrow, New Jersey will become the 11th state to impose a comprehensive ban on smoking in indoor public places like restaurants and bars. The exceptions are the gambling floors of Atlantic City's casinos — a compromise that was essential for the ban to win legislative approval in January.

The lead of this article fills the first two paragraphs and includes description and quotations. Not until the third paragraph — the nut graf — does the reader get answers to most basic questions:

WHO: The state of New Jersey.

WHAT: Imposing a smoking ban.

WHEN: 12:01 a.m. tomorrow.

WHERE: In indoor public places.

HOW: Through new legislation.

WHY: Not stated.

This example should clearly show why a delayed lead needs a strong nut graf.

ASSIGNMENT DESK 5.2

Pick three stories from today's newspaper. At least one should use a delayed lead. For each, highlight the lead and the nut graf, if one is used. Find the 5 W's and an H for each story, indicating whether the information is in the lead or the nut graf.

The Body of the Story

Past the lead (and the nut graf, if one is used), the writer has to determine what further information to include. Just as in the example about apartment hunting that started this chapter, a writer probably will not use all of the information available. Therefore, developing the body of the story means deciding what additional information readers *need* to know to understand the story and its significance. The best way to do this is for the writer to step back and put himself or herself in the reader's place, trying to anticipate the questions that an intelligent reader might ask next.

Let's look at how this works in practice.

A naked man climbed a fence at Los Angeles International Airport, ran across the tarmac and climbed into the wheel well of a departing plane before firefighters talked him out, airport officials said.

The lead summarizes the most unusual aspects of this story. A weaker lead might have read, "A flight was delayed departing from Los Angeles International Airport today after a man tried to stow away on the plane."

The 31-year-old Canadian man, who was described as mentally unstable, had been turned away hours earlier when he tried to buy a ticket on a Qantas Airways flight to Australia with only a credit card receipt.

After the lead, most readers would be asking, "Who is this man and why did he do this?" So the second graf provides additional identifying information on the man and background to the events.

Neil Melly told authorities he stripped naked to protest the airline's decision to deny him a ticket, said Nancy Castles, an airport spokeswoman.

This paragraph names the man, provides more details on the information given so far, and attempts to further answer the question of why the man did what he did.

In the incident Monday, baggage handlers saw Melly climb over an 8-foot barbed-wire fence and sprint to the Boeing 747 as it backed away from the gate.

This graf begins a two-paragraph chronological account of the events that provides further details. Readers do not need to know this information, but it is pertinent: type and size of fence, type of plane, what the plane was doing while the man was headed for it.

He climbed into a landing gear wheel well of the plane, which came to a stop. He initially ignored police officers' commands to come out but complied when city firefighters arrived. Melly later was booked on trespassing charges.

More details of how the events unfolded and what happened to the man. Because many readers would be asking that question from the start, it might be better to move it higher in the story.

Melly suffered from bipolar disorder and had been listed as a missing person in Canada, Castles said.

A possible explanation for the man's actions.

The plane, bound for Melbourne, departed an hour late.

Paul Haney, a spokesman for the agency that operates the airport, said authorities will look into improving the fence because of the incident. (AP)

So what happened to the flight? We finally get the answer. Some might argue that this information should come earlier, but a one-hour delay is not all that significant and not unusual these days. If the flight had been delayed several hours or canceled, that information would demand higher placement.

Notice that at any point in the story, the information already presented is more essential than that which follows. That makes it easy for the editor of a print publication to reduce the size of the story if less space is available than originally anticipated: Cutting from the bottom leaves the most important parts of the story intact.

Find a news story written in inverted pyramid format. Read it thoroughly. Delete the last paragraph. Has any essential information been lost? Continue removing paragraphs from the bottom up, each time checking to see if any of the deleted paragraphs contain information more essential than that in the remaining paragraphs.

Next, write an inverted pyramid story using the information that follows. Try the same test with your story.

The local police department purchased new weapons last month, 12 beanbag shotguns. They are less lethal than traditional firearms and designed to be used when a police officer feels his or her life—or the life of another—is in jeopardy. The guns shoot a rounded Kevlar sack resembling a sock. The bags are fired at almost 300 feet per second. Getting hit with one is like being hit by a major league pitcher's fastball.

The police got their first chance to try one of the shotguns last night on a man identified as Timothy Lee Carnathan. After the incident, he was booked on two counts of first-degree assault, two counts of felony assault and one count each of resisting arrest, failure to obey a police officer and destruction of property. He is being held on $5,000 bail.

According to police reports, two officers were pursuing Carnathan after seeing him throw a brick through the window of a shop on Main Street. At one point, he stopped and turned toward the officers. He was holding a steak knife, and he lunged at them.

In such situations, officers are permitted to use lethal force. But one of the officers had a beanbag shotgun, so he used that. He fired one shot into Carnathan's chest, knocking him to the ground. The other officer disarmed Carnathan while he was on the ground.

Beyond the Inverted Pyramid

The inverted pyramid format works well for a wide range of hard news stories, even fairly long ones. But some news stories benefit from alternate approaches.

The Summary and Chronology Story

Some stories are best told chronologically, that is, in the order in which events happen. Chronological accounts typically follow a summary lead (and, in many cases, a nut graf). Here's a good example by Heather Rawlyk of the Annapolis (Md.) Capital:

Cpl. Jeff Bauer has used a portable defibrillator to save a life twice in his five years with county police—once Wednesday, and again last night.

The writer gives this summary lead a little flair to catch readers' attention.

The 43-year-old Cape St. Claire resident is being credited with saving two lives in a little more than 24 hours this week using the heart jump-starter that helps victims of cardiac arrest. Until Wednesday, Cpl. Bauer had never used the device on anything other than a training dummy.

Elaboration on the lead provides more detail and background.

"I had never pushed the button on a real person," he said. "Then, I use it twice in two days."

Cpl. Bauer said he was in his patrol car around 7:30 p.m. when he got a call that a woman was stopped on the side of Solomon's Island Road with her brother, who was having a heart attack.

The first part of the chronology relates the events of the first emergency.

"I just happened to be one block over," he said. "When I made my right turn, they were in front of me."

Inside the car, Cpl. Bauer found a 67-year-old Harwood man slumped over in the passenger seat. With assistance from the man's brother-in-law, Cpl. Bauer pulled the man out of the car.

After starting CPR, he hooked the man to the automatic external defibrillator and pressed the button.

County firefighters showed up and took the man to the hospital. The man has been discharged from the hospital, according to Cpl. Mark Shawkey, a county police spokesman.

About 24 hours and 45 minutes later, Cpl. Bauer did it all again.

The second emergency is detailed in the next several paragraphs.

A woman said her husband had collapsed on Tarragon Lane in Edgewater. He was lying down and not breathing when Cpl. Bauer and Sgt. Eric Scott arrived.

Sgt. Scott started CPR. Cpl. Bauer pulled out his trusty defibrillator and went to work.

Thanks once again to Cpl. Bauer's quick moves with the special equipment, the 53-year-old man, who had suffered cardiac arrest, survived.

People around the county police station were calling Cpl. Bauer a hero this morning.

The final grafs deal with reaction to Bauer and his own feelings, wrapping up with a nice quote from him.

Cpl. Shawkey said the county executive plans to honor Cpl. Bauer next week.

"It's kinda weird," Cpl. Bauer said, laughing. "I did my job. That's all I did."

Writing about Crime

News Pointers

Many news stories concern criminal actions and charges. Until a person is formally charged with a crime, it is safest to not report the person's name. Printing a name before a person is charged can be an expensive mistake. Further, once people are identified as criminal suspects, they might never be able to totally reclaim their good names—whether they are innocent or not.

Even after a person has been charged with a crime, a writer needs to distinguish between the actions of the person or people committing the crime and the person or people charged with the crime, as the following example shows:

> A local man was in serious but stable condition after an apparently unprovoked attack in a local bar last night.

Bryan Dobson, 40, of Amsterdam Avenue, is being treated for a mild concussion as well as multiple cuts to the head and neck.

Police said Dobson was having a beer with a friend, Larry Griffin, at the Evergreen Lounge when a man walked over and smashed a beer bottle on his head. Witnesses said the attacker said, "Oh, you're back for more, huh?" Griffin said the men had never been to the bar before last night.

Police have charged Jason Wayne McKinley, 22, with aggravated assault in the attack. He is s being held on $10,000 bond.

Notice how the suspect's name is not mentioned in the first three paragraphs, which describe the attack. That's because at this point, McKinley has

ASSIGNMENT DESK **5.4**

Using the information provided, write a summary and chronology story.

Paramedics were called to Lake Ann yesterday. The call came about 4 p.m., after receiving a cell phone call from the mother of Gmerice Taylor, 21. Margaret McClean said her daughter had been struck by lightning.

Paramedics arrived quickly and were able to stabilize her. "I was having problems staying awake," Taylor said. "They kept telling me not to fall asleep, but it took everything I had to remain conscious." Paramedics took her to a local emergency room, where she was treated and released after about three hours.

She's OK now. Taylor suffered no serious injury but did get a welt on her chest.

The next time she goes to the lake, Taylor said, "I'm going to be paying more attention to the sky. If I see a cloud, I'm leaving."

Taylor was struck while visiting Lake Ann yesterday with her mother and some friends. A sudden storm moved in, and they gathered their things to leave. It was then that she noticed a puppy chained out nearby. She looked for its owners but could not find them. Taylor decided to take the puppy to her car and wait until the owners returned.

After putting the puppy in the back of her Jeep, Taylor walked toward her front door. At that moment, lightning struck her.

Taylor's mother and friends were in another car and saw the flash. They immediately called 911.

not been convicted of any of the charges, so although it's OK to say he has been charged with the crime, it is not OK to say that he committed it.

Some writers think that they can get away with just about anything if they pepper their writing with *allegedly* every now and then. That idea is simply wrong — and dangerous. *Allegedly* means that someone has made an accusation without proof. Although it can be used in detailing official charges against a person ("The men allegedly fired into the crowd, according to the police report"), the word *allegedly* by itself provides *no* protection from a libel suit. If no official charge has been made, using *allegedly* will not provide protection.

Further, the words *alleged* and *allegedly* work only in certain ways. A person cannot be an alleged anything; only an action can be alleged. So it's wrong to write:

> The alleged vandals entered the building at 9 a.m.

This revision is OK, though:

> The vandals allegedly entered the building at 9 a.m.

The Multiple-Element Story

Writers often find themselves coming up with more than one answer to the question "What's the most important aspect of this story?" Sometimes, one of the aspects merely elaborates on or explains the other, so the writer constructs a typical **single-element story,** like the examples we've seen so far. At other times, though, two or three distinctly different ideas compete for the spotlight and require a **multiple-element story.**

In a multiple-element story, the writer features each element in the lead — in one or more paragraphs — then elaborates on each aspect in the order in which it appeared in the lead. For example:

Music legend Eric Clapton is expecting his fifth child at the age of 59, he revealed today. His 28-year-old American wife Melia McEnery is seven months pregnant.	First paragraph of lead summarizes first element of story.
Clapton revealed the news as he accepted a CBE for services to music at Buckingham Palace.	Second paragraph of lead summarizes second element of story. Because this example is taken from a news source in the United Kingdom, CBE would be better known and more acceptable. For U.S. audiences, it would need to be spelled out as Commander of the Order of the British Empire, with a paragraph of explanation of that rank added in the body of the article.

"My wife is pregnant and she is expecting in January," he said.

The couple, who married three years ago in a secret ceremony, already have two daughters: Julie Rose, 3, and 18-month-old Ella Mae.

Clapton also has a 19-year-old daughter, Ruth, by previous partner Yvonne Kelly.

His four-year-old son, Conor, died in 1991 when he fell from a window of Clapton's Manhattan apartment. The star wrote the song "Tears In Heaven" as a tribute.

The guitarist, nicknamed Slowhand, was accompanied to the palace by McEnery, who wore a long gray dress and black shawl.

Clapton left their two young daughters at home for the occasion, joking: "They don't like you to bring anyone under 5 because it can get a bit chaotic."

The rock guitarist was presented with his CBE for services to music by the Princess Royal and described it as the "icing on the cake" of his glittering career.

The honor made him feel as though he had "grown up" and was no longer a young rebel, he said.

"I had a rebellious streak in me," he explained. "As a kid I would not have been able to accept this. I was very immature about the way I looked at that. I was against the establishment.

"Now I have grown up, I really think it is an important thing to be able to set an example of some kind.

"To say 'I did this all my life because I loved it' and to be recognized for that in this part of my life is good.

"It makes me feel like I have grown up in a way.

"I remember when the Beatles gave theirs back. At one time of life I probably would have identified with that, but I don't now."

He added: "This is the icing on the cake. Although I have been a rebel most of my life and most of the music I have made I have not done for any kind of success, it is a recognition for tenacity." (The Press Association via Scotsman.com)

These following six paragraphs elaborate on the first element. Notice that the details are provided in typical inverted pyramid fashion: From most pertinent to least.

The second element is restated with elaboration, as a transition point.

These seven paragraphs provide details of the second element. As there is not much to report about the honors ceremony itself, most of this section is given over to Clapton's remarks.

The trick to keeping a multiple-element story under control is to deal with the major elements one at a time. The writer needs to avoid hopping back and forth between the main themes, instead giving readers everything they need to know about theme No. 1 before moving on to theme No. 2.

Most multiple-element stories feature two main themes, but sometimes a third competes for top placement and is included. When there are more than three things worth focusing on, it's best to write multiple stories.

ASSIGNMENT DESK **5.5**

Find a multiple-element story (two or more main points). Analyze its structure: Does it conform to the model discussed in this chapter or does it differ? Then rewrite the information into two or more individual stories, each focusing on one of the elements. Compare your rewrites to the original: Which is more successful?

Updates and Second-Day Stories

One of the benefits of using inverted pyramid style with summary leads is that the format allows writers to update stories easily. In many cases, stories can be changed during the day as new information comes in, merely by rewriting the lead and adding another paragraph or two.

For example:

OPENING OF INITIAL STORY:	**OPENING OF LATE AFTERNOON STORY:**
Three people were killed and the westbound Bay Bridge was shut down indefinitely after a flatbed trailer being pulled by an SUV became unhitched.	Structural engineers have examined the site of a fatal crash on the Bay Bridge earlier today and pronounced the span free from structural damage.
The loose trailer resulted in a seven-vehicle pileup, including a tow truck and a tanker truck containing animal fat.	"Once we finish clearing the wreckage, we're good to go," lead engineer Todd Manx said.

After the new opening, the later version picks up material from the original article.

Some stories disappear after the first day, but most require follow-up stories a day or two afterward (see Figure 5.2). Unlike updates, these **second-day stories** require a complete rewrite. Although second-day stories follow the same rules as the originals, they differ in two important ways. First, the lead must reflect what has happened since the initial report was published. Second, the story must provide new details and also summarize the

FIGURE 5.2

As new developments occur in stories, writers and editors need to focus on the new information.

original report for those who might have missed it. For example, here's the lead on a New York Times article about a fire in New Jersey:

> A flare dropped by an F-16 fighter jet at a bombing range in southern New Jersey ignited a wildfire yesterday that burned thousands of acres of brush and pine forest, closed highways, forced thousands of residents to flee and damaged some homes, state officials said.

And here is the newspaper's second-day lead on the same story:

> Two days after fleeing 20-foot flames that licked at their backyards here, residents began returning to their mobile homes Thursday, though some came back to piles of charred rubble where their homes once stood.

Beyond the lead, there are important similarities and differences between first-day and second-day stories. The following article illustrates how a typical second-day story is organized:

The county court complex remained closed Thursday morning as investigators probed smoldering rubble from a fire that devoured a 123-year-old building.	Lead begins with the latest information: The complex is still closed while investigators search for causes.
It is not yet known what caused Wednesday's wind-driven blaze, which began on the roof area as work progressed on a $27-million renovation.	This graf recaps the original story.
The building's hose taps and sprinklers had been disconnected during the construction, and firefighters decided to let the flames gut the red-brick structure so they could save the modern courthouse next door.	This graf seeks to explain why the fire was able to do so much damage: Firefighters were more concerned with the adjacent building.

That building, which opened in 1991, contains the county's criminal files, land records and other documents.

Crews were expected to continue aerating the undamaged section Thursday. It could reopen for business Friday.

This graf explains what actions are likely to happen in the short term.

The modern building had not opened for the day when fire broke out in the so-called Duvall Wing. Officials believe more than 55 construction workers were on site.

Fuller background information amplifies the second paragraph.

Old beams, wooden flooring and construction materials provided ample fuel, and wind gusts of more than 25 mph spread the flames quickly.

Calling the building a county treasure, County Executive Jack Johnson said he would seek state assistance for restoration.

Another look ahead, offering information on what might happen in the long term.

Court operations have been conducted at the site since 1720. The burned building was completed in 1881.

Historical background on the destroyed building completes the article. In inverted pyramid style, this information could be cut without much loss to the overall story.

A cupola and columns added during renovations in the last century were damaged, but officials hope to salvage and restore them. Officials also hoped to find a bell used to sound the daily opening of court. (AP)

News Pointers | Correlation and Causation

Writers sometimes mistake correlation (events happening at the same time) for causation (one event causes another). So, for instance, if a car crashes during a heavy rainstorm, a careless writer might assume that the storm caused the crash. In actuality, the accident could have resulted from a blowout, drunken driving or any of a number of other causes. A journalist needs to be careful about making such assumptions about causation, removing any that are not supported by facts.

For example, an article quoted a college professor talking about a new faculty handbook:

He said the handbook is "anti-faculty" *because* it states that professors must hold office hours and turn in students' grades on time.

An alert reader would question why the professor would label such traditional requirements "anti-faculty." In fact, the professor had done nothing of the sort. What he told the reporter was that he considered the handbook to be disrespectful *because* professors at the school already held office hours and turned grades in on time. That's why the professor called the handbook "anti-faculty." As you can see, the writer's interpretation was far different from the professor's message.

Check Your Facts

No matter how good the writing, if a journalist messes up facts, the work is worthless. Legendary publisher Joseph Pulitzer made that point when he stressed that the main rule of good journalism is "Accuracy, accuracy, accuracy."

Before handing in any story, the writer should carefully review it to make sure there are no mistakes in handling facts. The following types of facts demand special attention:

- Names: All names should be double-checked to verify that they are spelled correctly. A writer must not rely on listings in directories and elsewhere. When in doubt, the writer should check with the person himself or herself.
- Dates: Dates should be verified with reference materials. A writer must not assume a date is correct just because the source is a knowledgeable person.
- Places: Many cities across the United States and around the world share the same name. For instance, more than a dozen states have cities named Athens—and several more have a New Athens. And of course, the most famous Athens of all is not in the United States but in Greece.
- Corporate names: In this era of rampant corporate mergers, some companies have taken on lengthy and confusing names. Others have changed their names over and again. For example, over the years Time Inc. became Time-Life Inc., then Time Warner Inc., then AOL Time Warner—and then back to Time Warner Inc.
- Titles: Many job titles sound similar, so a writer should always verify which one a person holds. There's a big difference between *assistant to the superintendent* and *assistant superintendent.*
- Numbers: Many journalists pride themselves on being bad at math. Nevertheless, there's no reason to let math errors slip into a story. In most cases, writers should be able to catch errors quickly with a calculator or simple spreadsheet program.
- Graphics: If information graphics are being created to run with an article, the writer should make sure that all the information in them is correct. Prepared graphics should be checked against the article to make sure there are no inconsistencies.

ASSIGNMENT DESK 5.6

The following selections include errors found in published news stories. Each contains at least one factual error. Using library or online resources, try to find the errors and correct them.

1. The three predatory breeds of sharks that can be found in waters off England are the mako, the poor beagle and the thresher.
2. The symphony is inspired by the works of Edgar Allen Poe.
3. Warren E. Buffet was best known for his role as CEO of Enron Corporation.

Continued ⁙

Assignment
Desk **5.6**
Continues

4. ABC anchor Brian Williams graciously agreed to deliver the commencement address.
5. The assassination of President John F. Kennedy in 1965 was the subject of Harry Livingstone's 1989 book, "High Treason."
6. Mohammed Ali's most memorable quote was "Float like a bumblebee, sting like a bee."
7. If scientific predictions for the next century prove accurate, global temperatures could rise as much as 7.7 degrees Celsius by the year 3000.
8. The Eiffel Tower looks delicate, but it is a massive structure, weighing nearly 7,000 pounds.
9. James Dobson, a well-known minister and psychologist, is also founder and chairman of the group Focus on the Family.
10. Those visiting Myrtle Beach, S.C., on vacation will find the Sun-Times newspaper published there to be a good read.

Using Quotes

Most news stories include quotations from one or more people whom the writer interviewed. Good quotes add life to writing, give a sense of a source's personality and often add important or useful information.

Unfortunately, many quotes add nothing to a story or, worse, slow it down or confuse the reader. To make sure every quote is worth using, a writer always should run through this checklist:

Make sure the quote adds to the story. If a quote does nothing more than repeat an idea written in the writer's own words, it should not be used. Even when a quote is not an exact repeat, if it says nothing, it should be cut. Quotes such as "That's interesting" are not interesting.

Make sure the quoted words are the person's exact *words.* Most print news outlets require writers to stick with a speaker's exact words, even if the speaker has omitted words or made grammatical errors. (Some publications require that writers use *sic* to indicate such errors were the speaker's.) Some media outlets permit corrections to minor grammatical errors, but a writer needs to make sure such corrections are acceptable to his or her employer. Similarly, some publications allow writers to revise phonetic spellings such as *gotta* (got to) and *gonna* (going to). But again, a writer must make sure it's OK to do so before changing anything in a quote.

If a quote adds to the story but needs to have material changed or inserted to make sense, the added material should be enclosed in parentheses to indicate it wasn't the speaker's words:

"It's not every day that (local students) get an opportunity like this," he said.

Paraphrase when necessary. If a quote requires more than minor clarification, it's probably better to paraphrase it:

Direct quote: Boswell said she "plan(s) to (resign)... before (the report) is released."
Paraphrase: Boswell said she plans to resign before the report is released.

Don't put words in a speaker's mouth. Writers don't have to use complete sentences from their sources; sometimes a partial quote works just fine. But in those cases, writers need to make sure that partial quotes could have been spoken. The most common problem is the use of the incorrect personal pronoun:

> He said completing the marathon "has been one of the greatest accomplishments of his life."

Unless the speaker has identity issues, he probably would not refer to his life as "his" life.

Place attribution carefully. Attribution usually works best placed after the quote:

> "I never thought the pain would end," she said.

However, when quotes run more than a sentence or two, attribution should be placed either at the beginning of the quote or in the middle. When placing attribution in the middle of a line, it should be placed at a natural break:

> Incorrect: "If our success," he said, "is measured by whether local residents feel safe in the community, it sounds like we have succeeded."
>
> Correct: "If our success is measured by whether local residents feel safe in the community," he said, "it sounds like we have succeeded."

Avoid inverted attribution. Many beginning news writers tend to invert the noun and the verb when they put attribution at the end of a quotation or paraphrase:

> "We will not end this investigation until we determine who was interfering with those facilities," said Waltham.

Such constructions are unnatural and clumsy. Much better is conventional subject-verb construction:

> "We will not end this investigation until we determine who was interfering with those facilities," Waltham said.

The one exception is when a lengthy title is needed to identify the speaker:

> "The international community must be united and send a very firm message to Iran on its nuclear program," said U.S. Undersecretary of State Nicholas Burns.

Make sure it is clear who's speaking. If more than one person is quoted in a story, attribution should come before the first quote from each new speaker. When that is not done, confusion often results. For example:

> "This execution accomplishes nothing," Lubliner said. "It demeans everyone."
> "I do not believe the evidence presented warrants the exercise of clemency in this case," the governor said after reviewing the petition.

Placing the second attribution at the start of the second paragraph would eliminate reader confusion:

> "This execution accomplishes nothing," Lubliner said. "It demeans everyone."

But after reviewing the petition, the governor said, "I do not believe the evidence presented warrants the exercise of clemency in this case."

Choose verbs carefully. Nine times out of 10, *said* works best for attribution. Other supposed synonyms convey a range of opinion and judgment. Consider:

"I am the father of two children," he said.

"I am the father of two children," he admitted.

"I am the father of two children," he blurted.

"I am the father of two children," he confessed.

A reader hardly notices *said*, but other words may stop the reader and may change the meaning of the quote. *According to* can be particularly troubling because it suggests that doubt is being cast on a speaker's words. While the phrase is fine to use when referring to a nonhuman source (a report or record, for example), it should be avoided when quoting people.

ASSIGNMENT DESK **5.7**

The passages here all incorporate quotes. Rewrite any passages that violate the standards for handling quotes.

1. She said the new position has "given her a brand new perspective on things."
2. "Well, I guess, I mean it's hard to get excited—to get pumped up—when, the fans isn't—uh, aren't—behind you, you know?" Lopez said.
3. "We found the study results worthy of attention," he indicated.
4. Weiss explained, "Our support staff. . . have really handled [the crisis] with flying colors. . . and made [us] proud of them."
5. "We expect the investigation to be completed within 48 hours, and we plan to bring charges at that point," according to Detective Kathryn Beene.

Conclusion

In this age of multimedia, writers working with only text might feel that they are at a disadvantage. But the range of tools for writing leads and stories can help them deliver the news with impact and clarity. To make the most of those tools, writers need to immerse themselves in newspapers and magazines and understand the steps of the news writing process. Good print news writing is not hard, but it does demand thoughtfulness and attention to detail.

KEY TERMS

delayed lead, 76
hard news, 73
inverted pyramid, 73
multiple-element story, 85

nut graf, 77
second-day story, 87
single-element story, 85
summary and chronology, 84

DISCUSSION QUESTIONS

1. Look at several leads on print news stories. What types of leads seem to be the most common? Which ones are best at grabbing your attention? At giving you the essential facts of the story? How many do both?
2. Can a writer's decision to use a delayed lead make a story seem less important than it is?
3. How often do you read an entire news story as opposed to only the lead? What are the primary factors that determine whether you will read the entire story?
4. How often do you read a news story only because the lead grabbed your attention?

NOTES

1. Jacqi Banaszynski, "Nut Grafs Create Sanity," American Press Institute, 25 April 2003, **www. americanpressinstitute.** org/content/p1763_c1385.cfm.

Chapter 6

Writing the Advanced Text Story

The previous chapter focused on the workhorse of the news business: the hard news story. The job of the hard news story is to convey information about an important or interesting event. Most people get most of their news from these types of stories.

But many stories, particularly those that do not concern a specific event or pronouncement, are better written as feature stories. Although features can be a refreshing change of pace for the writer, they also can present serious challenges. This chapter explores the range of feature articles and offers strategies for writing them.

The Feature Story

Features work particularly well in a range of situations:

- When a story is more interesting or unusual than important. The "just the facts" approach of the hard news story works well with serious and important topics, but it does not fit as well when the story topic is light. Therefore, writers often turn to the feature format when dealing with information of less-than-earth-shattering importance. In addition to making a better match, the feature story format also gives writers a chance to showcase their creative talents to help lure readers into stories they might otherwise pass by. For instance, many people will happily skip past a hard news story about a man who has just entered the record books for amassing 1,497 valid credit cards. But in the right hands, that same topic can be molded into an engaging feature article. (One warning: Resist the temptation to make light of serious stories. For example, after two caretakers at the San Francisco Zoo were fired for refusing to bare their breasts to bond with the gorilla they attended to, some writers—and headline writers—might have had a hard time resisting the temptation to have some fun with the story. But considering that the story focused on charges of sexual discrimination and wrongful termination, that would have been a bad idea.)

- When the focus of a story is the *how* or *why* and not the *what*. Although the hard news format can effectively handle stories in which two or even three things have happened, feature stories work better in recounting how or why those things have happened or putting together the pieces that explain a trend. For example, after the tsunami rocked Asia in late 2004, thousands of hard news stories reported the details of the devastation, suffering and aftermath. At the same time, journalists around the globe wrote feature articles that explained what had caused the tsunami and why it had not been anticipated.

- When a story depends on substantial background information. Although many hard news stories contain at least a little background—previous related events or likely motives behind an action or statement—when the background itself becomes a story, the feature format works better. For instance, when privatization of Social Security became the key item of President Bush's domestic agenda following his 2004 re-election, the Washington Post ran a feature titled "Private-Account Concept Grew From Obscure Roots" explaining the origins of the plan.

- When a story defies easy categorization and demands the writer look at it—and present it—in a fresh light. Sometimes the story doesn't fit into a traditional model of news writing. In those cases, the solution is a feature that's crafted to fit the topic. For instance, Diana Sugg of The Baltimore (Md.) Sun used the feature format to write a compelling four-part series about the long and drawn-out process of keeping a dying child alive with modern medicine.

As these different examples illustrate, the feature story can capably cover a vast range of topics and approaches. There's a catch, though: The reason the feature story is so versatile is that it's not a single story format as much as it is a form that grows organically from the material the writer is working with. A feature writer needs to take as much time as possible to gather information, including the sights, sounds, smells, tastes and textures that will help take readers on a journey. To aid in that process, Peter Perl, a longtime feature writer for the Washington Post and now director of Training and Professional Development there, recommends that feature writers carry a camera while researching stories to help record detail that might escape them while they're there. The proliferation of camera (and video) cell phones makes that easier than ever (see Figure 6.1).

Once finished with research and interviews, the feature writer needs to develop a clear theme for the story. In a sentence, he or she must be able to answer this question: What is this story all about? It's not enough to merely have a topic (for example, female motorcyclists). As part of that process, a writer must consider what would pique a reader's curiosity about the topic, why he or she should read it, and what will make him or her want to read it all the way through. Therefore, the writer needs to zero in on one aspect of that topic and have a clear point of view (for example, "More professional women are turning to motorcycling for adventure and exploration").

Some writers think it's good practice to develop a point of view before they begin research, but Perl disagrees. "You need to keep yourself open and really listen to the people you're talking to," he says. "Stories can change, so you need to be ready to change gears."

While writing a feature story, many writers find it helpful to discuss parts of it with another writer or editor. Perl notes, "Often a writer will have a sense of what needs to

FIGURE 6.1 Cell phones with built-in camera capabilities allow anyone to capture an image and share it immediately.

happen in a story. Talking it out with someone helps that along. Ultimately, though, you've got to go by your own instincts."

Some writers find it useful to tell their stories out loud to the wall. "So many reporters can verbally tell a great story," freelance writer Yvonne Feeley says, "but they can't transfer what they just said to print." For those writers, she recommends telling the story out loud and quickly writing a draft of it.

Story Length

While hard news stories do not have set word-length limits, they tend to be short, with the vast majority running between 200 and 500 words and few reaching 1,000 words. Feature stories however, have a much wider range of lengths. They also *can* be short, as this example from the AP shows:

> Who says cats and dogs don't get along?
>
> Workers at the Meriden Humane Society are marveling at a short-haired mother cat that has adopted a 6-day-old Rottweiler puppy that was rejected by its mother.

The tiny pup, named Charlie by Humane Society volunteers, nurses alongside a jumble of black and gray kittens recently born to Satin, who was taken to the shelter by an owner unable to care for her.

Charlie's mother was found by the side of the road in Meriden a couple of months ago. She gave birth to two puppies, but one was stillborn. As sometimes happens with a stillborn in the litter, the mother refused to accept Charlie.

Volunteers bottle-fed him every two hours, but the effort was exhausting for them and insufficient for the puppy, volunteer Chris Chorney said.

Research indicated that a suitable substitute could be Satin, who had given birth to four kittens that have quickly warmed to Charlie.

"The kittens scrum up with him, and the kittens treat him like one of their own," Chorney said. "There's a certain social benefit of small animals being with each other." (AP)

That sort of touching little story, known as a **brite** or **bright**, regularly appears in newspaper or online news feature sections, where it gives readers a chance to sit back and have a chuckle, no matter how sad or depressing the rest of the day's news is. This example uses just eight words for its lead and wraps up the entire story in 186 words.

Most feature stories, however, run substantially longer—and often use 200 or more words just to get the story started. For instance, the lead of this New York Times feature story runs 189 words over four paragraphs:

At 20 weeks pregnant, Courtney Monardo, a 40-year-old processor for a mortgage company in Scottsdale, Ariz., was—to quote Madeleine Kahn in "Blazing Saddles"—"so tired."

"After work, I'd sit down on the couch, take a cat nap, eat dinner, and I'd be in bed by 8:30," she said.

So her husband, who is also her boss, did something about it. "He walked into my office and told me to shut my computer down," she said. The couple soon arrived at the Westin Kierland Resort and Spa, also in Scottsdale (www.kierlandresort.com). "He explained to me that this was a getaway, to be pampered, that I needed it." First on the agenda was an in-room ice cream sundae. Next, a couples' massage. Then a shopping trip for baby clothes, a room-service dinner ordered from the 24-hour cravings menu and a movie. The next morning included breakfast in bed, a round of golf and a pedicure.

The appeal of this brief but indulgent experience—known as a babymoon in travel industry parlance—is pure escape. "Everything was done for us," Ms. Monardo said. "We didn't really need to plan anything."

Two leads, one of eight words and one of 189 words: Which is better? It depends. Obviously it would make no sense to write a 189-word lead on the first story because that story just doesn't have much substance to it—the writer used fewer words than that to tell the entire story. But for more complex stories, a longer lead can set the scene and introduce important background to prepare the reader for all the details to follow. The most important point is that each has its place in feature writing, and it's the writer's job to choose the appropriate length for the story, as well as the appropriate structure and ending. As always, writers need to remember the advice mentioned previously: Use just as many words as are needed to tell the story, and no more.

Feature Leads

Many feature writers devote the bulk of their time and energy into crafting just the right lead. If the lead does not entice the reader into the piece, all the work the writer puts into the rest of the story doesn't matter.

Many shorter feature stories begin with summary leads. Unlike their hard news counterparts, however, summary leads used on feature stories do not try to pack in the 5 W's and an H, but rather they focus on providing a quick preview of what's coming. For instance, this lead tops a story that explores a new tourist destination:

> Few tourist attractions at the Grand Canyon have generated as much hype as the Skywalk, the mammoth glass-bottomed deck that extends 70 feet past the rim of the Grand Canyon and offers breathtaking views 4,000 feet over the canyon floor. (AP)

This lead begins a story about a unique form of artistic expression:

> Since New Year's Day, 29-year-old artist Emily Katrencik has been eating the wall of her gallery in Brooklyn, N.Y., tearing off small chunks of plaster with her teeth as though it were a gingerbread house. (The Guardian)

Rather than try to cram a wide range of facts into their leads, the writers of the preceding leads merely tried to tempt the readers to wade into their stories to find out more.

That's not to say a summary feature lead *can't* include details, as this example makes clear:

> People have been eating soy for more than 5,000 years, but only in recent times has it been dubbed a "miracle food." And it's not just tofu we're eating any more.
>
> We're gobbling soy nuts, soy burgers, soy hot dogs, soy drinks, soy flakes, soy flour, soy cereals, soy yogurt and soy bars. You can fill your sandwich with soy turkey and top your burger with soy cheese. Want more? Sip a soy latte. (The Globe and Mail)

Some summary feature leads add description to try to set a scene for the reader, such as this one from the San Diego (Calif.) Union-Tribune:

> With football season over and baseball season more than a month away, there is another season in full swing — wildflower season. Sand verbena and evening primrose are now gracing the floor of the Anza Borrego Desert. The land is rife with fossils, from mammoths to crabs and clams, but in the early spring, especially after record rainfalls such as those this year, it is the flowers that run wild and steal the show.

Why Choose Journalism?

Journalism will never be a job I leave behind at the end of the day. I carry it with me all the time, and at times, honestly, that's a burden. I think about the stories I need to do and the stories I'm afraid to do. The ones I've nailed and the ones that nailed me. So choosing journalism isn't a matter of selecting a 9-to-5 grind. You'll have to give much more than that. The sound of a far-off siren will make you want to check with 911 dispatchers. A surprising piece of gossip in conversation will spur you to sneak away and call the city desk. You'll develop an insatiable desire to know every ounce of what's going on, and eventually people will want to tell you. It takes a while to get there — building sources, writing on deadline, knowing a good story when it bangs down your door — but no other job rewards and robs and glorifies and vilifies like journalism. Every single day.

MOLLY MOORHEAD
St. Petersburg (Fla.) Times

Because of their versatility, summary leads are often the first choice of feature writers. But writers need to realize that the summary lead is just one of many alternatives. Like the stories they introduce, feature leads come in a staggering range of guises. These various types of feature leads can give writers room to stretch out and gradually draw the reader into the story.

Anecdotal Leads

In many cases, the best way to make a general point is by starting with a specific example or anecdote. In such situations, a news writer looks for a "case study" that will bring a story to life for the reader. The writer then tells that story in the compressed form of an anecdote, which is a short story format that consists of a beginning, a middle and an ending. The ending often is a surprise.

Good **anecdotal leads** require that the writer carefully isolate the major point of the story and then find an anecdote that makes that point simply and clearly. Too often, a writer finds anecdotes that *almost* do the job and then struggles to make them work. This is one of the easiest traps to fall into: It's hard to resist using a good anecdote, even when it's not the right one for the given story. What separates the best writers from the rest is their skill at using only the right ones.

Richard Schapiro used an anecdotal lead to begin his story on a new trend in body modification:

> When George Chase, a stout man with a shaved head and a penchant for tattoos, strode into Sacred Tattoo in New York's Chinatown several months ago, he had already made the decision to get three X's emblazoned across his chest. The design is the commonly accepted symbol for indicating that he has sworn off cigarettes, alcohol and controlled substances. But instead of getting the letters tattooed on his body with ink, Chase wanted to have his resolve memorialized in a far more striking fashion: carved into his body with a scalpel.
>
> "To me, it's like the difference between a watercolor painting and an oil," said Chase, 39, a customer service representative for a telecommunication company. To prove his point, he lifted his shirt to reveal three slightly raised X's spanning 5 inches just above his right nipple.
>
> Scarification, the act of creating designs out of scar tissue by cutting the skin or branding it with heated metal, has been performed for centuries among tribal cultures in Africa, Asia and Polynesia. Now, people are being scarred in tattoo shops and piercing studios in cities across the United States and Canada. (Columbia News Service)

Opening the article with this anecdote, while likely to make many readers wince, gives this story a much more powerful beginning than a simple summary lead would. For example, notice how much less effective this summary lead is:

> A new trend in body modification creates designs out of scar tissue by cutting the skin or branding it with heated metal.

Notice also the nut graf beginning "Scarification, the act of creating designs out of scar tissue..." Such a bridge is critical in moving from the specific anecdotal lead to the general body of the story.

Judy Foreman used an anecdotal lead in a syndicated article, with the goal of drawing readers into a story about the frighteningly common occurrence of patients being awake under anesthesia:

> Seven years ago, Carol Weihrer, a flutist and office administrator, had her right eye removed. Weihrer had been living in pain from a severely scratched cornea for years and had had 17 surgeries to try to fix it.
>
> Just before she was given general anesthesia, she remembers, she felt relieved that her trauma would soon be over. Suddenly, she woke up hearing disco music and thinking, "I must be done."
>
> The next thing she said she heard was someone saying, "'Cut deeper. Pull harder.' I realized: They are not done. They are just starting."
>
> She felt no pain, but was terrified.
>
> "I can remember praying to God, screaming, but no sound came out," said Weihrer, now 53, whose vocal muscles had been paralyzed by the anesthesia.

> Such "anesthesia awareness" is not as rare as one might think. Up to two of every 1,000 patients—or as many as 40,000 Americans a year—wake up while under general anesthesia, according to a large study by Emory University researchers published last year. (MyHealthSense.com)

Again, notice how the nut graf moves the reader from Weihrer's specific story to the bigger issue of anesthesia awareness.

Anthony Faiola of the Washington Post used an anecdotal lead to begin his article on a new generation of robots being developed in Japan:

> Ms. Saya, a perky receptionist in a smart canary-yellow suit, beamed a smile from behind the "May I Help You?" sign on her desk, offering greetings and answering questions posed by visitors at a local university. But when she failed to welcome a workman who had just walked by, a professor stormed up to Saya and dished out a harsh reprimand.
>
> "You're so stupid!" said the professor, Hiroshi Kobayashi, towering over her desk.
>
> "Eh?" she responded, her face wrinkling into a scowl. "I tell you, I am not stupid!"
>
> Truth is, Saya isn't even human.

Once again, the nut graf effectively moves the story from one specific example to the big picture: That Japan is leading the world in production of robots. This article is not just about one sassy robot; it also is about a major cultural shift.

Anecdotes typically come from the experiences of others and not from the writer's life. Occasionally, however, a first-person anecdote offers the best way to drive home the main point of a story. In the following example, Tom Haines of The Boston Globe uses a first-person anecdote to show the tensions in modern-day Turkey:

> A Muslim man motions for me to follow: Weave among the noontime worshipers, find a space, and kneel.
>
> It is only days before spring, and the subject of the imam's speech, dictated to this eastern outpost by government officials in Ankara, the capital, is a battle on March 18, 1915, that laid a foundation for the Turkish republic. Gather around the mosque, then, in the name of the secular state that rose from the ashes of Ottomans. Yet it is ritual prayer, honoring Allah, that moves these men.
>
> Side by side we rise in sun and shadow. My arm presses hard against that of a robed elder. We bow, then kneel again. The silent sound of a thousand bending bodies surrounds me. Hands, then foreheads, press onto carpets. The weave is rough against the skin. My eyes settle inches from ankles. Turkish, Kurdish, and Arabic prayers rush around my still mouth.

Anecdotal leads can also be used when a writer wishes to convey the idea that something is happening in many different places at the same time. In those cases, three anecdotes can be compressed into what's sometimes referred to as a **bam-bam-bam lead**. This type of lead attempts to illustrate the scope of a story by combining a range of short, disparate anecdotes. The anecdotes might illustrate various aspects of a topic, come from various geographical areas, or show how a wide range of people are involved or affected by an event, as the following example by Rick Weiss and Nancy Trejos of the Washington Post shows:

> In Nevada, the chief executive of an import company examines the lawsuit that just hit him, wondering how much it will cost to ensure that his next purchases of pet food ingredients are free of industrial poisons.
>
> In Kansas, wheat growers wonder how China usurped the once-bustling market in gluten, a protein-rich byproduct of those amber waves of grain that once symbolized America's bounty.
>
> And at a park in Washington, the owner of a soft-coated terrier says that after learning the food he had been giving his beloved Checkers for the past six years was on the recall list, he will never again buy pet food brands with foreign ingredients.

Ian Urbina of The New York Times used a bam-bam-bam lead to introduce a story on shelters for gay youths:

> One girl said she started living on the streets after her mother beat her for dressing like a boy. Another said she ran away from home after her father pulled a gun on her for hanging around with so many "tomboys." A third said she left home after a family acquaintance raped her because she was a lesbian and he wanted to "straighten her out." (The New York Times)

Both of these bam-bam-bam leads do an excellent job of giving the reader a sense of the many dimensions of the stories.

Narrative Leads

Like anecdotal leads, **narrative leads** also present a story to the reader, but they typically run longer and include dialogue and quotes and set up scenes. Rather than offering a specific example to illustrate a general point, a narrative lead typically sets the stage for a story about a specific individual or place. For instance, Barbara Karkabi of the Houston Chronicle used a narrative lead to set the stage for a story that focused on one man's search for his ancestors:

> It took six weeks for James Jacobs to find out about his long-lost ancestors —
> a life-changing event capping years of research.
>
> Jacobs had traced his paternal family back to his great-great-grandfather Francois Jacob, born into slavery in 1820. Like other African-Americans documenting family history, Jacobs then hit a wall.
>
> Then he read about a company that could take his DNA from a cheek swab and trace his lineage to an ethnic group within an African country.
>
> When Jacobs received his answer from African Ancestry in December 2003, he handled it like precious cargo. His DNA sequence on his father's side matched

the Yoruba people of Nigeria. His mother's side matched the Bamileke people of Cameroon.

"It made me feel wonderful. It was a feeling of: 'My God, that's how it all happened,'" Jacobs recalls. "The woman came from Cameroon, and Nigeria is right next to it, so they all came to a common place to go to the ship. The feeling is hard to describe, like having a long-lost parent and you found them. I was able to make this huge leap, and now all I have to do is go back and visit." (Houston Chronicle)

Michael Liedtke of The Associated Press used a narrative lead to begin his article about a latter-day dot-com success story:

Like so many other 20-somethings hoping to mine the Internet gold rush of the late 1990s, Mena Trott was thrown for a humbling loop by the dot-com bust, yet still craved stardom. Her unassuming husband, Ben, just wanted another computer programming gig in Silicon Valley's depressed job market. The couple's odd chemistry cooked up Six Apart Ltd., a startup that has helped popularize the "blogging" craze, with millions of people worldwide maintaining online personal journals that dissect everything from politics to poultry.

The Trotts, both 27, have amplified the buzz about Web logs, or blogs, by making them easier to set up and write.

San Francisco–based Six Apart provides two widely used blogging tools — a software publishing program, Movable Type, and a hosted service, TypePad, for people who don't want to do the technological grunt work themselves.

Descriptive Leads

Stories that focus on a specific place, person or group of people often are best served by a **descriptive lead**. Good descriptive leads are not just grab bags of sights, sounds, smells and tastes. Instead, they include only those details that support the main point of the story.

Diane E. Foulds used a descriptive lead effectively to give readers an immediate sense of a person she was profiling in a piece published in The Boston Globe:

He has an indefinable presence, a gentle attentiveness that makes you feel good just being around him. Most of his patients do, which is why, at 92, Dr. Harry Rowe is still practicing medicine.

He still drives, still sings in the church choir, and attends numerous community meetings. Though he has cut down on house calls, patients still fill the cramped waiting room of the white clapboard clinic he shares with three other health professionals in his home on Main Street in Wells River, Vt.

"I don't do very much now," he said. "I only see two or three or four patients a day."

Cindy Loose's article in the Washington Post uses a descriptive lead to make readers feel like they have landed on a desert island:

The small wooden cottage atop a steep hill has no air conditioning, but a soft breeze through louvered windows flutters the sheer white curtains at my balcony door. The trade winds that once carried tall ships from around the world to Antigua today carry to my room the smell of tropical flowers.

Andrew Michelin, whose family came from Europe to the Caribbean several generations ago, says he planned every detail of his small resort so that visitors would have a true Caribbean experience. The roof of each cottage, for example, is made of galvanized metal, so if there happens to be a shower during your stay, you'll hear the sound of raindrops popping off a tin roof.

"When you first wake up, I don't want you to think even for a second, 'Where am I?'" Michelin says. "I want you to awaken and feel where you are, smell where you are, hear where you are."

When Vince Beiser of the Los Angeles Times wanted to demonstrate the lengths to which prescription drug addicts go to seek help, he found a descriptive lead the perfect way to lure readers in:

The hallucinations are coming fast and vivid. Faces, shapes, colors rush toward him, melting and swirling into each other, sometimes coalescing into more concrete visions. He sees himself floating underwater. By turns, his four children drift by. Sometimes they blow bubbles and float happily up to the surface; sometimes they sink straight down, disappearing into darkness. Then there are three ships, coming in to dock at three tubes; he knows, somehow, that they are building a bomb, and if all three dock successfully it will explode. He tries to direct them away, but can't. The final ship enters the final tube. A titanic explosion collapses everything into darkness.

Then it all starts again.

While Craig's mind reels through this visual cacophony, his body lies quietly in a darkened room in a house near Tijuana, deep in the grip of a powerful psychedelic drug. His wife, his children and his upper-middle-class home in Salt Lake City are all far, far away.

Craig is not some crystal-collecting spiritual seeker on a Carlos Castañeda trip. He is a prosperous, respected restaurant owner, age 50. He is friendly with the mayor and active in mainstream charities. Other than family vacations to the Bahamas and Mazatlan, Mexico, this is the only time he has been outside of the United States.

Craig is here because he is desperate. He is addicted to painkillers—OxyContin, Lortab and other illegally obtained prescription opiates. His habit is costing him $1,500 a month, and he knows he must stop. Conventional detox programs have failed to help, so he has slipped over the border to try a treatment that is as much an urban myth as a scientifically proven medication....

The powerful images that begin this story help to draw in readers who would turn the page if they encountered a summary lead like this:

Some prescription drug addicts are crossing the border to Tijuana to try psychedelic drugs that might help them break their addictions.

Question Leads

Question leads rarely are the best choice for feature articles. A writer should be telling (or showing) readers information, not giving them a quiz. Occasionally, however, a lead that poses a question of widespread interest or one that completely catches readers off guard can succeed. Su Lum of The Aspen (Colo.) Times uses the former approach:

> Which is more ecological: paper or plastic? Are milk, coffee and/or wine good for you or not?
>> Which will kill you faster: carbs or fat?
>> These and other questions mystify us as we tiptoe through the minefield of our extended lives, a winding path through a thicket of warning Do and Don't signs that randomly reverse themselves.

Dan Rafael of USA Today takes the second approach, raising a couple of outrageous questions to capture reader curiosity:

> Did you get punched in the nose by your boss at work today? Did he split open your lip with a right hand or crack your rib with a left hook?
>> Maybe he hit you so hard in the mouth that he cut your tongue and now it will take months to fully heal.
>> Perhaps he did all of that damage and didn't even pay for the medical bills. Don't bother calling the cops either because it's entirely legal.
>> Welcome to the world of a pro boxer's sparring partner, where daily pain and the ability to not fight back too hard are part of the job description.

Other Feature Leads

Not all feature leads fit into one of the preceding categories. Sometimes the material for a story suggests an offbeat way of starting it: a list, a powerful quote, a joke, a diary entry, a bit of conversation aimed at the reader, or a burst of staccato phrases. As long as the lead serves its purposes of getting readers' attention and luring them into the article, it's appropriate for the story.

For example, Washington Post television critic Lisa de Moraes began her piece on Dan Rather's last broadcast with a lead that plays off television newscast style:

> March 10: Day 1 of Conservatives Don't Have Dan Rather to Kick Around Anymore — otherwise known as Bob Schieffer's First Day as Temporary Permanent Anchor of the "CBS Evening News."

Christine Pittel of The New York Times began an article on an unusual undertaking this way:

> Let me explain why my 12-year-old had a chicken coop in her bedroom.

Ellen Gamerman of The Baltimore (Md.) Sun used a combination of lyrics and description to begin her multi-part story about life at a retirement home:

> "Start spreading the news," the singer wails.
>
> "I'm leaving today. I want to be a part of it: Leisure World, Leisure World."
>
> A wave of gray and white heads floats past the band. Light bounces off the spangled dresses and sparkling jewelry of women keeping time with partners in sports coats and hair pomade. In the past month, there have been ambulances, funerals, broken bones, heartbreak. But it is Saturday night in spring. The bandleader croons, the couples step forward and back, and the seniors-only community known as Leisure World spins happily in its own orbit.
>
> The room is dark, shadowy, romantic. So, naturally, someone complains.
>
> Ben Oliver is used to this; these are senior citizens, after all. He turns up the surrounding lights and lets a few minutes pass. Then, when no one's looking, he dims the crystal chandelier.
>
> Dark again.
>
> Perfect.

A writer should not expect to be able to write the best lead for a feature story on the first attempt. In fact, feature writers often write several types of leads before settling on one as the best for a given article. If a writer tries only one type of lead, chances are he or she will end up missing the one that would have worked best for the story.

ASSIGNMENT DESK 6.1

For each of the following story summaries, write at least two different types of feature leads. Be prepared to discuss which you think works best for each story.

1. Kyle MacDonald, 26, lives in Canada. Until recently, he lived in an apartment. But he got tired of that and decided he wanted a home of his own. Unfortunately, he did not make enough money or have enough savings to buy a house.

So MacDonald decided he would try to trade something he had for a house. He chose a red paperclip. He posted the paperclip on Craig's List last year and offered to trade it for something of more value. Then he traded each new item for something of more value. The items he received and then traded included a fish pen; a doorknob sculpted to look like a face; a keg of beer; a day with rock sensation Alice Cooper; a recording contract; a role in a movie; and then, on his 15th trade, a three bedroom, one-and-a half bathroom house in Saskatchewan, Canada.

MacDonald and his girlfriend plan to move into the house later this year. They have invited everyone in the world to attend their housewarming party.

Continued

Assignment Desk **6.1** Continues ⁝

2. Last week, Brian Buck, 35, released a bouquet of bright orange balloons, prompted by his 9-year-old daughter Anna's curiosity about how far they'd travel. Buck, a stay-at-home father who works part-time at a store that sells balloons, called it "all just a bit of fun, really."

"We once saw a TV report about a balloon that was released on St. Valentine's Day and ended up in France, so my daughter said we should try to do the same thing," Buck said. "We have to get rid of the balloons every night anyway because the helium inside can affect the store's security detection system."

The day after the balloons were released, Marcella Lourd, 80, who lives in the western Connecticut town of Sherman, found them on the tennis court of her home. "They still have air in them so I think I'll just keep them," she said. "They'll make a nice little ornament." The balloons had traveled about 630 miles in 13 hours, despite or perhaps because of strong storms that were heading east to Connecticut during that time.

Lourd noticed a business card on the balloons and sent an e-mail to the address. When she received a reply explaining their origin, she was shocked.

3. Robert Forrester dropped out of Weymouth High School in Massachusetts in 1965 and joined the Navy soon after, serving in Vietnam. After he returned, he got married, had kids, got divorced, remarried and retired from the U.S. Postal Service.

After reading about a 72-year-old high-school dropout who went back to Weymouth High School to get his diploma, Forrester decided he should do the same thing. He enrolled in the evening program and received his diploma last week, graduating with high honors.

For the first time in 27 years, the high school decided that evening students would be allowed to attend the prom with the other students.

When they gave Forrester the news, "I was jumping up and down and dancing like a giddy teenager," he said.

Forrester asked his wife, Jane, to be his date. She accepted. "I'm very proud of him," she said.

"It was a dream that I thought would always just remain a dream," Robert Forrester, now 57, said. He is considering going to college.

Bridging to the Body

In the previous discussion of anecdotal leads, special attention was given to the nut graf that shifts each one from the specific example to the more general issue. But it's not just anecdotal leads that call for well-written nut grafs; all feature leads need them. For example, look at the lead on this story by Tyrone Beason of The Seattle Times:

"We hardly need to be reminded that we are living in an age of confusion — a lot of us have traded in our beliefs for bitterness and cynicism or for a heavy package of despair, or even a quivering portion of hysteria. Opinions can be picked up cheap in the marketplace while such commodities as courage and fortitude and faith are in alarmingly short supply."

Legendary CBS newsman Edward R. Murrow spoke those words in a radio broadcast 54 years ago to introduce an experimental new program called "This I Believe," which gave prominent and everyday citizens a quiet forum to state their guiding life principles.

It was a counterintuitive idea. No rebuttals, no posturing, no putting other people down.

The nation loved it. Millions tuned in each day to hear the likes of Harry S. Truman, Helen Keller, Jackie Robinson and Albert Einstein talk about perseverance, integrity, individualism, responsibility and simple kindness.

"This I Believe" quickly grew into one of the most popular radio programs in the nation before the series unexpectedly lost its funding and ended in 1955.

But if Murrow, who died in 1967, felt so strongly about the need for such a show back then, what would he think of its value in today's superheated civic climate?

Beginning with a provocative quote, Beason leads the reader into a short history lesson, then ends the lead with a question that will serve as a bridge to current events. It is those events that give the story news value—and that need to be clearly stated in the bridge. Beason uses two short paragraphs to make the transition:

National Public Radio and a team of producers in Kentucky and New England, at least, felt it was high time to revive the show.

This spring, "This I Believe" returned to the airwaves after 50 years, with weekly audio essays recorded in the same "open mike" vein as the original program. The three-minute segments air during NPR's rush-hour "Morning Edition" and "All Things Considered" broadcasts on alternating Mondays.

For another example, look at how Patty Jessome of the Edmonton (Canada) Sun constructed a bridge after a narrative lead. First, the lead itself:

A lengthy illness spurred a love affair for gardening that stands as a testament to Harry Niemi's late wife, Patricia.

When Patricia was diagnosed with lung cancer back in the late '90s and she couldn't care for her large perennial garden, Harry volunteered to do it for her.

"She couldn't do much in a wheelchair," he says about Patricia, who had created a thriving garden in their Highlands-area home.

And the bridge:

So they gardened together. She gave instructions, he supplied the muscle. Along the way, he discovered how much he enjoyed the experience and after she died in July 2000, he kept at it, knowing that each year it would come back as a reminder of her.

"I do it in her memory more than anything else," says Harry, who found solace in the garden where Patricia left a lasting impression. Her irises, day lilies, gas plants and sea holly thrive in a large perennial bed that sways to the soft breeze blowing on this cool summer morning.

What makes this bridge particularly successful is that it serves not merely to connect the lead and the body of the story, but that it also includes descriptive details that help create an appropriate mood for the rest of the article.

ASSIGNMENT DESK 6.2

Pick your favorite lead for each of the summaries in Assignment Desk 6.1. For each, write a bridge to take the reader into the body of the story. Your bridges should be as brief as possible but include all necessary information.

The Body of the Feature Story

As was mentioned previously, features cannot be molded into a simple format. Instead, the details of a story determine the best way to shape it. That often results in one-of-a-kind story structures that are both dazzling and exactly right for the facts.

However, it takes time for a writer to reach the point at which he or she is able to let the material dictate the structure of a feature article. Therefore, it's helpful for new feature writers to master a handful of common feature structures.

The Wall Street Journal Formula

Probably the most used feature story structure is the **Wall Street Journal formula**. The WSJ formula consists of four main sections:

1. The story typically opens with a specific example (presented in an anecdotal, descriptive or narrative lead).
2. A nut graf relates that example to a more general point and explains what the story is about.
3. The body of the story provides support for the general point (quotes, facts, developments, and so on).
4. The story typically ends with another anecdote or description—often featuring the person or people featured in the lead—or speculates on a future development related to the lead.

Karen Schwartz of Columbia News Service used this structure in an article on fans' efforts to get "Star Trek: Enterprise" back on the air:

Anita Balestino, 50, is fighting to save her favorite television show. She's been working four to five hours a day since January to try to make sure the cast and crew of "Star Trek: Enterprise" can continue their weekly space adventures.	Anecdotal lead focuses on the experience of one person who has run up against a problem.

She, her husband and now-grown children gather Friday nights at 8 p.m. in their Columbia, Md., home to watch the adventures of the crew they've come to love over the past four seasons.

Though "Star Trek: Enterprise," the latest series in the 39-year-old space saga, was officially canceled by UPN and Paramount Network Television in early February, thousands of the show's loyal viewers have joined forces to protest what they see as its early termination.

Fans say the show presents a uniquely positive view of humanity and its potential. "It has historically promoted tolerance and acceptance, and its stories comment on the human condition by translating that to other cultures, alien cultures," said Balestino, a medical technologist.

Fans from the United States to the United Kingdom to Malaysia lit up message boards, voicing their dismay over the end of a show. Many wanted to see the show come full circle: "Enterprise" is a prequel to the original series, and was intended to end where the first "Star Trek" began.

With its cancellation, efforts shifted from trying to raise ratings to trying to get the show picked up by another network. Rallies were held in Washington, Los Angeles, New York, London and Tel Aviv in early February, and by the end of the month fans had already donated $48,000 to trekunited.com, where Tim Brazeal, the campaign leader and also the founder of saveenterprise.com, hopes fans can raise enough to pay for a fifth season.

Not counting the original show, which ran for three seasons, each of the show's other spinoffs—"Star Trek: The Next Generation," "Star Trek: Deep Space Nine" and "Star Trek: Voyager"—ran for seven seasons.

None of the spinoffs drew Balestino in like the original, until "Star Trek: Enterprise."

Nut graf shifts from to the larger story and explains its significance.

Supporting material includes quotes from fans, details of fan action and history of the show.

The show has been in jeopardy before. Marsha Robertson, 46, who acts as a liaison between enterpriseproject.org and saveenterprise.com, said the show was almost canceled at the end of its second and third seasons. She joined in the effort to save it because she thinks it's worthwhile.

"It's still something all ages can enjoy and can discuss," she said. "There aren't very many shows on evening television my friends can watch with their kids."

And being a "Star Trek" fan means more than watching the show, she said. Regardless of what happens with the program, she'll still have the friends she's met through it, she said. A passion for "Star Trek" often serves as a social outlet, connecting Trekkies first through their common interest.

Mark Williams, 38, from Anderson, Ind., says he's met "some of the nicest people" traveling in "Star Trek" circles. As a child, Williams watched "Star Trek" after Saturday morning cartoons.

"As a kid I watched that and I thought 'That's cool,' and that's before real life gets in the way," he said. "I guess I still follow in those ideas, from being a kid trying to look on the bright side of things."

Story concludes with quotes from another fan that reinforce the importance of the show to its fans.

This flexible model can accommodate a wide range of stories and can be adapted to work with stories running from a few hundred to several thousand words. The greatest challenge for the writer is to keep supporting material clearly organized by theme so it does not become an overwhelming jumble of facts for the reader to wade through.

The Trend Story

The Wall Street Journal also served as the originator of another great feature story structure, the **trend story**. A trend is a collection of small changes across society. Articles about trends are popular. Good trend stories provide readers with a sense of what's going on in the world and why.

The challenge in writing trend stories is that by definition they cover a wide range of events happening all over the place. Add to that the fact that every trend encompasses elements of the present, the past and the future, and the writer faces a daunting task of organizing material if he or she doesn't have a clear plan.

A trend story begins like a WSJ story, often using an anecdotal or bam-bam-bam lead, then quickly moves to a nut graf that lays out the main thrust of the trend. After that, things change. The structure:

- An anecdotal or bam-bam-bam lead opens the piece to provide one or more specific examples (descriptive or narrative leads are sometimes used instead).
- A nut graf relates that example to a more general point and explains what the story is about.
- The first major section of the story describes what's going on right now, indicating the amount of change, the areas where it is happening, and so forth.
- The next section explains the trend, trying to find its roots and explaining what events in the past brought about this trend.
- The final major section evaluates the trend, anticipates what lies ahead and tries to forecast the future.
- The story ends with a quote, a prediction or another anecdote that ties back to the lead.

Because the three major sections of this model are description-explanation-evaluation, it is sometimes called the D-E-E model, a designation bestowed on it by Syracuse University Professor Jake Hubbard.

The following example is drawn from an article about companies "going green," written by Katie Arcieri for the Annapolis (Md.) Capital:

For the Brick Cos., "being green" isn't just about a recycling bin in the office.

The Edgewater real estate developer makes preserving the environment a priority: It has a "green roof" to manage storm water at the company's headquarters. The Brick Cos. powers its main office and two company golf courses with alternative energy from cow manure. Rain barrels catch runoff at its marinas and employees are encouraged to carpool, a policy that last year saved the company $10,000 in reimbursement expenses.

These policies have helped the environment, but they also have translated into a backlog of resumés from talented employees, officials said. Experts say green businesses such as the Brick Cos. have a leg up when it comes to recruiting talent in a tight job market. There's tremendous cost in finding good employees

The story starts with a bam-bam-bam lead that illustrates the steps one company is taking.

The theme is succinctly stated in this nut graf.

that will be a good fit for the organization," said Lex Birney, the company's chief executive officer. "If you can attract people that have the same values that you have...that puts you, I think, at a significant competitive advantage."...

The trend is not limited to one type of business. Locally, companies ranging from auto dealers to financial intuitions are embracing the challenge to go green....

The description section details the scope of the trend.

The trend has grown out of the acknowledgement that more potential young employees, coming of age in the post-9/11 world, are considering the culture and community of an organization.

The explanation section attempts to show the factors that have led to the trend.

John Challenger, chief executive officer of Challenger Gray and Christmas, an outplacement firm in Chicago, said eco-friendly companies are attractive to new college graduates focused on work that provides "meaning."...

Companies expect the green movement to become a permanent part of how they do business. Rob Smith, vice president of Fitzgerald Auto Malls, which recently announced it will purchase wind power for 100 percent of its electricity needs, said feedback from associates and customers has been "very positive."

The evaluation section looks ahead.

While it's too early to predict how the initiative will affect retention, he said, new hires will be asked how much the company's green policies factored into their decision to join Fitzgerald....

Steve Sutton, a Kent Island resident, is a prime example of how the Brick Cos. has attracted talent.

The article ties up nicely with a return to the company introduced in the lead.

After watching a PBS show in which Birney was interviewed about his company's environmentally friendly policies, Sutton "applied the very next day" and took a job as a greenskeeper.

"Those are the kinds of values I wanted to align myself with," he said.

The Personality Profile

Another common type of feature story is the **personality profile**. Personality profiles are used to present an overview of a person so that readers feel like they have had a glimpse into his or her life. Like trend stories, profiles can be challenging: People tend to be complicated and full of contradictions, and most profiles combine elements of past, present and future.

Good profile articles depend on good research. A writer needs to find out as much as possible about a person before interviewing him or her. The writer also should talk with the person's friends and enemies to try to get a true picture of the subject.

The problem is, once all that information is gathered, some writers fall into the trap of trying to write a biography rather than a profile. Instead of trying to cover every aspect of a person's life, a writer needs to look for the facet of a person that readers would most likely identify with or care about. To help you accomplish that task, the writer needs to develop a **theme statement** about the person. In a nutshell, is he or she an overachiever, a dependable friend, a diehard activist, a paradox or something else? This theme will help the writer determine what to use and what to leave out.

Just as with feature articles in general, profiles come in a wide range of shapes and sizes. Beginning writers might want to try a model that follows the same general structure as the trend story model.

- An anecdotal lead capturing the distinguishing theme of the character opens the article.
- The justification section provides three quick points to suggest that the person is worth knowing more about, beginning or ending with a nut graf that states the theme.
- The amplification section describes the person's achievements.
- The flashback section turns to the person's roots and recounts significant life events that led to his or her current status.
- The flash forward section looks ahead and give readers some insights into what the person is likely to move on to next.
- A closing anecdote or strong quote reinforces the central theme and provides a sense of continuity.

Between each of the three major sections (amplification, flashback and flash forward), it's a good idea to insert short sections that bring the profile subject back down to earth. Here's how it all comes together:

Leigh Phoenix was excited when he first heard about a tandem race that was being held in Syracuse last year. The race was only 18 miles, and first prize was $200. "That sounded like a reasonable thing to go after," Phoenix said.	The lead of this article written for a bicycling magazine focuses on an anecdote that says a great deal about the profile subject's determination. This profile was a sidebar to coverage of a 24-hour bicycle race that the subject had recently won.

There were a few obstacles, though. For one, Leigh had never ridden a tandem before. For another, the Paris-Sport team had, and they were not coming all the way from New Jersey to lose.

That didn't bother Leigh. He borrowed a tandem and talked a friend into training with him for the race.

"At first we were terrible," Leigh said. "Fear kept us from working together. Single riders were passing us."

But when race day rolled around a week later, "the Paris-Sport team was beaten by two hairy-legged monsters from Ithaca," Leigh said, grinning broadly.

If Leigh Phoenix had a motto, it undoubtedly would be, "If I don't know it can't be done, I'll do it."

The justification section includes three disparate anecdotes to show the range of his accomplishments. The first line of this section states the theme of the article.

Although he began racing at the age of 29, he managed within two years to win the country's only 24-hour time trial. A week after that, he placed fourth in the Lake Luzerne (N.Y.) Cup race, coming in behind three of the best riders in the nation. And in his spare time, Leigh is finishing a textbook on mechanical reliability, his specialty at Cornell University.

"I used to think the guys who wrote those books were gods," Leigh said. "Now I'm a god."

It takes discipline and practice to be a god, though, and Leigh is acutely aware of the amount of effort it takes to keep in racing shape. He rides year-round, taking off only on days when the roads in Ithaca are buried under ice and snow. Then he trains on rollers and cross-country skis. If he has to contend with a wind-chill factor of a mere 20 degrees below zero, Leigh rides an hour and a half a day. He stays warm by fine-tuning the number of T-shirts he wears....

The amplification section begins here, looking at his current accomplishments and the effort they require.

Leigh also is organizing a stage race in Ithaca this summer.

"I hate it when I see events not run properly," he said, "but you shouldn't complain unless you run one and see what a hard job it is. I'm very sensitive to the attitude of a lot of cyclists—gimme, gimme, gimme, without ever giving back. There will be a lot more and better races if more people volunteer to set them up."

Leigh may seem to be a natural sportsman, but actually it was difficulty with other sports that got him into cycling.

As the subject is starting to sound a little too good to be true, the transition to the flashback section acknowledges that he's only human, too.

"I swam for five years as an undergrad in Ontario," Leigh said. "I wasn't any good. Then I started running. I wasn't any good at that, either. And I injured my knee."

Leigh had moved to the United States by then and was teaching at Cornell.

The flashback section recounts the subject's accomplishments to date.

"I found another prof in the department who had taken up cycling because his legs were giving him trouble. I started training with him, my knee didn't hurt, and I got the bug." Undoubtedly inspired by his brother Skip's selection to the Canadian diving team in the 1976 Olympics, Leigh started racing at the end of the year. He placed seventh in the 30-mile Corning Winefest race, then fifth in an 87-mile race around Cayuga Lake....

Leigh kept going longer. Before the 1976 season was over, he entered the Onondaga Cycling Club's 24-hour time trial. He was not to get past Jim Black that year, though.

The transition to the flash forward section again brings the subject back to earth by recounting how he had previously lost the race that is the subject of the accompanying article.

However, in 1977 Leigh got his revenge, and he could set a national record this year....

The flash forward section talks about several goals that lay ahead for the subject.

Whether or not he sets a record, Leigh hopes to move to U.S. Cycling Federation Class 1 this year, the national competition class. All he has to do is place within the top three of three races, such as the Lake Luzerne Cup....

With his drive, enthusiasm and talent, Leigh easily could find a sponsor. But he doesn't care to.

"I enjoy being part of a non-sponsored club," he said. "It's fun to ride with nothing on my jersey and beat guys who look like riding billboards."

The article closes with a quote to once again showcase the subject's individuality and confidence—it would have been harder to find a better way to close this piece than with the subject's own words.

The Human Interest Story

Although virtually every feature story contains elements of human interest, one particular type of story commands that title for its name. The **human interest story** recounts how one or more people come to terms with a situation—either good or bad—outside their control. In contrast to a news article that might be based on statistics, studies and official pronouncements, the human interest article looks at things from a human perspective. A human interest story might focus on someone who has won the lottery, a group of hikers stranded by an avalanche, a kidnap victim or any of a million other possibilities.

Different human interest stories are best served by different structures. For some, a pure chronological format might work well. In other cases, the following format, based on the legendary Reader's Digest "Drama in Real Life" articles, will help the writer craft a gripping story:

- Lead with a description of the incident that set the story in motion.
- Follow with a statement of the problem or challenge.
- Recount the events following the precipitating incident, all the way through the moment when all hope looks lost (the darkest hour).
- Move to the big picture: relatives' concerns or reactions, rescue plans, technical explanations, all the things taking place outside the knowledge of the subjects of the story.
- Return to the darkest hour.
- Wrap up with a resolution that provides uplift for the reader.

The following excerpts come from a nearly 5,000-word article written by Thomas Curwen for the Los Angeles Times. The article—and a second article that followed—tells the story of an encounter between a California man and a grizzly bear and the man's long recovery.

Johan looked up. Jenna was running toward him. She had yelled something, he wasn't sure what. Then he saw it. The open mouth, the tongue, the teeth, the flattened ears.

Jenna ran right past him, and it struck him—a flash of fur, two jumps, 400 pounds of lightning.

The lead sets up the incident.

It was a grizzly, and it had him by his left thigh. His mind started racing—to Jenna, to the trip, to fighting, to escaping. The bear jerked him back and forth like a rag doll, but he remembered no pain, just disbelief....

The attack had just started, and it had been going on too long. He grabbed the bear by the fur on its throat. The feeling of the coarse hair, as on a dirty dog, was unforgettable, and for a moment the animal just stared at him, two amber-brown eyes, its snout straight in his face. It showed no emotion, no fear, no anger. There were just those eyes looking down at him....

Amid the isolation and the cold, he grew sore and stiff and numb. Lying down, sitting up, nothing helped. Forty-five minutes later, he heard Jenna talking with someone. She called to him. "Dad, there are people here now. They're getting help."...

Three hours had passed since the attack, and Johan's metabolism was slowing down. The blast of adrenaline triggered by the attack was long gone; the 15-minute torrent of thought and reaction had dissipated in a miasma of pain, discomfort and boredom. Why was the rescue taking so long?...

With Johan and Anderson still beneath him, Justus accelerated down the valley to the helipad at Many Glacier. A waiting crowd was asked not to take pictures. Johan was transferred into an ambulance while Justus went back to pick up Jenna. Finally Johan was out of the wind and in a warm place.

Then he heard the news. "Jenna is here," someone said. "Hi, sweetie," he called out as they prepared to fly him to the medical center in Kalispell. With his head wrapped in bandages, mummy slits for his eyes and the C-collar on his neck, Johan couldn't see her. "Make sure when they call Mom that you talk to her."

The next several paragraphs provide a sense of the problem.

The section that begins here recounts the attack. The section ends at the moment when all hope looks lost (the darkest hour).

The "big picture" section discusses efforts to bring in outside help. This section runs for several paragraphs.

After all rescue details are recounted, the article returns to the darkest hour.

The resolution recounts the final steps of the rescue. It's an emotional roller coaster ride for the reader until things finally end on an upbeat note.

ASSIGNMENT
DESK **6.3**

1. Using the leads and bridges you have written in Assignment Desks 6.1 and 6.2, write the body of each story. Don't worry about the ending yet.
2. Following your instructor's directions, choose a topic for a story that fits into one of the formats discussed in the previous section—WSJ formula, trend, personality profile or human interest—and research and write a story.

Transitions

Transitions are an important component of any successful feature story. Although simple transitions sometimes are used to connect sections of hard news stories (for example, "Earlier in the day," "In addition," "In other developments"), not much attention is paid to carefully joining the parts of an inverted pyramid story. The whole idea of that structure is to allow readers to stop reading at any point.

Feature stories, on the other hand, are designed to be read from start to finish. Transitions help make that happen. Rather than depending on common and simple transition words and phrases, good feature writers look for transitions arising from the material itself. The easy—and boring—way to do that is by echoing words:

> Why do identical twins turn out not to be so identical? The answer lies in the relative new field of research called epigenetics.
> The field of epigenetics is the study of how environmental influences on a parent can result in changes in the genetic makeup of offspring.

Although repeating the words connects the paragraphs, this type of transition is the clunkiest and most obvious. Much better are transitions that clearly connect ideas without repeating things word for word:

> Why do identical twins turn out not to be so identical? The answer lies in the relative new field of research called epigenetics.
> Scientists working in that field are studying how environmental influences on a parent can result in changes in the genetic makeup of offspring.

Like much of feature writing, then, transitions work best when they are uniquely suited to the material the writer is working with. In the process of structuring each story, the writer should make sure paragraphs flow from one to another and look for natural transitions to connect those that do not.

ASSIGNMENT
DESK **6.4**

Reread the three stories you wrote in the first part of Assignment Desk 6.3. Look for places where transitions can be added to help the reader move along. Then do the same thing for the article you wrote for the second part of Assignment Desk 6.3.

Endings

Like transitions, endings also play a much more important role in feature stories than in hard news stories. Hard news stories typically just fade out, with the last paragraphs holding information that was not considered important enough to get higher billing. After all, if the ending might be cut for space reasons or ignored by readers in a hurry, why waste time worrying about it?

Feature stories, on the other hand, need to go out with a bang. The ending of a feature article serves both to wrap up the story and to provide a sense of completeness. A good ending reflects the tone of a story and seems exactly right for it.

Like feature leads, many of the best endings are unique bits of writing that spring from the material at the writer's disposal. Although some writers strive to figure out how a story will end before they even begin writing it, Peter Perl of the Washington Post says that's usually not the best approach.

Perl describes the story's end as "a discovery process" that evolves as a writer learns more about a topic. He suggests that a writer remain open-minded "and not predetermine what the ending is going to be until [he or she has] written most of the piece."

While the only limit in writing an ending is the writer's imagination, three types of feature endings appear frequently enough to make them good models for the beginning writer.

Summary endings used on feature articles differ from the boring summary endings students use over and over in composition class: "In summary, the purpose of a constitution is to…" The function is the same: to wrap things up in a tidy package, pointing out to readers that the writer has kept the promises you made in the lead of the story. But a feature summary ending has to have more pizzazz if it's to leave the reader feeling satisfied.

For example, Philadelphia Inquirer writer Eils Lotozo's feature on couples who are bucking the trend of super-sizing tiny beach houses wraps up the article by focusing on one of the couples he's written about:

> Except for an outdoor shower and storage shed, the Farneses have had no desire to add on to the tiny, two-bedroom house.
>
> "We love this place," Maria said. "We come down here and we spend 90 percent of our time puttering around the garden or sitting on the front porch reading.
>
> "This is a vacation home," she said. "And when you walk into it, there's a feeling of peace that its simplicity seems to create."

The ending nicely summarizes the main point of the article, and it does so using the words of one of its subjects, to give it a little more life.

The **circle ending** lives up to its name: The writer uses it to circle back to the lead and neatly close the story. Here's the opening of an AP story on how the Chinese are treating young people for "Internet addiction":

> "I'm 12 years old," one boy says with a smile. "I love playing computer games. That's it."
>
> Another boy, five years older with spiky hair, adds, "It's been good to sleep."
>
> The youths are patients at China's first officially licensed clinic for Internet addiction, a downside of the online frenzy that has accompanied the nation's breathtaking economic boom.
>
> Their days begin at 6 a.m. on a machine that stimulates nerve impulses with 30-volt charges to pressure points. Other treatments include receiving a clear fluid through intravenous drips to "adjust the unbalanced status of brain secretions."
>
> The youths usually stay 10 to 15 days, at $48 a day — a high price in a country where the average city dweller's weekly income is just $20.
>
> "All the children here have left school because they are playing games or in chatrooms every day," the clinic's director, Dr. Tao Ran, said.
>
> "They suffer from depression, nervousness, fear and unwillingness to interact with others, panic and agitation. They also have sleep disorders, the shakes and numbness in their hands."

After walking the reader through more details of the treatments, the scope of the problem, and so on, the article wraps up with a quote from one of the patients in the clinic where the lead was set:

> Says a youth from Beijing: "It would be hard to give it up completely. I'll take it step by step."

Not only does that ending tie things up neatly, it also clearly shows how seriously addicted some of the patients are: still hanging onto their habits despite IV drips and 30-volt shocks.

Like any other good ending, a circle ending must deliver a punch. Merely tying back to the lead is not enough. Here's an example of a circle ending that just peters out. It closes an article on the huge debts that college students are running up charging their daily Starbucks fixes. The lead includes this paragraph:

> "A latte a day on borrowed money? It's crazy," said Erika Lim, director of career services at the (Seattle University) law school.

Lim is featured in a few more paragraphs, then crops up again near the end. There, a few paragraphs focus on her concern that debt-burdened law school graduates will have to turn down jobs such as public defender, which do not pay high salaries, and instead will enter corporate law. The last paragraph reads:

> Lim, by the way, is not a latte drinker, unless someone else pays.
> (Washington Post)

And so at its conclusion, a long, well-written, interesting story ends up just lying there like a dead fish. It's not hard to imagine that the author could have gotten a strong quote to wrap things up—maybe something from one of the caffeine-fueled students reflecting on the strength of his or her addiction, sort of like the Chinese Internet addict who wraps up the previous example. But even without such a quote, the author could have massaged the ending into something with a little zing, such as this:

> Lim, by the way, loves an occasional latte—when someone else pays.

The final type of closing is the **surprise ending**. As the name implies, it should give the reader a jolt, but at the same time it has to feel exactly right for the story. Surprise endings must be short and crisp and logically follow what's come before.

Jodi Mailander Farrell, formerly of Knight Ridder Newspapers, combines the elements of summary and surprise in an article on celebrity posture. The piece begins with a description of runway models who have abandoned perfect posture and slump and sag instead. The article concludes:

> But David Wolfe, creative director of a New York consulting firm that analyzes and forecasts trends for retailers and designers, predicts that fashions—and postures—will swing away from sloppy.
>
> "It may take a couple of years," Wolfe says. "Clothes coming in will be simpler, more luxurious. Maybe they'll bring with them a new body language. By then, of course people might be so slumped over they'll be falling out of their chairs."

Another good example of a surprise ending wraps up an article written by Angie Wagner of The Associated Press. The article begins:

> Down a dim staircase in a place known for wild concerts and late-night partying, something very un-Vegas rings out from the depths of the House of Blues at Mandalay Bay hotel-casino.
>
> "Make a joyful noise unto the Lord!" comes a woman's throaty voice. "For the Lord is good!"
>
> Wait. This is Vegas, den of sin, where what happens here stays here, right?
>
> Absolutely, but inside the Sunday Gospel Brunch, not too far from the clinking slot machines and ticking roulette wheel, tourists and locals are raising their hands, tapping their feet and singing about Jesus.

Wagner proceeds to paint a vivid description of the Sunday Gospel Brunch and ends with these two short grafs:

> If this keeps up, Vegas' reputation may be on the line.
>   Salvation City anyone?

In just a few words, she plays on Las Vegas' famous nickname ("Sin City") and gives the reader something to smile at.

Another good surprise ending can be found on Washington Post writer Vanessa de la Torre's article about a local man's invention of Why Knot, a robot that can tie a necktie—in 350 steps. The article recounts how inventor Seth Goldstein spent years obsessed with the robot that he was now about to donate to a museum in Philadelphia. ("I gotta get this thing out of here and have a life!" he told the writer.) The article ends with a description of the machine in action, followed by a quote from the inventor's wife, Paula Stone, and another from Goldstein:

> Stone's gaze lingers on Why Knot. "It's going to be sad to see it go," she says.
>   "It's going to be traumatic," says Goldstein, who will drive his creation to Philadelphia next week. "Gonna be like empty nest syndrome."

Suddenly, the inventor who wants his life back has a change of heart—a nice ending that shows how much a labor of love the project has been.

Roy Peter Clark of the Poynter Institute for Media Studies warns that just as writers can bury their leads, they can also bury their endings: "Avoid endings that go on and on like a Rachmaninoff concerto or a heavy metal ballad," he warns. "Put your hand over the last paragraph. Ask yourself, 'What would happen if my story ended here?' Move it up another paragraph until you find the natural stopping place."[1]

ASSIGNMENT DESK 6.5

For each of the stories you have been working on in the previous Assignment Desk exercises, write at least two different types of endings. Be prepared to discuss which you prefer for each story.

Conclusion

Writing a good feature story is one of the biggest challenges in journalistic writing. But the payoff is huge. When a writer conducts careful and thorough research, creates a clear theme statement, and lets the material shape the article, the result is an experience in which readers can lose themselves, meet interesting people—and feel like the writer has taken them to someplace new.

KEY TERMS

anecdotal lead, 100
bam-bam-bam lead, 102
brite or bright, 98
circle ending, 122
descriptive lead, 104
human interest story, 118
narrative lead, 103
personality profile, 115

question lead, 106
summary ending, 121
summary lead, 99
surprise ending, 123
theme statement, 115
trend story, 112
Wall Street Journal formula, 110

DISCUSSION QUESTIONS

1. Choose a recent sports event. Look up news coverage from the day of the event. Then look for feature articles that were published about the event. How do they compare? How have the writers of the features managed to keep the story fresh and interesting?
2. Look through several issues of a recent newspaper (or on its Web site) and select three feature articles on different topics and of different lengths. Analyze the story structures. Do they fit any of the models discussed in this chapter? If not, do they provide any alternate models that might be useful to a journalist?
3. Using the same articles you chose for Question 2, analyze the leads and endings of each article. What types of leads and endings are used? Are they effective? If not, try to create better leads and endings.
4. Once more using those three articles, analyze each one for the use of transitions. How well does the article flow? Has the writer worked hard to create seamless transitions that arise from the material, or are the transitions more generic?

NOTE

1. Roy Peter Clark, "Write Endings to Lock the Box," PoynterOnline, 10 November 2004, **www.poynter. org/content/content_view.asp?id=73058.**

Writing the Basic Online Story

The past decade has seen a major shift in how people get news and information. Great numbers have moved from getting their news from traditional print and broadcast sources to what's collectively known as "New Media," which deliver content via computer, cell phones, PDAs and a range of other devices (see Figure 7.1).

Even though these new media delivery devices are fundamentally designed to offer multimedia, the fact remains that most people get the majority of their news and information in the form of text.

Unfortunately, many news organizations, short on time and resources, have taken that fact to mean that they could simply take stories that were written for print and dump them online, producing content that is referred to derisively as **shovelware**. Little if anything is done to differentiate the online and print versions; in most cases, links in print stories are not even made active when a story is put online.

That is hardly the ideal state of affairs. Not only does that practice result in many dull online news sites, it also actively discourages people from visiting many news sites because one is pretty much like the next.

The good news is that with a minor investment of time, a writer can enhance print stories to provide extra value to the online reader. In this chapter, we'll look at strategies for doing that. We'll also look at a unique online writing format that is growing in popularity, the blog.

Fundamentals of Online News Writing Style

Although the best online writing clearly differs from its print counterpart, many of the fundamental rules for good print writing also apply to online writing. In part, that's because stories are harder to read on a computer screen than on paper (resolution is much lower), so readers fatigue quickly. In addition, unlike the print reader who has paid for a publication, the online reader has virtually no investment in most news sites and may

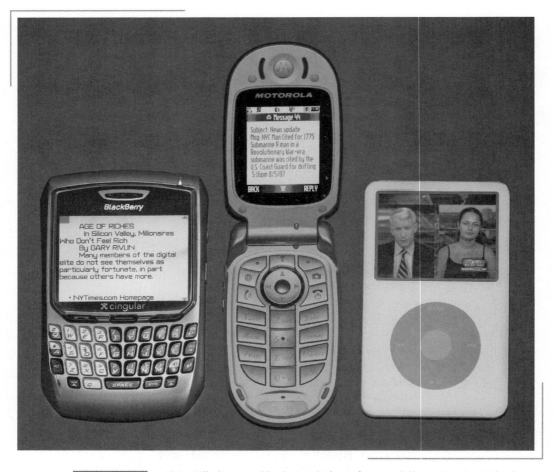

FIGURE 7.1 PDAs, cell phones and iPods are platforms for news delivery that are gaining in popularity because of their ability to deliver the news anytime, any place.

move to another site in an instant. Finally, the online reader is more likely than the print reader to multitask, searching for news and information while working, watching television, sending instant messages, and so on (see Figure 7.2).

For those reasons, online readers are best served by stories in which the main points and key facts jump off the screen. Stories written with summary leads and structured in the inverted pyramid format offer a good first step in that direction. Kathy McAdams, a University of Maryland professor who has worked for the online edition of the Washington Post, says: "In the space of one screen, the reader must quickly decide whether to participate. Leads are more important than ever."

Another good step is keeping stories short to hold the reader's interest. Writers for

FIGURE
7.2

Long respected for its well-designed Web site, the International Herald Tribune underwent a major redesign in mid-2007 to make it easier for readers to get the news they were looking for. Different editions are available for various parts of the world.

the BBC News Web site (news.bbc.co.uk/), for instance, are required to limit main stories to no more than 400 to 500 words and other stories to 250 to 350 words—the equivalent of a little more than one typed, double-spaced page.[1] Short, punchy sentences also help.

When a story needs to run longer to cover all the essentials, a writer can help readers navigate by offering informative headlines, blurbs and subheads.

- **Headlines**: Good headlines help the writer and the reader by narrowing the focus of a story. In as few as three or four words, a headline lets the reader know what the story is all about; in turn, that "theme statement" will ensure the writer stays on track.

  Unlike many headlines written for print publications, which rely on word play and clever ideas to get their points across, online headlines almost always provide a simple, straightforward summary of the story. That's important because in the online environment, headlines often appear independent of their stories: on home pages, in indexes, on search engine result lists, and so on. The following are good examples of online headlines:

  Ukraine court annuls poll results

  Lesbian minister defrocked

  Crude oil prices soar above $70 a barrel

  Notice that headlines are written in present tense so they say to the reader "Here's what's happening." The second example might look like it is written in past tense, but that's only because the word *is* is understood.

Why Choose Journalism?

Choose journalism because you want to tell stories. It's not just fun, but also offers a chance to meet real people and to delve into their lives, to experience realities different from your own and to find out what makes people and places tick. Choose it because it matters. Someone has to care enough to dig deeper and not stop at the obvious. Someone has to work late nights to find out what's really going on. Someone has to tell these stories: to document them and collect them, to arrange all the details just so and then pass them on to readers in an accurate and meaningful manner. I love that every day is different, and that every person I meet in the course of doing my job tells me a story in a way only he or she could tell it.

KAREN SCHWARTZ
Mergermarket Online Financial News Service

- Blurbs: A Web **blurb** sits just below a headline and in 20 to 50 words summarizes the story. A blurb can be used on a news home page to link to the story, or it can sit directly above the story itself. In either placement, a blurb helps readers decide whether they should take the time to read the accompanying article.

  Because of their position, blurbs generally complement headlines rather than repeat information in them. A few good examples:

  ### From Teachers to Trainers

  College graduates looking for jobs that fit their values as well as their skills are turning to life coaches and personality tests for help.

  ### Concerns Grow over Web Sites that List Informants

  Fearing witness intimidation, retaliation and harassment, the Justice Department pushes for fundamental changes in access to electronic court files.

  Blurbs should offer enough information to pique the reader's curiosity, but they shouldn't give away the entire story. Writing a good blurb requires walking that fine line: Too mysterious and no one will read further; too detailed and no one will read further, either.

- Subheads: To help readers find the sections of stories of most interest, the writer can add subheads of two to six words each throughout the story. A **subhead** helps break down the story into bite-sized chunks (a subhead every three to four paragraphs, for instance), guides readers to pertinent sections of an article, and offers skimmers a sense of the overall content of the article. Here's an example:

> Last summer was the worst in history for airline delays, and so far 2007 looks worse, Federal Aviation Administration officials said Wednesday. But government officials and airline executives said they hoped weather delays could be minimized by software innovations.
>
> For all of 2006, there were almost half a million delays of 15 minutes or more for airplanes flying under the jurisdiction of air traffic controllers, said Marion Blakey, the agency's administrator, speaking at its Strategic Command Center here. For the first four months of 2007, there were 142,000 delays, up from 126,000 in the same period last year, she said.
>
>
> **Weather likely to add to problem**
>
> "It wasn't good news when we learned just yesterday from the National Weather Service that in fact we're also looking at a very tough weather season for this summer," she said, referring to the latest forecast for hurricanes and strong tropical storms.
>
> The level of traffic is higher at the major airports, in many areas surpassing the peak reached in 2000, she said. International traffic is also up sharply.
>
> "It's hard to know this summer will be worse," Ms. Blakey said. "What I can tell you right now is that 2007 so far has been worse."
>
>
> **New software could help**
>
> To cope, the F.A.A. is trying a piece of software that will identify small areas of bad weather, usually thunderstorms, and then search the flight plans of thousands of planes to see which ones intended to go through those spots. Controllers will offer pilots a choice of accepting a departure delay or a detour. The past practice was simply to order takeoff delays for airplanes bound for airports near bad weather, without having information whether their intended route would take them through the problem area.
>
> "Planes originate and land at airports, but the congestion is in the airspace," said Michael J. Sammartino, the director of system operations at the command center. The result, he said, is that airlines get a choice of whether to wait on the ground or fly a longer route, and fewer planes are affected by weather.
>
> The program began last summer and is being expanded this year to cover most of the East and Midwest, including the line running from Canada to Mexico where thunderstorms tend to develop.
>
> Another computer program will look ahead about two hours in the predicted arrivals at busy airports. If some planes are likely to be delayed

by weather anywhere on their route, leaving their precious landing slots unused, the computer will identify others that could be brought in to land, keeping the runways at capacity.

"If you look at 55,000 airplanes a day, you can't do it by telephone," Mr. Sammartino said. (The New York Times)

ASSIGNMENT DESK 7.1

Pick a feature article from a newspaper or news Web site. Write a five- to 10-word headline, a 25- to 50-word blurb and at least two subheads for it.

Bullet Point Lists

Bullet point lists are among the most commonly used tools for online writing. Bullet point lists allow writers to present a great deal of information to readers in a manner that makes it easy to comprehend.

Here's an example of how a list is used within a news story. In this case, the list summarizes a "traffic light" plan by the British government to label unhealthful foods:

- Red light: Fatty, salty or sugary foods, to be eaten sparingly
- Amber light: Fatty but nutritious, to be eaten in moderation
- Green light: Fruit and vegetables, to be eaten often (BBCNews.com)

Bullet point lists also serve as the online equivalent of multiple-element leads. After a short summary statement, a list can be used to introduce the major aspects of the story. Each point in the list can then be addressed in the body of the story. For example:

Local motorists may need a triple-strength headache remedy next week, when three major road projects will be in the works at once:

- The 13th Street Bridge will be closed to westbound traffic between midnight and 6 a.m. so crews can repair support beams.
- Intermittent lane closures will occur on Route 214 to allow for shoulder widening.
- Traffic will be detoured around Route 9 in Georgetown while sinkhole damage is completed.

In many cases, detailed information in a story can be used to create a sidebar using bullet points to help the reader get to important information as quickly as possible. For instance, in a story about a product recall, the specific brands and model numbers could be presented in bullet point format. Here's an example using information from a recall of KTM off-road motorcycles:

Year and model of recalled motorcycles

- **2005:** 250SX-F

- **2006:** 200XC, 200XC-W, 250XC-W, 250SX-F, 250XCF-W, 300XC, 300XC-W, 400EXC-G, 450XC-G, 450EXC-G and 525EXC-G

- **2007:** 125SX, 144SX, 250SX, 250SX-F, 450SX-F, 505SX-F, 200XC, 250XC, 300XC, 450XC, 200XCW, 250XCW, 300XCW, 400XCW, 450XCW, 525XCW, 250XC-F and 250XCF-W (Source: U.S. Consumer Product Safety Commission)

ASSIGNMENT DESK 7.2

Present as much of the following information as possible in a bullet point list.

Most Americans eat less than half the amount of fiber that they should consume each day. Fiber is important in lowering cholesterol and risk of heart disease. In addition, a diet rich in fiber can reduce the chances of developing diabetes, colon cancer and rectal cancer. There are several easy ways to increase the fiber in your diet. The first is to eat more whole grains, substituting brown rice and whole wheat bread for white rice and Wonder bread. Snacking on fruit instead of candy, pretzels and chips also helps. In addition, you should eat plenty of vegetables; they provide the most fiber when served raw. Finally, try to have a source of fiber at every meal: oat bran cereal for breakfast, a salad for lunch, brown rice and vegetables as side dishes at dinner, for instance.

Finding and Adding Links

Another popular tool for online writing is the **hyperlink**. Hyperlinks are, in fact, the basis of the online universe, so it shouldn't be surprising that many online stories contain one or more links. Yet for a long time many online news sites resisted adding links to their stories, fearful that readers would click off their sites, never to return. They needn't have feared; as Web expert Jakob Nielsen has written, "Well-selected links enhance the value of your own service with the best of all the Internet has to offer, driving up user loyalty and repeat traffic to your site."[2] Media critic Jeff Jarvis goes even further, arguing that links offer news organizations a chance to play to their strengths: "[News organizations] should stop wasting resources covering what everybody else covers just to feed their institutional ego under their own bylines. They should stand out not by sending the 100th correspondent to a news event that witnesses are covering anyway but by doing what journalists should do best: reporting. . . . [D]o what you do best. Link to the rest."[3]

Links can direct readers to a range of destinations:

- Definitions: Links can be used to offer definitions for unfamiliar words or specialized terms. One common source for definitions is Wikipedia, the free online encyclopedia (http://en.wikipedia.org/wiki/Main_Page) that provides hundreds of thousands of hyperlinked entries in the areas of culture, geography, life, mathematics, history, science and technology (see Figure 7.3). For topics not covered by Wikipedia, writers can do a Google search and embed the resulting URL into the story.
- Previous stories: Although pertinent background information always should be included in a news story, a link to previous stories can let readers delve even more deeply into the background of a story.
- Related stories: When a story offers a new twist on a topic that's recently been in the news, steering readers to related stories can help them understand the big picture. For instance, a story about a new type of online fraud might link to one or more recent stories about other types of online fraud. Links also can be used to offer readers alternate viewpoints on a topic.

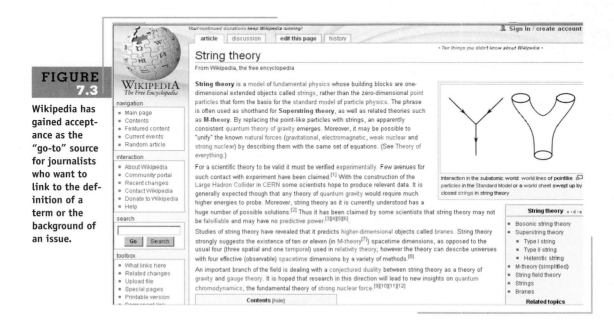

FIGURE 7.3

Wikipedia has gained acceptance as the "go-to" source for journalists who want to link to the definition of a term or the background of an issue.

- Resources for further research: Often, an online article serves to merely whet a reader's appetite for information on a topic. Therefore, whenever possible, writers should search for sources that offer information and other resources to let readers continue their exploration. For example, a story about the suicide of a teenager could be accompanied by links to Web sites dealing with teen depression and suicide.
- Source documents: Of all of the facets of the World Wide Web, one of the first to excite journalists was the ability to link to the documents on which stories are based. For example, a speech story can be linked to the full transcript of the talk, a budget story to the full text of the budget.
- Related Web sites: People, agencies and events mentioned in a story often have Web sites of their own. Writers often include links to these sites so that readers can learn more about the topics. However, ethical questions arise when a story covers controversial topics. For instance, in recent years writers and editors have had to struggle with whether they should link to Web sites showing Middle Eastern terrorists killing U.S. citizens and other Westerners. Some argue that doing so helps the terrorists promote their agendas, but others say interested readers can find the sites on their own, so embedding the links in a story makes no difference.
- Related audio, video and animations: The Web offers the ability to mix text, photos, audio and video like no other medium. In many cases, linking to multimedia elements—produced by professional journalists or eyewitnesses—can help increase reader understanding and comprehension.
- A form or e-mail link to contact the author or editor: Until the Web came along, journalists stayed hidden from the public and rarely interacted with them. Now the public expects to be able to reach writers and editors, and links that pop up a form or open a blank e-mail have become commonplace.

Working Links into the Story

Renowned journalist Gay Talese once observed that good writing is like glass: so smooth that readers don't realize they're being swept along. All too often, however, Web writing is more like a potholed road, with hyperlinks drawing attention to themselves or to their destinations.

To avoid that problem, writers need to choose carefully which words they use for hyperlinks. Just a couple of words or at most a short phrase should offer the reader enough information to know what lies ahead. Choosing precise link words helps readers not only in determining where they're headed but also in interpreting the information they find once they get there.

Links should be transparent and compelling. The phrase "click here" should be avoided. Instead, link words should give readers a sense of what's around the corner should they choose to go there. For example: "The National Association of Poodle Breeders offers 10 suggestions on choosing a pet."

Because links can disrupt the flow of the text, they should be placed carefully. Some writers prefer to place them all at the end of the story so readers can explore them after finishing the story.

ASSIGNMENT DESK 7.3

Read through the following New York Times story, underlining passages that can be enhanced with external links. Next, find Web sites to link to those passages. Finally, rewrite the story to include links to those sites.

BY JESSE MCKINLEY

The Navy and several environmental groups reached an agreement Friday allowing the service to use a powerful form of sonar during military exercises under way near Hawaii. The accord ends a brief court battle that the Navy had said could threaten national security.

At issue was whether the so-called midfrequency sonar, which blasts strong sound waves under water in hopes of detecting foreign submarines, causes harm to whales and other marine mammals.

Under the agreement, the Navy will use that technology but will be required to post observers who will look for whales or other animals that might be affected. It will also have to limit the sonar's use to areas more than 25 nautical miles from the Northwestern Hawaiian Islands Marine National Monument.

The legal skirmish was touched off a week ago when the Pentagon, in an effort to ensure the Navy's ability to use the sonar during the war games, gave the service an interim national security exemption from the Marine Mammal Protection Act.

But on Monday a federal district judge in Los Angeles, Florence-Marie Cooper, granted the environmental groups a temporary restraining order, declaring that the Navy's failure to look closely at the environmental effects of the sonar was an "arbitrary and capricious" violation of another federal statute, the National Environmental Policy Act.

Joel Reynolds, a senior lawyer for one of the plaintiffs, the Natural Resources Defense Council, said there was scientific consensus, including a study by the International Whaling Commission, that the sonar could cause "a wide spectrum of injury, from behavioral change to mass stranding and death."

The Navy appealed Judge Cooper's ruling to the federal appeals court in San Francisco, contending in a brief filed Wednesday that suspending the sonar during the exercises, which began on June 26 and are to continue through July 28, could cause "definite and serious damage" to national security, foreign relations and the good of the public.

The exercises, in which the Navy had planned to begin using the sonar this Thursday, are known as the Rim of the Pacific, or Rimpac, and involve military units from the United States, Canada, Britain, Australia, Japan, South Korea, Chile and Peru.

"Rimpac is the only opportunity for these participating nations to train together," the Navy said in the brief. "It is the only exercise scheduled in the next two years in which Pacific Rim forces can engage in realistic antisubmarine warfare training."

Blog Posts

Recent years have seen the emergence of blogs as a unique form of online writing. Blogs can be used to provide breaking news, commentary, corrections and background on items in the news. A typical blog post runs between two to five paragraphs, although some take no more than a sentence and others go on for 10 paragraphs or more.

Although blog posts are as different as the individuals who write them, the simplest are short inverted-pyramid summaries with links to full stories, such as this example:

> The government, as part of its "Operation Big Fat Lie," has filed suit against a Westport man and his companies it said promised weight-loss regimens that were too good to be true.
>
> It was one of six similar complaints announced today by the Federal Trade Commission (FTC), which, for the first time, also pressed publications that advertised the programs to identify and reject them instead.
>
> An FTC announcement said the complaint against Martin Howard, whose address was listed as the Regents Park condominium in Westport, was filed last Thursday in U.S. District Court in Bridgeport.

News Pointers

Some of the Best Blogs on Journalism

- Best of Journalism Blogs (www.journalism.co.uk/bestofblogs.php): A "mash-up of posts from the best blogs about journalism."
- BuzzMachine (www.poynter.org/column.asp?id=31): Jeff Jarvis on news.
- CJR Daily (www.cjrdaily.com/): Media criticism from the Columbia Journalism Review.
- Cyberjournalist Net (www.cyberjournalist.net/cyberjournalists.php): About 400 blogs by journalists.
- E-media Tidbits (www.poynter.org/column.asp?id=31): A group blog about online media/journalism/publishing.
- Eat the Press (www.huffingtonpost.com/media/the-news/eat-the-press/): Media news, commentary and analysis.
- Journalism.org (www.journalism.org/): Project for Excellence in Journalism provides overview and analysis of the field of journalism.
- Journerdism (www.journerdism.com/): News and commentary on journalism, multimedia storytelling, Web design and other topics.
- MediaShift (www.pbs.org/mediashift): Notes from the digital media revolution.
- News Gems (www.spj.org/blog/blogs/newsgems/): Hosted by the Society of Professional Journalists, this blog highlights the best of U.S. journalism.
- PressThink (http://journalism.nyu.edu/pubzone/weblogs/pressthink/): Media commentary.
- Regret the Error (www.regrettheerror.com/): Corrections from The New York Times and other news sources.
- Romenesko (www.poynter.org/column.asp?id=45): Daily notes on what's happening in the business of journalism.
- Teaching Online Journalism (http://mindymcadams.com/tojou/): Great for students and teachers.
- The X Degree (www.melissaworden.com/blogs/xdegree/): Examples and discussion of multimedia storytelling.
- The Tyndall Report (http://tyndallreport.com/): Monitors the weekday nightly newscasts of the three U.S. broadcast television networks.
- TVNewser (www.mediabistro.com/tvnewser): News about how television covers the news.

It named Howard and Bronson Partners LLC, doing business as New England Diet Center and Bronson Day Spa.

MORE "Government Sues Westport Man Over Weight-Loss Ads" (Courtesy WestportNow.com)

Most blogs, however, contain more than just a summary of a story. One typical pattern:

- A snappy headline grabs the reader's attention.
- A lead summarizes a recent news report or other online posting and includes a link to that item.
- One or two paragraphs provide pertinent quotes from the item.
- One or two paragraphs offer comments from the blogger.
- A link connects to comments others have made on the blog entry.

For example:

SHOT BY YOUR OWN GUN

When Baltimore City Detective Troy Chesley lost his life, it was truly a sad day. The man that killed him was Brandon Grimes. Shortly after Chesley's death, police learned that Grimes had been in the system numerous times. Many in the police force were outraged that Grimes had been arrested 17 times and was still allowed to roam the streets of Baltimore City.

As tragic as this story is, it gets even worse. According to the Baltimore Sun article "History of gun points to tracking problems," the gun used to kill Chesley was in the hands of police not once, but twice! The article states that the gun was "one of eight weapons seized by police in a 2001 firearms investigation." The gun was later returned to its owner because the case fell through. This gun was not a simple little handgun. It was modified to have a laser sight on it. A laser sight may be legal, however I don't know why you would ever need a laser sight unless you were planning to shoot someone.

To add to the craziness of this story, the gun used to kill Chesley belongs to a man named Mustafa Alif, a milk delivery driver. The article claims that "about a half-dozen of the weapons he once owned are linked to crimes in the area." Yea, you may want to investigate him. I am glad that we don't have those milk delivery guys that come up to your door any more because Alif is packing some serious heat.

However this gun ended up back into Grimes' hands is inexcusable. The police department had the gun twice in its possession and now a good cop is dead. Interim Mayor Sheila Dixon recently announced that a new gun unit will be created and they will target gun stores and violent criminals. This is a step in the right direction and I feel after this tragedy, something like this won't happen again. The police department got lazy and this is what happens when you are lazy.

Posted by Ryan Reed at 8:52 AM

0 comments

ASSIGNMENT DESK 7.4

Using the software specified by your instructor, create a blog account to use in this class. Choose a topic — or use the one assigned by your instructor — and create at least two posts on that topic. Each post must link to and comment on at least one pertinent and recent Web page, Web site or specific blog post by another author. Your posts should run between 75 and 150 words each.

Not all journalistic blogs exist to comment on news stories or other blogs. In many cases, reporters use blogs for a host of other reasons:

- To relate stories from their beats that do not make it into their regular stories.
- To give a "behind-the-scenes" look at the reporting process.
- To engage readers in a discussion of a story topic.

One good example of a writer using a blog for a combination of these purposes is Crocker Stephenson's "Meeting Baby Doe" blog (www.jsonline.com/ blog/?id=204) (see Figure 7.4). That blog accompanied a Milwaukee Journal Sentinel online story titled "In a

FIGURE 7.4

Crocker Stephenson found that incorporating a blog into his work made for a much richer experience for readers — and for himself.

Child's Best Interests" (www.jsonline.com/index/index.aspx?id=99), the story of 19-year-old Tim Krahling, whose birth raised questions about the rights of parents and the society in caring for a severely disabled child. The blog was designed to allow readers to watch and participate "as Stephenson gathers the facts he will use to tell Tim's story, and explore with him the ethical, emotional and moral issues that inevitably arise when a reporter journeys deep into the lives of private people to make public their most personal stories."[4]

Stephenson calls the blog "an experiment that turned into one of the most exciting projects in my career." He recounted in an e-mail: "We had people posting from all over the U.S., and a couple of people from the U.K. and South Korea. Opening the process to them, deconstructing it for our readers, not only made me a better informed, less myopic, journalist, but—and this is critical—deepened the story's credibility."

The Writer's Voice: When Is It Appropriate?

News Pointers

From its earliest days, the online environment has been seen as the "Wild West" of publishing. Largely as a result of the ease of access and low cost of admission, pretty much anything goes online.

Because of that, many people who get their news online expect a more personal and edgier tone than they get from conventional print and broadcast news. Most independent publishers and bloggers have been happy to oblige; there's no mistaking Wonkette (www.wonkette.com/) for The Wall Street Journal.

But traditional online media sites typically have stuck with a more straight-laced and blander style of writing. Partly, that's because online sites largely rely on wire service and newspaper copy. But it's also partly the result of traditional media wanting to preserve an aura of seriousness.

Things are changing, however, partly as a result of online news sites (and other sites such as AOL.com) experimenting with **dayparting**. In brief, dayparting means offering different content at different times of the day, similar to what the broadcast media have long done.

As publishers have begun shifting content away from hard news at various times of the day, they also have become more likely to accept edgier, more personalized writing. And that has been paying off. AZCentral.com, the Web operation of the Arizona Republic, found evening page views and visits rose substantially after it launched azcentral@night, its lighter, riskier evening package.[5]

On news sites that do not have their origins in print outlets, writers are often encouraged to break out of the conventional journalistic writing style and write more conversationally and less formally. Writers often use first person, a practice explicitly prohibited in conventional news writing. For example, here's the lead of Slate.com travel writer Seth Stevenson's piece on "Why I Hate India":

> It's OK to hate a place.
>
> Travel writers can be so afraid to make judgments. You end up with these gauzy tributes to the "magic" of some far-off spot. But honestly, not every spot is magical for everyone. Sometimes you get somewhere, look around, and think, "Hey, this place is a squalid rat hole. I'd really rather be in the Netherlands." And that's OK.
>
> For example, the last time I went to India I just haaaaaaaated it. Delhi was a reddish haze of 105-degree dust. And while, of course, the Taj Mahal was great...the streets outside it were a miasma of defecating children. I could not wait to go home.

This style of writing is the standard for many blogs, and it's slowly making its way onto more established news sites as well—at least at certain hours of the day.

Conclusion

Although online writing often looks remarkably similar to print writing, good journalists understand how to enhance material originally written for print so that it offers extra value for the online reader. Headlines, blurbs, subheads and bullet point lists all make it easier for multitasking readers to find the information they want. Hyperlinks allow the writer to provide a wealth of related information to the reader, opening gateways to source documents, related stories, multimedia enhancements and much more. In addition, blogs offer writers the chance to expand the range of stories they write about, to let readers see what goes into their reporting and to engage readers in important and interesting topics.

KEY TERMS

blurb, 130
bullet point list, 132
dayparting, 140
headline, 129

hyperlink, 133
shovelware, 127
subhead, 130

DISCUSSION QUESTIONS

1. Look over the online news sites you most often visit. How do the stories on those sites use the features discussed in this chapter (headlines, blurbs, subheads and bullet point lists)?
2. How often do you click on a link from a news story? What types of links are most interesting to you?
3. What blogs do you regularly read? How does the writing style on them compare with your other news sources? Is writing style part of your attraction to the blog?

NOTES

1. Mike Ward, "Journalism Online" (Woburn, Mass.: Focal Press, 2002), p. 112.
2. Jakob Nielsen, "Fighting Linkrot," UseIt.com, 14 June 1998, **www.useit.com/alertbox/980614.html.**
3. Jeff Jarvis, "Hacks Should Do What They Do Best and Link to the Rest," The Guardian, 30 April 2007, **http://media.guardian.co.uk/mediaguardian/story/ 0,,2068253,00.html.**
4. Crocker Stephenson, "Meeting Baby Doe" blog, October 2006 through March 2007, **www.jsonline.com/blog/ ?id=204.**
5. "Successful Dayparting in Arizona and More Insights Beyond the Printed Word," CyberJournalist.net, 9 November 2004, **www.cyberjournalist.net/ news/001709.php.**

Writing the Basic Audio Story

Although the news stories we have focused on so far may appear in a range of media—newspapers, magazines, the Web, and so on—they share one common element: They are written primarily for the eye. People gather the information in them primarily through reading words on a page or screen.

A good deal of the news that people get, however, comes to them through their ears, via radio, computer, cell phone or portable MP3 player. Even television news—regarded as "visual storytelling"—is written primarily for the ear, not the eye: Think about how often you're engaged in another activity while you have your television on, and you'll realize that a lot of the time you're not watching television but just *listening* to it (see Figure 8.1). For an audience that has to depend mainly or solely on its ears, audio news stories must resemble normal conversation as closely as possible—something that's not always a priority with text and online stories. If audio news is not written conversationally, the audience will have difficulty comprehending it.

In this chapter, we will examine the differences between stories written for print and online delivery and those written for audio delivery. We will look at the most common audio story structures and then focus on three essential components of the basic audio story: leads, transitions and endings. Next, we will look at the issue of timing a story. Finally, we will explore how to update audio stories as new information comes in.

How Audio Stories Differ from Text and Online Stories

Just as print and online writers follow a standard style, so do audio (and video) writers. Appendix B to this book covers the basics. Beyond those rules, audio stories differ in several other important ways from print and online stories:

Sentences tend to be short and contain no more than one idea each. Unlike the audience for print and online news, people listening to

FIGURE 8.1

Even though people refer to the activity as "watching television," in many cases televised news is heard rather than seen.

audio stories typically do not have the opportunity to replay the news if they miss something or don't understand it. Therefore, they need things presented in a simple, easily understandable manner. That's not to say, however, that audio stories should consist only of five-word sentences composed in subject-verb-object order. As with any writing, variety helps hold audience interest. The best bet is to alternate between short and longer—but not too long—sentences. This audio story provides a good example:

> The owner of a western Pennsylvania convenience store that sold a winning Powerball ticket says he told his workers, "We're all going to Cancun next year."
>
> The Country Food Mart in New Castle earned a 100-thousand-dollar payout for selling the ticket worth more than 171 million dollars.
>
> The storeowner says he's been fielding crank calls from people claiming they bought the ticket. He says, "It's nerve-wracking."
>
> Lottery officials haven't yet identified the winner.
>
> Once he or she claims the prize, the winner will have 60 days to decide whether to take the 171-point-four million dollars over 29 years or as a lump sum of about 93 and a-half million dollars.
>
> Powerball tickets are sold in 27 states, the District of Columbia and the Virgin Islands. (AP)

The sentences in this story vary distinctly from one to the next. The first two are relatively long for an audio story, at 26 and 22 words, then a mid-size sentence slips in at 15 words, followed by two short sentences of five and seven words, one long one of 37 and a final one of 15. That 37-word sentence is a good example of why shorter is usually better: It tries to combine several ideas and four numbers into one sentence. The result is just too much for a listener to comprehend. Breaking the sentence into several shorter ones would be better:

> Once the winner claims the prize, he or she will have 60 days to decide how to take the payout. One option is to take the 171-point-four million dollars over 29 years. The other option is to take a lump sum of about 93 and a-half million dollars.

Sentence fragments are acceptable. Because audio stories need to be conversational, a writer is allowed to use fragments in an audio story. It's critical, however, that the writer know he or she is writing a fragment and use it for a specific reason. For example, a story about growing security lines at airports might begin, "Bad news for the nation's vacationers." That would never be permitted for print and online writing.

Audio stories focus on people, not things, events, policies or statistics. The best audio stories feature people who are directly affected by the events of a story. Although print and online stories are sometimes criticized for focusing too much on official "experts," audio stories should try to balance those experts with people who have firsthand experience with the subject.

Ground Rules for Audio Story Leads

Just as with print and online news stories, every audio story must begin with a strong lead that draws the audience in. Audio story leads do, however, differ from print and online leads in two substantial ways: First, audio leads contain fewer details; second, they place a higher premium on action.

Audio story leads contain fewer details. While most audio and video leads summarize the news, they do it in a far more bare-bones way than their print and online counterparts. Rather than trying to cram in the who, what, when, where, why and how, audio and video leads typically offer one key fact and feature just one or two of the 5 W's and an H. Shorter leads help audience comprehension because the ear (and brain) can only process so much material at once. Further, there's only so much an announcer can read before running out of breath.

For instance, here are the opening sentences of a Reuters news service story written for print and online publication. The sentences run a total of 60 words:

> Six people were missing after a U.S. Coast Guard helicopter crashed into the stormy Bering Sea after plucking the last remaining crew members from a disabled Malaysian cargo vessel, officials said on Thursday. Those missing after the helicopter crash late on Wednesday included crew members plucked from the stricken Seledang Ayu, a 738-foot Malaysian-flagged freighter that later split in two.

In contrast, here is the AP lead intended for audio stories. It runs 28 words, five less than just the first sentence of the Reuters lead:

> Coast Guard rescue teams are searching for six people lost in the Bering Sea after one of its helicopters crashed while carrying crew members from a powerless freighter. (AP)

The audio lead still packs a lot of information, including answers to all of the essential questions except "How." But it sounds more like the way a person might tell the story to a friend. It doesn't include words like "plucking" and "disabled," language that most people wouldn't use in talking about the event. And it omits all the information about the origin of the ship, its size and cargo—facts that only serve to slow the lead and dilute its impact.

Some news writers would argue that even the example used here is too long, and that it would benefit from being cut after "Bering Sea" or "crashed," as in these two alternatives:

> Coast Guard rescue teams are searching for six people lost in the Bering Sea after one of their helicopters crashed.

> Coast Guard rescue teams are searching for six people lost in the Bering Sea.

These shorter versions more closely follow the guideline of presenting one key idea in the lead. The remaining essential details can be parceled out in the subsequent paragraphs.

Audio leads place a higher premium on action. Look back at leads on the Coast Guard story in the previous section, and you'll notice how the writer of the audio version has chosen a different subject than the writer of the print/online version. That change was made to make the audio lead more active.

The first print/online lead begins with the passive "six people were missing." Although technically accurate, this lead contains no action to move the story forward. In

Why Choose Journalism?

Why choose journalism? I wouldn't. The hours are farshtunken, the pay is crap, and the public hates you. However, if you're not a clock-watcher, you're not looking to get rich, and you have thick skin, there is no more fun career to be had. You get to know stuff before everyone else. You get to write the first draft of history, and no two days are the same. Plus, you get to shine the light in those dark places where the truth sometimes hides from the public eye. That can be very satisfying.

MIKE MCMEARTY
WTOP Radio, Washington, D.C.

contrast, the audio lead begins "Coast Guard rescue teams are searching," which uses active voice to drive along the lead—and the rest of the story.

Here's another example. The first lead comes from the print and online editions of The Boston Globe:

> A Marine who was reported abducted in Iraq and later turned up in his native Lebanon was charged Thursday with desertion.

This version is the AP audio lead:

> The Marine Corps has charged a corporal who disappeared from a U-S military camp in Iraq earlier this year with desertion.

Not only is the audio lead written to avoid passive voice ("A Marine who was reported" becomes "The Marine Corps has charged"), but it also manages to keep the subject and verb much closer together. Those techniques help create forward momentum for the story, whereas the print lead just sort of sits on the page.

Even when the story is that nothing has happened, a writer will try to get action into the lead. For example:

> Denver prosecutors say they won't charge a police officer who killed a bedridden man after mistaking his soda can for a weapon.

Although the story here is that the prosecutors are *not* going to act, the writer wisely focused on what they did do—which in this case was *say* that they were not going to act. The only real alternative would have been to turn the sentence around and write it in the passive voice:

> A Denver police officer who killed a bedridden man after mistaking his soda can for a weapon will not be charged, prosecutors say.

In addition to being wordier, passive writing such as this is also harder to read and comprehend. In this case, not only is the lead passive, but it also puts way too much distance between the subject and the verb, a surefire way to confuse listeners and viewers.

There's only one case in which action should be held off in the lead of an audio story: when some historical or other aspect of an event is what makes it newsworthy. For instance, when a United Airlines flight left San Francisco for the first direct flight to Vietnam in nearly 30 years, the AP lead read:

> For the first time since 1975, a U-S passenger jet is flying from the U-S directly to Vietnam.

In this case, the context of the event is what makes the action significant. It wouldn't be a story if the plane had been heading for a more routine destination such as Hawaii. So the lead begins not with the action but with the context.

Types of Audio Story Leads

While most print and online news stories rely on summary leads to get things rolling, audio story writers can choose from a range of options for beginning their stories. Main point leads are most common. As the name implies, a main point lead strives to deliver the major impact of the story quickly. Main point leads come in four varieties: the hard lead, the soft lead, the throwaway lead and the umbrella lead.

The **hard lead** is the audio equivalent of the print and online summary lead. It takes a "just the facts" approach to the news, presenting a simple and uncomplicated summary of events. The hard lead perfectly complements simple but serious stories:

> Former governor Parris Glendening is recovering at home in Annapolis after undergoing prostate reduction surgery last week. (AP)

> A Michigan woman is charged with five felonies, including attempted murder, for allegedly serving her husband and son lethal milkshakes. (AP)

> Immigrants who come to America in search of a better life may actually be harming their health. (AP)

For hard news stories that are more than a few hours old, a variation on the hard lead is often used. The **reax lead**—the equivalent of the print second-day lead—begins with the reaction of someone affected by the event. This type of lead adds freshness to a story that the audience might have already heard or read about. For instance, a story about changes in a city's housing rental laws might initially start with this lead:

> City Council members have approved a law that will make it harder for landlords to evict renters.

A story a few hours later might begin with a reax lead like this:

> Local landlords are warning that a new law that makes it harder for them to evict renters will hurt good tenants who will have to put up with problem renters for longer periods.

The **soft lead** delays the main point of the story for a sentence while easing the listener or viewer in with a teaser. Soft leads work well to set up the main point on lighter stories as well as more complicated stories. Some examples:

> In Chicago, one mother is calling her small daughter a great blessing. The little girl was born weighing a mere eight-point-six ounces but managed to survive. (AP)

> Sauerkraut isn't just for hot dogs anymore. The Fremont Company in Ohio has come up with a martini featuring an olive filled with sauerkraut. (AP)

The **throwaway lead** offers even less information than the soft lead, and in that respect, it earns its name. In a sentence, or even a fragment, the throwaway lead attempts to give a general sense of a story, create a mood or tie stories together:

In the asphalt jungle, it may be survival of the meekest. *(story on strategies used by holiday shoppers to find parking places)* (AP)

There's a new favorite gizmo on the market. *(story on the rise in popularity of the digital camera)* (AP)

The **umbrella lead** serves as the audio story equivalent of the multiple-element lead. An umbrella lead either can tie together two or three main ideas in one story or can tie together two or three separate stories:

The City Council is just saying no to requests for five new liquor shops…but is welcoming a big-box retailer to town. *(one story with two main points)*

More than two-thousand residents in three counties are still without power following yesterday's high winds. Manuel Delgado is standing by in Clark County with our first report. *(several separate stories)*

Other Types of Audio Leads

Not every story is best served by a main point lead. In some instances, more novel approaches work better. The delayed lead, a common alternative, begins telling a story in chronological order (along the lines of "once upon a time"). The entire story then proceeds to unfold along the timeline until it's played out. Obviously, that's not a good idea for stories of importance to the audience. But for lighter stories and stories that depend greatly on human interest, it's a smart strategy, as this short example shows:

An unidentified woman was driving in the six-hundred block of Howe Street about 5 a-m when she noticed smoke coming from the second floor of a home.
The woman banged on the door until the family got out, then returned to her car. The family of two adults and three children never got the chance to ask her for her name.
Firefighters think a space heater might have started the fire.

Notice that because it recounts events in chronological order, a delayed lead requires past tense. That's a change from the style used on other audio leads.

The question lead poses a question of general interest to introduce the point of the story. Like the soft lead and throwaway lead, its job is to set up the main point of the story:

Planning to head to the beach this weekend? You might want to get an early start, as traffic is expected to hit record levels.

How much could you spend in three minutes? One lucky Montana woman found out yesterday. (AP)

If the question doesn't command widespread interest, it can't do its job of luring the audience into the story. Here's an example of a question lead that doesn't work:

In the market for an icon? For five million dollars, you might be able to purchase the 16-foot bronze sculpture of a charging bull in New York City's Bowling Green Park, just across the street from the stock exchange. (AP)

Is anyone *ever* in the market for an icon? Do most people even know what that means? This one just doesn't work, and it misses what is the most interesting aspect of the story: The buyer needs to leave the sculpture in its current location.

The humor lead can help draw audience members in, but it needs to be genuinely humorous, and it needs to be appropriate for the story. Here's one that succeeds:

> Drivers should be experiencing less gas pain soon. An increase in the crude oil supply means prices will be dropping as much as 10 cents a gallon.

And one that doesn't:

> Santa might just want to pass on the milk and cookies this year — or at least the cookies. Archway Cookies is recalling holiday snacks that may contain pieces of glass.

That's serious news that needs to be presented in a straightforward manner.

ASSIGNMENT DESK 8.1

For each of the following scenarios, write at least two different types of leads.

1. Police stopped a local man last month for driving erratically. The driver, Henry Michaels, 52, failed a breath test and was charged with driving under the influence of alcohol. While police had him stopped, they searched his truck and found the dead body of a neighbor's Jack Russell terrier stuffed into a Morton's salt bag. The dog had been shot. Its owners said that Michaels had threatened to kill it if he saw it on his property. Today, Michaels agreed to plead no contest to the charge of killing the dog, which means he did not admit to or deny the charge. In return, he was fined $125, will spend three days in jail and was ordered to pay his neighbors $500 in restitution. In addition, he pleaded guilty to the DWI charge — his third — and agreed to participate in an alcohol awareness and intervention program. If Michaels breaks any laws or is charged with any serious motor vehicle violations, he will have to serve 90 days in jail.

2. Margaret Hudson, 85, a lifelong resident of the community, has agreed to comply with a judge's order. A few years ago, Hudson hired a contractor to work on her home. In the process, he installed vinyl siding. Hudson said she did not realize that because the house is in a protected historic district, that was not allowed. Because of Hudson's health problems and age, she appealed the decision, which could cost $25,000. But today her lawyer announced that with the help of donations from the community, Hudson had agreed to have the siding removed and the original wood finish restored.

Story Structure

When we looked at print and online stories, we found that most rely on the inverted pyramid structure. As you'll recall, that structure presents facts in order of declining importance until the story just peters out all together. That's fine for print and online, where few readers make it to the end of a story. But people listening to audio news stories generally cannot hit a fast forward button to get to the next story. Therefore, stories must be crafted so they hang together from start to finish.

To accomplish that, most audio stories are presented in logical order; that is, the writer tries to anticipate the listener or viewer's next question and answer it in turn. This demands that the writer, who might be an expert on the story after researching and interviewing, be able to act as though he or she knows nothing about the story. Here's a simple example:

A Texas family has filed a 25 million-dollar lawsuit against Wal-Mart, alleging that the retail giant should not have sold a shotgun to their suicidal daughter.	A hard lead introduces the main idea.
Twenty-four-year-old Shayla Stewart killed herself last year.	The next logical question is, "Who was the girl who died?"
Her parents argue that Wal-Mart should have known she was a risk because she had assaulted a customer at another Wal-Mart store—and Wal-Mart pharmacists were filling Stewart's prescription for anti-psychotic medicine.	Why do her parents believe Wal-Mart should be held responsible?
Wal-Mart isn't commenting on the case, but some mental health advocates say mental health records—including prescriptions—should stay private.	What's Wal-Mart say about the case?
In Texas, it's against the law to access such records without explicit permission.	Why didn't Wal-Mart check its own records when she bought the gun?
Federal law prohibits stores from selling guns to people who have a history of serious mental illness. But Stewart's name didn't show up when Wal-Mart did a background check. (AP)	Isn't there a law that prevents stores from selling guns to people like the suicide victim?

There is no secret formula to this type of structure; it depends entirely on careful thinking by the writer.

In other cases, chronological order—telling the story from beginning to end—works well. It's the obvious choice for human interest stories that build to a climax:

An Arkansas man had more than a sticking throttle to worry about, after his dog got behind the wheel of his truck.

Michael Henson took his dog with him when he drove to an auto parts store in Springdale, Arkansas, Sunday, so he could fix the throttle problem.

He left the truck running while he was in the store. The dog jumped over and knocked the truck into gear, sending it crashing into the store.

Henson told police he was standing there in the store when he looked up and saw his dog driving his truck through the window.

No one was hurt and no humans or animals were cited. (AP)

For more important stories, chronological order also can work well when coupled with a hard lead:

> Twenty central Florida homes are being threatened by a sinkhole that swallowed a four-lane road.
>
> The hole formed today as workers were pumping cement under a damaged section of road.
>
> The hole grew to 50 feet deep and at least 150 feet wide, and authorities say it isn't stabilized yet.
>
> Residents in all but three houses are expected to return tonight, but one house is in imminent danger of falling in. A major power line is also being threatened. (AP)

ASSIGNMENT DESK 8.2

Write an audio story for each of the following sets of facts. For the first, write a story using logical order; for the second, write a story using chronological order.

1. A local woman was walking with her granddaughter at the intersection of 28th Street and Boulevard Place around 10 p.m. Thursday. As they were walking, a man approached them and demanded money. He held out a carving knife, and the woman handed over her purse. The man fled on foot and the woman ran to a nearby house and asked the owner to call 911.

A short time later, K-9 officer Andrew Branham apprehended Aaron Tatum, 31, in the 3000 block of North Capitol Avenue. Tatum, of the 2900 block of Rolling Dunes Drive, matched the description of the robber.

Tatum struggled to get free and fled on foot. Branham again apprehended him a block north on North Capitol. Tatum then punched Branham's dog several times, police said. Branham was able to handcuff Tatum after a scuffle, police said.

The police dog suffered a minor injury, causing a limp. Police said Tatum was treated at Wishard Memorial Hospital.

2. Paramedics found Brian R. Pancherodich, 24, lying in a pool of blood in a car last evening. Paramedics had responded to a 911 call from a man who said he was an "associate" of Pancherodich's. The caller said they were at an auto-parts salvage yard on Cross Street. The caller has been identified as Brock Parks, 20. Waiting with him in a car outside the salvage yard was Kevin Brescia, 28. Parks and Brescia said they had just returned to the site after waiting eight hours for their friend to return home. They found him unconscious and bleeding from the head. Pancherodich had been knocked unconscious by an airbag he had been trying to remove from a car in the salvage yard, authorities said.

The three men initially arrived at the salvage yard yesterday morning, and Pancherodich jumped a fence, sheriff's spokesman Sgt. Carlos Torres said. When Parks and Brescia heard what sounded like a gunshot coming from the other side of the fence, they fled the scene. Pancherodich is listed in stable condition at a local hospital.

Transitions

As soon as a writer completes the lead of an audio story and begins thinking about the next paragraph of a story, he or she also has to start thinking about transitions. Those words, phrases and sentences help connect one point with another and are critical in guiding the listener through even simple stories.

Transitions link sentences and paragraphs in a variety of ways. In most cases, transitions are used to show how the information in a sentence or paragraph supports, opposes, neutralizes or draws conclusions from the information in the preceding sentence or paragraph. In other cases, transitions are used to compare information in two sentences or paragraphs. In yet other instances, transitions help show how material in two sentences or paragraphs is related by time or causation.

Transitions

Although transitions are best determined by the material being connected, several common transitional words and phrases also can help the listener or viewer understand connections:

Supporting transitions connect to a sentence or paragraph that lends support to the preceding material:

In addition
Not only... but also
Besides
For example
For instance
Furthermore

Neutralizing transitions connect to a sentence or paragraph that undercuts or dismisses the preceding material:

Still
Regardless of
In spite of
Nevertheless
Unfortunately

Opposing transitions connect to a sentence or paragraph that contains an idea contrary to the preceding material:

In contrast
Contrary to
Conversely

On the other hand
Although
But
Yet

Concluding transitions connect to a sentence or paragraph that builds to a conclusion based on the preceding material:

Therefore
Consequently

Temporal transitions establish a connection over time between two passages:

Before
Earlier
Then
Previously
Later
Next
Until
No sooner
Formerly
Previously

Causal transitions connect to a sentence or paragraph that contains information that results from the preceding material:

Because of that
As a result

In the following audio story, the writer has effectively used transitions to tie the pieces together:

Missouri is legalizing a new type of fast food. **But** you have to do the work.	Opposing transition *but* used to create contrast in the lead.
Next summer, people will be able to jump into the state's rivers and grab their own catfish by hand. It's called "noodling" — **and up until now**, it's been a misdemeanor offense. Conservationists were worried that people would pull too many large, mature catfish from logs and river bottoms.	Temporal transition *next* used to indicate that the law will not take effect immediately. The transition including *until* ties past practice to the future change.
But authorities have changed their minds and are giving the idea a chance next year. They're offering a seven-dollar noodling permit that lets anyone hunt for fish the old-fashioned way. The permits say each person can walk away with only five fish a day.	Another opposing transition (*but*) contrasts past thinking with the change of mind underlying the new law.
Before you try it, there's one warning: Many noodlers come up with fistfuls of angry snakes or turtles instead of fish. (AP, [emphasis mine])	Another temporal transition (*before*) moves the story to the next — and final — paragraph.

Audio Story Endings

Although most hard news stories written for print and online just fade out at the end, every audio story needs to have a strong and clear ending to alert listeners that the story is finished. The type and tone of story largely determines the best way to bring it to an end. While some endings defy categorization, most endings—or **closes**—belong to one of five types: the summary/main point close, the future ramification close, the information close, the opposition POV (point of view) close and the punch line close.

The **summary/main point close** brings a story full-circle by restating its central point. It's particularly good for complex stories that include a lot of information. This type of close should not mirror the exact words of the lead but should restate the same idea in another way. For example, a story reporting the arrest of a man on drug charges opens with this lead:

An Arlington man is one of three people charged with drug trafficking after Mississippi investigators seized eight-and-a-half kilograms of brown heroin.

The story closes like this:

Investigators arrested Jimmy Castillo Cuenca of Arlington, Javier Ararata Diaz of Charlotte, North Carolina, and Alba Mosquera of Jamaica, New York. They were booked into the Harrison County jail and are awaiting their initial court appearance. (AP)

The **future ramification close**, probably the most common type of ending, gives the audience a peek into what is likely to happen next. This type of ending often wraps up stories about weather emergencies, trials and other types of stories that have the potential for further consequences. It provides viewers or listeners with a clear indication that the story has ended while trying to provide a glimpse ahead.

Here's a future ramification close from a story about a heavy rainstorm in California:

> The powerful storm is expected to linger for days. Forecasters say it could dump up to 15 inches of rain and three feet of snow before moving east. (AP)

This close was used to wrap up a story about the disappearance of school milk cartons in favor of plastic jugs:

> The use of bottles also could be a financial boon for school lunch programs, which depend on sales to stay afloat. Fast-food chains Wendy's and McDonald's recently replaced their milk cartons with bottles — and sales soared. (AP)

The next example ends a story about doctors and pharmacists being charged with illegally selling free drug samples:

> If convicted, the doctors and pharmacists could be fined and possibly get jail time. (AP)

The **information close** provides additional information that is related to what's already been reported in the story. For example, a story reporting that Amazon.com had just completed its busiest holiday season ever closes this way:

> The hottest music seller was U2's "How to Dismantle an Atom Bomb." On one day, more than 13-thousand orders were placed for the D-V-D "Lord of the Rings, Return of the King." (AP)

Here's how an information close was used to wrap up a story about a revival of the oyster population in the Chesapeake Bay:

> Last year, as the region recovered from the drought of 2002, the harvest was only 26-thousand bushels. This year, the Department of Natural Resources says the harvest is already about 20-thousand bushels. The season doesn't end for another three months. (AP)

The final example comes from a story about airports testing new equipment that could eliminate the need to pat down passengers to check for explosives:

> The testing is part of the intelligence reform bill, which urged the security administration to expand the use of explosive-detection equipment and other measures. (AP)

The **opposition POV (point of view) close** lets a writer work in a contrary viewpoint. Often used to end stories dealing with controversial topics, this type of close gives a chance for the writer to air "the other side of the story." For instance, for a story about a controversial report by a state Home Builders Association claiming that new houses generate more tax revenue than the cost of the services they require, the writer wrapped up like this:

> Critics say the report underestimates the cost of building schools, roads and fire stations to accommodate growing populations. (AP)

This type of close has two potential problems. On one hand, it can serve to dismiss an important point of view. If one side gets 25 seconds and the other gets only five, it seems as if it is not to be taken seriously. On the other hand, the position of this oppositional information—at the end of the story, where it tends to stick with the audience—can artificially inflate its importance, even if it comes from a person or group that should *not* be taken seriously. A writer needs to carefully evaluate all sides of a story before structuring it, using this type of ending only when he or she is sure it won't fall into either trap.

The **punch line close** works on a range of lighter stories. Designed to leave the audience smiling, the punch line close often wraps up chronological stories or soft news features. For instance, this close wraps up a story on how to avoid overeating at holiday parties:

> But Moore says the key to not overeating starts before a person even leaves home. He says…What you have to do is disobey your mom before you go to the party, meaning you should spoil your appetite before you go. (AP)

ASSIGNMENT DESK 8.3

Using the two stories you wrote in Assignment Desk 8.2, write two different endings for each. Be prepared to discuss which of the endings works best and why.

Pulling It All Together

We've now looked at all the major parts of a basic audio news story. Typically, such a story is designed to be read live by an announcer and is therefore called a **reader**.

Readers are typically combined to create a newscast. All the pieces of a newscast must fit snugly together so it does not run too long—or conversely, too short. This is most critical when audio stories are to be broadcast on radio: Even in this era of round-the-clock news, radio newscasts typically run between one and five minutes each. That tight time frame provides no margin for error.

FIGURE 8.2

Even when broadcasting, a journalist finds that everything starts with the written word.

Therefore, the audio story writer must be sure that every story fits its prearranged time. The trick is finding a correlation between words on the written page and words as they are spoken. There is no simple formula, such as "x words per minute." It takes much longer to say *multimillionaire* than it does to say *one*.

Fortunately, most broadcast newsroom computers automatically provide an estimate of the time it will take to read a story. Nevertheless, it's a good idea for the writer to know how much copy is needed before he or she begins work on a story. A good rule of thumb is that a typical person reads at a rate of 16 lines per minute when copy is written with margins set so that lines hold a maximum of 65 characters each. The following passage, therefore, should take about 15 seconds to read:

> Another 25 classic American films are being added to a government archive.
> They include Jerry Lewis' 1963 comedy "The Nutty Professor," and the 1950s civil
> defense movie "Duck and Cover" that was shown in thousands of American class-
> rooms. (AP)

Beginning news readers should time themselves on several stories to see how close they come to the typical reading time and adjust accordingly. Doing so will help them work with writers to create stories that run just the right amount of time.

Read the following story to yourself to become familiar with it. Then, using a stopwatch, read it aloud. Don't race through it; instead, try to deliver it at a conversational pace. The story should take you 25 seconds to read. If you run more than a few seconds short or long, try again until you get close to that goal.

The Sudanese government and the Darfur region's largest rebel group are supporting a peace agreement to end three years of fighting that has claimed tens of thousands of lives.

But after negotiations in Nigeria, two other rebel factions have rejected the deal. The chief mediator from the African Union says the agreement between the main rebel group and the government is still a major contribution to restoring peace in Darfur.

Updating Stories

Breaking news audio stories may be rewritten several times a day—in some cases, several times in an hour. In updating stories, a writer needs to lead with the latest news while continuing to include information from previous stories so it all makes sense to the audience. Accomplishing both tasks takes skill and attention.

Following are three examples of how the Associated Press handled the story of a major fire in Chicago. All together, AP provided seven versions of the story: The first five were written within the 24 hours after the fire was first reported, and the last two versions ran over the next two days.

MONDAY 11:37 P.M.

A high-rise fire in Chicago has left at least 25 injured, including a dozen firefighters.

Eight firefighters and five others were hospitalized in serious condition. The rest were treated for smoke inhalation.

The fire happened in the 43-story LaSalle Bank building.

A fire department spokesman says there are no reports of anyone trapped, but the stairwells and floors are still being searched.

The fire was reported on the 29th floor at about six-thirty p.m. One witness says the smoke was "horribly thick" and the halls were "completely dark."

More than one-third of the city's fire equipment was dispatched.

The fire comes 14 months after a 35-story downtown building owned by Cook County caught fire, killing six people.

TUESDAY 7:16 P.M.

Chicago fire officials say several companies have been called back to deal with a lingering hot spot at the site of last night's high-rise blaze.

A fire department spokesman says the problem appears to be on the 29th or 30th floor of the Art Deco-style LaSalle Building.

Earlier in the day, Chicago Mayor Richard Daley praised the Fire Department's "well-organized" response to the stubborn blaze. He said people inside the building "refused to panic" and firefighters led them to safety "as soon as possible."

Officials say the fire burned for more than five hours, and sent at least 37 people to area hospitals — including 23 firefighters. Most had been released by this afternoon, though four firefighters are still hospitalized.

An investigation continues into what started the fire. The building remains closed.

THURSDAY 4:30 A.M.

Chicago city officials are preparing to debate ordinances that would require fire sprinklers in commercial skyscrapers.

Those discussions come as the investigation continues into a high-rise fire this week that injured more than 30 people.

The City Council's buildings committee is expected to advance one ordinance tomorrow. It would require sprinklers in commercial high-rises built before 1975, when they became mandatory.

Monday's fire in the LaSalle Building was the second blaze in a Chicago skyscraper in 14 months. Six people died in a fire at the Cook County Administration building last year.

Sprinklers weren't required in either building because both were built before 1975.

Mayor Richard Daley's administration wants to exempt residential properties and give building owners 12 years to comply.

Conclusion

Although audio news stories are built on the same principles as print and online stories, they differ significantly in style and structure. Taking the time to become familiar with these differences allows a writer to create audio stories that can reach a wide range of people who might not be willing or able to sit down with a newspaper or computer.

KEY TERMS

DISCUSSION QUESTIONS

1. Listen to a five-minute national audio newscast. You can probably find one on a local public radio station. If not, you can listen to the hourly newscast at www.npr.com. Make a list of the stories covered. Compare that coverage to what you find on a major online news site that day or in a major newspaper the next day. What types of stories are most effective in the audio format? The print/online format?

2. Again using a five-minute national audio newscast, analyze the order of stories, number of stories and kinds of stories used. What trends do you notice?

Writing the Advanced Audio Story

Chapter **9**

As we saw in Chapter 8, delivering news in the audio format makes it more convenient for many people, allowing them to tune in while on the go. But the basic audio format—the reader—hardly takes full advantage of all the resources that a writer can use when working with sound.

In this chapter, we'll look at how elements such as sources' voices and natural sound are gathered and edited into compelling audio stories. Then we'll see how to integrate them into a common audio news story, the wraparound. We'll also look at the most advanced form of audio story, the documentary. And along the way, we'll examine an audio format that's growing in popularity, the podcast.

Using the Voices of Sources

Most people are familiar with the phrase **sound bite.** It refers to a short video clip of someone talking and is a staple of television news reports. In audio news writing, the corresponding type of clip—less the video part, obviously—is called an **actuality**. Actualities typically run 10 to 30 seconds in length. Shorter ones can be difficult for listeners to comprehend, and longer ones demand too much listener attention.

An actuality is the equivalent of a direct quotation in a print or online story. But it goes one better than the printed quote: Not only does an actuality let a listener hear a speaker's exact words, it also lets the listener hear those words in the speaker's own voice. Just like a direct quote, an actuality adds seasoning to a story. It should never serve as the basis of a story; in most cases, actualities make up a minor part of a story.

Good actualities can improve audio news stories in several ways:

They add variety. No matter how skilled the newscaster, even a minute of a single voice reading the news can become dull. Adding the voices of sources mixes things up, grabs the attention of listeners and keeps a newscast interesting.

They add emotional impact. One of the first rules of good writing is "Show, don't tell." In audio news stories, the best way to *show* is by letting listeners *hear* for themselves. An announcer saying that the scene of a storm was a disaster is far less convincing than a witness describing the destruction.

They add credibility. Actualities let listeners hear directly from the people who make their laws, police their streets, and assess the damage caused by man-made and natural disasters. In addition, actualities let listeners hear the voices of people directly affected by tragedies, crime and changes in the law.

Let's look at an example. A story on federal hearings on steroid use among athletes included this actuality from Rep. Henry Waxman, D-Calif., a member of the House Government Reform Committee:

> The bill would require leagues to test for a broad range of performance-enhancing drugs. It would have true, random testing, and it would have tough penalties — two years for a first offense, and a lifetime ban for the second — that would make athletes think twice before resorting to cheating.

Although the announcer could have summarized that information, letting the listener hear it directly from the source adds interest.

ASSIGNMENT DESK 9.1

For each of the following scenarios, create a list of at least three people you could interview to get actualities for an audio news story.

1. The state legislature has just approved the budget for next year. Included in the budget is a provision to raise tuition 7 percent at all state colleges and universities. That increase is the highest in almost 10 years.
2. Next week marks the 20th anniversary of the worst storm ever to strike your area. Dozens of people were left homeless and more than 20 businesses were destroyed. You are to write a story commemorating the tragedy.
3. A graduate of your local high school has just been elected to the National Baseball Hall of Fame. He played baseball while in high school and then left town for college in the 1980s, eventually entering the major leagues.

Finding Actualities

Actualities generally arise from routine newsgathering procedures. Many are recorded at news conferences, speeches, panel discussions and presentations. The rest typically come from interviews, conducted either in person or over the telephone.

The key question that the writer needs to ask in determining which—if any—actualities to use in a story is, "How will actualities help listeners better understand or envision my story?" An actuality that is no more than a routine quote or simply repeats a point already made adds nothing to a story, and may in fact hurt the story by taking away time better used for other information.

An Associated Press story about four teenagers being shot to death in Huntington, WV, following an after-prom party illustrates the proper use of actualities. The first example comes from a woman who lives near the scene of the shooting:

> This is a wake-up call. We've had many of them. But this, I think, is one of the largest murders in this area with four dead, you know, and it makes absolutely no sense.

That quote captures the sense of frustration and outrage from a resident of a community that had recently experienced escalating violence and drug activity.

A second actuality featured the captain of the Huntington Police Department urging outraged community members to stay calm and cooperate with police:

> We certainly don't know who shot these individuals, right? And the people that are screaming "retaliation"—if they know who did it, let us know.

Both actualities add to the story by letting listeners hear the voices of people who were involved in the story. They present different perspectives from one another. Both of the actualities also convey information to the listener and don't just add superfluous comments such as "It's a tragedy."

ASSIGNMENT DESK 9.2

In the following interview transcript, pick out the two or three best actualities. This transcript is from an interview with your local chief of police.

Q: Judging from recent crime figures, it looks like our city is becoming more dangerous. Is that perception accurate?

A: Well, uh, you're right—this is a bad year for our city. Violent crime has risen almost 15 percent over last year. Most of the increase has been in the form of armed robberies.

Q: What do you attribute the increase to?

A: We're seeing more people falling through the cracks. Unemployment is up, the cost of living—food, gasoline, utilities—is way up, and some people, some residents have decided that the way to deal with all that is by taking what they need from someone else. That's bad enough, but in many cases the robberies include senseless violence.

Q: How are the police working to contain this problem?

Continued ⁝

Assignment Desk 9.2 Continues

A: We're using computer modeling to define the most dangerous areas of town, and we're stepping up patrols in those areas. We're also asking officers to get out of their cars and walk around. Just the sight of officers can have a great impact on reducing crime. And we're also asking residents and visitors to be alert and act intelligently. People are safer if they travel together rather than alone, and if they don't flaunt jewelry and other valuables. And if they see anyone acting suspiciously, we want them to call 911 immediately.

Recording Actualities

Creating broadcast quality actualities takes surprisingly little skill and investment. At a minimum, a reporter needs a digital recorder (Olympus and Sony digital recorders are available for as little as $50), a good microphone (several models from Audio Technica, Beyer, ElectroVoice and Shure offer professional results for $75 and up), and a cable that connects the microphone to the recorder. After recording, files are transferred to a desktop or laptop computer and edited with a program such as Adobe Audition, Apple Garage-Band or the free alternative, Audacity (available at http://audacity.sourceforge.net/).

In recording audio, the reporter needs to remember that many audio news stories are heard in cars, where the sound of the report competes against traffic, road noise, sirens, wind and storm noise, and so on. Therefore, actualities should be as clear and free from noise as possible. Quiet locations without distracting background noises and chatter are best. Busy restaurants make the worst locations for gathering audio; conventions and other noisy gathering spots are not much better. If a reporter's only choice is such an environment, he or she should look for a quieter out-of-the-way spot for the interview—a back room in a restaurant or a hallway in a convention hall, for example.

That rule is sometimes broken, however, when the sounds of the location add impact to a story: sirens blaring, fire hoses spraying, protesters chanting, and so on. As long as those background sounds do not overwhelm the actualities, they can help listeners feel like they are on the scene with the reporter.

For best results, a reporter should use headphones during interviews. Headphones will let the reporter hear exactly what is being recorded. If problems or unexpected noises are encountered, he or she can pause and figure out what's causing them. That's much better than finding out at the last minute that the recording is useless.

Although it's always good to encourage sources during an interview, when a reporter is recording audio, it's important that the reporter does not pepper the comments with the sounds of his or her own voice. Any time the reporter says "Uh-huh," "Wow," "Sure" or anything else in response to an interviewee's comments, those comments will be recorded as well—and they will be virtually impossible to erase later. For that reason, reporters should limit themselves to nodding and other nonverbal cues.

The type of microphone used makes a big difference in the quality of audio. A cardioid microphone picks up sound from in front and a little off to the sides but essentially ignores all other sounds—making it great for close-up interviews. In contrast, an omnidirectional microphone picks up sound from all around—making it the perfect tool for capturing background sound (see Figure 9.1).

FIGURE 9.1   **To get best audio quality, a high-performance microphone is a must.**

When conducting interviews, a reporter should keep the microphone close to both himself or herself and to the interviewee — but not too close. Typically, 6 to 12 inches works best. It's important to practice to find the best compromise between losing clarity and being so close that the listener will hear popping noises when the speakers utter words with hard B's and P's. Holding the microphone to the side of the speaker's mouth rather than directly in front of it also helps avoid this problem. Again, headphones can be helpful in avoiding sound problems.

Phone interviews, once frowned upon as a means of gathering actualities for audio news stories, have become increasingly acceptable. Phone interviews take much less planning and expense than on-the-spot interviews, and they allow reporters to talk with experts and other great sources around the globe who may otherwise not be accessible. Telephone interviews also bring with them an immediacy that many listeners prefer.

The biggest challenge in getting good actualities via the telephone is the quality of the phone lines themselves. A reporter should always ensure that his or her phone line is up to the task before staking an important story on it. To increase the odds of getting usable audio, it's best to ask the interviewee to use a wired landline phone — not a cell phone or cordless phone — and to avoid using a speaker phone or headset: Both of those can degrade audio quality.

The process of recording audio over the phone is not particularly tricky, but it does require care to get professional sounding results. Journalists most often use a **coupler**, which is a device that accepts a telephone line input. The coupler's audio output can then be fed to a handheld recorder or computer hard drive. For better results, a **hybrid** lets the reporter adjust the volume between the incoming and outgoing audio; without that capability, the interviewer's questions will likely be much louder than the interviewee's responses. Couplers come in both analog and digital varieties, with the latter offering

Why Choose Journalism?

Journalism gives a person the opportunity to use a very broad skill set. You can be a writer, a storyteller, an investigator, and the eyes and ears for the public when you cover breaking news. When I was in college, a professor once told me that the most important trait of a journalist is curiosity. Now, after more than a quarter-century in journalism, I couldn't agree more. You have to be a curious person to succeed in journalism. You have to want to know how things work, what makes a person tick, why things around you are the way they are. I guess I've always been a curious person, and for me, a journalism career was a no-brainer.

MARK S. MILLER
WBAL Radio

much higher quality. But that quality comes at a price, both in terms of cost (up to $600) and complexity (instead of using a phone, the reporter needs to use a microphone and a mixing board).

Editing Audio

Once audio has been recorded, it must be evaluated: Is it technically good enough to use? Will listeners be able to hear the speaker's words? Is background noise distracting? Does the speaker talk loudly enough? Does he or she mumble? Do regional accents or dialects make it hard to understand what the speaker is saying?

If the technical quality of the recording passes muster, it's ready to be captured to a computer. Rather than capturing the entire interview, most reporters capture only the clips they intend to use. The best clips include powerful quotes, unique ways of saying things or good summaries.

The simplest way to organize material for capture is for the reporter to play back the interview and take notes on the times at which good segments begin and end. Each good segment can then be saved as a separate clip.

For best results, many reporters working with audio create a **log**, or rough transcript, of the entire interview. The log is generally created on the fly while the entire recording plays. The goal is not to create a word-for-word transcription but just the essence of each part of the interview, using a word or short phrase to identify the passages. Logs often run long—10, 20 or even more pages, depending on the length of an interview. But it's easier to work with even a long log than with raw recordings. (See the sample tape log form on page 178.)

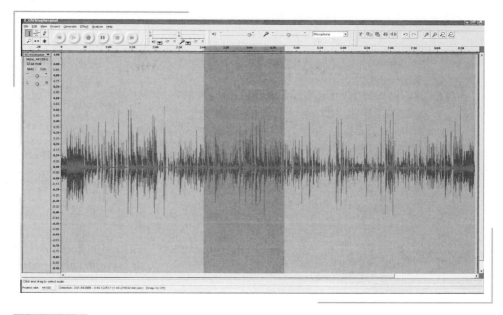

FIGURE 9.2   Easy to use and free, the Audacity software program offers quick and easy access to basic audio editing functions.

Once recording has been logged and decisions have been made about which actualities will be used, an audio editing program lets the reporter remove extraneous material at the start and end of clips, as well as long pauses, hems and haws, redundancies, and so on (see Figure 9.2). The reporter needs to be careful not to remove too much from long pauses, however, as the results will sound clipped and unnatural. It's also important to be careful not to remove words that could change the meaning of what the speaker has said. (A good guide for determining when cuts are acceptable, as well as other ethical questions about recording and editing audio, can be found at http://source.ca/english_new/detail.php?id=1638.) Finally, if there is background sound—and there usually is some, even if it's just the hum of an air conditioner or the whirr of passing traffic—it's crucial that edits do not create discontinuities in it.

ASSIGNMENT DESK **9.3**

Using campus news sources, find a recent story of interest to you. Choose someone who is an expert on the topic or has been affected by the story, and draw up a list of at least 10 questions to ask him or her. Make sure your questions are not simple yes-no questions; instead, you want to ask questions that solicit longer answers, preferably ones that have some emotional content. Record your interview. If hardware and software are available, capture your interview on a computer and pull out at least two good actualities. Otherwise, transcribe the best actualities.

Adding Actualities to a Story

Just as important as picking the best actualities from an interview is setting them up so they feel like a natural part of a story, not an intrusion. Typically, the first actuality follows a lead-in. The two pieces should complement each other. For instance, an actuality that contains specifics is usually introduced by a lead-in that provides a general overview or offers background.

> *Reporter*: You can get incredible deals at government auctions of seized or unclaimed property.
>
> *Actuality*: There's lot of stuff like cars and boats and jewelry and furniture and all kinds of stuff you can find at these places. (AP)

Conversely, actualities that are less specific require lead-ins with more details:

> *Reporter*: Expectations for a very busy summer travel season have emboldened hotels to boost their room rates by as much as 15 percent as compared to last year. So where do you find the deals?
>
> *Actuality*: That's going to be difficult.
>
> *Reporter*: Hotels analyst Bjorn Hansen with PriceWaterhouseCoopers says resorts are looking for a lot of business and are raising prices even in places like Miami, where summer is usually the off season. (AP)

An actuality should be set up in a way that allows the story to be understood even if technical problems prevent listeners from hearing the actuality. For that reason, actualities typically run a sentence or more; partial quotes are avoided. The following two examples—the first bad, the second good—show how actualities were used in a report on a new MP3 player from Gateway:

> *Reporter*: John Schindler with Gateway says as far as music downloads are concerned...
>
> *Actuality*: We offer a three-month promotion right now on our MP3 player that includes Napster to Go service, so that's access to over a million titles.
>
> *Reporter*: Schindler says the big plus factor for the Photo Jukebox is accessibility.
>
> *Actuality*: Our MP3 player works with subscription-based services, which makes it very easy for consumers to continuously update and get the latest and greatest stars and titles that they want on their MP3 player. (AP)

Notice that if the first actuality fails to play, the story does not make sense. However, if the second actuality does not play, the story still would work—even though the listener would not get all the specifics.

Traditionally, lead-ins have been used to identify the person featured in an actuality and establish his or her credentials. As the examples cited above show, however, it's becoming increasingly common for an actuality to be followed by the name and credentials of the speaker (in most cases, it makes more sense to give the title of the person first and then his or her name, so the listener can grasp the information better). In either case, it's always important that the speaker's identity be close to the actuality, so the listener can clearly identify the source of the voice.

The lead-in should never repeat words or information from the actuality that follows; doing that merely wastes time, as this example shows:

Lead-in: McKellan says that the Battle of the Bands will attract groups from all over the country.

Actuality: We've got bands from all over the country coming in.

The solution to this problem is to rewrite the lead-in or drop the actuality. Here's an example of a rewrite that works better:

Lead-in: McKellan says that word has gotten out about the event.

Actuality: We've got bands from all over the country coming in.

In years past, stories that begin with actualities—known as **cold opens**—were rarely used. Today, however, they are becoming more acceptable. But that does not mean they don't have problems. By their nature, cold opens cannot include any identification before the actuality begins. Unless the speaker's voice is well known, using a cold open will leave many listeners wondering who is talking and will also leave them unable to judge the credibility of the information because they will not know who said it. In most cases, preceding an actuality with a lead-in gives listeners more context and lets them anticipate a change in voice.

ASSIGNMENT DESK **9.4**

Write lead-ins for each of the actualities you captured in Assignment Desk 9.3. Each lead-in should set up the following actuality and identify the speaker.

Writing the Wraparound

Actualities are most commonly found in audio news stories known as **wraparounds** (or **wraps**). A wraparound takes its name from its structure: It begins with narration (either live or recorded), blends in at least one actuality and then returns to narration to finish. At its simplest, a wraparound includes:

- Two or three lines of lead-in to establish what the story is about.
- An actuality of 10 to 20 seconds.
- A one-line **write-out** or **tag** to give additional facts and provide a sense of closure.

This sample script below is from a story filed by an Associated Press reporter accompanying first lady Laura Bush on a visit to Egypt.

> It was not her first visit to the pyramids. That came on a Nile cruise with her mother-in-law when her husband was Texas governor.
>
> But it was the first visit on which Mrs. Bush was shown newly discovered tombs near the Sphinx at Giza.
>
> START: HAWAS
>
> OUTCUE: "…THE TWO TOMBS NOW."
>
> TIME: 05
>
> That's Egyptian antiquities director Zawi Hawas (ZAH-wee ha-WAHZ), who says one of the tombs was just found, the other comprises six rooms, including one cut out of solid rock containing a box with 400 statuettes inside. (AP)

A few things are worth noting about this script.

- The word *start* and the one-word name of the sound clip (in this case, *Hawas*, the name of the speaker) signal that the anchor should stop reading the story and the actuality should be played.
- The word *outcue* followed by the final words of the actuality signal the end of the actuality. (The actuality in its entirety is "We did announce to the public; we are actually announcing the two tombs now.") The outcue signals the anchor to pick up again.
- The length of the clip (*time: 05*) follows the closing words of the actuality to help the anchor gauge how long it runs.

ASSIGNMENT DESK **9.5**

Create a 30-second wraparound using the material provided. If you have access to recording equipment, record your story, having one or more other students read the actuality or actualities you select.

A mile-long section of the highway that runs by town was shut down early today. Officials do not know when it will reopen. The closure followed a chemical spill. Between 300 and 500 gallons of hydrochloric acid leaked from a container on a truck headed through town. Hydrochloric acid is a strong and corrosive chemical that is used to clean metals.

U.S. Environmental Services, a local company, used lime to neutralize the acid and decontaminate the truck. Another truck was being brought in to collect the remaining acid from the trailer.

The interstate remains closed, and dozens of state and local officials are manning roadblocks and supervising cleanup.

Actualities (you may use material from the actualities in the narrative part of the wraparound):

County emergency management director, Mildred Lamar: "We are taking all precautions to protect people."

Continued

Assignment
Desk **9.5**
Continues

Cindy Longo, local resident, who was stuck in the closure: "I thought maybe it was a huge wreck. I've never seen all four lanes closed down, and the officers would not let anyone stop to find out what was going on."

Volunteer Fire Chief Frank Ridgeway, on what he did when he arrived at the scene: "I saw the truck and smelled the acid. I used my car, which is equipped with emergency lights, to block the highway."

Using Natural Sound

If actualities help convey information to the listener, **natural sound** (also called **background sound**, **ambient sound** or **nat sound**) helps create a mood or sense of place. Natural sound can be anything related to a story: crowd noises; emergency vehicle sounds; thunder, wind and other weather noises; and so on.

Natural sound is a great way to bring the listener into the story. Natural sound often serves to introduce an audio news story, either on its own or with a voice-over that begins the story. For example, a story about a 100-year-old seamstress might open with the sound of her sewing machine or of the sound of her ripping seams. Those might not be the first choices that come to mind, but sometimes the most effective natural sound isn't the most obvious choice. If natural sound makes listeners ask "What's that?" they're going to listen more closely.

Natural sound also can be interspersed in a story to continue or shift the mood. For instance, a story about an athlete being injured in a traffic accident might open with the sounds of a stadium and then later shift to the sounds of a hospital.

Natural sound usually plays a supporting role in audio news stories, but in some cases natural sound has a higher profile. For instance, National Geographic's Pulse of the Planet stories (http://pulseplanet.nationalgeographic.com/) often devote much of their time to natural sound, such as the sounds of a traditional celebration in a remote country. Jim Metzner, founder of Pulse of the Planet and a regular contributor to Saturday Weekend Edition on National Public Radio, notes that it's important to balance words and sound: "What's enough to bring the listener in? What's too much? The only answer I have is to keep this question in mind." Metzner says that in general music can run longer on its own than other types of natural sound, "I suppose because we can follow the changes and patterns in it."[1]

Virtually anything can be used as natural sound—the sound of crowds at a festival or open-air market, telephones ringing in an office, birds singing in a forest, police sirens blaring, even the voice of a non-native speaker. In fact, using some of a non-native speaker's voice can bring the person to life in a manner impossible to achieve by merely translating his or her comments.

ASSIGNMENT DESK **9.6**

Find an upcoming campus or local event — a fair, a rally, a festival or other public activity. Attend the event and take notes. Interview and record at least two participants and one organizer. Also record at least five minutes of natural sound. Your recording should include at least two different types of natural sound (for example, crowd noise, music playing, and so on). If hardware and software are available, capture your natural sound on a computer.

Adding Natural Sound to a Reader

The easiest way to work sound into an audio news story is by using natural sound in the background of a reader (see Figurer 9.3). Just inserting a little outside sound can help bring an otherwise routine story to life. For instance, when Democratic senators threatened filibusters to block judicial nominees, The Associated Press's Jerry Bodlander filed a fairly straightforward report over background sound of cots being rolled into a room off the Senate floor. Here is the report presented in typical script format:

> Filibuster Vote
>
> May 23, 2005
>
> (NAT SOUND UNDER/COTS ROLLING)
>
> RUNS: 20
>
> As the Senate gears up for a key vote on judicial filibusters, custodians rolled cots into ironically enough the Strom Thurmond Room, ahead of what's expected to be an all-night debate.
>
> A dozen moderates are running out of time in their effort to hammer out a compromise that they can force on both leaders in the effort to avoid triggering the so-called nuclear option.
>
> The Senate will vote later today instructing the sergeant at arms to make sure all 100 senators are present as the debate heads into its final hours.

The directions at the top of the story indicate that natural sound of cots being rolled in should start as the reporter begins speaking and should run under his narration for the first 20 seconds of the 30-second report.

FIGURE 9.3

To give the listener a sense of being at the scene of a story, reporters will use audio recorders to capture a range of natural sounds, from chirping birds to buzzing saws.

ASSIGNMENT
DESK **9.7**

1. Using the materials you gathered for Assignment Desk 9.6, write a 20-second reader with background sound.

2. Once you've completed the reader, review your recorded interviews from the event and pull out the best actualities. Then write a 45-second wraparound using one or more actualities.

Documentaries

The most ambitious audio stories combine narration, actualities and natural sound and run anywhere from a few minutes to an hour. These **documentaries** often require more time to research and prepare than news writers can spare, so documentaries tend to be feature, rather than news, stories.

At their best, audio documentaries offer great examples of the medium's capabilities. With nothing more than words and sounds, audio documentaries can create vivid pictures for the listening audience. Although the techniques of assembling a great documentary could fill an entire book, the following tips can help a reporter create his or her first short documentary, or **mini-doc**.

Be on the lookout for story ideas. Good reporters always remain alert to ideas for documentaries. In many cases, the ideas come from other stories in the news that the reporter would like to know more about. Many reporters keep a clip file for such ideas. In addition, ideas often pop up from daily life. Reporters look for things they see or do every day or people they come across that make them stop and think. Broadcast writer Jenny Atwater calls these "What's up with that?" moments. "If it sparks your curiosity," she says, "it might be making other people wonder as well."

Try to find a focus before heading out. While a good reporter is always open to new information and new directions, an *efficient* reporter begins fieldwork with a good idea of what the story's focus will be. Without some idea of where the story is going, the reporter is likely to return with an unmanageable amount of information and recordings.

Look for a character or characters to build the story around. Although most documentaries deal with an issue of one sort or another, the best way to catch a listener's attention and hold it over time is by putting a strong person or people at the center of your story. More listeners are likely to stick around to hear the story of someone facing the devastating prospect of losing a job than to stick with a more theoretical story about the costs of outsourcing.

Let the sources tell the story. Reporters should resist the urge to paraphrase most of what sources say. People's stories are usually most powerful when told in their own words, and in many cases they do a better job of telling their stories than a reporter can.

Make sure the story has narrative flow. Like all good stories, documentaries need a narrative to keep the story flowing. The writer needs to look for conflict and change to drive the story.

Show, then tell. Documentaries need to build toward something; that something often is a lesson or reflective thought that will have broad appeal. So after sharing the story with listeners by showing them, it's a good idea to wrap things up by explaining what it all means.

Remember the importance of description. Listeners depend on the reporter to paint a picture in their minds. Although natural sound can let listeners hear what a museum sounds like (foot steps on the stone floors, guards ripping tickets, or the whispers of people looking at paintings), it's up to the reporter to describe what it looks like. Description shouldn't take up the entire piece, but it definitely has its place.

Don't go too long without a change of pace. Ira Glass, one of the creators of the well-known documentary series "This American Life" (www.thisamericanlife.org; see Figure 9.4), notes that reporters working in this longer form need to be aware of how audio news is usually presented:

> The length of a [typical NPR audio] news spot...is 45 or 50 seconds. Usually, there's a couple of sentences from the reporter, then they do a quote from somebody, and kind of two or three more sentences from the reporter, and you're at 50, 45 seconds.
>
> It turns out that we public radio listeners are trained to expect something to change every 45 to 50 seconds. And as a producer you have to keep that pace in mind. For example, in a reporter's story, every 45 or 50 seconds, you'll go to a piece of tape.
>
> So if you have a four-minute story, you figure you're going to have four quotes or maybe five. And even in a format like ours, where it just sounds like people talking and music washing all over the place, we have to adhere to that pace.[2]

Use natural sound for transitions. Not only can natural sound help create great ambience for a documentary, it also can be used to tie the pieces of the documentary together.

Try to offer surprises. The best documentaries often catch listeners off guard, offering a fresh perspective or an unexpected twist. If a reporter can tell listeners something they have not heard before, the result will probably be a winner.

Interview sources in their natural environment. A reporter should not pull the 100-year-old seamstress away from her sewing machine, but rather should try to interview her while she's working. She'll feel more comfortable, and the reporter will have the natural sound under her bites. Of course, this works only when someone has a fairly quiet job—interviewing the foreman of an assembly plant while at work would probably be a disaster.

FIGURE
9.4

This American Life is widely regarded as one of the best sources of audio documentaries. Its Web site offers access to recent episodes, updates, bonus audio and other features.

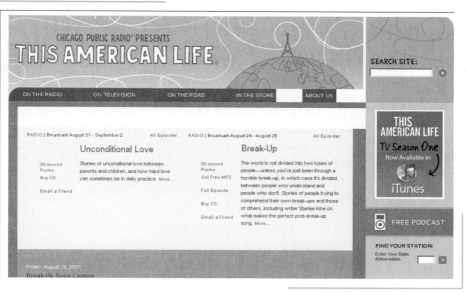

ASSIGNMENT DESK 9.8

For this assignment, you will write and produce a three- to five-minute audio story (mini-doc) about a person, place or thing in an area assigned by your instructor. You will need to do this in steps:

1. Prepare a proposal for your instructor's approval.
2. Using an audio recorder, conduct interviews with at least three different people. Do not include any members of your family.
3. Write a script for your mini-doc, incorporating at least three audio clips.
4. Using an audio recorder, record your narration.
5. If hardware and software are available, edit your audio clips and narration into a finished package.

Creating Podcasts

Podcasts have become one of the most talked-about phenomena of the last several years. News organizations of all sorts have embraced them, and many individuals also have started podcasting. Sites like Apple's iTunes Store and Podcast Alley (www.podcastalley.com) list tens of thousands of podcasts. Most allow listeners to subscribe so that new episodes are downloaded to their computers automatically.

Still, many people don't understand podcasting, even though it's a straightforward concept. "Simply put, podcasting is distributing audio files in a radio-show format over the Internet," technology expert Russell Morgan explains. "And despite the name, listeners do not need iPods; if you offer the broadcast in multiple formats, any digital music player will do. Many people listen to podcasts right on their PCs."[3]

So a podcast is not a form of news story so much as a technique for delivering an audio story. As such, any audio program can be packaged as a podcast, and indeed that's what a lot of podcasts are: Repurposed radio news programs, interviews and documentaries. But many of the best podcasts are unique items created expressly for online distribution.

Podcasts come in a wide variety of shapes and sizes. As one online podcast guide states:

There is one rule to keep in mind:

1. There are no rules with podcasting (just keep it legal)
You can cough into the mic once a week and post it to the Internet if you want. Just know that I won't listen to it.[4]

Although it may be true that "there are no rules—at least in terms of structure; legal issues are another matter—it is just as true that a podcast should stick to a format to create a professional feel. One widely used podcast model follows these steps:

1. Intro theme music.
2. Welcome and introduction of guest(s).
3. Q-and-A with guest(s).
4. Final comments.
5. Outro music.

The key criterion for any podcast is that it offers listeners something unique that is particularly suited for audio delivery. A podcast that is nothing more than a writer reading a print story into a microphone is unlikely to spur much interest. But a podcast of the same writer having a conversation about the story with sources and officials offers the audience something they cannot get elsewhere.

As far as technical considerations go, creating a podcast does not require much knowledge or equipment. The key requirement is that that podcast be saved in the MP3 format; most audio editing programs can handle that quickly and easily. Uploading podcasts to the Web and creating a feed that listeners can subscribe to are typically handled automatically, although even the technologically challenged can accomplish those tasks with an inexpensive program such as FeedForAll. One of many good tutorials on the topic can be found at About.com (http://radio.about.com/od/podcastin1/a/aa030805a.htm).

Conclusion

By combining the voices of sources along with natural sounds, a writer can create compelling audio news stories that help transport listeners to the story locations. Given the time and resources, a writer can stretch out and use the audio documentary format, which creates an even more compelling audio environment. Among the newest technologies, podcasts help writers reach audience members no matter where they are. All things considered, the tools available to the audio writer can go a long way in increasing story quality and reach.

KEY TERMS

actuality, 161
cold opens, 169
coupler, 165
documentary, 173
hybrid, 165
lead-in, 168
log, 166
mini-doc, 173

natural sound (background sound, ambient sound, nat sound), 171
outcue, 170
podcast, 175
sound bite, 161
wraparound (or wrap), 169
write-out/tag, 169

DISCUSSION QUESTIONS

1. Listen to an audio newscast online or on the radio. What percentage of the stories contains actualities? What percentage contains natural sound? What do those aspects add to the stories?

2. Listen to an episode of "This American Life," either on the radio or online. What are the differences in this documentary format as opposed to traditional audio news stories?

3. Visit an online news site and locate podcasts available. (Hint: Choose "Edit">"Find on this page" from your browser's menu to search for the word *podcast*.) Listen to at least two episodes. How successful is the podcast in providing information of interest to you? How likely are you to subscribe to the podcast? What other types of podcasts might the site offer to appeal to you?

NOTES

1. Jim Metzger, "How I Use Sound in a Story," Radio-College.org, **www.radiocollege.org/readingroom/articles/story_sound.php.**

2. Ira Glass, "More Better Radio," Minnesota Public Radio broadcast journalists' lecture series, 11 February 1998, **www.current.org/people/p809i1.html.**

3. Russell Morgan, "Believe the Hype," PC Magazine, 20 March 2007, p. 87.

4. Jason Van Orden, "How to Podcast," 2005, **www.how-to-podcast-tutorial.com/05-choosing-your-podcast-format.htm.**

Sample Interview Recording Log

Name of person(s) interviewed: _____

Other people present: _____

Interviewer: _____

Date of interview: _____

Location of interview: _____

General description of contents: _____

Tape/disc number: _____

Page _____ of _____

Topic Summary

Time/counter #	Contents
_____	_____
_____	_____
_____	_____
_____	_____
_____	_____
_____	_____
_____	_____
_____	_____
_____	_____
_____	_____
_____	_____
_____	_____
_____	_____
_____	_____
_____	_____
_____	_____
_____	_____
_____	_____
_____	_____
_____	_____
_____	_____
_____	_____
_____	_____
_____	_____
_____	_____
_____	_____
_____	_____
_____	_____

Chapter 10

Writing the Basic Video Story

Moving from writing audio stories to video stories is not as dramatic a step as might be imagined. As noted previously, even when people are "watching" a video story, they process most of its information through their ears.

That doesn't mean that visuals are unimportant in video news stories. To the contrary, properly used graphics and video footage can enhance any story. In this chapter, we'll look how those elements can be used effectively in the two basic types of video news stories: the video reader and the voice over.

The Video Reader

The simplest form of video news story is virtually identical to the audio-only readers discussed in Chapter 9: a 15- to 30-second story that an announcer reads, with no supplemental material. However, video readers typically include one or more graphics (abbreviated as GFX) shown on screen. Graphics are used to do several things:

- Illustrate a place or process.
- Provide a photographic image of a person.
- Provide relevant factual information, such as phone numbers, Web site URLs or serial numbers.
- Highlight a quote from a person or a report.

In some cases, these goals are combined. For example, a graphic might include a photo of a person's face and a quote from that person.

The keys to good graphics are clarity and simplicity. Viewers should be able to understand the point of any graphic, and they should be able to grasp all pertinent information at a glance.

Graphics either take up a corner of the screen **over the shoulder** of the news reader—(abbreviated as OTS), or they fill the screen (called **full screen**, abbreviated as FS).

FIGURE 10.1

Examples of television graphics. Clockwise from top left: An OTS showing a person, an OTS showing a place, a FS bullet-point list and a FS quote.

Missing

BALTIMORE LANDMARK

"We're sympathetic to the neighbors' concerns, but our work doesn't threaten the environment or public health. We've been in communication with the neighbors and will continue to be."

-Brooke Henderson
Synagro Spokeswoman

TIPS TO AVOID ROAD RAGE

- DON'T MAKE EYE CONTACT WITH OTHER MOTORISTS
- DON'T TAILGATE
- IF SOMEONE IS TAILGATING YOU, MOVE OVER
- BE COURTEOUS
- DON'T ALLOW YOURSELF TO BE PROVOKED

SOURCE: AAA MID-ATLANTIC

Why Choose Journalism?

Sometimes I like to think of my job in terms of a quest. The quest for a great story, the quest for great pictures, great sound, great moments. What's out there that's new to learn, see and hear? Who's suffering? Who's stealing? Who was born? Who died? Why? Why is the world the way it is?

I help shape how my city imagines itself. With my camera I take viewers to places they've never been and meet people they've never met. If I am doing my job well, my stories describe the way the world is, so just maybe, we can make it a better place.

JOHN ANGLIM
WMAR-TV, Baltimore

In many cases, OTS graphics appear as soon as a story begins. In such cases, the reader does not need to explicitly acknowledge the graphic if it merely shows a familiar person, place or other object. For instance, a story about humor columnist Dave Barry's decision to take a hiatus after 22 years might be accompanied by a photo of Barry. In that case, this unadorned lead would work just fine:

> Dave Barry says he's not joking this time. The Pulitzer Prize-winning humorist insists his piece in today's Miami Herald will be his last, at least for a while. (AP)

Other familiar graphics, such as corporate logos, can be handled the same way. For instance, this lead could run on a story that begins with an OTS graphic of the Weight Watchers logo:

> A new study of 10 popular diet programs finds only one has strong scientific evidence to back weight loss claims: Weight Watchers. (AP)

The same is true for generic graphics, such as a photo of a boat show that ran with this lead:

> It's being billed as a showcase of boats for every budget and lifestyle. There are more than one-thousand vessels on display at the 100th edition of the New York National Boat Show. It runs through Sunday at the convention center. (AP)

It would sound silly to try to work in an explicit mention of the graphic:

> It's being billed as a showcase of boats for every budget and lifestyle, just like the ones shown in the photo you can see here.

As long as the graphic clearly depicts something that obviously ties to the story, it does not need to be referred to in the story.

CG Graphics

In some cases, graphics require nothing more than a photo, as in the preceding examples. When the subject of a visual is not well known or is not obvious, however, it is common to add text created by a **character generator** (hence the designation of these as **CG graphics**).

When a CG graphic appears on top of a photo or illustration, it's referred to as a **super**, for superimposed. Such text alleviates the need to specifically refer to the graphic in the story when the subject of the graphic might not be widely known. For example, the following story uses a photo of Cindy Sheehan with "Cindy Sheehan, Antiwar Activist" superimposed. Notice that the script is presented in a typical two-column TV format. The left-hand column includes information on the visuals, including the anchor on camera

TV Speak

News Pointers

"President Bush in Washington today, meeting with Condoleeza Rice."

"A teen in custody, his parents dead of stabbing."

People listening to television newscasts might be forgiven for wondering what language the broadcasters are speaking. Full of fragments and delivered in a staccato style, the words that come out of many broadcasters' mouths sound nothing like the way most people talk.

The style that's come to be known as ***TV speak*** was born of a laudable goal: letting news writers convey as much information as possible in a short period of time. Over the years, the style has become ingrained as a method of encouraging viewers to look at graphics and video.

The idea is to provide just the bare minimum of words and information so the viewer can concentrate on the visuals.

TV speak has become so common that it's advocated in leading broadcast writing books, such as John Hewitt's "Air Words: Writing for Broadcast News," which encourages the use of "elliptical sentences — sentence fragments with implied but unspoken words or phrases."[1]

Many observers and former news people find these changes decidedly unpleasant. Tom Phillips, former writer and editor for The CBS Evening News, explains his feelings: "This is television being self-conscious about what it is. It's saying, 'Hey. We've got pictures here. We want you to look at the pictures.' And what's sacrificed there is the standard English sentence. Does it help? As they say, you decide."[2]

(sometimes abbreviated as AOC, or simply ON CAM). The right-hand column contains the story itself:

SHEEHAN	
Anchor on camera:	((On Cam)) THE FACE OF THE ANTIWAR MOVEMENT SAYS SHE IS ENDING HER CAMPAIGN AGAINST THE WAR IN IRAQ.
Anchor with OTS graphic of Cindy Sheehan:	((OTS)) CINDY SHEEHAN ATTRACTED NATIONAL ATTENTION WHEN SHE SET UP A PROTEST CAMP OUTSIDE PRESIDENT BUSH'S TEXAS HOME IN 2005. HER SON WAS KILLED IN IRAQ IN 2004.
	SHEEHAN SAYS SHE HAD HOPED THINGS WOULD CHANGE WHEN DEMOCRATS TOOK CONTROL OF CONGRESS…BUT NOW FEELS THERE IS NO POSSIBILITY THAT THE WAR WILL END SOON.

Not all CG graphics are used in combination with photos. CG graphics can be as simple as a headline or background used to dress up a story. For instance, on a story reporting concerns about mad cow disease, a graphic might show a photo or illustration of a hamburger under a super reading "Unsafe Beef?" Such a simple graphic would require no adjustment in news writing style. For instance, this lead would work fine either with or without an OTS "Unsafe Beef?" graphic:

It's not just poor grammar that troubles people like Phillips, it's what this style does to comprehension. "[S]ometimes leaving out the verb can get you in a little bit of trouble," he said:

> I heard on one of the networks the other night. "At the UN, desperate pleas today for help against the AIDS epidemic." Well, that sentence not only doesn't have a verb, it doesn't have a subject even. Who made these desperate pleas? How were they made? We don't know. And, to me, that's a deficient sentence because it leaves the viewer wondering, "Am I dumb? Am I supposed to know who said this?"[3]

Although video news writers should avoid this style whenever possible, life is not always that simple. As journalist Robin Mazyck says, "Many anchors prefer TV talk. So even though it's best to avoid it, you want to make the anchor happy. It does no good to get into a shouting match because of a script — something I've seen happen repeatedly."

Mazyck also recommends that

> writers try to write in the voice of the anchor or reporter. Once a person has worked for a particular talent long enough he or she will be able to hear that person's voice and write in the talent's tone. Many times this will be grammatically incorrect, but there are some anchors/reporters that can make a script sound like music — even though it is hard to decipher on paper.

Some cattlemen in Texas — the nation's leading beef producer — say the government is jumping the gun on lifting a Canadian beef ban. (AP)

That doesn't mean that all CG graphics are devoid of content. In many cases, CG graphics are used to convey information. These graphics are generated completely by computer, with no photos or other added items. For instance, a graphic accompanying a story about a sporting event might list the individuals, teams or countries leading the competition. The example that follows shows the eight teams in the division championships leading up to the 2006 World Series.

**FIGURE
10.2a**

MLB Division Playoffs

New York Yankees vs. Detroit
Minnesota vs. Oakland
New York Mets vs. Los Angeles
San Diego vs. St. Louis

Another common use is to present telephone numbers or Web site URLs that will be useful to consumers. For instance, a graphic like this one could accompany a story about a major storm:

FIGURE
10.2b

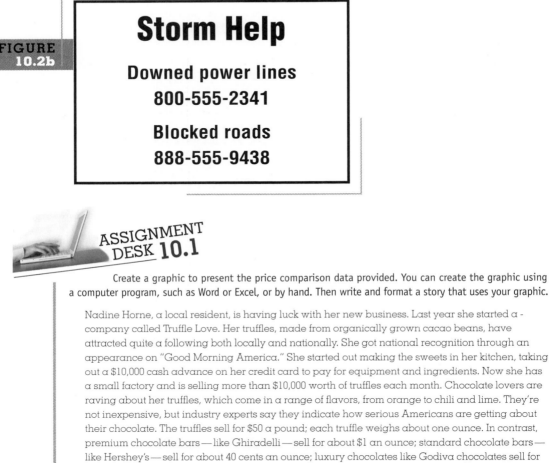

Storm Help

Downed power lines
800-555-2341

Blocked roads
888-555-9438

ASSIGNMENT DESK 10.1

Create a graphic to present the price comparison data provided. You can create the graphic using a computer program, such as Word or Excel, or by hand. Then write and format a story that uses your graphic.

Nadine Horne, a local resident, is having luck with her new business. Last year she started a company called Truffle Love. Her truffles, made from organically grown cacao beans, have attracted quite a following both locally and nationally. She got national recognition through an appearance on "Good Morning America." She started out making the sweets in her kitchen, taking out a $10,000 cash advance on her credit card to pay for equipment and ingredients. Now she has a small factory and is selling more than $10,000 worth of truffles each month. Chocolate lovers are raving about her truffles, which come in a range of flavors, from orange to chili and lime. They're not inexpensive, but industry experts say they indicate how serious Americans are getting about their chocolate. The truffles sell for $50 a pound; each truffle weighs about one ounce. In contrast, premium chocolate bars — like Ghiradelli — sell for about $1 an ounce; standard chocolate bars — like Hershey's — sell for about 40 cents an ounce; luxury chocolates like Godiva chocolates sell for about $2 an ounce; and the top-of-the line Godiva "G" series chocolates sell for about $7 an ounce.

CG graphics also are used to present an important phrase: a key statement from a speech, a specific charge of criminal activity or a controversial remark. Generally, such phrases need to be strong and short, usually 15 to 25 words. The exact words also should be included in the story that the anchor reads, not only to reinforce the importance of the phrase but also to let people who are not watching the screen get the key idea. For example, when news broke about a Dutch television reality show in which a terminally ill woman was to choose a recipient for one of her kidneys (the "reality" turned out to be a hoax), an Italian newspaper was among many media outlets criticizing the program. A quote from the paper could have been used to create a CG graphic:

FIGURE
10.2c

"**Desperation becomes a spectacle in the**

Netherlands"—Italian newspaper

Del Corriere Della Sera

That quote packs a punch and makes a nice CG graphic to air while the anchor read the story.

Occasionally, a CG graphic of a phrase is combined with a photo of the person who said it, but mixing photos and text greatly restricts the amount of text that can be used.

ASSIGNMENT
DESK **10.2**

Create a graphic to present the best quote in the material provided. Then write and format a story that incorporates your graphic.

Grace Sherwood, a resident of Virginia, was convicted 300 years ago this week of being a witch. Sherwood, a midwife who at times dressed as a man, lived in what today is the rural area of Pungo. She became known as the Witch of Pungo. She was brought to court several times on charges of witchcraft. In her final case, she was accused of using her powers to cause a neighbor woman to miscarry. On the day of her death, Sherwood, 46, was dropped into the Lynnhaven River and floated—proof she was guilty because the pure water cast out her evil spirit, according to the belief system of the time. In a ceremony before this morning's reenactment of Sherwood's trial by water, Sherwood was formally exonerated. Mayor Meyera Oberndorf read aloud a letter from Gov. Timothy Kaine exonerating Sherwood.

"Today, I am pleased to officially restore the good name of Grace Sherwood," Kaine wrote in the letter. "With 300 years of hindsight, we all certainly can agree that trial by water is an injustice. We also can celebrate the fact that a woman's equality is constitutionally protected today, and women have the freedom to pursue their hopes and dreams."

On rare occasions, the only graphic available at deadline might be one that depicts an unfamiliar person or subject, with no superimposed text. In such a case, the writer needs to ensure that viewers will be able to identify the subject of the graphic as soon as it appears. Viewers should not have to wait to find out who or what they are looking at.

When a graphic shows a person, the story can identify that person simply by naming him or her as the graphic appears. For example, here's how a writer would handle a story in which a graphic of a newly elected governor appears partway into the story. Most viewers would have recognized the governor, but they might not be able to identify him:

Anchor on camera:	((On Cam)) A GROUP OF DOCTORS IS BACKING A MEDICAL MALPRACTICE REFORM BILL PASSED LAST WEEK. EVEN THOUGH THEY DO NOT BELIEVE THE BILL IS PERFECT, THEY THINK IT SHOULD BECOME LAW.
Anchor with OTS graphic of governor:	((OTS)) GOVERNOR WASHINGTON HAS SAID HE PLANS TO VETO THE BILL, BECAUSE IT CALLS FOR A TAX INCREASE TO COVER THE BILL'S COSTS.

Notice that the writer doesn't have to specifically explain that the graphic is a photo of the governor. Mentioning his name when his picture appears does the job. (Technical note: The left-hand column of the script shows just one of many ways to indicate an over-the-shoulder graphic. Another common method is to use the anchor's initials followed by a slash, the word *box*, a colon and a brief description of the graphic (for example, *JS/Box: Governor*.)

When a photo of a less familiar person appears, the writer has to be more obvious. If the Cindy Sheehan story discussed previously did not identify her with CG text, the writer could handle identification like this:

Anchor on camera:	((On Cam)) THE FACE OF THE ANTIWAR MOVEMENT SAYS SHE IS ENDING HER CAMPAIGN AGAINST THE WAR IN IRAQ.
Anchor with OTS graphic of Cindy Sheehan:	((OTS)) CINDY SHEEHAN...SHOWN HERE AT A RECENT ANTIWAR PROTEST...ATTRACTED NATIONAL ATTENTION WHEN SHE SET UP A PROTEST CAMP OUTSIDE PRESIDENT BUSH'S TEXAS HOME IN 2005. HER SON WAS KILLED IN IRAQ IN 2004. SHEEHAN SAYS SHE HAD HOPED THINGS WOULD CHANGE WHEN DEMOCRATS TOOK CONTROL OF CONGRESS...BUT NOW FEELS THERE IS NO POSSIBILITY THAT THE WAR WILL END SOON.

Similarly, a graphic that shows an unfamiliar product, place or other subject needs to be specifically tied to the written report:

Anchor on camera:	((On Cam)) TRAFFIC IS BACK TO NORMAL IN DOWNTOWN TARRYTOWN…AFTER A MANHOLE EXPLODED THERE THIS MORNING.
Anchor with OTS graphic of scene of explosion:	((OTS)) THE EXPLOSION HAPPENED AT THE INTERSECTION OF MAIN STREET AND PENNSYLVANIA AVENUE SHORTLY BEFORE 9 THIS MORNING. UTILITY CREWS HAVE SURROUNDED THE MANHOLE WITH TRAFFIC CONES AND ARE REPAIRING DAMAGE TO UNDERGROUND CABLES. NO ONE WAS HURT IN THE EXPLOSION.

ASSIGNMENT DESK 10.3

Write a 30-second video reader based on the following information. At 10 seconds into the story, a graphic of Castlewood State Park will appear OTS; identify this graphic as it appears.

A group of about 50 youngsters with the local chapter of Dream Center, an interdenominational church, celebrated a volunteer appreciation day with a barbecue and swimming in Castlewood State Park yesterday. During the festivities, one of the children jumped into the Merriman River to swim. When he became caught in the undertow, five other children jumped in to rescue him. All six of the children then were swept away in the river. The children were between 9 and 15 years old, and their parents said all of them could swim.

Rescuers were called to the scene and managed to pull the children from the water. Rescue workers were hampered by inconsistent reports about how many children were missing, said Becky Haskamp, a dispatcher for the state Water Patrol. Two of the children were still alive, but one died in the hospital during the night last night, Haskamp said. She said the only survivor remained in the hospital today, but she had no details on the child's identity or condition.

"It was just so sad," Panus said. "The group was out there for a good cause, not drinking or getting stoned. It's just a tragedy."

The Voice-Over

Only slightly more complicated than the video reader is the **voice-over**. Also called a voicer or VO, this type of story typically runs under 45 seconds and incorporates video that plays while an announcer reads the story. The video usually begins after the first few lines of the story are read so that the announcer can set up the clip. Typically the video is played without audio, although in some cases the background sound—called natural sound and abbreviated NATS—may be played at a low volume to create a mood.

Just as with background graphics, this type of video typically plays in the background without any explicit mention. For instance, a news report on a 17 percent drop in the stock price of the Krispy Kreme Doughnut company—following allegations that the company padded shipments to hide declining sales over a two-year period—was read over video footage of workers and customers at a Krispy Kreme location. Footage like this, often referred to as **wallpaper**, does not add any specific information to the story; in fact, it would be nearly impossible to find video footage that explains a story such as this. What the footage does instead is to add visual interest to a report that would otherwise be a fairly straightforward and dry story.

A little more useful than wallpaper is **generic VO** (also known as **cover video** or **B-roll**). This refers to video that provides some information about the story, relieving the writer of having to include all that information. For example, when unseasonably warm weather settled over the East Coast one recent January, video of people bicycling, running and picnicking played while the announcer related the specifics of the warm spell: what was causing it, what records were being broken, and how long it was supposed to last. Viewers were able to gather more information from the video—for instance, that people were taking advantage of the warm spell to bicycle, run and picnic.

When working with generic VO, stories usually work best when they are written loosely, that is with time for the announcer to pause and let the viewer learn from the visuals. Nonstop chatter can interfere with the viewer absorbing the visual information.

Choosing Video and Graphics

News Pointers

To make the most of video news stories, the writer needs to pick video clips that are useful, not just thrown in as eye candy. Indiscriminate use of worthless video may confuse or disorient viewers rather than help them gain a better understanding of the story.

Video should accomplish one of the following objectives:

- *Show action:* Lets viewers see for themselves what has happened. Such shots are important for dramatic or confusing stories.
- *Create a mood:* Used in feature stories to give the viewer a sense of the atmosphere of a place or event.
- *Connect a name with a face:* Shows a person in the news to bring the story to life.

Sometimes video is not available, either because no footage exists or the story is more of an issue story that does not lend itself to video. CG graphics generally are used in those circumstances. Some basic guidelines for creating graphics:

- Simple graphics with bold lines work best.

- Text should be large, kept to a minimum and clearly contrasted with the background: white text on dark backgrounds, black text on light backgrounds. Use no more than five lines containing 15 characters or less each.
- Complex backgrounds call for simple text and other foreground elements; more ornate foreground elements require simple backgrounds.
- Colors should be kept to a minimum, with multiple shades of a few colors rather than a large number of different colors.
- For conventional television broadcasting, highly saturated colors should be avoided. As one guide explains: "NTSC video is notorious for its poor ability to handle bright, saturated colors. The rich reds and magentas that look great on a computer screen will bleed, flicker, and generally look awful on a TV monitor."[4] PhotoShop includes an NTSC filter to "legalize" graphics for broadcast.
- Graphic elements should be kept well away from the edges, which may cut off when they are displayed on broadcast television.

Video footage sometimes includes details that the viewer needs to pay close attention to. In such cases, the story should refer to those details. Those references have to occur at exactly the right moment. Otherwise, the announcer will be asking viewers to look at something that either has already been shown or has not yet aired. The only way to prevent such embarrassing moments is by having the announcer time the story to the video before the story is aired, then watch a feed of the video as the story is presented live. That allows the announcer to adjust his or her speed to keep the story and video synchronized.

Here's an example of a voice-over that incorporates an informative video clip:

Anchor on camera:	((On Cam)) FINALLY TONIGHT, A COLORADO MAN BUILT HIS DREAM BOAT.
	BUT HE NEEDED A LITTLE HELP GETTING IT OUT OF HIS YARD.
TAKE VO	((VO)) ED KENNEDY WORKED ON HIS 32-FOOT SAILBOAT IN HIS BACKYARD FOR THE LAST 10 YEARS.
	EVENTUALLY HE REALIZED IT WAS TOO BIG TO MOVE.
	SO A LOCAL CRANE COMPANY CAME IN AND LIFTED THE SAILBOAT RIGHT OVER HIS HOUSE.
	NEIGHBORS SAID IT WAS THE MOST EXCITING THING TO EVER HAPPEN IN THE AREA.
	KENNEDY PUT 67-THOUSAND DOLLARS INTO BUILDING THE BOAT.
	AND NOW THAT IT'S OUT OF HIS BACKYARD…HE PLANS ON SAILING IT AROUND THE WORLD.

(Reprinted with permission, Copyright 2007, The Christian Broadcasting Network Inc.)

Creating Visual Sequences

Voice-overs generally contain more than one shot. Short clips are joined together to help tell the story visually. In that respect, the voice-over—and other video news story formats we'll cover in future chapters—is a form of photojournalism.

Creating effective visual sequences demands close attention to several basic rules:

- *Lead with the best video.* The first footage shown should be thought of as the "lead" of the sequence: that is, the material most likely to get the message across quickly and capture audience attention. Therefore, the most compelling video should be used upfront.

- *Emphasize variety.* While close-ups work best on television, medium shots and wide shots help create variety and heighten interest (see Figure 10.3). For stories that will be used exclusively online, however, most shots should be close-ups. In addition, panning should be kept to a minimum online. Variations in camera angle also help; not every shot should be from the same perspective. Similarly, clips should run for different lengths of time, with more interesting and informative shots getting more screen time.
- *Watch the logical structure.* The visual story should follow the same rules as the spoken story, with shots from different times and places carefully placed in the proper order.

ASSIGNMENT DESK **10.4**

Materials for more Assignment Desks for this chapter are available at the book Web site: www.mycommkit.com

News Pointers

Using Video News Releases

With ongoing budget cuts, many newsrooms have found themselves with a skeleton crew of reporters. Given that situation, video news writers often succumb to the temptation to use **video news releases (VNR).** These video versions of standard news releases are prepared by companies, organizations or government agencies.

Some VNRs provide insider or behind-the-scenes footage that can offer viewers a glimpse into things they otherwise would not see. The slickest come prepackaged with introductions and endings (known as **intros** and **outcues**) handled by "reporters" hired by the producers.

As one critic notes:

One of the stealthiest marketing tools ever created, the VNR is heat-and-serve coverage, a fully polished news segment created by PR professionals to be seamlessly blended into local and national broadcasts. As long as it looks like news, acts like news, and smells like news, stations have no problem running the piece as their own.

The publicists, unlike the rest of us, enjoy having their work stolen without credit.[5] And stolen it is. One 2003 survey reported that "100% of stations polled said they use VNRs. We spoke with ABC, NBC, CBS and Fox affiliates in top 40 markets and while the frequency of VNR usage varied, not a single station said they do not use outside produced video."[6]

The important thing for journalists to remember about video news releases is that they always have something to sell or a cause to advocate. When journalists fail to identify the source of the footage or to identify the reporters as hired outsiders, they abdicate their responsibility to provide honest and accurate information to the public, a move that will ultimately cost them respect.

Identifying the source of video news releases is just the start, however. Because the material contained in video news releases is one-sided, reporters must make every possible effort to explore other aspects of and opinions on the story.

Recent news reports have raised the issue of government agencies improperly using video news releases to advance the agendas of those in power. In one case, several local television newscasts ran a story by Mike Morris that detailed a new White House ad campaign on the dangers of drug abuse. However, viewers were not told that Morris was not a journalist and that his report was produced by the government. An investigation by the Government Accountability Office resulted in the finding that the report constituted illegal "covert propaganda."

For the second time in a year, the GAO reprimanded the administration for distributing the phony prepackaged news reports "that include a 'suggested live intro' for anchors to read, interviews

FIGURE 10.3

Variety is important in video storytelling. A close-up shot works very differently from a medium shot. For stories to be delivered online, close-ups usually dominate.

with Washington officials and a closing that mimics a typical broadcast news sign off."[7] (The other instance, a few months earlier, concerned the Medicare drug bill.) Using tax money to influence public opinion in this way violates federal law.

Responding to the first of those two cases, the board of directors of the Association of Health Care Journalists requested that the practice be stopped. The board's statement explained:

> Viewers expect that anyone identified as a reporter is a journalist employed by a news organization. In this case, the so-called reporter was working for a public relations firm hired by a government agency. We find that misidentification unacceptable.
>
> The Association of Health Care Journalists calls on all news organizations to preserve their journalistic independence by avoiding the use of such video news releases. We warn the public to question the integrity of any such message.[8]

The Public Relations Society of America supports the use of video news releases by its members but has adopted a series of principles for producing and distributing them:

1. Organizations that produce VNRs should clearly identify the VNR as such and fully disclose who produced and paid for it at the time the VNR is provided to TV stations.

2. PRSA recommends that organizations that prepare VNRs should not use the word "reporting" if the narrator is not a reporter.

3. Use of VNRs or footage provided by sources other than the station or network should be identified as to source by the media outlet when it is aired.[9]

The Radio and Television News Directors Association offers similar recommendations:

- If this video/audio is available in no other way but through corporate release...then managers should decide what value using the video/audio brings to the newscast, and if that value outweighs the possible appearance of "product placement" or commercial interests.

- News managers and producers should clearly disclose the origin of information and label all material provided by corporate or other non-editorial sources.

- [M]anagers and producers should ask questions regarding whether the editorial process behind the story is in concert with those used in the newsroom. Some questions to ask include whether more than one side is included, if there is a financial agenda to releasing the story, and if the viewers and/or listeners would believe this is work done locally by your team.[10]

Conclusion

Video news stories offer journalists a wide range of creative opportunities to inform the audience. Graphics and video clips can bring stories to life in a way that other media cannot. But with those benefits come potential problems in preserving the language, selecting useful visuals and avoiding the temptation to use prepackaged stories.

KEY TERMS

B-roll (or cover video, generic VO), 188
CG graphics, 181
character generator, 181
cover video, 188
full screen (FS), 179
generic VO, 188
intro, 190

outcue, 190
over the shoulder (OTS), 179
super, 181
TV speak, 182
video news release (VNR), 190
voice-over (or voicer, VO), 187
wallpaper, 188

DISCUSSION QUESTIONS

1. Record and watch a half-hour television newscast. Keep a list of the types of stories used. What percentage are video readers? What percentage are voice-overs? Does the video used in the voice-overs help tell the stories?

2. Now watch the newscast again, this time looking at how graphics are used. What percentage are OTS graphics? What percentage are FS graphics? How useful are the graphics in telling the stories and increasing comprehension?

NOTES

1. John Hewitt, "Air Words: Writing for Broadcast News" (New York: McGraw-Hill, 2002), p. 49.

2. Tom Phillips, excerpt of interview with The NewsHour with Jim Lehrer, 27 June 2001, **www.pbs.org/newshour/media/verb/phillips.html.**

3. Phillips.

4. Sonja Schenk, "Making a DVD Video Portfolio: Onscreen Menus," CreativePro.com, 15 April 2002, **www.creativepro.com/story/feature/16286-3.html.**

5. "The Sell-a-Vision News," Abusedbythenews.com, 22 March 2004, **www.abusedbythenews.com/columns/col003.htm.**

6. Larry Saperstein and Barbara Kelly-Gutjahr, "VNR Usage Remains High," WestGlen News, August 2003,

www.westglen.com/pr_news/westglenaug03.html#larry.

7. Ceci Connolly, "Drug Control Office Faulted for Issuing Fake News Tapes," Washington Post, 7 January 2005, p. A17.

8. "Journalists Cry Foul," 17 March 2004, Association of Health Care Journalists, **www.ahcj.umn.edu/files/AHCJ%20statement_HHS_VNRs_FINAL.pdf.**

9. Statement of the Public Relations Society of America (PRSA) on Video News Releases (VNRs), **www.prsa.org/_News/leaders/vnrs0404.asp.**

10. "RTNDA Guidelines for Use of Non-editorial Video and Audio," April 2005, **http://rtnda.org/foi/finalvnr.shtml.**

Chapter 11

Writing the Advanced Video Story

For most types of news stories, the writer's words do the majority of the work. But when it comes to advanced video stories, it is the audio, video and graphic elements that work the hardest. Those elements dictate the structure of the story as well as the actual words the news writer will craft. In this chapter, we will explore the most common types of advanced video stories and emerging video story forms for online delivery. We will also look at shifts in the job of the video news writer.

Using Sound Bites

The fundamental building block of advanced television news is the **sound bite**. Like an actuality, a bite is used to let viewers hear words just as they come from the source's mouth. A bite—also called an **SOT** (variously pronounced "ess-oh-tee" or "soht"), for sound on tape—can lend authority, variety and emotion to a story. Like an audio actuality, a bite should *not* merely repeat words from the script. Rather, a bite should be used to emphasize key points of a story or present opinions on the events.

A bite typically runs from five to 10 seconds. Bites usually are not used on their own, but rather in the middle of related video. This common structure is called a **VO-SOT** or **VO-SOT-VO**. That is, as the story begins an anchor reads a script over top of video (VO), then pauses for a sound bite (SOT), and finishes by reading over a final video segment (the other VO). A VO-SOT-VO typically runs from 30 seconds to a minute, but the range is from as little as 15 seconds or as long as several minutes. Here's an example of a VO-SOT-VO:

Anchor on camera:	((On Cam)) THE WEATHER MAY HAVE PLAYED A ROLE IN A FIRE THAT DESTROYED A MOBILE HOME IN WESTMORELAND COUNTY.
//VO// CG: Ligonier Twp./Westmoreland County	(VO) THIS BLAZE BROKE OUT AROUND 11 IN THE MORNING AT THIS MOBILE HOME IN LIGONIER TOWNSHIP. THE FIREFIGHTERS HAD TROUBLE GETTING UP THE SNOW-COVERED DIRT DRIVEWAY. THEY HAD TO USE A FOUR-WHEEL DRIVE VEHICLE TO GET TO THE HOUSE. FIREFIGHTERS THEN USED HOSES FROM PUMPER TRUCKS AT THE BOTTOM OF THE DRIVEWAY.
//SOT// //Larry Shew/Neighbor//	(SOT) IN: "They had enough pumper trucks. It's just that trailers go up fast. By the time they got there, it was fully engulfed in flames." RUNS: 11
//VO//	(VO) 37-YEAR-OLD DONALD HOOPER WAS INJURED IN THAT FIRE. HE IS BEING TREATED FOR BURNS. A FEMALE RESIDENT ESCAPED UNHARMED. (Used with permission of Mark Barash, Station Manager, Pittsburgh Cable News Channel.)

Notice that instead of providing only an outcue (as an audio script would), the VO-SOT script provides the entire contents of the bite. This is done so that closed captioning can be provided for those with hearing disabilities. Also note that the time of the SOT is designated right after it. (For rare occasions when an SOT runs more than a minute, its length is designated this way: 1:15.) Finally, notice how instructions are added to place computer graphics (CG) over the video images.

Technically, writing a VO-SOT is not much different from writing a VO. One key distinction, however, is that timing is even more critical. The SOT should begin while the anchor is still delivering the VO, not start several seconds after the anchor finishes. For that reason, many writers keep the copy to a minimum before the SOT. That way, various reading speeds, mistakes, and so on won't make much difference in the time at which the anchor arrives at the beginning of the bite. (In practice, SOTs generally are kept separate from other video clips, so they can be started when the anchor gets to the correct spot in the story.)

Storytelling for Television News

In comparison with shorter video stories, the SO-VOT offers more of a chance to tell a story. To accomplish that, the video writer should follow some basic ground rules:

Try to find a new angle. In today's always-on world of news coverage, it can be hard to break through all the clutter. The video story writer's mission should be to find a fresh angle on each story so that viewers will stop what they're doing and pay attention. Whether a story focuses on a car crash, a city council meeting or a campus march, the writer should be able to find a unique aspect to make it stand out. One way to do this is by looking for contrasts. At a time when motorists are griping about rising gasoline prices, for example, a writer might focus on drivers who are still buying the biggest gas guzzlers—or focus on people who have given up on driving in favor of bicycling, skating or walking. Another strategy is to look for small stories within bigger ones. For instance, when assigned to cover a major event, many writers look for one fascinating small story that is part of the event.

Look for a person or people to wrap the story around. Typically, the best way to find those small stories is by focusing on individual characters. When Hurricane Katrina ripped through the southern United States in 2005, it was the small stories of individuals coping with loss and tragedy—and others reaching out to help in any way they could—that proved to be much more powerful than the "big" stories about infrastructure loss and rebuilding efforts. Journalists need to remember that people are most interested in other people, and every story ultimately affects people. The writer's job is to find those people and tell their stories. In his book "It Takes More Than Good Looks . . ." Wayne Freedman offers a simple formula for good television storytelling: "Find a person. Tell a story. Weave the facts of the news inside of it."[1]

Make sure every story contains emotional content. One reason personalized stories work well is that they tend to be emotionally powerful. Bringing things down to the human level lets the writer help viewers comprehend the joy, anger, fear or other emotions of those affected by or connected to a news event. Emotion lives at the heart of every story, and the writer's job is to find it and make it an integral part of each story.

Don't try to cover too many points. A writer should strive to convey one or two points in a VO-SOT. That's pretty much the limit of what can effectively be accomplished in a short television news story. If a story contains more than two major points—a rare occurrence—the writer must carefully consider all of them and choose only the best two. Viewers can't grasp more than that in a short period of time.

Carefully craft a story structure. Good television news stories are first and foremost stories, and therefore require attention to narrative structure. The beginning of every story should pique the viewer's interest, the middle should develop the theme, and the ending should leave a strong impression. When everything wraps up, viewers should feel satisfied that they have just digested a full meal, not merely ingested some morsels.

ASSIGNMENT DESK **11.1**

Assignment Desk exercises for this chapter are available at the book Web site: www.mycommkit.com.

The Package

While the VO-SOT format works well for most news events, a story deemed particularly interesting or important may be upgraded to a **package**, a prerecorded self-contained story filed by a reporter. Packages run from as little as 90 seconds to as long as 10 minutes.

Packages dominate video news. That's because more than any other type of video story, they provide the writer a chance to incorporate all the makings of a great story: good script, video and bites, all in one.

A package contains elements from two categories:

- *Reporter narration:* Because a package is assembled in the field, a reporter rather than an anchor handles narration. The narration is split among three or more tracks that join together the field elements.
- *Field elements:* These are the bits and pieces that are gathered in the field—B-roll video, bites, natural sound, and so on. Another field element is the stand-up, in which the reporter appears on camera while delivering part of the narration. Although stand-ups can be placed anywhere within a package, they most commonly are positioned not at the beginning or end but somewhere in between, where they connect two pieces of video—hence their designation as **bridges**. Stand-ups are most useful when they allow the reporter to point out relevant locations or other details of a story (see Figure 11.1).

Planning and Gathering Materials for a Package

Because of the length and complexity of packages, they require more planning than other video stories. Generally speaking, the steps in assembling a package are:

1. Start planning the package as soon as possible. Draw up a list of video shots needed to create sequences and serve as B-roll.
2. Make a list of people who should be interviewed. Look for sources who represent various viewpoints, and look for people who are directly affected. Veteran TV reporter Charles Raiteri recommends that every story contain one "real person"—somebody who is affected by the situation—and one or more officials who can provide a broader perspective.[2]

It's important for a video reporter to not just keep an eye on the scene but to listen carefully to what is happening, as well.

3. Consider locations for shooting stand-ups. The locations should make visual sense. In a story about runaway housing development, for example, one logical place for a stand-up is a construction site.

4. Begin preparing the package as soon as interviewing and shooting are wrapped up. The drive back to the studio offers a great opportunity to begin prep work. Some video news writers use a portable audio recorder to let them review their interviews and select the most promising sound bites before they arrive at the studio for video editing.

5. Review the video and select the best background video and bites. The best video will generally determine how the package begins: The strongest video should open the package.

6. Select bridges, using both natural sound and stand-ups.

7. Write the narration to fill in any gaps. Resist the temptation to write long stretches of narration. Let the pictures tell the story.

Structuring a Package

Once the package is complete, there is still work to do before it's finished. Generally, a package opens with a lead-in to be read by the anchor. The lead-in sets up the package, but it should *not* give away the story. In addition to introducing the story, the lead-in can provide updates on any information that changed since the package was created: casualties, arrests, and so on. Including such details in the package itself could render it out of date by airtime. Further, the lead-in allows the anchor to identify the reporter who will provide the voice-over in the opening section of the package.

Next comes the package itself. While packages vary from story to story, it helps to think of each one as having a beginning, middle and ending:

- The beginning most often consists of a voice-over running on top of the best video. Sometimes the natural sounds of the video play under the reporter's voice. The opening typically focuses on recent events that will draw viewers' interest. Background information should be kept to a minimum and placed later in the opening or in the closing voice-over.
- The middle consists of one or more interviews, event footage (with or without the reporter's voice-over narration), and other pertinent video. This section may include one or more stand-up bridges. These tracks often echo some of the wording of the bites that lead into them.
- The ending is where the reporter signs off, either in a stand-up or in a voice-over. Often, the ending looks to the future: What's likely to happen next. In other cases, it serves as a place to stick any information that did not fit into the story up to that point.

Once the package is finished, the anchor reads a **tag**, a line or two that wraps up what the reporter has said and works to make the anchor seem like he or she is also on top of the story (see Figure 11.2).

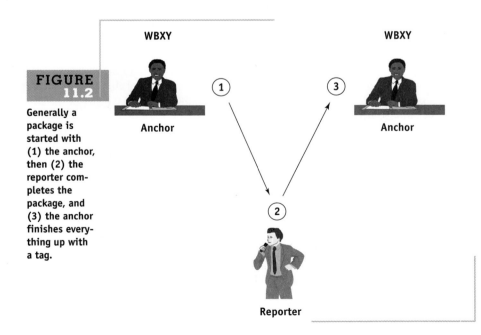

FIGURE 11.2

Generally a package is started with (1) the anchor, then (2) the reporter completes the package, and (3) the anchor finishes everything up with a tag.

WBXY

Anchor

① ③

WBXY

Anchor

②

Reporter

Here's a good example of a package. It begins with a lead-in read by the anchor in the studio:

Anchor on camera:	((On Cam)) A LOCAL MOTHER-TO-BE FOUND OUT JUST HOW LARGE HER EXTENDED FAMILY IS TODAY. MARY JO EBO'S (EE-BO) HUSBAND IS A MARINE IN IRAQ… BUT AS ABC 2'S JENNY ATWATER SHOWS US—SHE KNOWS SHE WON'T BE ALONE WHEN THE BABY COMES. (PKG)

And now the package itself. Notice the format differs from anchor-read copy, using just a single column:

//NATS of Mary Jo Ebo greeting people//
IT'S NOT USUAL BABY SHOWER PROTOCOL THAT YOU MEET YOUR GUESTS FOR THE FIRST TIME THE DAY OF THE PARTY.
BUT FIRST-TIME MOM-TO-BE MARY JO EBO'S STORY IS DIFFERENT.

//SOT//
(Sue Updike/Doula)
"She's wonderful, she's an amazing, amazing woman. She's very strong."

EBO'S HUSBAND WAS DEPLOYED TO IRAQ IN AUGUST…SOON AFTER FINDING OUT HIS WIFE WAS PREGNANT.

//SOT//
(Mary Jo Ebo)
"We had our first pregnancy in January of 2002 and four miscarriages later…we found out we were pregnant."

BOTH ARE MUSIC TEACHERS AT GILMAN SCHOOL. NEITHER HAS FAMILY IN TOWN.

//NATS of guests//
"I wouldn't have missed it!"

BUT NOW MARY JO IS CONVINCED SHE DOES.

//SOT//
(Mary Jo Ebo)
"For someone else to recognize what we're going through on a day-to-day basis is just overwhelming."

THIS BABY SHOWER AT GREATER BALTIMORE MEDICAL CENTER…CAME INTO BEING THROUGH A PROGRAM CALLED OPERATION SPECIAL DELIVERY…A PROGRAM THAT PROVIDES FREE DOULA SERVICES FOR PREGNANT WOMEN WHOSE HUSBANDS ARE OVERSEAS.

//SOT//
(Sue Updike/Doula)
"It's very difficult. Many of them are out of state, they have no family in state and no real support services. We provide support through phone or e-mail and then we're there for the deliveries."

MARY JO SAYS WHILE SHE MISSES HER HUSBAND…

//SOT//
(Mary Jo Ebo)
"Ken's words are the best, he'd rather be gone and have a baby than be here and not have a baby."

BESIDES, HER NEW FRIENDS HAVE GIVEN HER A MINIATURE STAND-IN…

//NATS of guests//
"Special response team!"

IN BALTIMORE COUNTY, JENNY ATWATER, ABC2NEWS.

To close the story, the following tag is read while a full-screen graphic appears:

Anchor on camera:	((On Cam)) MARY JO EBO IS DUE IN JUST A FEW WEEKS…NO WORD ON WHEN HER HUSBAND MIGHT MAKE IT HOME TO MEET THE BABY. (WMAR-TV)

Tags often provide contact information or a Web site URL for viewers who want more information on a topic. For instance, the tag for this story could have gone something like this:

Anchor with OTS graphic GBMC Web site URL	((OTS)) FOR MORE INFORMATION ON OPERATION SPECIAL DELIVERY, VISIT THE GREATER BALTIMORE MEDICAL CENTER'S WEB SITE AT WWW.GBMC.ORG.

Basic Package Formats

Every package includes a unique mix of elements. The mark of a good video writer is blending those elements to best tell the story.

Nevertheless, many stories can be successfully presented in one of two common formats identified by former television news reporter and producer John Hewitt in his book "Air Words": the altered chronology model and the particular to general model.

The Altered Chronology Model

Many breaking news stories are handled with the **altered chronology model**. After the lead-in, the package begins with a description of the present events, segues into relevant details of the past, and then looks ahead to the future. If the story includes any controversial aspects, they fall between the past and future sections. Bites usually run only five to 10 seconds. Here's an example:

//SOT//
(Protesters)
"Ehrlich says death, we say no!" (:03)
A LITTLE MORE THAN A WEEK BEFORE CONVICTED MURDERER VERNON EVANS COULD BE PUT TO DEATH…

(NATS of protest)
A RALLY TO ASK GOVERNOR EHRLICH TO GRANT HIM LIFE.

//SOT//
(Protesters)
"There has to be another way…"(:03)
VERNON EVANS HAS SPENT MORE THAN 20 YEARS ON DEATH ROW FOR THE 1983 MURDERS OF TWO PIKESVILLE MOTEL CLERKS. DAVID PIECHOWICZ AND SUSAN KENNEDY WERE SHOT TO DEATH IN THE LOBBY OF THE WARREN HOUSE MOTEL…
EVANS' FAMILY SAYS HE WAS NOT THE SHOOTER.

//SOT//
(Gwen Evans, sister)
"He didn't have fancy lawyers, the evidence is right there in the court documents that proves he was nowhere near that hotel at the time of those shootings…" (:08)
GWEN EVANS TRIED TO DELIVER A LETTER TO THE GOVERNOR TODAY, BUT HIS OFFICE IS CLOSED. SHE SAYS THEY WANT HIM TO REVIEW THE CASE…

//SOT//
(Gwen Evans, sister)
"We're asking him to take five minutes out of his busy schedule to review the tape that his family and I have for him to review." (:08)

(REPORTER STAND-UP)
VERNON EVANS' ATTORNEYS HAVE ALSO ASKED A FEDERAL JUDGE TO DELAY HIS EXECUTION ON THE BASIS THAT MARYLAND'S METHOD OF EXECUTION BY LETHAL INJECTION IS UNCONSTITUTIONAL IN THIS CASE.

(WMAR-TV)

The Particular to General Model

The particular to general model is useful for covering trend stories or others that have widespread effects. This structure—also known as **personalization**—requires the writer to find an individual who exemplifies the situation. The piece begins with that person's story, pulls back to discuss the general trend, covers any controversy, looks at likely future effects or events, and then returns to the individual. Here's an example that begins with a lead-in read by the anchor in the studio:

Anchor on camera:	Anchor on camera: ((On Cam)) The key to understanding the next generation of college graduates may come from taking a closer look at what they consider trash.
Rollcue to pkg: "students leave behind"	As News Channel 8's Suzy Conway shows us now…it may be earning them the title "the throwaway culture."
Total Run Time: 1:30	//Take pkg//

It then moves to the package itself:

//NATS of packing boxes//
FOR PENN STATE STUDENT SARAH SMITH, IT'S AN UNAVOIDABLE SPRING RITUAL…

//NATS of packing tape//
PACKING UP A DORM ROOM'S WORTH OF STUFF WHEN IT'S TIME TO HEAD HOME FOR THE SUMMER…

//SOT//
(Sarah Smith/Junior)
"What am I going to do with all of this? It makes me want to throw some of it away!"

IF SMITH DOES DECIDE TO TOSS THE CLOTHES SHE CAN'T FIT IN HER BOXES, SHE WON'T BE ALONE.

//NATS of refrigerator door shutting//
TAKE A LOOK AT THIS HALLWAY IN HER DORM…REFRIGERATORS…COMPUTERS… COUCHES…CLOTHES…ALL LEFT BEHIND BY PREVIOUS OWNERS…

//SOT//
(John Paker/Resident Assistant)
"It happens this way every year. Students don't care about their things. They just leave them behind as trash."

(REPORTER STAND-UP)
AND IT'S NOT JUST HAPPENING ON THE PENN STATE CAMPUS. EACH SUMMER AT COLLEGES ACROSS THE COUNTRY, STUDENTS TURN THEIR DORMS INTO JUNKYARDS…

//SOT//
(Fred Pebbles/Association of College Housing)
"Students these days live in much more of a throwaway culture. They'll leave behind things in perfectly good condition because they know they can get the newest, updated version next fall."

//NATS of loading items onto cart//
BUT NOT EVERYONE SEES IT AS TRASH. THESE PENN STATE STUDENTS ARE COLLECTING WHAT'S SALVAGEABLE TO DONATE TO CHARITY.

//SOT//
(Parker)
"I found a couch in perfect condition, not to mention a microwave that looked like it had barely been used. We donate it all to charity."

//NATS of car door slamming//
THIS YEAR...

//SOT//
(Smith)
"That's the last of it."

SMITH MANAGED TO PACK IT ALL...

//shots of hallway full of junk//
UNLIKE SO MANY OF HER CLASSMATES...
AT PENN STATE, SUZY CONWAY, NEWS CHANNEL 8.

To close the story, the anchor takes over again, reading the following tag:

Anchor on camera	((On Cam)) Last year...students on the Penn State campus raised more than 50-thousand dollars for the United Way by selling more than 66 tons of stuff students left behind.

Creating Online Video News Stories

The types of video stories we have discussed so far—video readers, voice-overs, VO-SOT-VOs and packages—were developed for television broadcast. Unfortunately, many television stations and networks looking for a quick way to build an online presence have posted these types of stories to their Web sites without considering whether they work in the online environment. Even worse, newspapers and other non-television news organizations have largely followed that example, essentially creating "TV on the Web."

In all of those cases, the result has been video stories that fail to harness the power of the online medium. Travis Fox, the Washington Post video journalist who won the first

Emmy in the Web-video category, says, "A lot of time when people think of video on the Web they think of TV—which I don't think works at all."[3]

Mike Clemente, executive producer of ABC News Now, which streams about 14 hours of video each day, agrees. "We don't just do straight TV on the Web. Why would you watch something in linear form when you could choose the order?" Clemente said. "If I have a VCR from 25 years ago I can do that too. I just don't think doing straight TV on the Web makes sense."[4]

So what does make sense? The ground rules are simple, according to writer Kurt Anderson: "Don't do Web video if you don't have anything interesting to *show*, and don't compete with TV unless you can do something they can't or won't. In other words, *use* the medium."[5] Following those rules would eliminate video clips in which reporters simply read their text stories, as well as those in which editors interview writers. In both of those examples, the video stories are in no way superior to text stories. In fact, by requiring more of the viewers' time and offering less control, they are worse.

Adrian Monck, who has worked as a broadcast journalist and executive with CBS News, ITN and Sky News, offers four suggestions for creating online video on his blog (www.adrianmonck.blogspot.com):

1. *No newscasters.* While using a newscaster makes sense in complex TV studio broadcasts, Monck says there is no need for newscasters in the online video environment.
2. *Make sense.* "Reporters need to deliver their own intros/lead-ins, to camera or over picture or graphics," Monck notes. "Images and clips need labeling if they're raw. The most important thing video clips online require is standalone coherence."
3. *Stick to your part of the story.* Monck argues that reporters should not try to cover every aspect of a story but instead should remember that the online environment allows them to use other means of presenting information.

Why Choose Journalism?

Early on in my television journalism career I remember sitting in a control room after a particularly strong news broadcast and saying to a colleague, "You know, this is so important and so exciting that if they didn't pay me to do this, I'd pay them!"

I had better days and worse days during my 40 years in journalism, but I never once thought differently. The privilege of being an eyewitness to history — which is what a journalist is — is a unique way to spend one's life.

I constantly tell my teenage son, "Leave a mark, make a difference." That's what journalists do . . . and they are fulfilled and have fun doing it.

ERIC OBER
Crosstown TV and former president of CBS News

4. *Get graphics.* While audio and video are great for telling stories, Monck says, graphics are important, too. "We know that people will watch short video clips online, but the conventional TV news piece is no longer the way to hack it," Monck says.[6]

Journalism educator Paul Bradshaw sees two new types of online video stories emerging:

- **Moving pictures.** Bradshaw compares these to the newspaper in the Harry Potter stories in which images are magically animated. Video is used as an illustration, "without narration but in the same way as a still image might be used."
- **The video diary.** These come in two forms:

  1. The video blog/vlog, in which a person speaks directly into a camera about events or observations. One of the most widely praised examples of this was "The Show with Zefrank" (www.zefrank.com/theshow/). Although it was not everyone's idea of news (and many would argue it was not even remotely related to journalism), the yearlong program used fast-paced editing, user content and a strong sense of identity to produce short videos that many found riveting.
  2. The personal account, in which a person being recorded by someone else talks about his or her thoughts or experiences.[7] The Associated Press, which syndicates video to about 1,200 sites, has had success with personal accounts, including an interview with the wife of one of the miners trapped when a West Virginia coal mine collapsed and another with the wife of an astronaut from the space shuttle Challenger.[8]

A third emerging type of online video—**raw feeds** of news events, usually streamed live—also can have widespread appeal. Sandy Malcolm, executive producer of CNN.com's Pipeline, which streams video 24 hours a day, has found that to be the case. "I'd say one of the most popular Pipeline experiences so far was Coretta Scott King's funeral," Malcolm said. "We had multiple camera angles, it was commercial free, there were no reporters talking over it."[9]

A fourth emerging type of worthwhile online news content is the **video news summary**, which also can work well on cell phones and other mobile devices. The Associated Press' "One-Minute World," which summarizes major news events of the day, and Reuters' "World Updates" have both proven to be popular features.[10]

Some examples of people and sites that "get" online video are:

- Travis Fox's work for the Washington Post (search "travis fox" on the home page) sets the standard for online documentary video.
- David Pogue (http://pogue.blogs.nytimes.com/) and David Carr (http://carpetbagger.blogs.nytimes.com/) of The New York Times. Pogue blends humor with technology for his informative and often hysterical take on the latest tech gadgets. Carr, in his Carpetbagger videos, produced a series of man-on-the-street and celebrity interviews that were like nothing else the Times—or pretty much any other news organization—has ever done.
- Minnesota Stories (http://mnstories.com/) employs user submissions to highlight a multitude of interesting stories "that fall through the cracks of broadcast media." (See Figure 11.3.)

FIGURE 11.3

MinnesotaStories is a highly regarded Web site that is built on user contributions.

- Ken Broo's "BrooTube" video blogs on the countdown to the Cincinnati Reds' opening day (www.wlwt.com/openingday/index.html).
- ThePittsburghChannel.com's "Links n' @" online video newscasts (www.thepittsburghchannel.com/linksnat/index.html).

Shifting Responsibilities

Creating an advanced video story was once a major team effort. In the field, a reporter/writer would be joined by a lighting person to illuminate a scene, a photojournalist to shoot the video, and an audio technician. Back in the studio, an editor would distill the best video and audio, and a producer would pull everything together. Today, however, many "teams" include only a reporter and a photojournalist, with the photojournalist often also acting as editor. In some smaller markets, even the photojournalist is dispensed with. "One-man band" reporters have to do everything by themselves.

For instance, both KRON in San Francisco and WKRN in Nashville have moved to replace video news teams with what they label **video journalists,** or **VJs.** Although many video reporters have resisted the change and criticized it as a step toward lowering quality, some VJs have embraced the new style. Dan Adams of News10 in Sacramento, Calif., for example, pushed to take on all the duties of a traditional crew: reporting, shooting video, recording sound, and editing his packages. "I feel completely energized," he told the Sacramento (Calif.) Bee. "To me, it's an extension of an artistic being. You capture these images and craft a story and... that's how I wanted it to look."[11]

The move toward VJs will be a slow and controversial one. But underlying it is an important lesson: Although writing is the key component of a video news writer's job, today's writer likely will be expected to juggle a range of tasks.

Conclusion

With careful planning and good writing, video news stories built around strong audio and video elements offer compelling ways to tell journalistic stories. The ability to write strong VO-SOT-VOs and packages and to develop online-oriented videos is becoming increasingly important in this age of multiplatform journalism. The ability to juggle multiple tasks required to create video news stories is another desirable trait for today's journalist.

KEY TERMS

altered chronology model, 201
bridge, 196
moving pictures, 205
package, 196
particular to general model
   (or personalization), 202
raw feed, 205
sound bite (or SOT), 193

stand-up, 196
tag, 198
video diary, 205
video journalist (or VJ), 203
video news summary, 205
VO-SOT (or VO-SOT-VO), 193

DISCUSSION QUESTIONS

1. Record and watch a half-hour television newscast. Keep a list of the types of stories used. What percentage are VO-SOT-VOs? What percentage are packages? Are the audio and video elements of these stories used effectively?
2. Record and watch at least two different local newscasts aired on the same day. How are the newscasts similar to one another? How do they differ from each other? Does one channel do a better job than the other in structuring stories?
3. Audiences for television news have been shrinking in recent years. Suggest at least three ideas that could help television newscasts attract more viewers.

NOTES

1. Wayne Freedman, "It Takes More Than Good Looks..." (Chicago: Bonus Books, 2003), p. 15.

2. Charles Raiteri, "Writing for Broadcast News" (Lanham, Md.: Roman & Littlefield, 2005).

3. Kurt Anderson, "You Must Be Streaming," New York Magazine, 26 February 2007, **http://nymag.com/news/imperialcity/28152/**.

4. Steve Bryant, "What Works in Online Video News" Online Journalism Review, 22 May 2006, **www.ojr.org/ojr/stories/060522bryant/index.cfm**.

5. Anderson.

6. Adrian Monck, "Online Video on UK News Sites," Adrian Monck Online, 18 February 2007, **http://adrianmonck.blogspot.com/2007/02/online-video-on-uk-news-sites.html**.

7. Paul Bradshaw, "Stop Trying to Make Television—It's Video," Online Journalism Blog, 16 February 2007, **http://onlinejournalismblog.wordpress.com/2007/02/16/stop-trying-to-make-television-its-video/**.

8. Bryant.

9. Bryant.

10. Bryant.

11. Sam McManis, "Media Savvy: All-in-one revolution," Sacramento Bee, 25 July 2006, **www.sacticket.com/tv_radio/story/14281400p-15089578c.html**.

Writing the
Advanced Online Story

Having spent the last several chapters looking at various ways of preparing audio and video news stories, we now return to the online environment. In this chapter, we look at strategies for creating alternative story forms for the online environment. When combined with audio and video elements, the result is some of the most powerful journalism possible.

Multipart Storytelling

The basic premise of the Web is the interconnectedness of documents. The same technology that allows readers to click from one site to another also makes it easy for writers to break stories into multiple pieces so they are more easily digestible and offer readers a variety of ways to proceed through the story.

This practice—often called **chunking**—is based on two main points: First, despite the conventional wisdom that online readers will read only short articles, readers are willing to read longer articles online *if* they're well written. In fact, research conducted by the Poynter Institute found that close to 67 percent of those who began reading a story online read it all the way through, versus 59 percent of those who finished stories printed in broadsheet newspapers.[1] Second, while a 5,000-word article requires the same amount of time to read whether it's presented in one piece or five, readers find it psychologically easier to take when it's broken into chunks.

In its simplest form, **multipart storytelling** means simply breaking a long story into at least two pieces. No formal guidelines dictate how long a chunk should be or how many chunks a story should be broken into; writers typically just use common sense in finding a balance between overwhelmingly long articles and too many chunks that require nonstop clicking.

Some stories by their nature beg to be chunked: for instance, a story written in a diary format, with each chunk representing a new entry. One such case is MSNBC's daily coverage of mountain climber Ed Viestur's attempt to reach the summit of Annapurna in Nepal, thereby becoming the first American to summit all 14 of the world's 8,000-meter peaks. Each day, reporters Richard Bangs and Lindsay Yaw filed dispatches from the mission, with each presented as a separate chunk. (Their dispatches can be found in "Climbing Toward the Final Peak," at http://travel.msn.com/firsts/ annapurna/dispatch1.armx).

Another example of a story that is well served by chunking was Masha Gessen's "A Medical Quest," written for Slate.com. Gessen's work details the 37-year-old writer's odyssey of trying to decide what to do after she found out she had a genetic mutation that made her highly likely to develop breast or ovarian cancer. In eight chunks, Gessen walks her readers through her probing conversations with a range of medical specialists and shares her interior monologues as she decides what to do with the new information. (The story can be found at http://slate.msn.com/id/2102171/ entry/2102173/.)

The only downside to breaking a story into chunks is that readers can stop partway through the story (of course, they can do that with a single long article, too). To encourage readers to continue, the writer needs to make the links connecting one chunk to the next so interesting that readers will have no choice but to click. For instance, in his account for Fray.com of moving into his dead grandparents' home (http://fray.com/hope/ghosts/), Adam Rakunas ends the first chunk like this:

> We got to work cleaning, prepping, puttying, sanding, painting, ripping out carpet (and discovering a hardwood floor that demanded more work), varnishing. I have clothes that still stink of primer and Varathane. But in that week (and other weeks that followed, since I started work that following Monday), we got a lot done. We finished in mid-July and moved out of the one-bedroom into our own spaces. Then she moved out this September.
>   It was after that when the ghosts started to visit me.

Only a person with no curiosity could pass up the chance to click that link and move deeper into the story.

Although such enticing links are more commonly used on feature stories than on news stories, any type of article can benefit from them. Just because a story contains important information is no reason to assume readers will follow it to the end. For example, a routine MSNBC article on attacks in Iraq seems to have been split right down the middle with no consideration of whether doing so was a good idea. As a result, at the end of the first chunk the reader is confronted with a final line that just begs to be ignored: "Australia contributed 2,000 troops to the U.S.-led invasion of Iraq, and about 300 remain in Iraq." That sentence, restating an old fact, gives readers little incentive to continue—and no idea what they will encounter if they do. In fact, the second chunk begins with a summary of other violence during the preceding week, followed by explanatory information on suicide bombers. Now imagine if the first chunk had ended something like this: "Friday's attacks capped a week in which scores of Iraqis were killed by suicide bombers." That line provides much more incentive for readers to continue into the second chunk.

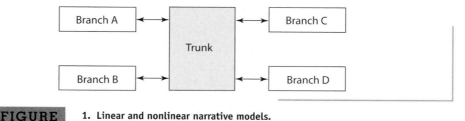

Linear narratives have logical beginning and end points.

Point A → Point B → Point C → Point D

A typical nonlinear narrative consists of a trunk that offers an overview of a story and branches that provide background and further explanation.

Branch A ↔ Trunk ↔ Branch C

Branch B ↔ Trunk ↔ Branch D

FIGURE 12.1   **1. Linear and nonlinear narrative models.**

Nonlinear Storytelling

The stories discussed so far have been broken into a number of parts designed to be read consecutively. Those types of stories—often called **linear narratives**—have logical beginning and end points. Merely breaking linear narratives into chunks fails to fully take advantage of the power of the Web. To take fullest advantage of the Web, writers need to think in terms of **nonlinear narratives**.

A nonlinear narrative offers readers several different possible paths (see Figure 12.1). Rather than saying, "Start here, then read this, then on to that," the writer hands over some control to readers and lets them make decisions about how to pursue the story. Nonlinear structure works best on feature stories because most readers still want the facts of news stories presented quickly and simply.

The most common form of nonlinear structure is that of the **trunk and branches**. Typically, it consists of a trunk that provides an overview of the story and several branches that provide background, elaboration and further explanation. Interested readers can follow those links, and others who are pressed for time or don't have as much interest in the topic still can get the basic message of the story.

The following example of a trunk shows how the writer has tried to present an overview of the community she's writing about, while also offering interested readers the opportunity to learn more about several aspects of it. Each underlined phrase represents a link.

Sights and Sounds in Roland Park

By Pamela K. Martin

One of the best ways to become acquainted with Baltimore's Roland Park is to stroll down its main promenade. Roland Avenue goes straight through the heart of the countryside community and is the hub of neighborhood activity.

Travel down the narrow sidewalks next to the avenue and the area's diversity comes to life. You see schoolchildren pouring out of the brick entrances to Roland Park Country School, local college students riding their bikes to work, and stay-at-home mothers scurrying out of the local supermarket, <u>Eddie's of Roland Park</u>, carrying brown paper bags stuffed to the brim. One of Eddie's <u>loyal workers</u> has been with the store for nearly 50 years.

Stroll a few steps south of the market and you are surrounded by lavish real estate and beautifully renovated homes, many of which date back to the 19th century. Community members were recently invited to tour one of these elaborate homes during the <u>Historic House Tour and Tea</u>, an event that raised money for a local charity.

Travel a few miles across town from the beautiful homes of Roland Avenue and you can hear the lively buzz of several college campuses. Johns Hopkins University, Loyola College and the College of Notre Dame of Maryland are situated in Roland Park along Baltimore's famed Charles Street. Loyola College sponsors a unique form of on-campus entertainment for students and community members who crave adventure. The <u>Banff Mountain Film Festival World Tour</u> has been bringing mountain adventure, culture and humor to Loyola's urban campus setting for the past five years.

Just a block south of the campus is a cluster of small local businesses where friends gather for coffee and shopping. This section of town is home to <u>Balance-the salon</u>, a trendy and tranquil spot for hair styling, cutting and coloring for Baltimore women.

Each of the links connects to a branch, a self-contained story dealing with that topic. As the following branch demonstrates, while all the pieces combine to make one story, readers do not need to read the branches in any given order—or even read all of them to understand the story.

Eddie's of Roland Park

By Pamela K. Martin

Elaine Herget is a 67-year-old Roland Park resident who lives by herself. Last year she was nearly bedridden with back problems that prevented her from performing everyday activities like cooking and grocery shopping. But because of her high cholesterol, Herget was wary of ordering meals from delivery places, and she had no family in the area to bring her food. She had no clue what to do until she called <u>Eddie's of Roland Park</u>.

"I just called them on the phone and they shopped in the store for me," Herget said. "They'll not only deliver [the groceries] but I've had them put it on the table in the kitchen for me. The service is superb. It really is."

Superb, like when Eddie's chefs make a local family's Christmas dinner each year using the family's own recipes. Like when customers call the store to request an off-the-wall item and see it on the shelves a few weeks later. Like when customers walk in the store and clerks greet them by name.

The service, selection and quality of foods available at Eddie's of Roland Park have made the supermarket a prime part of the Baltimore community and a popular spot for area food aficionados.

Despite the large legacy that it carries, Eddie's is a fairly small store. With less than 10 aisles in the supermarket—each only a fraction of the length of a normal grocery aisle—Eddie's resembles an old-world neighborhood store where community members gather to gossip and get groceries for the week. At Eddie's, neighbors and friends chat in the aisles and clerks greet customers by name, but the selection is far more diverse than any neighborhood general store. The supermarket is known for the wide variety of foods that it carries—everything from Maradol papayas to vegetarian pate.

"From the beginning, specialty foods were our hallmark," said Eddie's advertising director Jo Alexander. "Our customers ask for the finest foods in the world, and we try to cater to them."

Even if that means ordering a specific brand of soy-based cheese sticks or carrying milk in glass bottles. Eddie's sends employees to gourmet food shows across the country to stay up on new trends in the industry. If a customer requests something that their food hunters have overlooked, Eddie's will order it for them straight from the supplier.

"[Owner Nancy Cohen] is always in tune with customer requests. If they want something, she'll make sure they get it," Alexander said.

This never-say-no philosophy has carried over into Eddie's <u>"Gourmet to Go"</u> service as well. The supermarket employs classically trained chefs to create meals that are sold ready-to-eat at the deli counter. Items range from cocktail egg rolls to beef wellington, and the chefs will sometimes keep family recipes brought in by customers and rotate them into the general menu. Still, workers say the crab cakes and Caesar salad are the most popular choices.

"During a snowstorm, when the rest of the city goes to the supermarket for toilet paper and milk, our customers come in for our crabcakes and salad," Alexander said. Getting to Eddie's during a storm is not a problem for many of its loyal customers, as Alexander says that a majority of them are Roland Park residents who can make the trip by foot.

"We have a lot of customers that shop every day of the week just about," grocery clerk <u>Bob Miller</u> said. "That's how we get to know a lot of people by their names and their kids' names. It's the type of store we have, a friendly store that makes them keep coming back. It's more or less a neighborhood ritual to shop at Eddie's supermarket." Herget has lived in Roland Park for 26 years, and she says that she's been shopping at Eddie's since the day she moved to town. "I wouldn't say I'm in here less than once a week," Herget said. "I'm certainly in here every week."

Eddie's employees are just as loyal as its customers. Miller has worked for the company for 45 years, managing the store for nearly four decades and introducing his son to the business before cutting his hours as a form of early retirement. Now Miller works part-time as a clerk and his son Steve, who began working at Eddie's as a grocery bagger at age 13, is the seafood and meat buyer for the store.

Bob Miller says the store has changed a lot since his first day on the job. "We only had three aisles and didn't do near as much business," Miller said. "I think we maybe had 11 employees when I started. It was just a small little grocery store at that time."

<para> According to <u>Eddie's Web site</u>, the supermarket has undergone few changes since it was founded in 1944. In 1953, the store was moved from downtown Baltimore to its current location in Roland Park, and its name was changed from Victor's, for original owner Victor Cohen, to Eddie's. The name change was a result of the store banding together with several other local markets in order to stay in business against pressure from national chains.

Eddie's did stay in business, and sales grew steadily at its new Roland Park location. The store was so successful that in 1992 Victor's daughter Nancy Cohen opened a second location on North Charles Street. But the quality and service has always remained the same.

"It's the quality here that makes us different," produce clerk Sonny Hamrick said. "It's not that it's bad at other places, but it's the best at Eddie's."

In order to show off that quality, Eddie's will be holding an outdoor grill festival on May 7 and 8. During the festival, the public is invited to sample the food of Eddie's top chefs, who will be teaching customers how to smoke and grill vegetables, cheeses and meats.

"It's just one of the ways we thank our customers for being so good to us," Alexander said. "It's really just a fun, nice event."

<u>Home</u>   <u>Balance-the salon</u>   <u>Banff Mountain Film Festival</u>

<u>Historic House Tour and Tea</u>   <u>Links</u>

Why Choose Journalism?

Journalism is more than words and facts, these days especially. We have different options to create and convey our reporting — through video, Soundslides, interactive graphics, searchable databases and the like. And we try to further engage the public we serve with features such as message boards, online polls, reader-submitted photos and information, etc.

But at its core journalism remains spellbinding to those who practice it because of what it does. It helps us all make sense of the communities in which we live. It keeps honest public officials and institutions. It brings the stories of everyday people to everyone. And at its most intimate and powerful, it lets us, in particular those with little voice or influence, know we are not alone.

Few other professions help shape words and facts into such meaning.

ABE KWOK
azcentral.com/The Arizona Republic

Several things about this branch are worth noting. First, note that the branch can be read on its own as a separate story. Readers should not need to read any other parts to understand it. In the online environment, that's important because most Web site visitors reach their destinations through search engines. Therefore, writers cannot predict which part of their stories might be read first. For the same reason, even if some of the people mentioned in this branch have been identified by title and full name in other branches, the writer cannot take for granted that the reader has seen that information. So the first reference to a person in each branch should be complete.

Notice, too, that the branch contains four links. Three of these are external links; that is, they will take readers to other sites that are not part of this package. The link "Bob Miller," however, connects to a narrated slide show created by the writer. For that part of her story, the writer decided that photos and audio would be more effective than words alone. In the online environment, it's fine to mix and match internal and external links. The key point is to include all links that might help readers better understand the story.

Finally, notice that the story ends with five links. These are direct paths back to the other parts of the package. All multipart online articles should allow readers to move to any other part of the story with a single click. Few things are more frustrating than having to click two or three links (or keep hitting the Back button) to move to another part of a story.

ASSIGNMENT DESK **12.1**

One of the easiest ways to develop an understanding of multipart articles is by creating a how-to package. For instance, imagine you have decided to write about how to get your first internship in journalism. Next, come up with four to six steps. In this case, your list might look like this:

- Work to get strong grades in your basic courses.
- Get involved with campus organizations, such as the Society of Professional Journalists and the newspaper.
- Create a portfolio of clips.
- Investigate the requirements for an internship.
- Make friends with people in the campus internship office and let them know what you hope to find.

Next, you would find experts on the topic. You should look for a blend of students, faculty and staff, employers, and others who can lend unique and varied perspectives on the topic. Finally, you would create a trunk that summarizes and links to each of your major points, then create an individual branch for each point.

Now it's your turn: Come up with an idea for a how-to package, research your topic, and create a package with a trunk and four to six branches. Remember that because this package is written for the Web, it should not merely reiterate what's already been published on the Web. Instead, you will want to conduct original research, interviewing a diverse group of experts.

Primers, FAQs and Timelines

If there is one area in which the bottomless news hole of the online environment can help writers convey their stories, it is in allowing the addition of complementary material to articles and packages. Even trunk-and-branch packages can be improved with the addition of complementary material. WashingtonPost.com staff writer Dan Froomkin says that three types of complementary materials—primers, FAQs and timelines—help readers understand all the fine points of a story and its background. (Research by the Poynter Institute has confirmed Froomkin's point.[2]) Further, Froomkin says that such features— "particularly if they are produced in a way that encourages and responds to reader input"—can strengthen bonds between news sites and readers, a move that might help prevent readers from drifting away, "either to ignorance or to commoditized news on the likes of Yahoo."[3]

A **primer** is an overview of an area or topic. "A good primer is sweeping in scope," Froomkin writes. "It identifies and describes the big challenges in your chosen area. . . . Primers also force reporters to state the obvious—which is often left strikingly unstated in the hurly-burly of daily journalism."[4] Froomkin cites several primers as good examples for writers to follow. One of them is his own primer on affirmative action, which can be found at www.washingtonpost.com/wp-srv/politics/special/affirm/affirm.htm. The primer begins with an essay introducing the concept of affirmative action and explaining the politics of affirmative action. It links to related stories on the topic that had been published in the Washington Post, as well as to selected editorials and columns. A section of resources and links lists related Web sites and contains the text of President Bill Clinton's address on the topic. Finally, a talk section invites visitors to share their thoughts on the topic.

Froomkin's second recommendation is that writers create **FAQs**. Anyone familiar with modern technology has run into FAQs, which are lists of frequently asked questions. FAQs can help readers understand complicated stories and get up to speed on the background of stories they may be joining "in progress." For example, the following FAQ was put together as part of a package on Alzheimer's disease. Much of the information is based on the writer's interviews with medical specialists and caregivers who specialize in the disease, but she also incorporates (and links to) information from several online sources:

Alzheimer's FAQs

By Amanda Chaffman

What is Alzheimer's disease?

As defined by the Alzheimer's Association, Alzheimer's disease is a progressive, degenerative disease that attacks the brain and results in memory loss, impaired thinking and behavioral and personality changes.

What causes Alzheimer's disease?

Although it is still unknown what causes Alzheimer's, age and family history with the disease have been linked as risk factors. According to the Alzheimer's Association Greater Maryland Chapter, scientists are exploring the role of genetics in the development of Alzheimer's, with focus on Chromosome 19. Many researchers believe the disease is more complex than originally thought and caused by a variety of influences.

Is Alzheimer's disease hereditary?

Researchers are not certain but believe that a person's risk of developing the disease is slightly higher if a first-degree relative (meaning mother, father, sister or brother) has had the disease.

What are the symptoms of Alzheimer's?

Symptoms begin as mild forgetfulness, often confused with "getting old." Symptoms in the early stages of Alzheimer's often consist of trouble remembering events, activities or names of family or friends. As the disease progresses, simple forgetfulness begins to interfere with daily activities. Those with Alzheimer's may forget how to brush their teeth, drive or dress properly. Patients can no longer think clearly, failing to recognize people and places. Problems speaking, reading and writing quickly follow. In the final stages of Alzheimer's, total care is essential. Patients are unable to speak, bathe, eat or even walk without assistance. The Alzheimer's Association breaks down the progression of the disease into seven stages.

How old do you have to be to get Alzheimer's?

Symptoms of Alzheimer's have been found in individuals as young as 30, but it is most common in those 65 years or older.

How is Alzheimer's different from dementia?

The symptoms of Alzheimer's are much more severe than those of simple memory loss. Alzheimer's affects communication, thinking and reasoning, and can deeply affect a person's work and social life rather than subtle lapses in memory.

Can Alzheimer's patients live on their own?

Early stage Alzheimer's patients may live on their own, but it is highly recommended that once diagnosed with Alzheimer's patients seek additional care. This may mean living with family members or in an assisted living facility so proper care and attention is available for the patient.

What are the options for care?

Care options for Alzheimer's patients continue to change and grow. Families have started moving diagnosed family members into their homes, providing them with full care either by themselves or through Respite Care (a nurse comes to the home and tends to patients until family returns). Many patients are taken to adult day care (similar to a children's day care center). According to Carroll Nurse Monitor Maria Carr, the need for these two care options is growing.

"We have seen such an increase in requests for these services that we have continued to expand our staff," said Carr.

Specialized assisted living and nursing facilities are options for families unable to care for their loved ones at home.

Does being diagnosed with Alzheimer's affect life expectancy?

According to the Fisher Center for Alzheimer's Research Foundation, a recent study found that women diagnosed with Alzheimer's tend to live six years after diagnosis, while men diagnosed with the disease tend to live four years. The study also found that those diagnosed with Alzheimer's lived half as long as those of a similar age not diagnosed with Alzheimer's.

How is Alzheimer's diagnosed?

Diagnosis of Alzheimer's is done through a process of elimination to rule out other forms of dementia. This process is typically conducted by a family physician or a team of specialists. The process involves a thorough examination of the person's medical history as well as family history; an assessment of the person's mental status; lab tests; and physical, psychological and neurological exams. In Maryland, teams of specialists from Copper and AERS conduct such examinations.

Is there a cure?

At this moment a cure for Alzheimer's is not available, but medications that help slow down the process of deterioration of the brain are available to patients.

The final form of complementary material is the **timeline**. Used with stories that have developed over time—whether a few hours or several years—timelines let readers quickly see the sequence of events. For example, this timeline details events of the morning when a Virginia Tech student killed 32 people and himself at the university:

7:15 a.m.

A 911 call summons Virginia Tech police to West Ambler Johnston Hall, where they find two gunshot victims, one male and one female. Blacksburg police help set up a safety perimeter around the hall.

7:30 a.m.

Investigators begin following up on leads in the shootings.

8:25 a.m.

Virginia Tech's president and other officials begin determining the best way of notifying students about the deaths.

9:26 a.m.

Students and faculty are sent an e-mail alerting them to the shootings. A news release is posted on the university's Web site.

9:45 a.m.

Another 911 call is received. This one reports a shooting at Norris Hall, about a half mile across the campus from West Ambler Johnston Hall. Officers arrive to find the doors chained shut. Once inside, they follow gunshots to the second floor. The gunshots stop, and they find the gunman, who has killed himself.

9:55 a.m.

Another alert goes out to students and faculty, this time reporting the second event.

Timelines can be graphic based or text based. While in the past, an artist would have been required to create a graphic timeline in Figure 12.2, programs such as Adobe's Flash allow even technically challenged journalists to create eye-pleasing timelines.

For example, the following timeline covers major events in the professional bicycle racing career of Lance Armstrong. When the user clicks one of the six time periods on the timeline, text appears at the bottom of it to explain what happened that year. In this example, 1996 has been selected, and information about what happened that year is displayed at the bottom.

ASSIGNMENT DESK 12.2

Pick three stories from today's newspaper (either the print or online edition). For each of them, come up with at least one idea for a primer, FAQ or timeline. Next, research the topic of each article and create the primer, FAQ or timeline.

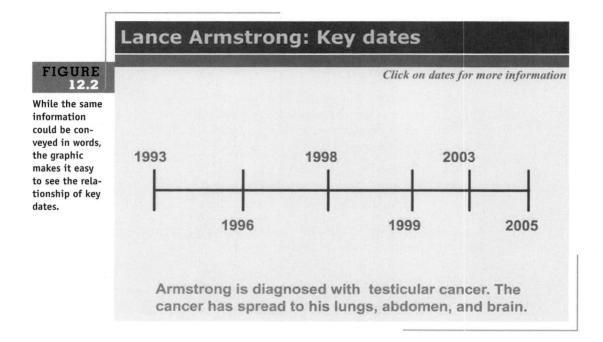

Lance Armstrong: Key dates

Click on dates for more information

**FIGURE
12.2**

While the same information could be conveyed in words, the graphic makes it easy to see the relationship of key dates.

1993   1998   2003

1996   1999   2005

Armstrong is diagnosed with testicular cancer. The cancer has spread to his lungs, abdomen, and brain.

Multimedia

Few online writers are masters of multimedia. Most find it challenging enough to create compelling text stories let alone incorporating audio, video, animation and other elements. Still, more writers are finding themselves as collaborators in creating multimedia or as maestros orchestrating multimedia packages (see Figure 12.3).

One of the simplest things for writers to do is to include **audio clips** from interviews in their work. The practice of including actualities or sound bites is long established in radio and television news; in the online environment, too, audio clips can help the audience get a sense of the people in and behind the news. Stories that can benefit from adding audio clips include those about important announcements, profiles of interesting characters, stories with strong emotional content, and so on. For example, the author of a piece on Baltimore's arabbers—a vanishing breed of vendors who travel through neighborhoods selling fruit, vegetables and other items from horse-drawn carts—wanted to let her audience hear the distinctive hollers of her subjects. So in addition to transcribing an arabber's pitch, she created an audio clip of it.

Adding **video clips** to an online story is not much harder. However, because of the difficulty of shooting content that is both technically good and interesting, few writers shoot their own video clips. Writers are much more likely to create slide shows.

FIGURE 12.3

The Montgomery Advertiser won an award from the Online News Association for its multimedia package commemorating the anniversary of the Montgomery, Ala., bus boycott. The package included front pages of newspapers, a timeline, video clips, a database of more than 500 stories, and much more.

Slide shows are a unique form of video storytelling, and when properly constructed they can present a story with power and grace. Good online slide shows have virtually the same impact as video clips but without the need for large crews or lengthy production times. An individual journalist equipped with a camera and digital audio recorder can gather everything needed for a compelling slide show. Brian Storm, president of MediaStorm.org and former director of multimedia for MSNBC.com, notes: "Shooting and producing a successful video package (see Figure 12.3) takes years to perfect. Succeeding with (photos and) a 10 to 15-second audio clip is a cakewalk in comparison."[5]

At its simplest, a slide show runs barely a minute long and contains six to 12 photos with captions. Just as with any other form of storytelling, a slide show should have a clear central theme and be tightly edited.

Even though the main focus of a slide show is its photos, printed words still play a significant role. Those words are included in **captions**, which must try to accomplish one or more of the following tasks:

- Clearly explain what is going on in the photo.
- Identify the people in the photo.
- Point out significant details the viewer might overlook.

Captions should cover the basics. According to Meredith Birkett, special projects multimedia producer at MSNBC.com: "Text captions are useful for the basic information related to an image. A reader should be able to see the picture and read the caption and take away all of the important information about the image and continue the thread of the story without listening to the audio."[6]

The first line of a caption is typically written in present tense, as if to say to the viewer, "Here's what is happening as you take a look." Subsequent lines, if any, are written in past, present or future tense, as appropriate. Here are a few examples of opening lines:

> Oana Stiehl , 6, has makeup applied before an annual recital at the St. Francis Academy.

> Children walk on the remains of a bridge destroyed by insurgents.

> Jack Kevorkian leaves prison in Coldwater, Mich.

More and more slide shows are bridging the gap with broadcast news by incorporating audio. Brian Storm explains, "Gathering ambient sound and interviewing the subject of a story are the perfect complements to a documentary photograph or essay."[7]

The advantages of incorporating audio into slide shows, Storm says, include giving a voice to the subjects of photos, adding realism and texture, providing extra details for use in the captions, and better communicating the emotions of a person or the feel of a place.

When audio is used in a slide show, it should complement the captions. For example, the audio track can provide background, let viewers hear the subject's emotions, or cover more abstract ideas than what the caption covers. Meredith Birkett provides this example:

> We have an image of a child's drawing of a relief plane in Sudan. The caption describes what the child drew, where the picture was drawn, and that this child has been receiving food aid from the World Food Programme for all of his life.
> In the audio, you hear the photographer describing how since ancient times, people have drawn what is important to their culture…animals they hunted, wars they fought. A child drawing a relief plane shows how important that aid is to their life.[8]

Like any other type of story, a successful slide show begins with careful preparation. For every image, the journalist should try to record corresponding audio; for every sound, he or she should try to find a matching photo. Every "asset" collected for the slide show should be logged to make sure nothing is overlooked. That process is best begun in the field to head off surprises at deadline.

Some ground rules on slide shows:

- *Each photo should make a distinct point.* Just as every paragraph in a text, audio or video story should convey additional information, so should every photo in a slide show.
- *Photos should span a range of perspectives.* Wide shots of scenes provide an overview of a scene, close-ups let viewers see fine details, and medium shots complement the other two types and add even more variety.

FIGURE 12.4

The New York Times online site is well respected for its slide shows, which feature great photography.

The New York Times
Thursday, August 30, 2007

Multimedia/Photos

Multimedia All NYT Search

WORLD U.S. N.Y./REGION BUSINESS TECHNOLOGY SCIENCE HEALTH SPORTS OPINION ARTS STYLE TRAVEL JOBS REAL ESTATE

U.S. OPEN

A Popular Women's Champion, and a Player Trying to Get There

By LYNN ZINSER

Serena Williams and Ahsha Rolle won second-round matches last night at the United States Open, separated by a few hundred yards that might as well have been a million miles.
· Nadal Grinds Out a Win | Interactive Brackets: Men | Women
· Slide Show: Day 3 | Blog
· At the Open, It Is the Evening That Becomes Electric | Video

Robert Caplin for The New York Times
Serena Williams defeated Maria Elena Camerin of Italy, 7-5, 6-2, in the second round on Wednesday.

Audio Slide Show

The World's Smokestack
Chang W. Lee, a Times photographer, traveled around China to document the impact of industrialization on the country's rural and urban landscapes.

New Podcasts
Listen to New York Times editors, critics and repc discuss the day's news and features.
· See All Podcasts

New York Times
RadioNews
Updated hourly weekdays from 6 a.m. to 6

You have to not see

- *Viewers should have some control.* It's not easy to inspect a photo, read a caption and listen to audio all at the same time. Therefore, many journalists take advantage of controls in the Flash software used to create their slide shows to let viewers pause, rewind or fast forward the slides, or step through them one by one.

Great examples of journalistic slide shows abound on the Web. Two places in particular that offer many excellent slide shows are MSNBC.com (click the "Multimedia" link, then "The Week in Pictures") and The New York Times on the Web (click "Features" then "Multimedia Photos").

Several programs can be used to create slide shows, but most of the slide shows online are created with Flash or Soundslides, which automates the Flash creation process. (See Figure 12.4.) While producing a Flash slide show from scratch requires a good bit of time and practice, many online news organizations employ Flash producers to handle the technical work, or they offer Flash slide show templates for their writers to use.

ASSIGNMENT DESK 12.3

Choose an upcoming campus event. Brainstorm as many ideas as you can for creating a multimedia news package about the event. Attend the event and write a story on it. If the tools and software are available, create an audio clip and a slide show to accompany your story.

Conclusion

The online environment offers unprecedented opportunities for journalists to tell compelling stories. By blending alternative story forms with photographic, audio and video elements, the writer can create powerful and immersive story packages that go beyond what any single medium can provide.

KEY TERMS

audio clip, 220
caption, 221
chunking, 209
FAQ, 216
linear narrative, 211
multipart storytelling, 209

nonlinear narrative, 211
primer, 216
slide show, 220
timeline, 220
trunk and branches, 211
video clip, 220

DISCUSSION QUESTIONS

1. Look at two or three copies of local or national newspapers published within the last week. Choose three stories that could be complemented with the types of things we've discussed in this chapter. For each, make a list of items that could be used effectively. Then find the online versions of those stories. How many of these types of things are included in the online version? Are there other online complements included that you did not think of?

2. YouTube has become one of the most popular online destinations. Many of the clips there include raw video footage: accidents, fights, and so on. Does a YouTube video clip ever qualify as journalism? Why or why not?

3. Check out two or three online slide shows produced by your local news media or by a national news source such as MSNBC or The New York Times. How effectively do the slide shows tell stories? In what ways are they better than simple text stories? In what ways are they worse?

NOTES

1. Joe Strupp, "Surprise: Study finds online users finish more stories than print readers," Editor & Publisher, 28 March 2007, www.editorandpublisher.com/eandp/search/article_display.jsp?vnu_content_id=1003563988.

2. Dan Froomkin, "Why Beat Reporters Could Be News Sites' Greatest Secret Weapons," Online Journalism Review, 26 August 2004, www.ojr.org/ojr/workplace/1093463778.php.

3. Froomkin.

4. Froomkin.

5. Brian Storm, "Made for the Medium: Photojournalism at MSNBC.com," http://digitaljournalist.org/issue0203/storm.htm.

6. Brian Storm, "Gathering Audio," MediaStorm.org, 1 March 2005, http://mediastorm.org/howto.html.

7. Storm, "Gathering Audio."

8. Storm, "Gathering Audio."

Key Story Types *Chapter* 13

Many news writers begin their careers as **general assignment reporters**, covering a wide range of stories. One day, they may cover a robbery, the next day a speech and the next day an accident. In each case, a good writer will try to determine what makes the story unique, trying to find a fresh perspective or a new way of telling the story. That's the only way to hold an audience's attention over time. Readers, viewers and listeners who get the same old same old every time will soon become former readers, viewers and listeners.

While it's important to find a fresh approach, it's just as important to make sure the basics are not overlooked in the process. In this chapter, we'll look at several types of stories that a beginning news writer is likely to be called on to write.

Public Events and Meetings

Much news originates from events in which one or more people speak to the public (see Figure 13.1). Such events typically fall into one of four categories:

- **Speeches**: Whether at college graduations, store openings, political campaign stops or any of a wide variety of other events, public figures deliver countless speeches every week. Many of these prove to be routine and self-serving, but occasionally a speech contains something newsworthy. Even when a speech itself produces little of note, news may emerge in a question-and-answer session afterward.
- **News conferences**: When there is no scheduled event available or when a politician, attorney, corporate officer, law enforcement official or other powerful figure has something important and wants to make sure the media take notice, he or she often will call a news conference. A question-and-answer session may follow.
- **Panel discussions**: Many of these sessions take place at industry and professional conferences and conventions, or at academic institutions. Typically, three or four speakers will discuss various aspects of or perspectives on a topic. For instance, a college communication department might sponsor a panel discussion on how new technologies are affecting journalism. In some instances, panel discussions take place in public settings, where

When the public conducts its business, reporters are there to get the story to relay to those who were not in attendance. *Source:* **Clayton Statler/ Jacksonville-Courier/The Image Works**

governmental officials, often along with experts and community members, discuss issues of concern, such as new highway construction.

- **Public meetings**: Many government bodies hold regular public meetings, as do some community groups and neighborhood associations. Some public meetings, such as those of a city council, are devoted primarily to the work of a formal body. Other public meetings, such as those announcing the relocation of a registered sex offender into a community, are designed to elicit a wide range of public feedback.

Covering the Event

Although news conferences and speeches sometimes last no more than a few minutes, most public events typically are long and full of information of varying degrees of interest and importance. That can seem overwhelming to a new reporter, especially if the topic of the event is unfamiliar. A writer can increase the odds of getting a good story by following these tips:

Obtain any available advance information. In virtually every instance, there is something available that the reporter can read before the actual event. For example:

- Someone who plans to deliver a speech often prepares his or her text well in advance and offers copies to journalists.
- A person scheduling a news conference will often send out a news release beforehand.

- A body or committee planning a public meeting will prepare an agenda.
- The planners of a panel discussion usually release an agenda for the discussion, along with names of the presenters and other biographical information.

Using the agenda or other advance information, a reporter should try to determine what the event will mean to the public. A meeting on a woodlands protection plan might sound like a good idea—Who doesn't like trees?—but if it substantially increases the cost of new homes, it might not draw public support.

Conduct research. If time permits, the reporter should find out as much as possible about the speaker or speakers and about the topic. To do so, the reporter might:

- Talk to experts and citizens who have taken a position on the proposal or will be affected by it.
- Call the drafters and ask for their rationale.
- Think about multimedia opportunities: What maps or graphics can complement the story, what original documents can be linked to, and so on.

Prepare questions. Just as in preparing to conduct an interview, a reporter should use research to draw up questions for those at a public event. Even if the event does not include a formal question-and-answer period, the reporter might be able to talk to one or more of the participants afterward. Questions should be short and to the point; asking long-winded questions is a good way to get cut off before obtaining any information.

Ask clarifying questions. As questions occur to a reporter during the event, he or she should feel free to add them to the list and ask them when possible. At all times, the reporter must remember that his or her job is to make sense of things for the audience. That's not possible if a reporter returns from an event with unanswered questions.

Listen and take notes. On occasion, every reporter is going to feel lost in covering a public event. Preparation will help, but it cannot guarantee that the reporter will understand everything. The best bet is to pay attention and jot down anything that seems important, even when it comes in response to another journalist's question.

Watch for sparks. Amy Gahran of IReporter.org advises that one good way to home in on what's important in a public event is to "Watch the faces of the participants. Listen to their tone of voice."[1] She suggests watching for people to change their posture, raise their eyebrows, or otherwise signal their concern.

Check details. The reporter always should make an estimate of the number of people in the audience. Before leaving an event, the reporter should confirm the names, titles and affiliations of all the major players. If the reporter does not already have a contact who's connected to the event, he or she should try to make one before leaving. Doing so offers a chance to verify details and ask follow-up questions.

Finding the News

In covering a spoken word event, the reporter's job is the same as it is when working on any other type of story: Find the most important or interesting thing (or things) that was said, and focus on that. As Amy Gahran says: "Don't try to recount absolutely everything that happened. . . . That makes for dreadful storytelling. Just focus on the newsworthy story you've discovered."[2]

Reporters always must remember that it is never the act of speaking itself that's newsworthy, but rather *what* was said or, even better, *how* the announcements and decisions made at the event will affect the public. That seems simple enough, yet one of the most common mistakes among beginning news writers is leading with the fact that someone spoke rather than focusing on what they said. The following lead is a typical example of that problem:

> In what has become an annual tradition, the governor spoke to students in the Business Leadership class Wednesday.

Right from the start, the writer seems to be saying, "Move along folks; there's nothing interesting here." Not only does this lead back in by noting the "annual tradition," but it also provides no hint that the governor said anything of importance in his speech.

Only a little better is a lead that names a topic without going into what was said about it, such as in this example from a student newspaper:

> The abortion debate hit campus Tuesday, when an acclaimed pro-life speaker led a discussion about being conceived in rape.

Again, the lead does little to draw in the audience. This type of lead may be effective for broadcast writing because it sets up the story, but for print or online use, it fails. A better lead for those media was buried further down in the story, when the writer noted that the speaker called for more assistance for women who chose to carry pregnancies to term.

Here's another example of a lead that fails to spotlight the news:

> Islamic Awareness Week got off to a strong start Monday with a motivational lecture by Islamic speaker Abu Omar Irfan Kabiruddin.

With editing, this might work for broadcast news, to set the stage for the story. But even in that setting, this one is a little dense and dull. One of the biggest problems is the use of a long and unfamiliar name. It's always better to instead use a title or description for an unfamiliar person; that establishes the person's credentials and credibility. In this case, however, the writer does not provide that information anywhere in the story, diminishing its power.

In a meeting story, unless something truly weird happens, the writer should try to focus on what the votes and decisions mean to the audience. Leads like this do not pass that test:

> The City Council met Tuesday night and in a unanimous vote changed its current R-2 zoning to light industrial.

Instead, the reporter must explain what that means:

Local residents may be doing battle against light industrial businesses in their neighborhoods after the City Council voted to allow them under certain zoning codes.

After a reporter has found the lead, the rest of a public event story follows the basic conventions discussed in previous chapters, typically presenting details in order of diminishing importance. This story focusing on a public meeting provides a good model:

After dozens of people expressed their concerns about a proposed watershed ordinance for Beaver Lake at a public hearing Wednesday night, the Benton County Planning Board voted to send the document back to the Environmental Committee for revision.	Lead focuses on the most important aspect of the meeting.
Justice of the Peace Bob Tharp, chairman of the Environmental Committee, said Thursday he is pleased with the outcome of the public hearing. "As uncomfortable as it was for the Planning Board and as (passionate) as it was for the people speaking, I felt like democracy was served and served very well," Tharp said.	Reaction to the decision follows.
Tharp voted to forward the ordinance out of the Environmental Committee to the Planning Board. He maintains that was the right decision, but now that he has heard from the public, he believes the Environmental Committee still has much work to do on the ordinance.	Background of the decision provides insight into it.
John Butler was the only member of the Planning Board to vote against sending the ordinance back to the Environmental Committee. Butler preferred to see the ordinance discarded completely.	Dissenting vote or votes and the reasons for them are noted.
About 100 people attended the hearing, which came at the end of the regularly scheduled Planning Board meeting. With no specific start time for the hearing, people waited in the lobby of the Benton County Administration Building until the Planning Board meeting ended. Once, Planning Director Michelle Crain asked the crowd to lower their voices. The crowd met first at the Arvest Bank Community Room, where Justice of the Peace Bill Adams offered snacks and a campaign speech.	Remaining details: How many attended, time and place of the meeting, and so on.
(Copyright 2006 The Benton [Ark.] County Daily Record)	

As this example shows, in most cases the lead and story should focus on the major point or points of the spoken comments.

Occasionally, however, an offhand comment can be the most newsworthy aspect of the story. For instance, in the course of a panel discussion a three-star Marine general made this off-the-cuff remark about fighting in Afghanistan:

> Actually it's quite fun to fight them, you know. It's a hell of a hoot. It's fun to shoot some people.... You go into Afghanistan, you got guys who slap women around for five years because they didn't wear a veil. You know, guys like that ain't got no manhood left anyway. So it's a hell of a lot of fun to shoot them.

Needless to say, news reports of the panel discussion did not focus much on the contents of the discussion, but rather on a top military leader calling killing Afghanis "fun."[3]

ASSIGNMENT DESK 13.1

Attend a public event or speech or watch a White House news briefing online (go to www.whitehouse.gov/news/briefings/, choose a briefing, then choose the video link). Write a 300-word story for print and online use.

Next, make a list of actualities, video clips and multimedia enhancements that could be used with this story.

Special Considerations for Broadcast and Online Reports

Not surprisingly, pictures of people standing at a lectern or sitting at a table do not make for fascinating video storytelling. And the audio from a spoken word event typically doesn't offer much appeal to an audio story. So to produce the best radio and television stories on news conferences, panel discussions and public meetings, you need to expand the story beyond the boundaries of the event location.

To illustrate, television reporter Jenny Atwater offers this example:

> If I were assigned a meeting story about a proposal to build a new jail, if time allowed—and most often this is a case of using your time wisely—I would first go to the neighborhood affected. I'd talk to the man raking leaves about how he feels about the new jail, shoot video of the spot where the jail will go, etc. I would find the "real people" affected and try to get as much video as possible before the meeting so I wouldn't have to rely on sound from the meeting and wallpaper video (boring video of people sitting still). I would work sound from the meeting into my story—and of course visuals to prove we were there—but the bulk would come from what I had shot earlier.
>
> Often you can get an official before the meeting as well. This all really helps with deadline time constraints, too. With much of the story shot before you go into the meeting, you can spend time writing during dull parts of the meeting or before.

Why Choose Journalism?

Journalism is about the stories you tell.

It's about hearing of a boy shot by police, arriving at the scene and listening to witnesses scream that the police are lying. It's about watching the neighborhood erupt in nonviolent protest. It's about gathering all those facts and emotions and setting them in ink.

There's a thrill in getting crucial information to the public. By keeping readers informed about their city, or digging deep into a well-camouflaged scandal, or simply writing a thoughtful obituary, you're illuminating a subject that most people would never encounter. Both the good and the nefarious are thrust into the light, and we're all better off for it.

And that, really, is why you get into the business. Because every day is different, and because every time you pick up your pen, you can *make* a difference that will reverberate far beyond the next morning's edition.

GERRY DOYLE
Chicago Tribune

So try to get as much done BEFORE you go into the meeting or news conference. Of course, sometimes this isn't possible—and sometimes big things happen at the meeting that throw your earlier stuff out the window.

The same advice applies to online coverage. The online medium offers one additional advantage, though, in the ability to post recordings and transcripts of an event. Although reporters probably do not need to do that routinely, offering the audience a way to hear or watch the proceedings of an event of wide community interest can be a nice bonus.

Obituaries

Some people would argue that there is no story more important than a person's obituary. It is typically the last story written about a person—and often the only one—and a good obit can serve as a fine summary of the good or not so good that the person did while alive. Especially for local and regional media outlets, where everyone tends to know everyone else, obits are critical. As James A. Raykie Jr., editor of The Herald in Sharon, Pa., has said, "In community journalism, the writing of obits is one of the most important things we do."[4]

Alana Baranick, an obit writer for the Cleveland Plain Dealer and 2005 winner of the award for best obituary writing given by the American Society of Newspaper Editors, agrees with that assessment:

> A well-written and well-researched obit can enlighten readers about contemporary history and a variety of ethnic, religious and socio-economic cultures. It also can provide information about agencies, events and individuals that can help the reader or benefit from the reader's support.
>
> If we're lucky, an obituary will inspire the living to be good to their neighbors, strive for success and keep hope alive.[5]

Unfortunately, many journalists find themselves challenged by the process of writing a good obit. One problem is that it's not always clear what an obit should be. In fact, it may be easier to define what an obit is *not* rather than what it *is*. For starters, an obit is not a death notice. These are put together from information supplied by families to funeral homes and are routine "fact sheets." The purpose of a death notice is to let readers know that someone has died and to provide information about survivors and services. It is not, by any stretch of the imagination, a journalistic story.

For that matter, most **standard** (or **news**) **obits** that appear in newspapers (and often their online counterparts) are not stellar examples of journalism, either. They differ little from death notices and are designed primarily to present essential information about a person's life and death:

- Name and age of the deceased.
- Date and place of death.
- Cause of death.
- Major life events.
- Education.
- Military service (when appropriate).
- Professional accomplishments.
- Club affiliations.
- Survivors.
- Details of services.
- Details on memorial contributions.

Accuracy in obits is critically important. There are no second chances with obits. Many families keep them as a tribute to their loved ones, and nothing is worse than to have a name misspelled or an age listed incorrectly. Therefore, the obit writer must double-check all facts.

The **feature obit** moves beyond the basics to create a more compelling story of a person's life. As Gregg McLachlan, associate managing editor of the Simcoe Reformer in Ontario, Canada, has noted, writing an obit should be like writing any other feature article:

> When we write news, we are forced to dig for details and information that is interesting. We look for themes. We think about how to hook readers. We look for the unusual. Obits should be no different. Probe. Ask a lot of questions. You're still investing in a main character and writing a human interest story...you just need the help of supporting characters to tell the story.[6]

A feature obit writer's primary job is to find the most interesting aspect of the subject's life. A good feature obit should offer "a defining line, an insight into the heart and soul of the life," says Carolyn Gilbert, founder of the International Association of Obituarists, editor of ObitPage.com and the host for a continuing series of events for obituarists.[7] Gregg McLachlan adds:

> The best obits are the ones where a reader finishes the article and can say, "Wow. I feel like I know this person. He/she seemed like someone who was very special." Some of the best obits can also inspire others by showing a person's courage and wisdom. . . . often, it's a circumstance that we may have faced, or may face in the future. Perhaps it's dealing with an illness. Or maybe it's a tale of achieving success.[8]

Here's a great example of a feature obit written by Amy Rabideau Silvers of the Milwaukee Journal Sentinel:

At the age of 86, LaVerne Hammond did something that she always wanted to do.

She became a writer.

The turning point came as she attended the Florida Suncoast Writers' Conference in St. Petersburg with her daughter, Margo Hammond, book editor for the St. Petersburg Times.

"I'm so glad you became a writer, because that was my dream," she told her daughter.

Margo Hammond said: "Well, Mom, you can still be a writer. It's not like you wanted to be a ballerina."

Hammond began writing letters to family members as a sort of memoir. Then the perfect find at a rummage sale—and the kindness of a stranger—inspired a story about framing a photo of her late husband. She submitted it as a guest column to the St. Petersburg Times.

"She was 86, and it was her first published piece," Margo Hammond said.

"That editor liked it so much, she asked if she would write a monthly column for a senior section."

Hammond wasn't sure whether she could write something every month, but her daughter encouraged her to try another piece, just to see how long it might take her.

"She wrote three pieces her first day trying," Margo Hammond said.

Hammond continued writing for six years, even as her health was failing.

"Her last piece—a letter to her first great-grandchild—will run this month," her daughter said. "She made her last deadline, and she was a writer to the end."

Hammond died Tuesday of kidney failure. She was 92.

A longtime Kenosha resident, she moved to Shorewood to be closer to her family, finding the perfect apartment across from the library and the Shorewood Senior Resource Center. She also began spending part of the year in St. Petersburg with her daughter, which led to her late-in-life writing.

The former LaVerne Nordstrom graduated from high school in Kenosha at 16. She first wanted to be a doctor, but applying to medical school was not an option for girls in 1930. Then she was told she was too young to be a nurse.

"So she went to business school in Chicago," Margo Hammond said, "and

(continued)

(Continued)

then to night school for journalism at Northwestern University for two years."

The Depression interfered with school plans, and the young woman began working at jobs that included switchboard operator, secretary and accountant. She was working as assistant head of payroll and accounting at Great Lakes Naval Station when she again met Paul Hammond. They had dated once while in high school.

The couple married in 1945.

The next decades were filled with raising their family and lots of volunteer work at their church and elsewhere. When the parish priest called, telling her that she was being "given the honor" of leading the church women's group, she didn't want the job. Instead, Hammond said she had a new job, and he asked where. The Kenosha school system, she said.

"She got off the phone and thought, 'My God, I've lied to a priest,'" her daughter said.

To make a long story short, she decided to try to get a job with the school system. Soon, Hammond was working as head of the English Resource Center at Tremper High School, helping students with their writing.

She worked until the mandatory retirement age and then kept busy with volunteer and other activities.

Her readers in St. Petersburg sometimes heard about life in Milwaukee.

One column told of how she always wanted to try yoga but was too timid to be the old person in the group. Her chance came with an "Ageless Yoga" class at the senior resource center.

Another column told of her experience at Harley-Davidson's 100th birthday bash.

"The bikers invited us to see their bikes up close and personal," she wrote. "One was truly an artistic expression on wheels.... I stood there admiring every detail.

"Suddenly, the man said to me, 'Would you like to go for a ride?'"

She loved her ride on the Harley.

"I gave my driver a hug and told my newfound friend that the rev of a motorcycle will now always remind me of a warm, beating heart," she wrote.

In addition to Margo Hammond, LaVerne Hammond is survived by daughters Joan Whipp, Diane Kavalauskas and Renee Hammond, grandchildren and a great-granddaughter.

Visitation is set for 10 a.m. today until the funeral service at 11 a.m., both at Three Holy Women Parish-St. Hedwig Church, 1704 N. Humboldt Ave.

Notice how the feature obit turns the standard obit on its head. Not until the 14th paragraph—about a third of the way into the story—is the subject's death even mentioned. As noted Washington Post obituary Editor J.Y. Smith once wrote: "The occasion for obituaries is death, which is sad. But the subject of obituaries is life itself, which is wonderful."[9]

Survivors and service information come only in the last two grafs, a long way from the start. Major life events are woven into the story as appropriate. Most importantly, along the way, the author weaves a great story, one that truly gives the reader a sense of what the subject was like. This example also makes it clear that a writer does not need a world-famous subject to create a world-class obit. Everyone has a story worth telling if the writer will only look for it.

Notice that the writer maintains a clear focus from start to finish: LaVerne Hammond, the writer. The writer wisely did not try to write her subject's life story, cramming in every detail she could find. That's a common mistake among inexperienced obituary writers and one that leaves their work with little impact and provides little insight. Gerry Goldstein, whose work for the Providence (R. I.) Journal-Bulletin has included obit writing, says the obit writer's job is similar to the jewelry maker's: "We take the rough diamond of a life as lived and rub away at it until facets emerge. Then the reader can hold it up and examine it—turn it around and around and cogitate on just how much light it reflects."[10]

Not everyone's life reflects as much light as the next person's, however: Some lives are markedly dark. That can be a touchy point for obituary writers. The best guideline is to treat each subject thoroughly and fairly; sweeping important but unsavory details under the carpet doesn't tell the whole truth about a person. J.Y. Smith was forced to confront this when the first deaths from AIDS began to occur while he was in charge of obituaries at the Washington Post:

> The newspaper has a duty to reflect the world as it really is. . . .That is the whole point of journalism, and it is the single best reason for citing AIDS as a cause of death. . . . People try to deny painful memories. In this way death is the enemy of common sense and, unless one is very careful, death always wins. Denying painful memories is to deny part of the life itself.

Young's point was powerfully made by the inclusion of information on his battle with alcoholism in his own obituary.[11]

Research

To polish their rough diamonds, the authors of feature obits have to conduct quite a bit of research. The obvious challenge in the research process is that the subject is no longer available. Therefore, the writer must seek out others who can help find the subject's story and can bring it to life with quotes, anecdotes and descriptions. These sources include friends, relatives, professional colleagues, and so on. Books and articles can also help provide insights, but the writer must to be extremely careful to verify any information that comes from such sources (and to credit any of them used for background).

Some beginning obit writers automatically assume that the immediate family would not want to talk right after a loved one's death. Sometimes that's true, but not always. In fact, for many people, such conversations can have a therapeutic effect. As Greg McLachlan has written:

> Over the years, I've seen it happen more than once. A family was not contacted for comment about a loved one. A journalist simply assumed they wouldn't want to talk in their time of grief. It was an incorrect assumption. The family wished someone had been given the opportunity. Let the family know that you would like to talk to them, if they wish. Contact the family, call a relative or use the funeral home as a go-between. If the family doesn't want to talk, respect their wishes. (When my grandfather, a former police officer and founder of a large police association, died about 20 years ago, our family called the newsroom of a large metropolitan daily newspaper. We hoped they would do a story. We were proud of grandpa and thought his story should be told. The newspaper agreed and did a story. We still have that article tucked away. It's a special keepsake.)[12]

The best advice for the writer is to inquire if the family is interested in being interviewed but not to count on them agreeing to talk.

ASSIGNMENT DESK 13.2

Select a classmate and conduct a 15-minute interview. Try to get a sense of what makes him or her "tick," and work toward getting anecdotes, quotes and descriptions that support that point. Then write a 250-word obit about the person, focusing primarily on that aspect of his or her life. Next, create a list of multimedia elements that could be added to the obit in an online setting.

Audio and Video Obits

On radio and television, obituaries tend to be either short standard obits or longer feature obits, generally reserved for highly notable people. Broadcast obits are written similarly to their print counterparts, with one notable exception: They should include audio and video of the subject. For instance, here's how the British Broadcasting Corp. began its three-minute report on the death of journalist and television personality Alistair Cooke in 2004; it is online at http://news.bbc.co.uk/1/hi/entertainment/tv_and_radio/3581573.stm:

> Alistair Cooke — it's been said — did more for Anglo-American relations than a whole string of ambassadors from both sides of the Atlantic. His weekly broadcasts of "Letter from America" for BBC Radio monitored the pulse of life in the United States, and in a relaxed yet informative style relayed its strengths and weaknesses to 50 countries.

Those words are read over stock footage of Cooke in a variety of settings. Then the video switches over to Cooke at work in the newsroom, and the reader's voice is replaced by Cooke's as he broadcasts an episode of "Letter from America":

> Good evening. It used to be liquor — bootleg liquor — that made vast illegal fortunes for underworld characters in Chicago.

The camera zooms out and the narrator returns:

> Born in Salford, he went to America on a grant and started working for the BBC in the 1930s. He developed a passion for jazz and golf, and as a film critic mixed with Hollywood stars. Later, as a correspondent for the Guardian as well as the BBC, he reported on the administrations of 11 American presidents in over half a century.

Throughout the remainder of the report, a combination of narration, natural sound and Cooke's voice — in some cases used as a voice-over — is matched with archival photos and video clips for a rich audiovisual portrait.

Online Obits

The online environment offers even more opportunities to present a full-featured portrait of a person (see Figure 13.2). In addition to audio and video clips of the person and of others discussing him or her, an online obit can include any or all of the following:

- Slide shows.
- Links to related stories and recent news stories.
- A link to an official site connected with the person.
- A text or visual timeline of the person's life.
- A guest book for visitors to sign (or a collection of their e-mails).

CNN.com did a particularly good job of packaging its online obit of entertainer Johnny Carson when he died in 2005. It is online at www.cnn.com/2005/SHOWBIZ/ TV/01/ 23/your.memories/index.html.

Although it might seem that multimedia obits would work for only well-known people, at least one online news site has experimented with bringing the concept to everyday people. The Web site of the Spokane, Wash., Spokesman-Review has been producing slide shows consisting of seven photos and 25 seconds of audio provided by family members; it is online at www.spokesmanreview.com/library/valley/obits/ cover.asp.

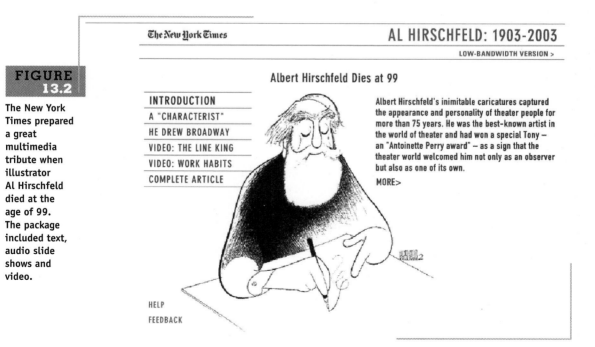

FIGURE 13.2

The New York Times prepared a great multimedia tribute when illustrator Al Hirschfeld died at the age of 99. The package included text, audio slide shows and video.

The New York Times

AL HIRSCHFELD: 1903-2003

LOW-BANDWIDTH VERSION >

Albert Hirschfeld Dies at 99

INTRODUCTION

A "CHARACTERIST"

HE DREW BROADWAY

VIDEO: THE LINE KING

VIDEO: WORK HABITS

COMPLETE ARTICLE

Albert Hirschfeld's inimitable caricatures captured the appearance and personality of theater people for more than 75 years. He was the best-known artist in the world of theater and had won a special Tony — an "Antoinette Perry award" — as a sign that the theater world welcomed him not only as an observer but also as one of its own.

MORE>

HELP

FEEDBACK

Accidents and Disasters

Another staple of journalism is the accident or disaster story. This type of story can include a wide range of events: plane and motor vehicle crashes, natural disasters, accidental shootings, mine cave-ins, and so on. While from a structural perspective, the accident or disaster story is relatively straightforward, it is sometimes tougher to write than the other stories we've discussed so far because it might need to be written before all the facts are in.

To prepare a good accident or disaster story, a reporter needs to gather lots of information, talking with law enforcement officials, witnesses and as many other people as possible. The reporter needs to find out:

- Names, addresses and conditions of victims (or estimates of number of victims for larger disasters).
- Locations where injured people are being held.
- Names and contact information for relatives of the casualties.
- Exact location of the accident or disaster.
- Law enforcement agencies investigating the event (and names and titles of those in charge of each agency's investigation).
- Damage estimates.
- Cause, if known.
- Weather at the time of the event (if pertinent).

The following story typifies the structure of an accident or disaster story:

A man has died after a dog apparently fell from a freeway overpass and crashed through the windshield of his car, police said Thursday.

> Lead begins with the most important information, in this case the death of the driver. Most of the 5 Ws and an H are answered in the lead.

Charles G. Jetchick, 81, was severely injured by the dog, which fell from an Interstate 96 overpass on Saturday afternoon. Jetchick died Wednesday at a Livonia hospital, Michigan State Police said.

> Second graf provides full identification and other details to fill in the basics outlined in the lead.

A passenger in Jetchick's car, whom police would not identify, suffered minor injuries, said Sgt. Michael A. Shaw.

> Other less important consequences follow—injuries, property damage, and so on.

Police don't believe the dog, a 60- or 70-pound black Labrador retriever, was thrown from the Schoolcraft Road overpass in suburban Detroit. The dog probably fell by accident while trying to avoid a car, Shaw said.

"We don't know," he said. "That's why we're looking for witnesses."

> The body of the story typically relates the events of the accident or disaster, answering the question, "How did this happen?" In this case, there is no clear answer. The writer cannot, however, ignore the question, but has to report on the attempts that are being made to answer it.

The passenger in the car didn't see anything other than the dog crashing through the windshield, police said. Despite his injuries, Jetchick was able to steer his westbound car in a straight line and stop safely, Shaw said.

Troopers also questioned the dog's owner, Shaw said.

Shaw, who has been with the State Police for 11 years, said he's never encountered a similar incident.

"We've had rocks and other stuff like that fall off of overpasses. This would be the first dog we've had," he said. (AP)

Any remaining details or interesting sidelights come at the end.

As with other stories discussed in this chapter, it's important that the reporter double-check all details and facts. In addition, a reporter should present estimates of casualties and damages as estimates, not as hard facts. Such predictions tend to change greatly as a story develops. For example, when the crashes of two hijacked planes into the World Trade Center on Sept. 11, 2001, led to the collapse of the towers, initial estimates speculated that 10,000 or more people were killed. In the final accounting, the number was less than 3,000. If answers to obvious questions are not available by deadline or are not being released, the reporter should say so (for example, "Police would not release the victim's name until the family was notified" or "No damage estimates were available by deadline").

Audio and Video Accident or Disaster Stories

Covering accidents and disasters can be exciting but difficult for audio and video news reporters. The first challenge is that stories are often prepared and delivered while the news is taking place. Stories need to be written quickly, and updates can come in at a blistering pace.

Another challenge is that audio from officials—the fire or police chief, FBI agent or whoever is in charge—typically lacks pizzazz and adds little to a story. Therefore, reporters should talk to as many witnesses as possible to piece the story together. (One word of caution, however: Some "witnesses" just want to be on the air. Reporters must be cautious and try to verify a person's status with police before using audio or video clips featuring him or her.)

Reporters preparing video stories face an additional challenge, in that officials often try to keep reporters far away from the scene, limiting opportunities to capture good video.

Therefore, video reporters need to be resourceful and look for video opportunities away from the main action: fire trucks racing in, rescuers looking exhausted, or anything else that expresses the urgency of the situation.

This voice-over is a typical example of the first report of an accident or disaster:

JET SKI DEATH	
Anchor on Camera: CG: Maria Sanchez/Action 11 News	We've got breaking news out of Belleville this morning. One man is dead after a jet ski collided with a motorboat on Ford Lake.
(VO) CG: Breaking News/Belleville, Michigan/Jet Ski Death	(VO) It happened just after 9 this morning. Police say the man died when his jet ski ran into the motorboat carrying two passengers.
	The passengers of the boat…a middle-aged man and a young girl…apparently suffered minor injuries in the crash. No identities are yet available. We will keep you updated on this story as more information becomes available.

The story uses the only video available—footage of the accident scene—and includes no sound bites. Throughout the day, the story would be updated several times as details become available about the identity and condition of the victims, the cause of the crash, and so on.

Online Accident or Disaster Stories

One of the biggest advantages of using online news to report accident or disaster stories is that the stories can be updated easily as information becomes available. The online environment not only allows but also encourages speedy posting of news reports and ongoing updates. As Steve Outing of the Poynter Institute has written:

> It wasn't very long ago that I bemoaned the local papers ignoring significant breaking news events—say, a fire in the hills above Boulder that everyone could see—until the end of the day, when print-edition stories were posted to the Web. Residents of a city should expect that a significant news event will be covered very quickly on a newspaper's Web site.
>
> Well, perhaps we're finally at the point where this kind of thing is routine, even for smaller community papers.... The deadline is now for big news, not tonight.[13]

ASSIGNMENT DESK 13.3

Using the information given here, write a short article for print and online use. Then write a short video news script.

Surgeons at a local hospital spent yesterday morning preparing a critically ill man for a heart transplant. Meanwhile, 45 minutes away a team of four transplant specialists boarded a Cessna plane along with a donor heart on ice.

Shortly after takeoff, one of the two pilots reported that he was having difficulty steering the plane because of trouble with the plane's trim system, according to an investigator with the National Transportation Safety Board. The trim system is used to control the bank and pitch of the plane.

The NTSB investigator said the pilot signaled an emergency and indicated that he was heading back to his airport of origin. Shortly after that communication, the plane crashed.

The crash killed all four members of the transplant team: cardiac surgeon Katherine Pinch, transplant donation specialists Richard Moore and Michael Shapiro, and physician-in-training Miram Longford. Also killed were pilots Dennis Wholey and Robert Sadera.

The patient who was awaiting the transplant was put back on a waiting list while the search began for another heart. The hospital did not release his name for privacy reasons, but a hospital spokesman said there was no telling how long the patient might be able to live without a transplant.

Justin Brain, the chief of transplant surgery at the local hospital, said when he heard the news: "Everyone in the operating room went quiet. This is such a tragedy for so many people."

Video footage: NTSB team at the site of the crash (17 seconds).

Crime Stories

Crime news accounts for a large percentage of all news stories and is always one of the most popular types of news. People want to keep tabs on what's going on around them so they can take any necessary steps to protect themselves and their families.

Crime stories can be written at many different stages. Depending on the stage of the investigation and criminal proceedings and the cooperation of law enforcement with the media, the writer should include as much of the following information as possible:

- Name(s) and condition of victim(s), if any.
- Status of investigation: Are police questioning someone, do they have a suspect, has an arrest been made, has anyone been charged?
- If someone has been charged, the name(s) of person(s) charged, age and address.
- If police are searching for a suspect or suspects, detailed description of the suspect(s) if available. Generic descriptions such as "a white male, 20 to 35 years old, approximately 6 feet tall, medium build" are useless in helping the public find the suspect and should not be included.
- Details of the crime (from police report if possible).
- Punishment if convicted of crime (e.g., "Each charge carries a penalty of up to one year in jail or a fine of $500 or both sanctions").

The biggest challenges in covering crime stories usually come in gathering information. The first issue is that victims often are reluctant to be interviewed. As the Covering Crime and Justice Web site states, "Many victims have never had contact with the media. They feel overwhelmed, distrustful and scared. Imagine that after a horrible crime, a pack of reporters, with cameras and tape recorders rolling, surround you and yell out questions."[14] (See Figure 13.3.)

Dealing with people in such a vulnerable position requires sensitivity and thoughtfulness. Ethics expert Bob Steele of the Poynter Institute offers several suggestions for working with victims:

- Be clear about what is on the record. For most victims, this will be the first time dealing with a journalist.
- When talking to relatives of someone who died in a crime (or accident), focus on the victim's life, not death. Ask if they have a photograph or video footage of the victim that they would like to be used in the story.
- Look for a victim's advocate when a victim or family cannot or will not cooperate. Don't be pushy—respect people when they decline to be interviewed.
- Be cautious about publishing information that might help identify suspects in a crime. Doing so might hinder law enforcement.[15]

The second challenge in covering crime is getting information from authorities. Law enforcement authorities often brush off reporters so they can focus on their investigations. Although journalists—and the public they represent—are entitled to such public information, sometimes getting it requires effort. One of the best tips for making authorities more receptive to questions is to talk with as many other people on the crime scene as possible. Doing so lets a reporter appear more knowledgeable when approaching authorities; that usually results in authorities providing more information.

FIGURE 13.3

Crime victims and other people in the news for the first time typically do not know what to expect when a pack of reporters shows up to interview them.

In the simplest crime stories, all that's known is that a crime has been committed:

Police are investigating an arson in the Broadwater community yesterday that destroyed four homes under construction. Damage to the homes is estimated at nearly $2 million. Police say they are looking for similarities with an arson that took place earlier this month in the White Oak area.

Such stories tend to be short because little information is available. More typically, crime stories are written after suspects are arrested and charged with a crime:

A three-week investigation into drug activity at a Glen Burnie home ended Tuesday with the seizure of 6 grams of crack cocaine and the arrest of two suspected drug dealers, county police said.

> Lead summarizes the news and answers who, what, when and where.

Citizen complaints prompted police to look at 1300 Howard Road. While conducting surveillance Tuesday, detectives saw a man driving a black Lincoln Navigator visit the house for about two minutes. Police said neighbors mentioned the SUV in their complaints, leading officers to follow it and pull it over for a traffic violation. A search of the SUV found 6.6 grams of crack.

> Next two paragraphs provide background on the arrests and answer the why and how.

The driver, Quentin Alexander Monday, 29, of 1517 Leslie Road in Severn, was charged with driving on a suspended license and possession of crack with intent to distribute.

> The final two paragraphs provide details on the suspects and charges.

Police then got a warrant for 1300 Howard Road and found a small amount of crack and drug paraphernalia. Diane Carol Sevick, 42, of 1300 Howard Road, was charged with possession of cocaine and possession of paraphernalia. (Annapolis Capital)

Notice that nowhere in the story are the two suspects referred to as criminals or drug dealers. Despite the fact that this seems like a straightforward case at this point, they have been charged, not convicted, of the crimes. Saying they are guilty—explicitly or implicitly—is libelous and could cause serious legal problems.

Audio and Video Crime Stories

Perhaps the biggest challenge to video news reporters covering crime is that audio and visual elements often are scarce. The crime scene might not be accessible or visually interesting; suspects might not have been apprehended; officials might not be talking; there may be no witnesses; and so on. In such cases, the reporter needs to be especially enterprising, looking for photos and archival video, seeking out residents who live near the crime scene, turning to friends and family members for comments. The following story illustrates how a television reporter prepared a two-minute package in such a situation:

Anchor with OTS graphic: Teenager Killed	((On Cam)) GRIEF COUNSELORS WILL BE AT COURTLAND HIGH SCHOOL TODAY FOLLOWING THE DEATH OF AN ATHLETE.
Take F/S graphic CG: Map Rollcue to pkg: "has the story" Pkg TRT: 1:53	((Fullscreen Map)) 16-YEAR-OLD BARON BRASWELL WAS STABBED TO DEATH LATE FRIDAY NIGHT IN SPOTSYLVANIA COUNTY. NEWS 4'S DARCY SPENCER HAS THE STORY.
CG: Spotsylvania County, Va. (26–29) CG: Christine Lynch/ Pres. Courtland HS PTSA (30–33) CG: Sheriff Howard Smith/Spotsylvania County Sheriff's Office (53–57) CG: Adam Lynch/family friend (1:21–1:32) CG: Mike Lynch/parent (1:40–1:46) CG: Darcy Spencer/News4 (1:46–1:53)	((PKG))

16-YEAR OLD BARON BRASWELL, A STAR ATHLETE AT COURTLAND HIGH SCHOOL...IN SPOTSYLVANIA COUNTY.

THE TEENAGER WAS STABBED TO DEATH IN A GANG-RELATED ATTACK IN THE PARKING LOT OF A HOWARD JOHNSON'S MOTEL NEAR THE SCHOOL FRIDAY NIGHT.

//SOT//
(Christine Lynch/Knew Braswell)
"This is something that I think we in our little high school feel pretty separated from, violence like this...and I think it's shocked everyone that it's reached us."

FIVE BOYS — AGES 15 to 17 — HAVE BEEN CHARGED WITH CONSPIRACY TO COMMIT MURDER . . . IN CONNECTION WITH THE KILLING. THEY ATTEND JAMES MONROE HIGH SCHOOL IN FREDRICKSBURG. POLICE SAY THERE WAS A CD RELEASE PARTY AT THE HOTEL THAT NIGHT.

//SOT//
(Sheriff Howard Smith/Spotsylvania County Sheriff's office)
"There was a particular song that was played there called . . . and I hope I get this right . . . Knuck if you Buck, which is apparently a mob lyric song. And it's a song talking about shooting and stabbing and beating people up."

BRASWELL WAS A JUNIOR AT THE HIGH SCHOOL, KNOWN TO HIS FRIENDS AS "DEUCE." HE EXCELLED IN SPORTS, PLAYED ON THE SCHOOL BASEBALL, BASKETBALL AND FOOTBALL TEAMS.

//SOT//
(Adam Lynch/family friend)
"Do you think he had a future in sports?"
"Absolutely, he was a great athlete. That's another thing, you know, the school teams are going to miss him because he was a bright spot for the football team especially."

FRIENDS SET UP A MEMORIAL AT THE SCHOOL, A NUMBER 5, SIGNIFYING HIS JERSEY NUMBER.
HIS PARENTS RELEASED A STATEMENT SAYING — THE FAMILY IS STILL TRYING TO MAKE SENSE OF WHAT HAPPENED AND DEAL WITH THE LOSS AS BEST AS WE CAN.

//SOT//
(Mike Lynch/family friend)
"It's just such a sad thing. I don't know how the family copes with it."

(REPORTER STAND-UP)

GRIEF COUNSELORS ARE SCHEDULED TO BE HERE AT THE SCHOOL WHEN CLASSES RESUME ON TUESDAY. BARON BRASWELL WILL BE LAID TO REST ON SATURDAY. IN SPOTSYLVANIA COUNTY, THIS IS DARCY SPENCER, NEWS 4. (Courtesy WRC-TV, NBC4.com)

The only downside of this report is that aside from the sheriff, all three people interviewed share the same last name and are likely related. Even when production time is tight, a reporter should make every effort to interview as many diverse sources as possible.

Online Crime Stories

The fundamental strengths of the online environment once again come to the fore in covering crime stories. Online stories can be posted and updated rapidly, and new stories can be linked to older related stories, to official documents and multimedia enhancements (for example, photos, maps and animations of crime scenes).

ASSIGNMENT DESK **13.4**

Using the crime report given here, write a short article and a 20-second reader.

CRIME REPORT

LAST Name	First	Middle	Race	Sex	DOB
Frank	Melissa	Ann	Caucasian	Female	3/11/73

Residence			City	Zip	Res. Phone
498 Royal Oak Drive			Hometown	12345	997-555-4398

Business			City	Zip	Bus. Phone
Second National Bank, 101 Main Street			Hometown	12366	997-555-6942

Do you know who is responsible?	If yes, Name and Address		
No			

Physical description of suspect		Race	Sex	Age
Dark hair and beard, 5–10 to 6–0, heavy build Wearing blue jeans and T-shirt		Caucasian	Male	20–25

Date and time of incident	Address or location of incident
12:27 p.m. 9/17/07	Second National Bank

Was a vehicle involved?	If yes, Model/Make/Color/Year/License No.
Suspect's _x_ Victim's __	Late-model red Ford F-150 pickup truck.

Method of entry of vehicle	Point of entry of vehicle

Brief Summary of Incident

Suspect entered bank, handed teller Frank a note demanding money and indicating teller would be hurt or killed if she did not comply. Suspect lifted his shirt and displayed semiautomatic handgun strapped to his chest. Teller complied and turned over contents of her cash drawer to suspect, who fled without further incident. Suspect was seen entering late-model red Ford F-150 pickup truck, where another white male was waiting in driver's seat. Vehicle fled area.

Continued :•

Assignment
Desk 13.4
Continues

Describe what was ___X___ **Stolen** _____ **Damaged** _____ **Lost**

Article	How many	Model/ number	Serial number	Color	Value
Cash	$6,570				

Note: It is VERY important to give the serial number of each item listed above.
IT IS A MISDEMEANOR TO MAKE A FALSE REPORT OF A CRIME.

Special Events

Most communities host at least one or more large events regularly: street fairs, book fairs, county and state fairs, food and wine festivals, and so on. The scale of such events offers writers lots of creative freedom but also presents logistical nightmares: Where should a writer start, and how much needs to be covered?

To answer the second question first: It depends. An overview provides a sense of what the event is about. For instance, Julie Sumper wrote this account of a popular Baltimore event:

> Maybe it's the live music, costumes, food and contests that bring people out to Oktoberfest each year, or maybe it's the 11 different breweries that participate in the event. Either way, Oktoberfest is a fall event that adds to the flavor of Baltimore throughout the month of October. The Maryland Brewer's Oktoberfest in Timonium, however, is the biggest and best of all of the local celebrations.

> Oktoberfest is an event surrounded by beer. It's a beer tasting in which one purchases beer tokens and then uses the tokens as cash to go around to all of the different breweries and taste their beer.

> "One beer is 4 ounces, and in the state of Maryland you have to do tastings. It's one of those crazy laws," said Gary Brooks, the owner of Barley and Hops, one of the breweries represented at the event. "So one token equals one tasting, and three tokens equals a beer."

> Barley and Hops is one of the original breweries to participate in this Oktoberfest.

> "This is one of our best events each year. We get to introduce our beers to more of a Baltimore-based clientele" said Brooks, whose brewery is located in Frederick, Md. "It's a good place to showcase all of the Maryland beers."

> Despite the German tradition behind Oktoberfest, the beers showcased at the event are not German. Instead, they represent local breweries such as Barley and Hops, the Brewer's Art, Fordham Brewing Co., Clipper City Brewing Co., DuClaw Brewing Co. and more. All of the breweries present are members of the Brewer's Association of Maryland.

> Brooks supports the idea of holding an Oktoberfest that is full of local breweries.

"In Maryland we think so much about wineries, but…there are so many different breweries here," he said.

Brooks said that his own favorite Barley and Hops beer is the Pale Ale, but during the fall the Oktoberfest brew is the brewery's best seller.

While it is true that Oktoberfest is an event focused on beer, you don't have to be a beer lover, or even a beer drinker, to attend. Even children can enjoy the music and contests that take place on two stages throughout the weekend. This year's Maryland Brewer's Oktoberfest featured music from local bands, as well as the German Edelweiss Band.

"We've been around for 36 years," said Brian Priebe, a member of the Edelweiss Band. "We've been here several times. We play at Oktoberfests all over the region, and this is one of the best."

Throughout the festival, the Edelweiss Band played German, Austrian and Swiss music, as well as some American jazz and popular songs that Germans like.

"When you go to Oktoberfest in Bavaria, you hear all kinds of American music," said Priebe. "Three years ago 'Country Roads Take Me Home' was the most popular tune over there."

The stages also hold contests such as the "Baltimore Best Beer Belly" competition and the "Miss Oktoberfest" contest.

"We just tried to incorporate something fun, and we started doing it a couple of years ago. It seemed to go over well. Both of the contests are fun for all of the attendees," said Alicia Woodward, who works for Moorea Marketing. Moorea Marketing helps to produce the event every year.

Woodward herself was born in Baltimore, and she sees Oktoberfest as way to impact the community.

"The Maryland Brewer's Oktoberfest gets the Brewer's Association's name out there. There are a lot of great breweries in Maryland that get sort of overlooked because of some of the powerhouse beers, you know, the big companies. There are some great brewing institutions here," she said. "This festival helps people to become aware that brewing is a craft. It supports a lot of jobs in the area. The more people that are aware and are patrons of these establishments, the better it is for the community in general. It's also just a fun event for people to come out to."

Despite the fact that the beer at this German event is not German at all, there are many other ways in which the German tradition behind Oktoberfest is incorporated into the Maryland Brewer's Oktoberfest.

Woodward hopes that next year will be an even better Oktoberfest, but until then she is satisfied with the results of the event.

"Our turnout is bigger than ever, but we are always trying to incorporate something new to keep people coming back," she said.

For long-standing events, however, such overviews can grow stale and repetitive. In those cases, instead of trying to cover every aspect of an event, the reporter should look for the most interesting, important or unusual aspect or aspects. For instance, rather than attempting to write an all-encompassing story about a farm show, the reporter should look for interesting people to focus on: a fruit-and-nut judge, a honey queen, and so on. If the reporter does a good job, the resulting stories will help the audience understand the ongoing appeal of the event in a way that a more generic overview cannot.

Audio, Video and Online Coverage of Special Events

Adding audio and video elements to special event stories goes far in helping audience members share the experience of attending the event. Sights and sounds that capture the energy and feel of the event are mandatory in preparing audio and video reports. Such elements also help flesh out online packages, which can incorporate a wealth of other elements to offer even more depth: links to event and performer Web sites, timelines, short audio and video interviews with those in attendance, and so on. For example, the online version of the Oktoberfest story includes a slide show with interviews and photos of participants, and links to the Web sites of the several local breweries and the state Brewer's Association.

ASSIGNMENT DESK **13.5**

Attend a special event on your campus or in your community and write an overview article on it. Interview at least three people at the event, representing different roles (for example, an organizer, someone attending the event, and a vendor or performer at the event).

Next, make a list of audio and video elements that could be incorporated to provide the sense of attending the event.

Conclusion

The number and types of stories to be covered can overwhelm the new journalist. But understanding the most common types and developing strategies for tackling them can make it easy to handle them. The most important things for a reporter to remember are to look for something original, be thorough and accurate, and use the medium or media to its fullest potential. That way, the result will be a good story every time, no matter what the news—and the audience will enjoy and learn from it.

KEY TERMS

feature obit, 232
general assignment reporter, 225
news conference, 225
panel discussion, 225

public meeting, 226
speech, 225
standard or news orbit, 232

DISCUSSION QUESTIONS

1. Using Google News (http://news.google.com), search for *transcript* to find the full transcript of a recent speech or news conference. Then find at least two stories based on the speech or news conference. How are the stories similar? How do they differ?
2. Again using Google News, find a local news site's coverage of a major accident or disaster. Search the site for coverage over the next several days. How do the follow-up stories differ from the originals? Would a new reader coming in on the second or third day find everything necessary to understand the story in the updated versions?
3. Using newspapers, online news sites or local television news, read or watch at least three crime stories. Are the stories interesting or routine? How good a job has the reporter done in each case of highlighting what makes the stories unique?

NOTES

1. Amy Gahran, "Embrace Your Learning Curve," I, Reporter, 15 December 2005, **www.ireporter.org/ 2005/12/embrace_your_le.html.**

2. Gahran.

3. "General: It's Fun to Shoot Some People," CNN.com, 4 February 2005, **www.cnn.com/2005/US/02/03/ general.shoot/.**

4. Chip Scanlan, "Summing Up a Life: Meeting the obituary's challenge," Poynter.org, 9 April 2003, **www.poynter. org/column.asp?id=52&aid=29333.**

5. Alana Baranick, "Writing About the Dead and Loving It!" Deathbeat.com, **www.deathbeat.com/ index.html.**

6. Gregg McLachlan, "Obit—Don't Bury Your News Values," No Train, No Gain, **www.notrain-nogain.org/train/ res/write/obits.asp.** Used courtesy of editor and journalist Gregg McLachlan.

7. Mark Singer, "The Death Beat," The New Yorker, 8 July 2002, **www.newyorker.com/fact/content/ ?020708fa_fact.**

8. McLachlan.

9. Adam Bernstein, "J.Y. Smith, 74; Raised Standards for Post Obituaries," the Washington Post, 19 January 2006, p. B7.

10. Gerry Goldstein, "Making Obits Anything but Routine," Providence Journal-Bulletin, 25 March 1998, **www.projo.com/words/tip325.htm.**

11. Bernstein.

12. McLachlan.

13. Steve Outing, "Breaking News Won't Wait," Poynter.org, 10 November 2005, **http://poynter.org/column. asp?id=31&aid=92012.**

14. Suzette Hackney, "Covering Crime and Its Victims," Covering Crime and Justice, 2003, **http:// justicejournalism.org/crimeguide/.**

15. Bob Steele, "Handle with Care: The victim's perspective," Poynter.org, 18 May 1996, **http://poynter.org/ content/content_view.asp?id=5582.**

Journalistic Principles

So far, we have concentrated on the mechanics of news writing. From sentence structure to story formats. We have focused on creating compelling news reports.

What we haven't talked about yet, though, are the guiding principles that underscore every action a journalist takes and every story he or she writes. In this chapter, we turn our attention to those principles, which help ensure journalism that is not just technically correct but is also responsible.

Shifting Values

Like much else that we've covered so far, the guiding principles of journalism are undergoing change and reevaluation. Rules that have seemingly been in force forever are changing or disappearing entirely. Although some observers bemoan these changes as evidence that journalism is becoming worse, others see the changes working to create journalism that does a better job of serving the public than it ever has before.

The journalistic value receiving the most scrutiny is **objectivity,** which has been the leading principle of U.S. journalism for many years. In a nutshell, objectivity requires that journalists stick to observable facts and avoid injecting their opinions into news reports. As sociologist Michael Schudson has noted in his landmark book "Discovering the News," "the belief in objectivity is a faith in 'facts,' a distrust in 'values,' and a commitment to their segregation."[1] As recently as 1999, a survey of local and national journalists and news media executives found that a full three-fourths of them believed "it is possible to obtain a true, accurate and widely agreed upon account of an event."[2]

Almost from the beginning, however, objectivity has been under fire. Just a few decades after objectivity became the accepted standard of U.S. journalism, it came under fire for helping obscure lynching and other attacks on blacks.[3] During the next 75 years, the rise of public relations, the McCarthy era, and "(g)overnment lies about the

U2 spy flights, the Cuban missile crisis, and the Vietnam War all cast doubt on the ability of 'objective' journalism to get at anything close to the truth."[4] The presidential campaign of 2004 prompted even more people to consider that it might be time for objectivity to be retired or at least be given a tune-up. Even many journalists who once staunchly defended the concept are having second thoughts. In fact, the Society of Professional Journalists no longer includes the word "objectivity" in its Code of Ethics.

Critics point out several failings of objectivity:

Objectivity's demand that journalists stick to only observable facts often keeps them from finding the truth in a story. As Mitchell Stephens has written, objectivity is based on "the pretense that news merely consists of collections of unbiased information, which had somehow passed, without contamination, directly from reality to notebook to typewriter."[5] The problem, he explains, is that "Facts, sadly, are often messy, difficult to isolate, dependent on context, and subject to interpretation."[6]

What is most important to the public is not the facts of a story but the truth of a story. Blogger Tim Porter notes: "News stories are supposed to provide answers, to assign reward or blame, to leave no ends lying loosely about. Journalists search for facts to explain complex issues, but facts alone are often not enough to provide readers with understanding."[7] In a piece titled "Re-Thinking Objectivity," Brett Cunningham adds, "Our readers need, more than ever, reliable reporting that tells them what is true when that is knowable, and pushes as close to truth as possible when it is not."[8]

Many journalists feel uncomfortable with this role. But as Steve Lovelady, former managing editor of CampaignDesk.org (which analyzed political claims and coverage during the 2004 election), told the Los Angeles Times: "Reporters can and do argue that it's not their job to ascertain veracity. But that *is* their job, especially when the facts are so easily available."[9] Another critic of political campaign coverage raises a related point that applies to all news stories: Suggesting that "campaign remarks are misleading could lead to screams of 'Bias!' But when the candidates have become so good at spin, the media need to understand that pointing out the truth isn't the same as taking sides."[10]

Closely attached to the concept of objectivity is the notion of **balance**. While the idea that a reporter should cover all sides of an issue is a good one, few reporters go beyond seeking comments from two opposing parties. "The media are awash in 'he said/she said/ we're mum' journalism, 'the practice of reporters parroting competing rhetoric instead of measuring it for veracity against known facts,'" the creators of the CampaignDesk.org Web site argued. "Instead of acting as filters for the truth, reporters nodded and attentively transcribed both sides of the story, invariably failing to provide context, background or any sense of which claims held up and which claims were misleading."[11]

Lovelady adds: "Reporters seem to think they've done an adequate job just because they give both sides the chance to state their case.... But if that's all you do, you may have satisfied the imagined constraints of objectivity, but often you haven't told the reader anything."[12]

When reporters claim that providing this type of false balance is good journalism, Washington Post ombudsman Michael Getler says, "News organizations need to look hard and fast at whether they are truly 'leveling with the reader.'"[13] Some journalists have made noble attempts to address this issue. For example, during major political races, some news organizations have analyzed campaign ads and pointed out misleading and untruthful information in them. Still, these cases represent the exception rather than the rule.

This issue is one of the key ones that has driven young people away from the mainstream media. As one wrote in the Washington Post, "The endless he said/she said reporting and the airtime given to questionable allegations highlight the reason why so many young people like myself are turning away from mainstream outlets such as newspapers and network newscasts."[14]

ASSIGNMENT DESK 14.1

Find a recent story in the news about a controversial issue in your community or at your school. Make a list of the sources cited in the article. Who do they represent? Can you think of any other viewpoints that are not covered? Who might be able to speak for people holding those viewpoints? What questions remain unanswered in the story?

Objectivity promotes the views of the powerful at the expense of their critics and the powerless. Journalists' tendency to rely on the powerful people who are enmeshed in the news net leads to stories that often favor the viewpoint of those in power at the expense of their critics.[15]

With ever-increasing time pressures, "The nonstop news cycle leaves reporters less time to dig and encourages reliance on official sources who can provide the information quickly and succinctly," writes Brent Cunningham. He adds, "More important, objectivity makes us wary of seeming to argue with the president—or the governor, or the CEO—and risk losing our access."[16]

The biggest problem with using official sources is that they typically have their own agendas, and they also often are accomplished in shaping media messages. "Sometimes there are no answers to difficult and persistent issues like poverty, racism, religious and moral differences or the role of government in private lives," writes Tim Porter. "Journalists have the opportunity to explore the questions, air the differences and enable civic debate." But those debates are not likely to occur if all the sources for a news story are officials who see things in the same way.[17]

Geneva Overholser, a longtime journalist and educator, has said, "The way it is currently construed, 'objectivity'... produces a rigid orthodoxy, excluding voices beyond the narrowly conventional." For that and other reasons, she adds, it is "unmistakably clear that objectivity has outlived its usefulness as an ethical touchstone for journalism."[18]

Objectivity tends to make journalists passive. If journalists are prohibited from going beyond the facts, they cannot select a topic to put into the news if no one is talking about it. Brent Cunningham calls this "a particular failure of the press: allowing the principle of objectivity to make us passive recipients of news, rather than aggressive analyzers and explainers of it."[19]

Washington Post economics reporter Jonathan Weisman adds, "News is driven by the zeitgeist, and if an issue isn't part of the current zeitgeist then it will be a tough sell to editors."[20] And those in power largely determine the zeitgeist.

As a result, journalists often find objectivity to be a straitjacket that prohibits them from putting important topics on the agenda. "Curiously, for all the technology the news media have, for all the gifted minds that make it all work," wrote David House, the reader advocate for the Fort Worth Star-Telegram, "it's a simple thing to stop the media cold. Say nothing, hide documents."[21]

Even after a topic makes it onto the agenda, a journalist who goes no further does not serve the audience. "What are needed are journalists who can connect the dots," says Mike Levine, executive editor of the Middletown, N.Y., Times Herald-Record. Levine argues that once reporters demonstrate they know as much or more about their subjects as their sources do, they should be given the freedom to make sense of the facts, not just report them as discrete objects.

The conditions that made objectivity a wise economic decision no longer apply. At the time objectivity became the standard for journalists in the United States, people had few sources of news, and those sources—the wire services and the penny press—were interested in attracting the widest possible audiences. In that climate, it made sense that news should be free of bias so it would appeal to as wide an audience as possible.

Today, however, the news media do not operate in a climate of scarcity. News is every-where, all the time, and the emergence of bloggers has added countless new journalists and commentators to the mix. (Of course, if mainstream media are not to be trusted, the bloggers often inspire even less trust, as the case of conservative blogger Jeff Gannon clearly revealed. Gannon, who wrote for the conservative online site Talon News, was revealed to be a former gay escort with no journalistic experience.[22])

In a climate of abundance, no one source of news has to be all things to all people. Instead, news outlets are now finding that having a clear point of view is the key to draw-ing people. Many people have shown that they prefer to get their news from clearly parti-san journalistic outlets that share their views, hence the rise of the Fox News Channel, which despite its motto of being "fair and balanced" is generally regarded as leaning toward a conservative Republican perspective.

"I think it's a watershed moment in the politicization of journalism," media con-sultant and former CNN executive David Bernknopf said after Fox's coverage of the 2004 Republican National Convention drew more viewers than any other network. "It really does show that people are choosing their news outlets based on what they per-ceive to be the politics of that news outlet. It's undeniable that a large number of people chose Fox because they thought it would cover the Republican National Convention in a respectful way."[23]

ASSIGNMENT DESK 14.2

With a group of classmates, record and watch several network newscasts from a single day. If possible, include CNN, Fox and other major cable networks. Make a list of stories that have been cov-ered on more than one newscast. Compare the stories to determine the perspectives used in them.

What Comes Next?

So if it's time to toss out objectivity—granted, not an idea with which all journalists agree—what should replace it? Dan Gillmor, formerly a reporter for The San Jose (Calif.) Mercury News and a leading proponent of citizen journalism, suggests "four other notions that may add up to the same thing. They are pillars of good journalism: thoroughness, accuracy, fairness and transparency."[24] Let's look at each of those in turn.

Thoroughness

Doing thorough journalism means looking into every aspect of a story. **Thoroughness** requires time to track down and talk with the best sources, find the best documentary evidence, and so on. The goal is to give the audience as much information as possible so they can understand what is happening and make informed decisions based on that information. "Thoroughness serves readers, not sources," writes Tim Porter. "Information, with more reporting, becomes education."[25]

But education precedes thorough reporting, too. Journalists need "to develop expertise and to use it to sort through competing claims, identify and explain the underlying assumptions of those claims, and make judgments about what readers and viewers need to know to understand what is happening."[26]

Timothy Noah addressed the issue of journalists' education in a 1999 symposium on objectivity for The Washington Monthly, writing, "Ultimately, it's best for reporting to strive to be neither 'analytic' nor 'neutral,' but simply to be fair-minded and truthful based on a detailed examination of the matter at hand." Noah argued that reporters need to take the time to get to know and understand their subjects so they can develop intelligent viewpoints.[27]

Accuracy

Legendary publisher Joseph Pulitzer once remarked that the three rules of journalism are "Accuracy, accuracy and accuracy." Most journalists would readily agree that **accuracy** is a vital aspect of journalism. In fact, if a piece of journalism is not accurate, it has no value. People turn to the news to learn what of importance is happening in the world. They base decisions and make plans according to the news, so the information *must* be accurate.

Bill Kovach and Tom Rosenstiel of the Project for Excellence in Journalism state the case simply:

> The essence of journalism is a discipline of verification.
> In the end, the discipline of verification is what separates journalism from other forms of communication—from entertainment, propaganda, fiction or art.... Journalism alone is focused first on getting it right.[28]

And yet, inaccurate information abounds in the news. A survey undertaken for the American Society of Newspaper Editors found that 68 percent of the public thinks that newspapers run many stories without checking them just because other papers have published them, not because they know they're true. In addition, nearly half of those surveyed reported seeing factual errors in their newspapers at least a few times a month.[29]

Even worse, an error-tracking system at the Chicago Tribune found that "at least half to two-thirds of all errors in the newspaper were preventable; most occurred through reporting or writing mistakes or were introduced during the editing process."[30]

At a minimum, factual errors can annoy the audience and send them elsewhere. Speaking of the Chicago Tribune project, Editor Howard Tyner has said:

> The slightest excuse is sufficient (for readers) to bail out. People get very angry when they see mistakes, especially mistakes that go uncorrected. It's a credibility issue. If people are thinking about getting rid of you anyway, why serve up a big softball?[31]

And it's not just errors in printed or spoken words that need to be watched for: Errors in charts, maps and other graphics also are common.

In addition to being annoying, a factual error also can be an inconvenience for an audience member. Even a minor error in an entertainment listing "can send a reader to a movie theater at the wrong time, to a restaurant on a night when it is closed, or to a museum exhibition that doesn't open for another week."[32]

For example, a reporter for the Fort Worth (Texas) Star-Telegram wrote a short item about a school board meeting scheduled at Parkview Elementary School—without double-checking his notes. The actual location was Park Glen Elementary School, a few blocks away. As a result, several people ended up at the wrong place wondering why there was no meeting. (This story had a happy, if unusual, ending. The reporter realized his error in time to drive to Parkview Elementary and hand out maps to Park Glen Elementary. He was later applauded by the audience at the meeting for taking the time and trouble to make things right.)[33]

Inaccurate information can have serious consequences. For instance, Judith Miller and Michael R. Gordon of The New York Times were widely criticized for their 2003 reporting that made a strong case that Iraq possessed weapons of mass destruction, thereby lending credence to and support for U.S. administration officials' claims that an invasion of Iraq was necessary. No evidence of WMDs was ever found, but billions of dollars were spent and thousands of lives lost in the invasion and subsequent occupation.

In another case, Newsweek magazine was forced to apologize "for an inaccurate report on the treatment of detainees that triggered several days of rioting in Afghanistan and other countries in which at least 15 people died."[34]

In recent years, a number of renowned journalists have brought disgrace on themselves and their organizations by displaying a blatant disregard for accuracy and truth. Among the more notable:

- Rising star Stephen Glass was fired from the New Republic for fabricating stories and creating fake Web sites and voice mail boxes to make his stories more credible. After his firing, researchers found many other articles he had written for Rolling Stone, George and Harper's to be full of lies.
- New York Times reporter Jayson Blair was fired after he pretended to file stories from the road while he remained home, made up comments and plagiarized from other news reports. A 7,239-word-long front-page article in the Times said of the case, "The widespread fabrication and plagiarism represent a profound betrayal of trust and a low point in the 152-year history of the newspaper."[35]

- Jack Kelley resigned from USA Today after the paper "found strong evidence that Kelley fabricated substantial portions of at least eight major stories, lifted nearly two dozen quotes or other material from competing publications, lied in speeches he gave for the newspaper and conspired to mislead those investigating his work."[36]
- Best-selling author and longtime columnist Mitch Albom was suspended by the Detroit Free Press after he wrote an advance column in which he described the presence, dress and behavior of two former Michigan State University players at an NCAA Final Four game. The former players did not attend the game, however, and the column ran without acknowledging that.

Striving for Accuracy

At a bare minimum, accuracy means getting the facts straight. That process should begin with the first questions a reporter asks a source: name, age (including birth date), profession and title. Reporters should read the information back to sources to verify that it is correct.

During the research process, a reporter should check information obtained from interviews against original sources: maps, directories, agencies, and so on. Reporters should not rely on secondhand information if there is any way to check it. Even when someone mentions a historical figure or event in a quote, a reporter should make sure the information is accurate before using it. Above all, a reporter never should assume anything, as reflected in this long-standing rule of journalism: If your mother says she loves you, check it out. (See Figure 14.1.)

Once a story has been written, it's important to do one more round of fact checking. John X. Miller, public editor of the Detroit Free Press, offers these questions for writers to consider:

1. Have you double-checked all names, titles and places mentioned in your story?
2. Have you tested and checked *all* phone numbers or Web addresses?
3. Are the quotes accurate and properly attributed? Have you run spell check?
4. Have you checked the math?
5. Have you fact-checked your information given to graphics or photography? Have you seen the completed graphic or photo?[37]

For an in-depth overview of what and how to check to ensure accuracy, check out Frank Fee's "Tips for Greater Accuracy" at www.unc.edu/~ffee/teaching/ accuracy.htm.

ASSIGNMENT DESK 14.3

Using a local newspaper or online news site, another online news site, or the Regret the Error Web site (www.regrettheerror.com/), examine at least 10 corrections. Do they tend to fall into any consistent pattern? How could they have been prevented? What lessons can be learned from them?

FIGURE 14.1

Regrettheerror.
com keeps tabs
on the many
ways in which
the media
stumble.

Beyond Accuracy — to Truth

In addition to verifying facts, a writer also needs to make sure the facts don't misstate the truth. That might not seem to make sense at first, but think of this: A long-running joke in the entertainment business is that the glowing quotes featured in ads ("Spectacular!" "One of the best!" "They don't get any better than this!") are often pulled out from negative reviews ("What a spectacular waste of time. This film is one of the best arguments ever made for shutting down Hollywood. I will have to stop seeing movies if they don't get any better than this!"). The quotes are taken verbatim from the reviews, but they also distort the originals. Although this might be acceptable behavior for a publicist, it is thoroughly unacceptable for a journalist.

To avoid such misinterpretations, a writer should be sure to follow these guidelines:

- Make sure quotes, actualities and sound bites fully capture what the speakers meant. It's easy to distort meaning by changing as little as a single word or by taking a passage out of context.
- Check that photos and video clips don't misrepresent an event. If only 12 people show up for a protest rally, photos and video should not make the event look like a major gathering. News photos should never be altered; altered feature photos should be published only if accompanied by a clear disclaimer.
- Don't rearrange events in time or place. Changing the chronology of events in a print or broadcast story to make it "more interesting" is a serious breach.

FIGURE 14.2

Although the old saying has it that the camera never lies, a photographer can tell very different stories just by changing positions or lenses.

Fairness

Fairness is a word that means different things to different journalists. At its simplest, however, it means an attempt to make sure all the bases are covered.

"I think perfect objectivity is an unrealistic goal," journalist and self-described food detective Michael Pollan has said. "Fairness, however, is not. Fairness forces you—even when you're writing a piece highly critical of, say, genetically modified food, as I have done—to make sure you represent the other side as extensively and as accurately as you possibly can."[38]

Dan Gillmor agrees:

Fairness means, among other things, listening to different viewpoints, and incorporating them into the journalism. It does not mean parroting lies or distortions to achieve that lazy equivalence that leads some journalists to get opposing quotes when the facts overwhelmingly support one side.

Fairness is also about letting people respond when they believe you are wrong...this is much easier online than in a print publication, much less a broadcast.

Ultimately, fairness emerges from a state of mind. We should be aware of what drives us, and always willing to listen to those who disagree. The first rule of having a conversation is to listen—and I know I learn more from people who think I'm wrong than from those who agree with me.[39]

All too often, reporters are guilty of coming into a story with a mindset of how the story will turn out. This tendency to "frame" a story before all the information is gathered is often exacerbated by deadline pressures and insistent editors. Such framing can cause a reporter to seek only sources that support the conclusions he or she has already drawn and avoid sources that challenge those conclusions. The end result is a story that's far from fair. As columnist Nat Hentoff has said, "Fairness means you get the facts, all of them if you can, especially when they surprise you into re-evaluating what you thought the story was going to be about when you began."[40]

That reevaluation occasionally can force a reporter to realize that there is *no* story. "Sometimes despite the best of intentions, fairness can get trampled in the rush to expose wrongdoing," writes Robert J. Haiman. "A reporter can get so wrapped up in tips about wrongdoing he or she can forget that a tip is only a tip. It has to be checked out thoroughly. But the checking process is best begun with a mindset that the tip is just as likely to be wrong as it is to be right."[41]

Transparency

With the ascendancy of the Internet as a primary news delivery medium, the term **transparency** has become part of many journalists' vocabulary. The idea is that to gain and maintain public trust, journalists must be as open as possible about what biases they bring to the job, how they get their information and how they make decisions on choosing and reporting stories. As a report from the Project for Excellence in Journalism notes, "If journalists are truth seekers, it must follow that they be honest and truthful with their audiences, too—that they be truth presenters. If nothing else, this responsibility means journalists [must] be as open and honest with audiences as they can about what they know and what they don't."[42]

Transparency is not a new idea. As the Committee of Concerned Journalists has noted: "When the concept of objectivity in the media originally evolved, it did not imply that journalists were free of bias. It called, rather, for a consistent method of testing information—a transparent approach to evidence—precisely so that personal and cultural biases would not undermine the accuracy of their work. It is the method that is objective, not the journalist."[43]

Professionals in other disciplines have practiced transparency for years. When scientists report the results of a study or pollsters the results of a survey, they provide information about how the studies were conducted, who the test subjects were, what the margin of error is, and so on. That makes their work credible to other professionals and to the public.

In addition, as Buzzmachine.com blogger Jeff Jarvis—among the leading evangelists of transparent journalism—notes, the news media have long demanded transparency of their sources. "It is our turn to open the shades, to reveal our process and prejudice, to engage in the conversation, to join in the community—to be transparent," he says. "Shouldn't we, of all people and professions, be the most transparent?"[44]

Steven A. Smith, editor of The Spokesman-Review in Spokane, Wash., finds real merit in being transparent:

> Transparency—which includes being open about mistakes—can kill rumors and conspiracy theories that breed distrust. It can soften criticism, or at least direct it to the appropriate targets. (Where the mistake was made.) It can enhance credibility, but only if consistently followed. That last is really the point. It's a little counter-intuitive. But raising the window, fessing up, speaking directly to readers with a genuine openness actually enhances credibility.[45]

At a minimum, being transparent requires that a reporter answer these questions:

- How do you know what you know?
- Who are your sources?
- How direct is their knowledge?
- Are there conflicting accounts?
- What don't you know?[46]
- Why was this story, photo or name published?
- Why were other words, photos and names withheld from publication?[47]

In many cases, the writer can answer those questions in the story itself. When not all the information will fit, the writer might prepare a separate article for print or online publication.

Journalists are constantly developing new methods of practicing transparency. A few of the more promising ones include linking to source materials, allowing the audience to

Why Choose Journalism?

I picked journalism over every other profession because I wanted to have a hand in the documentation of society's growth and changes. A journalist's most important task is to inform the public in a direct, concise and unbiased fashion on subjects they both should know about and want to know about. To be able to help someone develop an informed opinion due to the information you provided them is one of the most rewarding things about being a journalist.

AMANDA KROTKI
Baltimore.Metromix.com

take part in decision-making sessions, and offering a regular look behind the scenes. Some examples:

Linking to source materials. When it comes to transparency, online news has one big advantage over traditional news formats: the ability to link to source materials. Rather than just asking the audience to take their word for it, journalists publishing online can offer immediate access to the documents that led them to the conclusions they've reached. As one news critic has written:

> After all, much reporting is based on statements in the public record or other information that's available online. If you're writing about job losses, you can point readers to a specific place on the Bureau of Labor Statistics' Web site so they can decide for themselves if you...are doing the math right. It's hard to get away with a lie (or even subtle misinterpretation, as any blogger who has ever had to correct a piece will attest) when you link to the evidence itself. Yet as far as I can tell, no major news outlet provides such links from the online version of their stories.[48]

David Berlind of ZDNet News has carried that process a step further by providing direct access to recorded interviews: "By providing the uncensored, unedited raw data used to assemble a news story, opinion piece, or blog entry, the problems of misquoting, quote truncation, placing quotes out of order to arrive at an unintended meaning, quoting out of context, or manipulating interviews in the interests of a particular agenda could go away," he writes.[49]

In recent years, a wide range of news organizations have followed that lead:

- In covering a story about how Spokane, Wash., Mayor James West was using the Internet to search for young men, The Spokesman-Review posted audio and video interview clips, documents and letters concerning the story. (These are available at www.spokesmanreview.com/jimwest/).
- When reporting the results of polls, the Washington Post and The New York Times routinely post the full data on their Web sites. (See www. washingtonpost. com/wp-dyn/content/politics/polls/ and www.nytimes.com/ref/us/polls_index. html?8qa).
- In its ongoing coverage of sexual abuse by priests, The Boston Globe posted voluminous documents, video interviews, letters and much more. (See www.boston.com/globe/spotlight/abuse/).
- Throughout its coverage of the BTK killer case, The Wichita (Kan.) Eagle has posted everything from an audio clip of the killer's confession to his letter for a class reunion. (See www.kansas.com/btk/).
- For its series on corruption in the county housing agency, The Miami Herald posted video interviews, maps, information graphics and other materials on its Web site. (It is available at www.miamiherald.com/multimedia/news/houseoflies/ part1/index.html) [50]

Ken Sands, online publisher of The Spokane Spokesman-Review, sees these examples as just the starting point. He told Editor & Publisher magazine that he envisions posting all steps of the reporting process, from initial tip to final story. "You tell people what you are working on so they can help you," he said. "We have nothing to hide. You bring the same journalism practices into play."[51]

Offering even a modest level of transparency is not without its problems. David Berlind notes that offering podcasts of his interviews does not work in all cases. "The raw material behind a credible story may exist in a variety of media, and there's also the thorny issue of protecting sources," he wrote.[52] Another problem is one that journalists heatedly debate: just how much raw data people want to sift through, and just how useful unlimited data is to someone with little time or expertise.

In addition, posting source material opens a news organization to criticism that it missed important points or slanted its coverage. John Robinson, who writes a blog in his role as editor of the News & Record in Greensboro, N.C., said he is accustomed to having his every decision criticized. But he says that even the negative comments are useful. "If you pay attention to what some of the people say, you learn something," he said.[53]

Finally, there are also legal concerns about posting material online, especially when the material includes reporters' notes. Media attorney Bruce Sanford strongly advises against posting such notes. "It is very common to take notes about things you might forget, but not take notes about things you would not forget," he told Editor and Publisher magazine. In addition, he believes that posting audio and video interview clips is not a good idea: "It is too much information that invites scrutiny."[54]

Offering a regular look behind the scenes. In mid-2005, NBC Nightly News anchor Brian Williams became the first evening news anchor to write a blog. "The Daily Nightly" (http://dailynightly.msnbc.com/) was envisioned "as both a narrative and as a window into our editorial process." Williams and other NBC News employees use the blog to preview upcoming newscasts and explain editorial procedures.[55] Elsewhere, similar efforts are under way:

- The Spokesman-Review's "Ask the Editors" blog (http://spokesmanreview.com/blogs/editors/) answers reader questions about editorial decisions and operations, and the paper's "Daily Briefing" blog (http://spokesmanreview.com/blogs/briefing/) describes daily editorial meetings, explains editorial decisions and corrects errors in the print edition.
- Public Eye, a section of the CBS News Web site, attempts to explain how and why editorial decisions are made at the network (The site, at www.cbsnews.com/sections/publiceye/main500486.shtml, was shut down in late 2007.)
- The Seattle Post-Intelligencer's Virtual Editorial Board lists topics about which the paper plans to editorialize the next day, inviting readers to share their opinions (http://blog.seattlepi.nwsource.com/veb/index.asp?from=HPsn).
- The Ventura County (Calif.) Star uploads audio recordings of meetings in which the editorial board decides on political endorsements (www.venturacountystar.com).[56]

Allowing the audience to take part in decision-making sessions. It's one thing to let the public see what goes on behind the curtain. It's another thing—and a far more frightening one—to let the audience in on the decision-making process. At the Spokesman-Review, editors have faced their fears and undertaken just that process. Editor Steven A. Smith cites three examples of how his publication is approaching that goal:

- All of our daily news meetings are open to the public and we promote that opportunity on Page One several times each week. Those participating in morning critiques

Visit some of the sites mentioned in the section on transparency. As a prospective reader, what do you find that appeals to you, and what do you wish was online that is not? As a journalist, what concerns do you have with the material that's online?

often remain afterward to talk with editors about issues that concern them. Invariably, we learn something worth knowing or get a tip on a story worth pursuing.

- Eight citizen bloggers representing a cross-section of political and social views critique the paper daily in an online feature called "News Is a Conversation." Staffers can respond to the citizen posts; so can other readers. This generates an ongoing discussion of our news coverage, including our priorities, core beliefs and daily decisions.
- Perhaps the most interesting experiment . . . [is] Webcasting our morning and afternoon news meetings, inviting observers to participate through real-time chat-style interaction.[57]

Conclusion

Although some observers have seen a crisis in journalism in recent years, many people both inside and outside the industry have seen an opportunity to win back the public trust by conducting journalism in a responsible manner. When news stories are thorough, accurate, fair and transparent, the public gets the access it is due from the news media. At the same time, journalists and their institutions have a chance to regain the respect they deserve as a fundamental pillar of a democratic society and to win the confidence and loyalty of their audiences.

KEY TERMS

accuracy, 255
balance, 252
fairness, 259

objectivity, 251
thoroughness, 255
transparency, 260

DISCUSSION QUESTIONS

1. If you had to choose the three most important rules of journalism, what would they be? Why?
2. How important is objectivity to you in the news media you use?

3. Look at your campus or local newspaper or online news site. What efforts do they make to be transparent? What could they do better in the area of transparency?

NOTES

1. Michael Schudson, "Discovering the News" (New York: Basic Books, 1980), p. 6.

2. The Pew Research Center for the People and the Press, "Striking the Balance, Audience Interests, Business Pressures and Journalists' Values," 30 March 1999, Section I, **http://peoplepress.org/reports/display.php3? PageID=314.**

3. David Mindich, "Just the Facts: How 'Objectivity' Came to Define American Journalism" (New York: New York University Press, 1998).

4. Brent Cunningham, "Re-Thinking Objectivity," Columbia Journalism Review, July/August 2003, **www.cjr.org/issues/2003/4/objective cunningham.asp.**

5. Mitchell Stephens, "We're All Postmodern Now," Columbia Journalism Review, July/August 2005, p. 61.

6. Stephens, p. 63.

7. Tim Porter, "New Values for a New Age of Journalism," First Draft by Tim Porter, 10 April 2005, **www. timporter.com/firstdraft/archives/000436.html.**

8. Cunningham.

9. David Shaw, "Campaign coverage needs to read between the lines," Los Angeles Times, 5 September 2004, p. E20.

10. Bryan Keefer, "You Call That News? I Don't," the Washington Post, 12 September 2004, p. B2.

11. Shaw.

12. Shaw.

13. Michael Getler, "Is Balancing an Act?" the Washington Post, 17 October 2004, p. B6.

14. Keefer.

15. See for instance Edward S. Herman and Noam Chomsky, "Manufacturing Consent: The Political Economy of the Mass Media" (New York: Pantheon, 2002).

16. Cunningham.

17. Porter.

18. Jay Rosen, "Bloggers vs. Journalism Is Over," PressThink, 15 January 2005, **http://journalism.nyu.edu/pubzone/weblogs/pressthink/2005/01/21/berk_essy.html.**

19. Cunningham.

20. Cunningham.

21. Cunningham.

22. Eric Boehlert, "'Jeff Gannon's' Secret Life," Salon.com, 15 February 2005, **http://dir.salon.com/story/news/feature/ 2005/02/15/guckert/print.html.**

23. John Cook, "Glimpse at the Future Looks Neither Fair or Balanced," the Chicago Tribune, 19 September 2004, p. 1.

24. Dan Gillmor, "The End of Objectivity," 20 January 2005, **http://dangillmor.typepad.com/dan_gillmor_on_grassroots/2005/01/the_end_of_obje.html.**

25. Porter.

26. Cunningham.

27. Timothy Noah, "Just the Facts," The Washington Monthly, January/February 1999, **www.washington monthly.com/features/1999/9901.symposium.noah.html.**

28. Bill Kovach and Tom Rosenstiel, "The Elements of Journalism: What newspeople should know and the public should expect" (New York: Crown Publishers, 2001), p. 71.

29. American Society of Newspaper Editors, "Examining Our Credibility," 3 August 1999, **www.asne.org/kiosk/reports/99reports/1999examiningourcredibility/p7–10_Accuracy.html.**

30. Robert J. Haiman, "Best Practices for Newspaper Journalists," The Freedom Forum's Free Press/Fair Press Project, p. 10, **www.freedomforum.org/templates/document.asp?documentID=12828.**

31. Haiman, p. 11.

32. Haiman, p. 11.

33. Michele McLellan, "Details Matter: Accuracy," American Society of Newspaper Editors, 23 July 2002, **www.asne.org/credibilityhandbook/details matter.htm.**

34. Howard Kurtz, "Newsweek Apologizes," the Washington Post, 16 May 2005, p. A1.

35. "Times Reporter Who Resigned Leaves Long Trail of Deception," The New York Times, 11 May 2003, p. A1.

36. Blake Morrison, "Ex-USA Today Reporter Faked Major Stories," USA Today, 19 March 2004, **www.usatoday.com/news/2004–03–18–2004–03–18_kelley main_x.htm.**

37. John X. Miller, "Accuracy Checklists," Detroit Free Press, 2001, **www.freep.com/jobspage/academy/accuracy.htm.**

38. Russell Schoch. "The Food Detective," AlterNet.org, 7 February 2005, **www.alternet.org/envirohealth/ 21185/.**

39. Gillmor.

40. Haiman, p. 53.

41. Haiman, p. 59.

42. Project for Excellence in Journalism, "Developing Methods of Verification," Committee of Concerned Journalists, 29 May 2007, **http://concernedjournalists. org/developing-methods-verification.**

43. Haiman, p. 54.

44. J. D. Lasica, "Transparency Begets Trust in the Ever-Expanding Blog-o-Sphere," Online Journalism Review, 12 August 2004, **http://ojr.org/ojr/technology/ 1092267863.php.**

45. Steven A. Smith, "Guest Writer Steve Smith: Fortress journalism failed. The transparent newsroom works," PressThink, 23 November 2005, **http:// journalism.nyu.edu/pubzone/weblogs/presshink/ 2005/11/23/spk_ss.html.**

46. Project for Excellence in Journalism.

47. Haiman, p. 42.

48. Keefer.

49. David Berlind, "Can Technology Close Journalism's Credibility Gap?" ZDNet News, 18 January 2005, **http://news.zdnet.com/2100–9588_22–5539175.html.**

50. Most of the preceding examples are discussed in Joe Strupp, "The Inside Story: Newspapers go 'transparent,'" Editor & Publisher, January 2007, pp. 30–37.

51. Strupp, p. 32.

52. Berlind.

53. Strupp, p. 36.

54. Strupp, p. 37.

55. Brian Williams, "Welcome to 'The Daily Nightly,'" MSNBC.com, 31 May 2005, **http://www.msnbc. msn.com/id/8046841/#050531.**

56. The Seattle and Ventura County examples are discussed in length in Strupp, p. 37.

57. Smith.

Chapter 15

Legal Issues and Journalistic Ethics

The founders of the United States realized early on that the best way to promote democracy was to allow free and open dialogue. Only if people were allowed to hear all arguments and all sides of a story would they be able to make informed decisions as citizens. This initial impulse to allow unfettered dialogue was codified in the First Amendment to the Constitution, which states that Congress shall make *no* laws abridging freedom of the press. Over time, however, this idea was tempered with the adoption of a social responsibility model of the media. In essence, this model allows the media a wide range of rights and freedoms in return for the promise that they will behave responsibly.

We've already looked at some of the things that are viewed as journalistic responsibilities: thoroughness, accuracy, fairness and transparency. In addition, the behavior of journalists is bound by laws imposed from outside bodies and by ethics imposed by the profession itself. In this chapter, we examine those two topics.

Legal Issue 1: Libel

Many of the stories in the news focus on corruption, crime, scandal and other unsavory behavior. Some critics lament this focus on "bad" news, suggesting journalists should work harder to find stories about the many "good" things that people do. The reality, however, is that by definition journalism will always focus on these types of stories because stories generally become news only when they break from the routine. In addition, many journalists serve in roles that regularly require them to critique someone's actions or performance; political analysts, movie and music critics, restaurant reviewers and others fulfill this function. As a result, much of what gets published is at least critical, if not outright negative.

For the most part, that's all right. But a journalist has to be careful to understand the difference between defamatory material that is justified and that which is not—also known as **libel**.

Defamation and Libel

The obvious starting point in developing that understanding is with a definition of **defamation.** In essence, defamation occurs with the publication or broadcast of material that lowers someone's standing in the eyes of his or her friends, family, employer, coworkers or others.

Typically, defamation consists of one of the following:

- *Accusing a person of a crime.* This is perhaps the most common type of defamation in news stories.
- *Accusing a person of being incompetent or dishonest.* Either of these types of charges can hurt the chances of a person getting a job or could lead to the loss of a job he or she already has.
- *Charging a person with belonging to a generally disreputable group.* Accusation of membership in specifically named groups that most people hold in low esteem (for example, neo-Nazis, Pagans, Ku Klux Klan, and so on) must be verified.
- *Charging a person with a repugnant disease or mental illness.* Such charges include reporting that a person has a sexually transmitted disease, is mentally ill or suffers from alcoholism.
- *Charging a person with anti-Semitism or other religious, racial or ethnic intolerance.* In today's society, linking someone with racism or other forms of intolerance can cause irreparable damage to his or her reputation.
- *Charging a person or business with financial insolvency.* Reports of personal insolvency can hurt an individual's reputation, and reports of corporate financial problems can cause loss of clients and investors.

Such defamatory statements can be published or broadcast with no problem if the journalist has a defense for doing so. Without a defense, the statements move from defamation to libel, and serious problems follow.

Defense #1: Provable Truth

The best defense is **provable truth.** Just proving that someone else made a charge is not enough; a journalist has to prove the truth of that charge. In some cases, that can be accomplished with documentary evidence: for example, a bankruptcy filing, a recording of a person telling a racist joke or a video showing someone stealing from his office.

Alternately, journalists might be able to prove the truth of a reported action or behavior because they have witnessed it. For example, on a beautiful spring day, a man opened a window on the second story of his home and began shooting at people outside. As the day went on, reporters from many media outlets gathered to watch police try to capture the man. Finally, they subdued him and led him from the house in handcuffs. There was no doubt in this case that reporters could refer to the man they took into custody as "the gunman" because he had been seen throughout the day shooting at passers-by.

This defense applies only when a journalist can prove that a charge is true, *not* that someone made the charge. Attribution—"But he said it!"—is never a defense in a libel suit.

Defense #2: Qualified Privilege

Having a bird's eye view or documentary proof doesn't happen all that often, however, because much of what journalists write about comes from an outside source. In many cases, that source will be a government agency of some sort: the police department, a court, a legislative body, a grand jury and so on. In such cases, journalists can use another defense, **qualified privilege.**

If qualified privilege itself is somewhat complex, the idea behind it is simple. Much of the public's business is carried on by a variety of government agencies. Those agencies often move slowly, so investigations and litigation can drag on for years and charges are filed long before they can be proven. In addition, during trials, hearings and other inquiries, people sometimes are less than fully truthful. To encourage public discussion of these matters, journalists are permitted to report on these matters even while they are in progress. Qualified privilege protects a journalist against libel suits if the material gotten under these circumstances contains information that ultimately turns out to be false.

Although qualified privilege is a powerful defense, there are several important things to remember when using it as a defense:

- Reports of events that have not yet incurred some type of official action are *not* covered. If members of the public are organizing a petition to take before a government body, the material in that petition is not covered until it is accepted by the body. If someone is picked up by police for questioning about a crime, details are *not* covered until and unless the person is charged with a crime.
- The mere fact that a public official says something does *not* provide qualified privilege for those comments. Comments made by a detective speaking privately about an investigation or by a prosecuting attorney speaking outside a courtroom about a case being litigated will *not* be covered. Only comments made by public officials in official settings are protected.
- Charges made out of context are *not* covered. One of the requirements of qualified privilege is that the material provides a **full and fair account**. So while anything that is said in a courtroom is generally covered, that coverage is *not* guaranteed. For instance, if a witness accuses someone of selling illegal drugs, but the next three witnesses rebut that accusation, a journalist cannot just report the initial accusation and expect to be covered unless the rebuttals are also covered.
- Charges that go beyond what's in the official proceeding are *not* covered. When police charge someone with killing another person, that information can be reported with no fear of losing a libel suit, even if the suspect is later cleared. What the journalist *cannot* do is call the suspect a killer or murderer; at this point, that has not been proven.
- Charges that have been disproved or dismissed before publication or broadcast are *not* covered. For example, an article that reports defamatory charges in a lawsuit will not be privileged if the suit was dismissed before publication or broadcast.

Why Choose Journalism?

To my mind, the aspiring journalist possesses a combination of the following: curiosity about the world, a love of good storytelling, and a desire for the truth. It is said that some people are born with ink in their veins. One could argue that the "ink" part is growing outdated, but regardless, the sense remains: For many, this is a calling. Other journalists, including myself, are drawn to the profession by happy accident and then through the years find it hard to imagine doing anything else. Journalism offers rich possibilities to a variety of talents and personalities. Those who enjoy the chase may wind up dogged reporters. Those who enjoy the art may focus on becoming masterful writers or editors. There is room here for the aggressive inquisitor, the deep thinker, the quiet perfectionist, the skillful stylist. Journalism requires that you ask questions, work hard and stay honest. It can also be a rollicking good time. So if that's appealing, why *not* choose journalism?

JENNIFER BALDERAMA
The New York Times

Defense #3: Fair Comment and Criticismg

Truth and qualified privilege provide defenses for a large number of defamatory statements. But when defamation occurs in opinion, two other defenses prove more useful. The first is **fair comment and criticism.** This defense is based on the notion that the news media should be able to publish or broadcast criticism of people and companies that offer their goods or services for public consumption. The two most important aspects of this defense are highlighted right in its name: The comments must be fair, and they must be criticism. Let's look at each of those in turn.

Being fair does not mean that criticism has to be positive or even nice: Many celebrities have likely shed tears over mean-spirited comments published about them and their work. What it does mean is that the criticism has to be based on the actual product or performance under review. If a theater reviewer suffers through a miserably bad production of a Shakespeare play, then writes an unflattering review, it will be covered by fair comment and criticism. If, however, the play is good but the lead turns out to be played by someone the reviewer just broke up with—and is extremely angry with—an unflattering review will not be protected. In other words, the comments must be based on facts.

That should be simple enough. Where this defense becomes a little more complicated is in the criticism part. Although the comments must be based on fact, they should not contain facts that cannot be proven. Let's return to our theater reviewer, this time on another assignment. In a production of a play, the lead actor forgets his lines, misses cues and generally makes a mess of things. The reviewer has every right to rip apart the play. What the reviewer does not have, however, is the right to speculate that the actor was drunk. That's a factual allegation, and unless the reviewer can prove it, that's libelous.

One simple way to test whether something is criticism or a factual allegation is to ask whether it can be proved or disproved. So for instance:

- "She has done a poor job of running the state" is a criticism; it cannot be proved or disproved.
- "She has embezzled funds from taxpayers" is a factual allegation; it can be proved or disproved.

Merely labeling a piece of writing "opinion" or "commentary" does *not* protect it if it contains allegations of fact that cannot be proved.

Defense #4: Public Official/Public Figure Rule

A related defense is often referred to as the **public official/public figure rule.** This works on the same general concept, but it specifically applies to the actions of public employees or those in the public eye. It has grown out of what is arguably the most important libel case in U.S. history, The New York Times Co. v. Sullivan (see Figure 15.1). Decided in 1964, that case effectively said that the news media could publish almost any accusations about public officials (whose job it is, after all, to serve the public), provided they do it without **actual malice.** That phrase was defined as knowing that charges are false or showing **reckless disregard** for their truth or falsity. Reckless disregard generally means one or more of the following occurred:

- The reporter's sources were weak.
- The reporter's investigation was not adequate.
- The charges reported were inherently unbelievable.
- There were serious doubts about the story.

Later cases extended this coverage to public figures—that is, people who voluntarily put themselves in the public eye. Actors, athletes, singers, musicians and others obviously fall into the category, as do private citizens who thrust themselves into a controversy. Just like public officials, public figures can win a libel suit only when they can prove actual malice.

What makes dealing with public figures trickier, however, is that not all public figures are treated the same. Some are regarded as **pervasive public figures:** no dividing line exists between their private and public lives. Many entertainers, sports figures, authors and others fall into this category: They always must prove actual malice to win a libel suit.

On the other hand, otherwise private citizens who take active roles in public controversies or events are regarded as **limited,** or **vortex, public figures.** For them to win libel suits based on defamation that applies to their public roles, they have to prove actual malice. However, if the defamation applies to the private part their lives, they are regarded as **private figures.** Like other private figures, they need to prove only

FIGURE 15.1

At the center of the most famous case in U.S. libel law is this advertisement that appeared in The New York Times in 1960.

> "The growing movement of peaceful mass demonstrations by Negroes is something new in the South, something understandable.... Let Congress heed their rising voices, for they will be heard."
>
> —*New York Times editorial*
> *Saturday, March 19, 1960*

Heed Their Rising Voices

As the whole world knows by now, thousands of Southern Negro students are engaged in widespread non-violent demonstrations in positive affirmation of the right to live in human dignity as guaranteed by the U. S. Constitution and the Bill of Rights. In their efforts to uphold these guarantees, they are being met by an unprecedented wave of terror by those who would deny and negate that document which the whole world looks upon as setting the pattern for modern freedom....

In Orangeburg, South Carolina, when 400 students peacefully sought to buy doughnuts and coffee at lunch counters in the business district, they were forcibly ejected, tear-gassed, soaked to the skin in freezing weather with fire hoses, arrested en masse and herded into an open barbed-wire stockade to stand for hours in the bitter cold.

In Montgomery, Alabama, after students sang "My Country, 'Tis of Thee" on the State Capitol steps, their leaders were expelled from school, and truckloads of police armed with shotguns and tear-gas ringed the Alabama State College Campus. When the entire student body protested to state authorities by refusing to re-register, their dining hall was padlocked in an attempt to starve them into submission.

In Tallahassee, Atlanta, Nashville, Savannah, Greensboro, Memphis, Richmond, Charlotte, and a host of other cities in the South, young American teenagers, in face of the entire weight of official state apparatus and police power, have boldly stepped forth as protagonists of democracy. Their courage and amazing restraint have inspired millions and given a new dignity to the cause of freedom.

Small wonder that the Southern violators of the Constitution fear this new, non-violent brand of freedom fighter . . . even as they fear the upswelling right-to-vote movement. Small wonder that they are determined to destroy the one man who, more than any other, symbolizes the new spirit now sweeping the South—the Rev. Dr. Martin Luther King, Jr., world-famous leader of the Montgomery Bus Protest. For it is his doctrine of non-violence which has inspired and guided the students in their widening wave of sit-ins; and it is this same Dr. King who founded and is president of the Southern Christian Leadership Conference—the organization which is spearheading the surging right-to-vote movement. Under Dr. King's direction the Leadership Conference conducts Student Workshops and Seminars in the philosophy and technique of non-violent resistance.

Again and again the Southern violators have answered Dr. King's peaceful protests with intimidation and violence. They have bombed his home almost killing his wife and child. They have assaulted his person. They have arrested him seven times—for "speeding," "loitering" and similar "offenses." And now they have charged him with "perjury"—a *felony* under which they could imprison him for *ten years*. Obviously, their real purpose is to remove him physically as the leader to whom the students and millions of others—look for guidance and support, and thereby to intimidate *all* leaders who may rise in the South. Their strategy is to behead this affirmative movement, and thus to demoralize Negro Americans and weaken their will to struggle. The defense of Martin Luther King, spiritual leader of the student sit-in movement, clearly, therefore, is an integral part of the total struggle for freedom in the South.

Decent-minded Americans cannot help but applaud the creative daring of the students and the quiet heroism of Dr. King. But this is one of those moments in the stormy history of Freedom when men and women of good will must do more than applaud the rising-to-glory of others. The America whose good name hangs in the balance before a watchful world, the America whose heritage of Liberty these Southern Upholders of the Constitution are defending, is *our* America as well as theirs . . .

We must heed their rising voices—yes—but we must add our own.

We must extend ourselves above and beyond moral support and render the material help so urgently needed by those who are taking the risks, facing jail, and even death in a glorious re-affirmation of our Constitution and its Bill of Rights.

We urge you to join hands with our fellow Americans in the South by supporting, with your dollars, this Combined Appeal for all three needs—the defense of Martin Luther King—the support of the embattled students—and the struggle for the right-to-vote.

Your Help Is Urgently Needed . . . NOW !!

Stella Adler
Raymond Pace Alexander
Harry Van Arsdale
Harry Belafonte
Julie Belafonte
Dr. Algernon Black
Marc Blitzstein
William Branch
Marlon Brando
Mrs. Ralph Bunche
Diahann Carroll

Dr. Alan Knight Chalmers
Richard Coe
Nat King Cole
Cheryl Crawford
Dorothy Dandridge
Ossie Davis
Sammy Davis, Jr.
Ruby Dee
Dr. Philip Elliott
Dr. Harry Emerson Fosdick

Anthony Franciosa
Lorraine Hansbury
Rev. Donald Harrington
Nat Hentoff
James Hicks
Mary Hinkson
Van Heflin
Langston Hughes
Morris Iushewitz
Mahalia Jackson
Mordecai Johnson

John Killens
Eartha Kitt
Rabbi Edward Klein
Hope Lange
John Lewis
Viveca Lindfors
Carl Murphy
Don Murray
John Murray
A. J. Muste
Frederick O'Neal

L. Joseph Overton
Clarence Pickett
Shad Polier
Sidney Poitier
A. Philip Randolph
John Raitt
Elmer Rice
Jackie Robinson
Mrs. Eleanor Roosevelt
Bayard Rustin
Robert Ryan

Maureen Stapleton
Frank Silvera
Hope Stevens
George Tabori
Rev. Gardner C. Taylor
Norman Thomas
Kenneth Tynan
Charles White
Shelley Winters
Max Youngstein

We in the south who are struggling daily for dignity and freedom warmly endorse this appeal

Rev. Ralph D. Abernathy
(Montgomery, Ala.)

Rev. Fred L. Shuttlesworth
(Birmingham, Ala.)

Rev. Kelley Miller Smith
(Nashville, Tenn.)

Rev. W. A. Dennis
(Chattanooga, Tenn.)

Rev. C. K. Steele
(Tallahassee, Fla.)

Rev. Matthew D. McCollom
(Orangeburg, S. C.)

Rev. William Holmes Borders
(Atlanta, Ga.)

Rev. Douglas Moore
(Durham, N. C.)

Rev. Wyatt Tee Walker
(Petersburg, Va.)

Rev. Walter L. Hamilton
(Norfolk, Va.)

I. S. Levy
(Columbia, S. C.)

Rev. Martin Luther King, Sr.
(Atlanta, Ga.)

Rev. Henry C. Bunton
(Memphis, Tenn.)

Rev. S. S. Seay, Sr.
(Montgomery, Ala.)

Rev. Samuel W. Williams
(Atlanta, Ga.)

Rev. A. L. Davis
(New Orleans, La.)

Mrs. Katie E. Whickham
(New Orleans, La.)

Rev. W. H. Hall
(Hattiesburg, Miss.)

Rev. J. E. Lowery
(Mobile, Ala.)

Rev. T. J. Jemison
(Baton Rouge, La.)

COMMITTEE TO DEFEND MARTIN LUTHER KING AND THE STRUGGLE FOR FREEDOM IN THE SOUTH

312 West 125th Street, New York 27, N. Y. UNiversity 6-1700

Chairmen: A. Philip Randolph, Dr. Gardner C. Taylor; *Chairmen of Cultural Division:* Harry Belafonte, Sidney Poitier; *Treasurer:* Nat King Cole; *Executive Director:* Bayard Rustin; *Chairmen of Church Division:* Father George B. Ford, Rev. Harry Emerson Fosdick, Rev. Thomas Kilgore, Jr., Rabbi Edward E. Klein; *Chairman of Labor Division:* Morris Iushewitz

Please mail this coupon TODAY!

Committee To Defend Martin Luther King
and
The Struggle For Freedom In The South

312 West 125th Street, New York 27, N. Y.
UNiversity 6-1700

I am enclosing my contribution of $_____ for the work of the Committee.

Name _____
(PLEASE PRINT)

Address _____

City _____ Zone ____ State ____

☐ I want to help   ☐ Please send further information

Please make checks payable to:
Committee To Defend Martin Luther King

simple negligence—that is, that the facts are wrong. This can happen as a result of one or more of the following problems:

- The reporter did not contact the person being defamed to get his or her side of the story.
- The reporter did not use the best sources available.
- The reporter failed to resolve discrepancies between what he or she recalls someone as having said and what they recall having said.

Identifying People Who Are Defamed

A journalist always should double-check the names of people who are being defamed (and, if appropriate, any photos or graphics; incorrectly using a photo of a legitimate businesswoman named Mary Smith with a story about a drug dealer named Mary Smith is grounds for the businesswoman to sue for libel). For that reason, it is good practice to use full names including middle names or initials whenever possible. In general, a journalist should use as much information as possible to limit the identity of people who are being defamed.

Leaving identifying information out of a story to avoid a libel suit is never a good idea. A person does not have to be named in a story to sue for libel; if the story contains enough identifying information, that person can sue. And including less identification actually increases the chances that someone could prove that the information unfairly defames him or her.

In addition, a journalist needs to be careful to separate the names of people charged with crimes from the actions attributed to suspects in police reports.

Finally, a journalist never should count on being able to wiggle out of a libel suit because he or she only implied that someone did something unsavory. Under libel law, hinting that someone is a thief is just as bad as coming right out and saying it.

Nor will using the words *alleged* or *allegedly* offer protection from a libel suit. Alleged and allegedly mean only that someone has made an accusation without proof. It is fine to use when reporting actions detailed in official charges ("Howard allegedly supplied liquor to the children on four occasions, according to the police report."). But in such cases, it is qualified privilege and not the use of the word *allegedly* that provides protection from a libel suit.

Being Forthright about Mistakes Is Important

Despite the best intentions, a journalist might make an error that is potentially libelous. If that happens, a retraction must be printed or broadcast as soon as possible. Doing so makes it harder for the offended party to prove actual malice and in some cases might be enough to satisfy the injured party. Retractions should be conspicuous and frank, so they dispel any notion of reckless disregard for the truth, and they should not reprint any libelous material.

If the libelous material was published online, there's good news and bad. On one hand, the online environment allows almost instantaneous corrections and retractions, which can help defuse libel suits. On the other hand, that environment brings up the question of what to do with the original, libelous article. Some publications leave the original online, which risks further circulating the libel (the article may be found, for instance, by a search engine). Others correct the article with no notice made of the change, which strikes many as at least a bit dishonest. Perhaps the most honest way to handle a correction is to change the original and add a note that the article was changed after initial publication.

ASSIGNMENT DESK 15.1

Read through the following story excerpts. For each, write a brief summary of whether any defense is necessary and whether the material can be published or broadcast.

1. A pro wrestler used one of his signature chokeholds to kill his son, police reports show.
2. After the commentator said she hoped the presidential candidate would be "killed in a terrorist assassination plot," he used his appearance on a television show to call her "mean-spirited" and "shameless."
3. Police investigating the crash that left the actor hospitalized said they had no doubt that alcohol was a factor.
4. A local man was sentenced to five years in prison for selling drugs to neighborhood schoolchildren.
5. The action film does not include any instances of torture, aside from those inflicted on the suffering audience.

Legal Issue 2: Privacy

As we noted previously, journalism is essentially the practice of finding and reporting information of interest to an audience. In most cases, the information comes from a public source: a government report or action, a news conference, a public meeting, or an event the journalist witnessed firsthand.

Sometimes, however, information that might be of public interest is not readily available through public channels. A private citizen might have tried to keep private certain facts about himself or herself, or the information might come from a government proceeding in which some information is kept private. In those cases, journalists need to weigh whether the public benefit of reporting that information outweighs the right to privacy of the subject. If they are not careful, they might be sued for **public disclosure of private facts**.

Even then, when journalists can prove that such material is of legitimate public concern, they will likely be safe from lawsuits. Over the years, the courts have ruled repeatedly in favor of journalists who have published private information contained in public proceedings, even when that information is the name of a rape victim, a sexually abused child, a juvenile offender or the client of a prostitute. As the Reporters Committee for Freedom of the Press notes:

> Some states restrict the release of certain information, even though it is part of an official record, by sealing the files or restricting public and news media access to certain proceedings.
>
> However, if the press lawfully obtains truthful information about a matter of public concern from government sources, the state may not constitutionally punish publication of the information absent the need to further a substantial state interest.[1]

One potential trouble spot occurs when journalists create retrospectives on people who were once in the news. Repeating an old charge about a person could be construed as an invasion of privacy if that person is now a private citizen. But courts generally have ruled that even in such cases, the material is fine to publish.

In fact, about the only way a journalist can get into legal trouble over publishing private information is if a person can show that the material was of no legitimate public interest and was designed merely to embarrass the subject. That's rarely the case, but it can happen. PublishLawyer.com offers these examples that could lead to trouble:

> For example, publicizing the fact that your brother-in-law has failed to pay his mortgage for three months, although true, would be an invasion of his privacy. Other examples would be details of a person's sexual problems, physical or mental ailments.[2]

Note that this discussion applies only to private citizens. Government officials and other public figures have no reasonable expectation of privacy.

Another area of concern in privacy issues is **false light.** Simply stated, "False light invasion of privacy occurs when information is published about a person that is false or places the person in a false light, is highly offensive to a reasonable person, and is published with knowledge or in reckless disregard of whether the information was false or would place the person in a false light."[3]

People can sue for false light when a story creates a misleading—and usually negative—impression about them. That should sound a lot like the definition of libel, and indeed many states no longer recognize a distinction between libel and false light.

Where false light remains on the books, though, it carries some clear distinctions from libel. First, false light applies even when a story does not reflect badly on a person. For example, a person who had never been in the military could sue under false light if a journalist referred to him as a war hero. Second, "false light cases are about damage to a person's personal feelings or dignity, whereas defamation is about damage to a person's reputation."[4] Third, and perhaps most importantly, a person can win a false light case even when everything in a story is true—a distinct difference from libel cases. In one case in Florida, a jury awarded $18.28 million for a false light award based on a story in which no facts were disputed. As one report on the case noted, "The story's facts were all true. . . . But the jury found that the paper strung those facts together in a malicious manner, leaving the impression that Anderson killed his wife."[5]

A final area of concern is **intrusion.** While journalists are free to report on anything they witness in public places, they are prohibited from installing hidden cameras and from using audio recorders and cameras in private settings without permission. (A person who agrees to be interviewed in a private setting and can clearly see any recorder or camera implicitly grants such permission.) In addition, journalists may face civil and criminal penalties for entering private places without permission and for harassing private citizens. It doesn't matter whether a story was published or not; the actions undertaken by the journalist in the newsgathering process are what matter.

In any questionable cases concerning privacy, the best course of action is to get a person's written consent:

> If a person consents, there can be no invasion of privacy. However, the reporter should be sure that the subject has not only consented to be interviewed, but also consented to publishing or airing the interview or photographs. When minors or legally incompetent people are involved, the consent of a parent or guardian may be necessary.[6]

Legal Issue 3: Protecting Confidential Sources

The subject of confidential sources hit the public's radar in dramatic fashion after the leak of former CIA agent Valerie Plame's identity. In that case, reporters—including Judith Miller of The New York Times—initially refused to divulge the name of the person who had revealed Plame's identity, a revelation that was thought to have been politically motivated because Plame's husband had been a critic of the Iraq war.

Even setting aside the political and criminal aspects of the case, it was a complex one. Although Miller did not publish that information and columnist Robert Novak did, she spent several months in jail for refusing to name her source. Novak apparently was not a target of the investigation into the leak. Although many in the media and public initially were outraged that Miller had been singled out, subsequent revelations made it clear that she had not leveled with her editors about whom she had talked with, what she had said and what she had promised. Miller resigned from the Times shortly after her release from jail.[7]

As messy as the Miller affair was, at the heart of the case was one of the essential questions journalists face: How far should reporters go to protect the identity of sources who provide information in exchange for a promise of confidentiality? Many journalists believe that keeping their promises to sources outweighs any other considerations. At some news organizations, reporters do not have sole discretion to decide whether to turn over confidential information; instead, an editor makes that decision. It is important for reporters to understand the situation at their news organizations before making any promises to sources.

Some journalists mistakenly think they have universal protection from being forced to name confidential sources or divulge other confidential information. The reality is far different and far more complex. As of this writing, there is no federal **shield law** that would offer reporters "the right not to be compelled to testify or disclose sources and information in court."[8]

In 2004 alone more than two dozen reporters were subpoenaed or questioned about confidential sources in federal cases.[9] One outcome of that has been a push for a federal shield law that would force reporters to testify only when there is no other way to get information they have.

Until that happens, however—if it ever does—journalists have no protection against federal subpoenas and at best only limited protection at the local level, with that protection varying widely from state to state. As the Reporters Committee for Freedom of the Press summarizes the situation:

> Thirty-one states and the District of Columbia have adopted shield laws affording the media varying degrees of protection against subpoenas. Some shield laws protect reporters from forced disclosure of their confidential news sources, but not of unpublished material. Other laws provide absolute or qualified protection according to the type of legal proceeding involved (civil or criminal) or the role of the journalist in the proceeding (defendant or independent third party).
>
> In many states without shield laws, state courts have recognized some form of qualified privilege. In others, state constitutions may include "free press" provisions, which are similar to the U.S. Constitution's First Amendment protections and afford qualified protection. There are several states, however, such as Hawaii and Wyoming, where no privilege to protect unpublished sources or information has been recognized by the courts or legislatures.[10]

In locations with shield laws, the courts typically rely on a three-part test to assess whether a subpoenaed journalist should be forced to reveal information:

1. Is the information clearly relevant and material to the pending case?
2. Does the information go "to the heart of the case"?
3. Could the information be obtained from non-media sources?[11]

When courts rule against reporters, the reporters have to present the information or get ready to go to jail. In some cases, reporters have been jailed until they decided to cooperate with the subpoena; in others, they have been sentenced to a specific amount of time in jail with no chance for a reduction in the sentence even if they decide to cooperate. In addition to the jail time, reporters sometimes also face fines.

ASSIGNMENT DESK 15.2

Visit the Reporter's Privilege section of The Reporters Committee for Freedom of the Press Web site (www.rcfp.org/privilege/index.php). Look up the laws for your state. (If there is no information for your state, look at a neighboring state.) Write a short summary of the major points covered.

The Student Press Law Center's College Top 10 List

News Pointers

The 10 questions college student journalists most frequently ask about their rights:

Q: Do students at a public college or university have First Amendment rights?

A: Emphatically, yes. As the United States Supreme Court said back in 1969, "It can hardly be argued that either students or teachers shed their constitutional right to freedom of speech or expression at the schoolhouse gate." As agents of the government, public school officials are prohibited by the First Amendment from censoring most student speech. Students at a public school have the right to voice their opinions and write about the issues that concern them just like every other American. But because the First Amendment only prohibits government officials from suppressing speech, it does not prevent censorship by private school officials. Nevertheless, a state constitution or statute — or even a school policy protecting free speech — may give private school students important free press protections.

Q: But if school officials or student governments fund a student publication, radio or television station, can't they censor it like any other publisher or owner could?

A: Not at a public school. The courts have ruled that if a school creates a student news or information medium and allows students to serve as editors, the First Amendment drastically limits the school's ability to censor. Among the censoring actions the courts have prohibited are confiscating copies of publications, requiring prior review, removing objectionable material, limiting circulation, suspending editors and withdrawing or reducing financial support.

Q: But what about the Hazelwood decision?

A: The U.S. Supreme Court's 1988 Hazelwood decision, which gave school officials significant power to censor some school-sponsored student expression, only dealt with high school student publications. While a few college officials have tried to extend Hazelwood's reach to their campus, most courts have rejected such attempts.

Q: What about underground or independent student publications? Are they protected from censorship, too?

A: Absolutely. Schools can establish reasonable restrictions as to the time, place and manner of distribution, but non-school-sponsored student publications are entitled to at least as much First Amendment protection as school-sponsored student publications.

Q: Can a student publication be sued for libel, invasion of privacy or copyright violations?

A: Yes, and on rare occasions they are. In such cases the individual reporter who produced the story, the editor of the publication and the publication itself if it is separately incorporated can always be held liable if money damages are awarded. Court decisions suggest that a school that does not exercise content control over the publication will not be held liable for what students publish. In any event, most cases are dropped or settled before they ever get to court.

Q: Can student reporters protect confidential news sources or information when they receive a court subpoena asking that they turn it over?

A: In most cases, yes. Some states have "shield laws" and others have court-created reporters privileges that protect journalists from having to reveal

Ethical Issue 1: Using Anonymous Sources

Any discussion of the legal aspects of using confidential sources raises the question of the ethical implications of using them. Simply put, when is it proper to publish or broadcast a story based on anonymous sources?

That question was on the minds of many journalists in the wake of the Plame affair. The case followed a period of increased use of anonymous sources, a practice that had this kind of information. Most states have never explicitly applied these laws to student journalists, and the language of a few of these might not protect students. You should check your state law.

Q: How can I make use of freedom of information laws?

A: Freedom of information, or "sunshine" laws, require that government agencies such as public schools and police departments open to the public most of their official records and meetings. These laws, which vary from state to state, are usually simple to use and often require that a journalist simply make an informal request. Every newsroom should have a copy of their state's open records and open meetings laws.

Q: Since freedom of information laws only apply to the records or meetings of government agencies, are private school students out of luck in getting information about their school?

A: Not necessarily. There are a number of state and federal laws that now require private schools to reveal certain information. One of the most important access tools for private school journalists is the institution's federal informational tax return, the Form 990, which the law says must be available at your school's business office for public inspection. The form provides information about where your school gets its money and where it spends it.

Q: One of our star student athletes has been accused of stealing thousands of dollars of school computer equipment. Rather than going to the local court system, the school has decided to try the case before the University Judicial Board, or campus court. They have said the proceeding is closed and they refuse to release any information about the case's outcome. What can I do?

A: This is one of the hottest — and most important — issues confronting the student press today. Many schools claim that these proceedings are "educational" in nature and that releasing information about them will unfairly invade students' rights to privacy. Student journalists (and many commercial journalists as well) believe that schools are simply using campus courts to control or bury information that hurts the school's reputation. They argue that when these proceedings involve charges of criminal rather than academic activity, the public has a right to know what goes on behind closed doors. College students, they argue, are adults. And they should be treated as such. The public routinely has a right to attend criminal proceedings in public courts. Public access [e]nsures fairness and accountability, both to the accused and to the system and victims. Where schools take on the responsibility of a public criminal court they must be held to the same standards of openness and accountability. Invoke the power of your state's open records and open meetings law. If you are still denied access, appeal. Also, let your readers and other media know what the school is doing.

Q: Where can I go for more information about my rights and responsibilities as a student journalist?

A: The Student Press Law Center! (www.splc.org/) (See Figure 15.2.)

© 2000 Student Press Law Center. Used with permission.

drawn criticism both inside the industry and among the public. Some journalists blamed that increase at least partly on the round-the-clock news cycles that became common during the 1990s. As Amy Mitchell, associate director of the Project for Excellence in Journalism, told Editor and Publisher: "News organizations became a little more lax in their oversight, the sources gained more control and were able to demand anonymity more. . . . Reporters were in more need for information, there was more competition, and sources saw they could demand it — and they did."[12]

Few would argue for a complete ban on anonymous sources. People were reminded of the importance of anonymous tipsters when during the Plame affair, W. Mark Felt, former assistant director of the FBI during the Nixon administration, stepped forward to admit that he was "Deep Throat," the secret source who had helped to expose the internal spies, secret surveillance, dirty tricks and cover-ups that made up the Watergate case. Reporting on that case led President Nixon to resign and sent many of his aides to prison. Felt, like many other anonymous sources throughout history, believed his career would be at risk if he provided information on the record, so he reached an agreement with Washington Post reporters Bob Woodward and Carl Bernstein to keep his identity secret. He finally divulged it himself after more than 30 years of secrecy (see Figure 15.3).

Rebecca Carr, a former Justice Department reporter for Cox Newspapers, says that it is cases like Watergate that show how vital anonymous sources can be. "It's about telling stories that matter, and those stories often require anonymous sources to confirm records or the direction of a story. If those sources start drying up, then the future Watergates won't be told. The loser in all of this is the public, because they won't know what's really going on in the government they pay for."[13]

Washington Post national security reporter Dana Priest agrees. "Most everything I write about is something the government doesn't want people to know about," she told Editor & Publisher. "About 90 percent of the people I talk to not only don't want to be

FIGURE
15.3

The Washington Post, the paper whose reporters Carl Bernstein and Bob Woodward broke the Watergate story, prominently displayed a story about the identity of their source "Deep Throat" when he came forward more than 30 years later.

The Washington Post

Weather
Today: Partly sunny. High 79. Low 60.
Thursday: Mostly cloudy, showers. High 68. Low 59.
Details, B10

DISTRICT
HOME EDITION

35¢

WEDNESDAY, JUNE 1, 2005

Justices Overturn Andersen Conviction

Advice to Enron Jury On Accountants' Intent Is Faulted

By CHARLES LANE
Washington Post Staff Writer

The Supreme Court overturned the 2002 criminal conviction of Enron Corp.'s accounting firm yesterday, nullifying with a single stroke one of the government's biggest victories in the corporate scandals that climaxed the bull market of the 1990s.

The court ruled unanimously that the Houston jury that found Arthur Andersen LLP guilty of obstruction of justice was given overly broad instructions by the federal judge who presided at the trial.

As a result of the faulty instructions, the justices ruled, the firm was convicted without proof that its shredding of documents was deliberately intended to undermine a looming Securities and Exchange Commission inquiry in fall 2001. U.S. District Judge Melinda Harmon should have instructed the jury that the law required the government to prove that Andersen knew it was breaking the law, the court ruled.

"Indeed, it is striking how little culpability the [judge's] instructions required," Chief Justice William H. Rehnquist wrote in the opinion for the court. "For example, the jury was told that, 'even if [Andersen] honestly and sincerely believed that its conduct was lawful, you may find [it] guilty.'" Legal analysts said the decision was a major setback to the Justice Department's corporate crime prosecutions.

"To lose a case like this is huge," said William B. Mateja, a former official of the Justice Department's corporate fraud task force. "Arthur Andersen was the poster-child case

See ANDERSEN, A12, Col. 1

■ **No backing off on fraud prosecution.** | *Business, D1*

Bill Clinton Takes Spot On Global Stage

By JOHN F. HARRIS
Washington Post Staff Writer

In 2001, in the opening months of his ex-presidency, Bill Clinton confided to an aide that he had decided on his dream job for the next chapter of his life: secretary general of the United Nations.

The goal may not be realistic, he acknowledged, but he then went on to analyze all the factors in minute detail, as though he were preparing for a political campaign: whether a U.S. president would ever see fit to back him, for one, and what it would take to persuade other nations to bend the long-standing tradition that the top job does not go to someone from a country with permanent status on the U.N. Security Council.

His ambition, as the aide described it, was both breathtaking and entirely logical for a natural-born politician who had reached the top of the American political ladder: "president of the world."

Four years later, say several associates who have spoken with him in recent months, Clinton regards his dream of leading the United Nations as something more than a flight of fancy and something less than a serious prospect. Already, however, he has succeeded to a surprising degree in fashioning his ex-presidency to make himself a dominant player on the world stage. His ambitions are no less obvi-

See CLINTON, A13, Col. 1

FBI's No. 2 Was 'Deep Throat'

Mark Felt Ends 30-Year Mystery of The Post's Watergate Source

By DAVID VON DREHLE
Washington Post Staff Writer

Deep Throat, the secret source whose insider guidance was vital to The Washington Post's groundbreaking coverage of the Watergate scandal, was a pillar of the FBI named W. Mark Felt, The Post confirmed yesterday.

As the bureau's second- and third-ranking official during a period when the FBI was battling for its independence against the administration of President Richard M. Nixon, Felt had the means and the motive to help uncover the web of internal spies, secret surveillance, dirty tricks and coverups that led to Nixon's unprecedented resignation on Aug. 9, 1974, and to prison sentences for some of Nixon's highest-ranking aides.

Felt's identity as Washington's most celebrated secret source had been an object of speculation for more than 30 years until yesterday, when his role was revealed by his family in a Vanity Fair magazine article. Even Nixon was caught on tape speculating that Felt was "an informer" as early as February 1973, at a time when Deep Throat was supplying confirmation and context for some of The Post's most explosive Watergate stories.

But Felt's repeated denials, and the stalwart silence of the reporters he aided — Bob Woodward and Carl Bernstein — kept the cloak of mystery

See DEEP THROAT, A6, Col. 1

W. Mark Felt, with daughter Joan at home in Santa Rosa, Calif., acknowledged his role as a source for The Washington Post's coverage of Watergate.

Felt, in an undated photo, "knew he was taking a monumental risk," said Woodward, now a Post assistant managing editor.

■ **Key figures have mixed reactions.** | *Nation, A9*

Carl Bernstein, left, and Bob Woodward in the Post newsroom in 1973. The young duo's investigative reporting earned the newspaper a Pulitzer Prize.

Woodward, left, with Benjamin C. Bradlee in the newsroom yesterday. They and Bernstein had agreed not to identify Felt until after his death.

■ **The end of a cherished legend.** | *Style, C1*

Conflicted And Mum For Decades

By DAN BALZ
and R. JEFFREY SMITH
Washington Post Staff Writers

W. Mark Felt always denied he was Deep Throat. "It was not I and it is not I," he told Washingtonian magazine in 1974, around the time that Richard M. Nixon resigned the presidency in disgrace after a lengthy investigation and threat of impeachment, aided in no small part by the guidance Felt had provided to The Washington Post.

It was a denial he maintained publicly for three decades, until yesterday. Throughout that period, he lived with one of the greatest secrets in journalism history and with his own sense of conflict and tension over the role he had played in bringing down a president in the Watergate scandal: Was he a hero for helping the truth come out, or a turncoat who betrayed his government, his president and the FBI he revered by leaking to the press?

There were plenty of reasons that he felt such conflict. He was an FBI loyalist in the image J. Edgar Hoover had created for the bureau in its glory

See FELT, A8, Col. 1

■ **The scoop that almost wasn't.** | *Style, C1*

Prince George's Makes Sales Pitch For High-End Retail

By MICHAEL BARBARO and KRISSAH WILLIAMS
Washington Post Staff Writers

LAS VEGAS — Prince George's County has waited decades for high-end retailers, and this day brought no relief. Marc Guth, a representative for the Cheesecake Factory Inc., has agreed to hear the county's sales pitch at a major shopping center convention here, but he is running 10 minutes late, then 15, then 20.

He finally arrives but has no time to sit down.

A rushed County Executive Jack B. Johnson (D) hurries into his arguments, promoting "four to five really great opportunities" for an upscale restaurant in Prince George's.

"Sorry," Guth said after a few minutes and no promises. "I have to run."

For retail-starved Prince George's County, it has come to this. Passed over by the same luxury stores and white-tablecloth restaurants that have cropped up in suburbs across the region, county leaders are making an aggressive — and for Johnson, a personal — bid for high-end shopping, including a three-day trip to a retail industry trade show here.

It is a frustrating exercise, with the county's highest-ranking official scrambling to win five-minute meetings with restaurant executives and repeating the case for Prince George's in meetings with dozens of brokers and developers who are weighing proposals from throughout the country.

See RETAIL, A11, Col. 1

INSIDE

New Look for Business, New Place for Sports

Starting today, a redesigned and expanded Business section will begin appearing in front of the Sports section. With added coverage of local and international business, the section will also include an expanded table of contents on its front, to make all The Post's business-related coverage easier to find.

Today's contents are on A2

The Post on the Internet:
washingtonpost.com

Russian Oil Magnate Gets 9 Years

Mikhail Khodorkovsky, center, and an associate are sentenced, instigating criticism of the Kremlin at home and abroad.
WORLD, A14

Amplifying His Cause

Twenty years after Live Aid, Bob Geldof announces a worldwide concert to raise awareness of poverty before the G8 Summit in Scotland.
STYLE, C1

New Premier in France

Dominique de Villepin, a leading Iraq war foe, is appointed in the wake of voter rejection of the European Union constitution.
WORLD, A14

A Big Slice of Better Bread; Organic Milk In Short Supply

To make the artisanal bread and pastries that are enjoyed at more than 500 area restaurants, Uptown Bakers must carefully control all the variables.

Organic milk, once sold mostly in specialty stores, is becoming more difficult to find now that shoppers at supermarket chain stores have acquired a taste for it.
FOOD, F1

identified by name, but sometimes not even as a U.S. intelligence official."[14] Another Post reporter, Walter Pincus, agrees: "Protecting confidential sources, who provide me with material for many of the intelligence stories I write, is a key factor that enables me to write the stories I do about national security."[15]

United Press International White House reporter Richard Tomkins adds that anonymous sources can be extremely helpful even when they are not used directly in a story. "I bounce ideas off them and ask if I am headed in the right direction," he explained.[16]

So what's not to like about using anonymous sources? For one thing, many journalists are too quick to grant requests for anonymity. As a result, news stories end up being full of shadowy figures whose credibility is suspect. Over and over again, the public has expressed its discomfort with widespread use of anonymous sources—in surveys and in letters and phone calls to editors. In addition, sources sometimes ask for secrecy not because they fear for their jobs or lives but because anonymity provides cover for their personal vendettas. In those cases, "news" stories end up becoming propaganda.

With those factors in mind, some consensus has emerged on the best way to deal with anonymous sources. What follows is a collection of the "best practices" in the industry:

- Reporters never should volunteer to grant a source anonymity.
- Reporters should use anonymous sources only as a last resort when the story is of compelling public interest and the information is not available elsewhere.
- If a reporter has to grant anonymity to get information from a source, the reporter should follow up by encouraging the source to go on the record.
- Before conducting an interview with a source who insists on anonymity, a reporter should make sure both parties agree on the ground rules. The reporter should ask whether he or she has permission to share the source's identity with an editor; under what conditions the source will release the reporter from confidentiality; whether the confidentiality is eternal; and whether the confidentiality is unconditional (e.g., the reporter will go to jail rather than reveal the source).
- Reporters should weigh carefully the reliability and credibility of the source and his or her information. Ideally, the source should have firsthand knowledge of the information he or she is relaying, or the reporter should have access to a document confirming the information.
- Reporters should describe anonymous sources as specifically as possible, providing as much information as possible about the placement and motivation of the source: "a senior aide to a Democratic senator on the Commerce Committee" is preferred to "a Senate aide."
- Reporters should do their best to explain to the audience why the source requested anonymity.
- Reporters should make every effort to disclose to readers any potential source biases.
- Reporters should make every effort to find additional sources to verify the information or to go on the record with it.
- Reporters never should lie to protect a source.
- Reporters should not mislead an audience by doing things like citing "sources" when there is only one source.

- Reporters should carefully consider whether disclosing classified information would harm national security.[17]

Ethical Issue 2: Plagiarism and Fabrication

We've already touched on this issue in the previous chapter in dealing with the topic of accuracy. But it's an issue that's worth revisiting because cases of **plagiarism** and **fabrication** have exploded in recent years. In 2005, for example, more than a dozen major cases of journalistic plagiarism made headlines.[18]

This isn't a topic that needs a long discussion; in fact, this section can be summarized in four words: Don't plagiarize or fabricate. That would seem to be easy advice to follow, but it isn't always. A number of things that are highly prized in newsrooms—getting scoops, writing quickly and getting "killer" quotes—can pressure writers into taking short-cuts. That's a terrible mistake. In an age in which editors and the public have easy access to news archives, it's almost impossible to get away with plagiarism. And it's a mistake with a steep price: Dozens of journalists, some of whom have worked without incident for decades, have been fired or resigned in recent years for plagiarizing.

Catherine Manegold, a journalism professor and former reporter for The New York Times, told American Journalism Review that she sees "so many different things weighing in on the newsroom . . . all these little ways in which corners are cut to get the product out." She said she is particularly concerned about younger writers who enter the field without a strong sense of ethics. "I think it can be a real mess and a difficult thing for young people to navigate right now," she said.[19]

The following guidelines should help avoid most instances of potential plagiarism:

- A journalist does not need to cite a source for facts and quotations that came from his or her own reporting.
- Generally, a journalist does not have to cite a source for background information contained in stories prepared by the news outlet he or she works for. However, it's important that a journalist verify that this is the policy of his or her news organization.
- A journalist does not have to attribute common knowledge. If information has been published in or broadcast by three or more sources, it is generally presumed to be common knowledge.
- A journalist always should attribute direct quotations if they were not spoken in his or her own newsgathering.
- When a journalist was not present at a scene described in a story, he or she should indicate how the information was obtained.
- In all other situations, a journalist always should attribute the information, whether quoting it or paraphrasing it.

Attribution in a news story differs from citing sources in a research paper because a journalist is not expected to use footnotes or endnotes. Instead, the writer should weave sources into a story as transparently as possible, either by noting the source in a print or broadcast story or by linking to it in online work. For example:

Those findings come from a study published today in the journal Science. (*print or broadcast*)

Those findings come from <u>a study published today</u> in the journal Science. (*online, with link to the study*)

By following these guidelines, a journalist should avoid one of the most common ethical landmines.

Ethical Issue 3: Advertising Pressures

Nearly all U.S. news media outlets depend on advertising support to pay the bills. Unfortunately, that support sometimes brings with it the possibility of interference in the news process. Advertisers often threaten to pull their support if a news outlet publishes or broadcasts stories the advertisers do not like. They also lobby vigorously for coverage of stories that cast them in a good light, even though the news value of such stories might be minimal.[20]

In recent years, one of the most visible cases of bad decision making on this front was the Los Angeles Times–Staples Center scandal. In 1999, management of the Times agreed to share with the center's owners revenue made from a Sunday magazine issue devoted to the new sports complex. The decision was made without telling the editorial staff. Once the story broke, "a full-scale newsroom revolt produced petitions and angry confrontations with top brass."[21]

Unfortunately, the Los Angeles Times is hardly alone. In one study, 90 percent of newspaper editors surveyed reported that they had been pressured by advertisers to change or withhold copy.[22] That admission that would not surprise most of their readers: A 2003 study by the Radio and Television News Directors Foundation reported that nearly three-fourths of the public think that advertisers either often or sometimes improperly influence the news.[23]

Al Tompkins of the Poynter Foundation argues that studies like those point toward one clear plan of action:

Journalists should do all they can to erase that public perception. It should be clear that advertisers have no influence over news content. Journalists sometimes cover issues and events that conflict with the interests of advertisers. Journalists should be free to fairly and aggressively cover stories that involve advertisers, even if you show the advertisers in a "negative light."[24]

The Society of Professional Journalists' Code of Ethics sums up the issue even more simply: "Journalists should . . . deny favored treatment to advertisers and special interests and resist their pressure to influence news coverage."[25]

Ethical Issue 4: Conflicts of Interest

Advertiser pressure is the largest conflict of interest faced by journalists. But it is hardly the only one. Other conflicts can arise in relationships with sources, investments and financial ties, participation in public life, outside work, and so on. As The New York Times notes in its Code of Conduct:

Conflicts of interest, real or apparent, may come up in many areas. They may involve the relationships of staff members with readers, news sources, advocacy groups, advertisers, or competitors; with one another, or with the newspaper or its parent company. And at a time when two-career families are the norm, the civic and professional activities of spouses, family and companions can create conflicts or the appearance of conflicts.[26]

In its code, the Times also succinctly states why avoiding such conflicts requires constant vigilance: "(I)t is essential that we preserve a professional detachment, free of any whiff of bias."[27]

When journalists fail on this front and give audience members any reason to doubt their independence and integrity, they throw away their most valuable asset. Whenever reporters have any doubt about whether an action or a relationship might be a conflict of interest, they *always* should consult with their editors.

ASSIGNMENT DESK 15.3

Review the following scenarios and write a short response to each explaining why you do or do not consider it to be a conflict of interest.

1. A reporter covering real estate news learns that a bad area of town is about to undergo a major renovation and is expected to become one of the more desirable areas to live in. The reporter buys some property in the area with the hopes of cashing in on the development. Should the reporter still be allowed to cover the area — or real estate at all?
2. One of the biggest political issues in recent years has been gay marriage. Should a gay or lesbian reporter be allowed to report on the topic?
3. A reporter who covers the local school system has a child who is about to enter school. Should the reporter be allowed to continue covering that beat?
4. A sports reporter who covers football is known to be a fan of the local team. Should the reporter be reassigned to another sport?
5. A reporter who covers politics is asked to serve on the board of a local nonprofit organization that provides food and shelter for the less fortunate members of the community. Part of the reporter's volunteer work involves calling people in the community to request donations. There is a chance some of the people the reporter will be asked to call are among his or her sources. Is that a problem?

Ethical Issue 5: Deception in Gathering Information

One of the most contentious ethical issues for journalists is when, if ever, a journalist can use **deception** to help get a story. Some journalists have a hard time even accepting that as a legitimate question. The primary job of a reporter is to report the truth in an honest and fair manner, they say, so journalists have no business lying to get a story. The New York Times Code of Conduct, for instance, clearly states the news organization's position: "Staff members should disclose their identity to people they cover (whether face to face or otherwise), though they need not always announce their status as journalists when seeking information normally available to the public. Staff members may not pose as police officers, lawyers, business people or anyone else when they are working as journalists."[28]

Others don't see the matter as nearly as clear cut. They argue that if the only way to get a story of legitimate public concern is by using false identities, obtaining secret materials, eavesdropping or other questionable methods, the ends might justify the means. That was the thinking when ABC News' "PrimeTime Live" sent reporters posing as grocery store workers to investigate the food-handling practices of a Food Lion supermarket. As part of their news gathering, they also used hidden cameras. The report "showed stores in the Food Lion chain repackaging old, spoiled meat and fish; mixing old ground meat with new ground meat, and taking a rotting turkey, slapping some barbeque sauce on it and repackaging it for sale in the gourmet food section."[29] While the initial reaction to the story probably made ABC feel the deception was justified, Food Lion's massive public relations campaign and prolonged legal challenges afterward likely did as much if not more harm to ABC's reputation than the report had done to Food Lion's reputation.

To many observers, the PrimeTime case made a better argument *against* using deception than for using it because the program could have told the story without the deception. "Indeed, PrimeTime said that seventy current and former Food Lion employees had attested to unhealthful food-handling practices at more than 200 Food Lions in on-the-record interviews, and that others had done so off the record," Russ Baker wrote in Columbia Journalism Review. "Many journalists have argued that ABC could have done its story without violating the law, and that it went with the hidden camera because viewers find it sexy."[30]

Baker adds that journalists need to understand the difference between working undercover and actively practicing deception:

> The 1995 Pulitzer for national reporting went to The Wall Street Journal's Tony Horwitz for a series on dead-end jobs that included his undercover work in a chicken plant. Horwitz powerfully recounted the degrading and dangerous routines on the "disassembly" lines in the poultry industry. On his job application, Horwitz did not note that he worked for the Journal; instead he listed "Dow Jones," which, to some people, might look like a poultry wholesaler named "Don Jones." Just last year [1996], Jane Lii of The New York Times got a job in a garment factory, and catalogued the brutal fifteen-hour work days and fifteen-minute lunches of an invisible sector of society. Michael Oreskes, the Times metro editor, says Lii "was under express instructions to do nothing misleading." Still, she didn't have to make anything up, because the manager simply saw a young Chinese woman and asked if she was ready to work hard.[31]

In the end, any time the question of using deception arises, the best practice usually is to take a hard look at the story and see if there are other ways to get it. In virtually all cases, there is one.

Ethical Issue 6: Taste and Sensitivity

Occasionally, journalists face tough choices in determining whether using certain content might be in bad taste or lack sensitivity. This situation most often occurs with photographs, especially those that show people who have died. In an era of frequent global disasters, ongoing war and terrorism, some journalists are reassessing how they handle such photos. Ken Irby of the Poynter Institute told The Dallas Morning News that "Always in the past, we've addressed these as taste issues." If an image would offend readers having breakfast, it was not used. "I don't think these tests are relevant any more," Irby said. "We live in a graphic society, whether we choose to or not."[32]

A photo does not have to be gory or gruesome to powerfully convey a message. Tom Rosenstiel, director of the Project for Excellence in Journalism, has said that he believed that the strongest image to come out of the Hurricane Katrina disaster in 2005 was that of a dead elderly woman slumped in her wheelchair in the Convention Center. "People were informed by that image," Rosenstiel said. "I don't think anybody was offended."[33]

Stories about deaths and other tragedies also can raise questions of ethics, forcing journalists to balance the public's right to know against a family or community's privacy in a time of grief and mourning. For example, The Eagle-Tribune of North Andover, Mass., faced that question in reporting a story on an 11-year-old boy who had died at home. Readers of the story were left to wonder how he died after the paper decided to omit that information from the story. Upon reflection, Editor-in-Chief William B. Ketter decided that decision was not a good one:

> We didn't include that fact in the story out of sensitivity to the boy's family and because of the newspaper's policy of only reporting suicide that's committed in public or by a public or well-known figure. Self-inflicted death done in the privacy of a home usually doesn't make the paper.
>
> This, however, was not your usual private suicide, if there is such a thing.
>
> The victim was only 11 years old. Additionally, because of his popularity with his peers, the school's principal felt compelled to reach out to the community with advice on how to handle what she described as an "untimely death." That also is unusual.
>
> It is the exceptional that often makes life and death especially newsworthy. So does public interest and reader desire to know what happened, why it happened and how it happened. In other words, to know the complete story. Or as complete as we can assemble the details and still publish a timely story.
>
> All of which argues for making an exception to our suicide reporting policy in the case of the boy's death. We were not, in this instance, completely honest with our readers, and that is an obligation that we take seriously every day. It goes to the heart of our believability.[34]

Another sensitive issue is naming sexual assault victims and juvenile offenders. Some beginning journalists have the mistaken impression that they are not legally permitted to publish such information. However, as we saw earlier, in many cases there is no legal prohibition against publishing it. The question instead is one of ethics: When is publishing such details the right thing to do?

One high-visibility case that brought this question to the fore was the 2004 rape trial of basketball star Kobe Bryant. His accuser requested that the media not name her. Although many news organizations withheld her name, some decided to publish it. The Boulder (Colo.) Daily Camera, for instance, said it decided to publish her name after the accuser added her name to a refiled lawsuit. The Rocky Mountain (Colo.) News defended its decision to publish by noting that "fairness requires that both sides be named."[35] Journalists working for news outlets that combine print or broadcast and online operations faced an additional challenge: If the traditional outlet did not publish the name, under what circumstances would it be proper for the online site to link to another site that did publish her name?

Steve Outing of the Poynter Institute touched on this ethical question in a column he wrote during the Bryant case:

> News organizations, it would seem, no longer can shield the public from disturbing content—or protect rape victims or accusers from public scrutiny—in the way they once could. They no longer are effective gatekeepers, shielding their audiences from material deemed too sensitive, controversial, or disgusting. All they can do on the Internet—using whatever ethical guidelines they choose—is to regulate their own small slice of cyberspace.[36]

Journalists face perhaps even tougher calls when confronting the issue of publishing the identities of juveniles involved in crimes. Here the goal of informing the public must be balanced with the harm that could occur to a vulnerable juvenile. Al Tompkins of the Poynter Institute has put together a set of questions to guide journalists in making such decisions. Chief among the questions are these:

- What is the journalistic purpose in identifying the juvenile?
- If the juvenile is charged with a crime, how strong is the evidence?
- How likely are the charges to stick and the juvenile to be prosecuted?
- If the juvenile is charged with a crime, will he or she be tried as an adult?
- What is the severity of the crime and the nature of the crime, and how much harm was done in the process of the crime?
- What is this juvenile's record?
- How would shielding the juvenile's identification and history expose the public to potential harm?
- How public was the juvenile's arrest or apprehension, or the incident that landed the juvenile in the public eye?[37]

Only when a journalist is satisfied with the answers to these questions should the name be used.

Conclusion

Doing the right thing as a journalist means paying attention to many details, laws and ethical guidelines. But when journalists take the time to do all that, they can leave work at the end of the day knowing that they have served the public and their news organizations without exposing anyone to unnecessary risk or criticism. Taking short-cuts is the best way to undermine the only valuable thing a journalist has: credibility. Although the laws are generally clear-cut, ethical issues can be hard to negotiate. When in doubt, a journalist can turn to the Ethics AdviceLine for Journalists: www.ethicsadvicelineforjournalists.org, a free phone and online service dedicated to helping journalists choose the right course (see Figure 15.4).

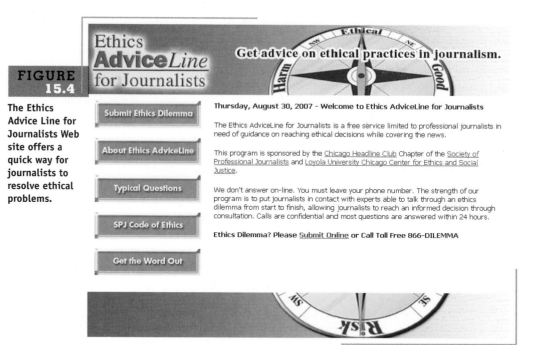

FIGURE 15.4

The Ethics Advice Line for Journalists Web site offers a quick way for journalists to resolve ethical problems.

KEY TERMS

actual malice, 271
deception, 285
defamation, 268
fabrication, 283
fair comment and criticism, 270
false light, 275
full and fair account, 269
intrusion, 276
libel, 267
limited (vortex) public figure, 271
pervasive public figure, 271

private figure, 271
plagiarism, 283
provable truth, 268
public official/public figure rule, 271
public disclosure of private facts, 274
qualified privilege, 269
reckless disregard, 271
shield law, 276
simple negligence 273

DISCUSSION QUESTIONS

1. Libel laws were created long before the Internet came into existence. Are changes needed to make them more useful in a time when most people get much of their news and information not from traditional media but from online media?

2. Millions of students and others post intimate details and revealing photos of their lives on Facebook, MySpace and blogs. Are the existing privacy laws sufficient given this situation, or should the laws be changed? If so, how?

3. Should citizen journalists be required to follow the same laws as professional journalists? If not, how should the laws governing the two groups differ?

4. Visit the Society of Professional Journalists Freedom of Information "Reading Room" (www.spj.org/rr.asp?t=foia). Read at least three of the articles there and write a short summary of the critical issues discussed in them.

5. Should citizen journalists and bloggers have the same legal rights as professional journalists? Why or why not?

NOTES

1. Reporters Committee for Freedom of the Press, "Invasion of Privacy: Publication of private facts," The First Amendment Handbook, 2003, **http://www.rcfp.org/handbook/c02p03.html.**

2. Daniel Steven, "When Truth Is No Defense," PublishLawyer.com, 2002, **www.publishlawyer.com/carousel4.htm.**

3. Reporters Committee for Freedom of the Press, "Invasion of Privacy: False light," The First Amendment Handbook, 2003, **http://www.rcfp.org/handbook/c02p04.html.**

4. Steven.

5. "True or False?" St. Petersburg Times, 5 January 2004, **www.sptimes.com/2004/01/05/Opinion/True_and_false.shtml.** See also Stephen Nohlgren, "When Truth Fails as a Defense," Poynter.com, 5 January 2004, **www.poynter.org/content/content_view.asp?id=58793.**

6. Reporters Committee for Freedom of the Press, "Invasion of Privacy: Defenses," The First Amendment Handbook, 2003, **http://www.rcfp.org/handbook/c02p08.html.**

7. Katherine Q. Seelye, "Times and Reporter Reach Agreement on Her Departure," The New York Times, 9 November 2005, **www.nytimes.com/2005/11/09/business/09cnd-miller.html?ex=1183089600&en=fe0b3102a2af5a2c&ei=5070.**

8. Reporters Committee for Freedom of the Press, "Reporter's Privilege," **http://www.rcfp.org/privilege/index.php.**

9. "Federal Shield Law," Newspaper Association of America, 31 March 2005, **www.naa.org/artpage.cfm?AID=6852&SID=1040.**

10. Reporters Committee for Freedom of the Press, "Confidential Sources and Information: Legislative protection of news sources," The First Amendment Handbook, 2003, **http://www.rcfp.org/handbook/c04p02.html.**

11. Reporters Committee for Freedom of the Press, "Confidential Sources and Information: Constitutional privilege protects sources," The First Amendment Handbook, 2003, **http://www.rcfp.org/handbook/c04p03.html.**

12. Joe Strupp, "Losing Confidence," Editor & Publisher, July 2005, p. 36.

13. Rachel Smolkin, "Uncharted Terrain," American Journalism Review. October/November 2005, p. 35.

14. Strupp, p. 36.

15. Walter Pincus, "Anonymous Sources: Their use in a time of prosecutorial interest," Nieman Reports, 59, no. 2 (Summer 2005): p. 28.

16. Strupp, p. 34.

17. This section is compiled from a range of sources: The New York Times policy on Confidential News Sources, 25 February 2004, **www.nytco.com/company-properties-times-sources.html**); the Washington Post's Policies on Sources, Quotation and Attribution, 20 February 2004, **www.poynter.org/column.asp?id=53&aid=61244;** "Report: Journalism without scandal," 17 July 2003, Poynter.org, **www.poynter.org/content/content_view.asp?id=41405;** the Walter Pincus article cited earlier; and the Rachel Smolkin article cited earlier.

18. See for example Kara Wedekind, "The Unethical Timeline," American Journalism Review, August/September 2005, **http://ajr.org/article.asp?id=3934,** and "2005 Plagiarism Roundup," Regret the Error, 13 December 2005, **http://www.regrettheerror.com/2005/12/2005_plagiarism.html.**

19. Lori Robertson, "Confronting the Culture," American Journalism Review, August/September 2005, **http:// ajr.org/Article.asp?id=3933.**

20. Lawrence C. Soley and Robert L. Craig, "Advertising Pressures on Newspapers: A survey," Journal of Advertising, XXI, no. 4 (December 1992): pp. 1–10.

21. James Risser, "Lessons from L.A.: The wall is heading back," Columbia Journalism Review, January/February 2000, **http://archives.cjr.org/year/00/1/lacron.asp.**

22. Soley and Craig.

23. Radio and Television News Directors Foundation, "2003 Local Television News Study of News Directors and the American Public," **www.rtndf.org/ethics/2003 survey.pdf.**

24. Al Tompkins, "Balancing Business Pressures and Journalism Values," Poynter.org, 9 April 2002, **www.poynter. org/content/content_view.asp?id=3806.**

25. Society of Professional Journalists, "Code of Ethics," 1996, **http://spj.org/ethics_code.asp.**

26. "Ethical Journalism: Code of conduct for the news and editorial departments," The New York Times, January 2003, **http://www.poynterextra.org/extra/ethics.pdf.**

27. "Ethical Journalism," p. 9.

28. "Ethical Journalism," p. 8.

29. Laurie Maisano, "ABC vs. Food Lion: Ethical questions raised by sweeps week," Associated Content, 7 December 2005, **www.associatedcontent.com/article/15562/ abc_vs_food_lion_ethical_questions.html.**

30. Russ Baker, "Damning Undercover Tactics as Fraud," Columbia Journalism Review, March/April 1997, **http://archives.cjr.org/year/97/2/greensboro.asp.**

31. Baker.

32. Bill Marvel and Manuel Mendoza, "Gruesome Images: Does taste trump newsworthiness?" The Dallas Morning News, 1 April 2004.

33. Gail Shister, "To Show or Not to Show Bodies," Philadelphia Inquirer, 8 September 2005.

34. William B. Ketter, "Death and Self-Censorship," The Eagle-Tribune, 15 August 2004, **www.presswise.org.uk/ display_page.php?id=803.**

35. "Collection of Newsroom Decisions on the Naming Issue," Poynter.org, 15 October 2004, **http://poynter. org/content/content_view.asp?id=72893&sid=32.**

36. Steve Outing, "The Thorny Question of Linking," Poynter.org, 21 October 2004, **http://poynter.org/ content/content_view.asp?id=73151&sid=32.**

37. Al Tompkins, "Identifying Juveniles," Poynter.org, 29 February 2000, **www.poynter.org/content/content_ view.asp?id=5555.**

Writing in a Diverse Environment

As Americans watched in astonishment at the havoc that Hurricane Katrina left in its wake in 2005, the nation's news media seemed astonished by another story: that many Americans—including thousands in the devastated areas—live in poverty. As CNN's Wolf Blitzer so indelicately put it: "You simply get chills every time you see these poor individuals... so many of these people, almost all of them that we see, are so poor and they are so black, and this is going to raise lots of questions for people who are watching this story unfold."[1] A few weeks later, Newsweek devoted its cover to a story on "The Other America." In the article, the magazine's reporters declared:

> It takes a hurricane. It takes a catastrophe like Katrina to strip away the old evasions, hypocrisies and not-so-benign neglect. It takes the sight of the United States with a big black eye—visible around the world—to help the rest of us begin to see again. For the moment, at least, Americans are ready to fix their restless gaze on enduring problems of poverty, race and class that have escaped their attention.... this disaster may offer a chance to start a skirmish, or at least make Washington think harder about why part of the richest country on earth looks like the Third World.[2]

A chorus of other reporters registered their astonishment as well (see Figure 16.1), prompting Rosa Brooks to respond in the Los Angeles Times:

> Apparently none of these ace reporters has ever set foot in Washington's Anacostia district, or South Central Los Angeles, or the trailer parks of rural Arkansas. Had they done so... they'd have learned what 37 million Americans already know from personal experience: The Third World didn't sneak in along with Hurricane Katrina. It's been here all the time.[3]

Brooks added that more than one in 10 Americans—and nearly one in five American children—live in poverty.

Washington Post media critic Howard Kurtz echoed Brooks' critique:

> A Sept. 12 Washington Post story was headlined "Katrina Pushes Issues of Race and Poverty at Bush." An equally apt headline would have been, "Katrina Pushes

FIGURE 16.1

The Shreveport (La.) Times provided prominent coverage of a tragedy that struck home for its readers.

The Times

shreveporttimes.com

SHREVEPORT ■ BOSSIER CITY ■ ARK-LA-TEX

WEDNESDAY, AUGUST 31, 2005

Despair, horror

Level of devastation still rising

Floodwaters fill the streets of New Orleans on Tuesday. **More photos, 8A, 9A.**

shreveporttimes.com

■ Expanded coverage   ■ How to help
■ Local shelters   ■ Photo galleries

Tell us your story

Send The Times your Katrina stories by e-mailing dturner@gannett.com or by calling (318) 459-3233.

Water among worries

In the aftermath of the storm, many worries are centered on mosquitoes and finding food and clean drinking water, **3A.**

Opening games altered

Due to Katrina, LSU and Tulane have postponed their season openers, and Southern's has been canceled, **1C.**

Police send help south

Law enforcement personnel are going south to help in the storm's aftermath, **4A**

Schools open doors

Schools in Bossier and Caddo parishes are opening classrooms to children who had to leave south Louisiana, **5A.**

Gasoline prices soar

The Gulf of Mexico's normal daily oil production was shut in because of Hurricane Katrina's approach, **6B.**

Death toll tops 100

One county in Mississippi alone reports at least 100 deaths, and officials fear the number is going to get much higher. **7A.**

By John Hill
jhill@gannett.com
and Mike Hasten
mhasten@gannett.com

BATON ROUGE — Stunned by the extent of devastation in the New Orleans area, a visibly shaken Gov. Kathleen Blanco said survivors will have to be evacuated to other parts of the state and residents may not be allowed back to their homes for weeks.

She acknowledged there is significant loss of life but said the search for survivors will continue to have the highest priority.

Blanco also called for today to be a day of prayer among all Louisianans, who are going to have to assist the victims.

"A lot of people lost their lives, and we still don't have any idea because the focus continues to be on rescuing those who have survived. We don't want to lose any more people than we absolutely have to."

State health officer Jimmy Guidry said rescue workers have not counted the casualties. "We're not retrieving bodies at this point. We want to save the living."

Emergency responders in boats and helicopters plucked hundreds of survivors off their rooftops, many having punched holes through their attics to escape the rising water Katrina left in her assault Monday morning.

Blanco, U.S. Sen. Mary Landrieu, U.S. Rep. David Vitter and federal and state disaster officials toured the area by helicopter, touching down at the Superdome for a briefing by New Orleans Mayor Ray Nagin, who said rescue and plugging two levee breaches are his top priorities.

"We have witnessed the most extraordinary devastation," said Blanco, obviously exhausted and fighting back tears. "The magnitude of the situation is untenable. It's just heartbreaking."

Things were so bad, Nagin said, that rescue boats are bypassing the dead. "We've not even dealing with dead bodies. They're just pushing them to the side."

The damage is the worst natural disaster in the country's history, said Bill Lokey of the Federal Emergency Management Agency, who is coordinating federal assistance. "This is the most significant disaster ever to visit the United States."

While Tuesday was a day of assessment, FEMA already was considering housing alternatives at property outside the damaged areas, he said. It may put people on cruise ships, in tent cities, mobile home parks or so-called floating dormitories, boats FEMA normally uses to house its employees, Lokey said.

■ See STORM 2A

FEMA personnel from Tennessee carry a man off a boat who was just rescued from his rooftop in New Orleans. Hundreds of people were plucked from high spots with helicopters and boats.

Evelyn Turner cries alongside the body of her husband, Xavier Bowie, after he died in New Orleans on Tuesday. Bowie and Turner decided to ride out Hurricane Katrina when they could not find a way to leave the city.

'My city is gone'

By Don Walker
donwalker@gannett.com

NEW ORLEANS — A flotilla of rescue boats behind her, Martha Smith stood Tuesday on the safe, dry pavement of Interstate 10 and glanced back over her shoulder at a Crescent City under a sea of floodwater. "My city," she said, "is gone."

Smith was among thousands of New Orleanians who chose to brave the ferocious winds and torrential rains of Hurricane Katrina, which moved inland early Monday. By afternoon, New Orleans was a catastrophic disaster, a city under water, with many — like Smith — stranded in the upper floors, attics and roofs of their homes and businesses.

On Tuesday, Jefferson Parish Sheriff Harry Lee mounted a massive search and rescue effort bolstered by Federal Emergency Management Administration search and rescue teams from Texas, Tennessee and Missouri. The plan is to

go door-by-door, but to first focus on rescuing people stranded on rooftops, said John Selberg, head of FEMA's Tennessee Task Force. The effort could take days.

"We'll go through thousands of homes. We have to work fast," Selberg said.

"I wish a lot more people would have gotten out. They get so complacent with these hurricanes."

Hundreds were rescued Tuesday, hundreds more waited for aid, and countless hundreds more were feared dead in the hands of Hurricane Katrina.

Judy Martin, 57, collapsed and fell to her knees when she was escorted off the rescue boat. The joy of being rescued couldn't touch the personal tragedy wrought by Hurricane Katrina.

"I give up," she said, quoting the final words spoken by her 95-year-old mother, Cecile Dupont Martin.

■ See RESCUE 2A

Helping hands reach out to soothe hurting hearts

By Doneciea Pea
doneciapea@gannett.com

Betty White celebrated her 55th birthday alone in a gymnasium with at least 800 strangers.

She stood among the throng of people inside the LSU-Shreveport gym when she was glued to the television set watching in sheer amazement, even gasping at times, at the latest news video of the toxic lake

White

that used to be their south Louisiana hometown.

Despite her constant pleas to her mother and sister, they stubbornly refused to stay behind at her home in New Orleans' 6th Ward.

Because of poor telephone connections due to the hurricane,

she's only been able to rely on her sister in San Diego to give her the latest status on her mother and sister.

"She said they're OK, but the house is flooded up to the second floor right now," White said.

But even amid of the dire circumstances surrounding her birthday, she had a smile on her face. "I'm just blessed. ... The people here have been so wonderful to us. If it weren't for the people here, this

shelter, Red Cross and everyone who's helped us out, I wouldn't be here. (Today) is my birthday and I just thank God that I'm still here and I'm not going anywhere."

White is one of many evacuees grateful for the community's outpouring of charity in the aftermath of Hurricane Katrina. Due to the devastation in New Orleans, some are predicting it could be months before its residents are able to return to their homes or whatever

is left of them.

The Red Cross shelter in the LSUS gymnasium and the shelter set up at Centenary College's Gold Dome for Dillard University staff members and students have been an overwhelming flow of contributions and support. Individuals from throughout the country have offered their help.

■ See HELP 10A

Price: 50¢

© 2005 The Times

To subscribe: 459-3322
800-525-4335

The area's leading source for news, entertainment and more

INSIDE

Former Shreveporter cloudy on future of her old house

Winnie Watson (left), 87, and Dora Mae Smith left New Orleans to escape Katrina. Neither know if their houses weathered the storm.
PAGE 4A

Weather

High: 97 Low: 80
Details: 2A

Index

Advice	4D	Lottery	2A
Classified	1E	M. Career	1B
Comics	3D	Money	6B
Crossword	6D	Movie Ads	6D
Deaths	3B	Scoreboard	5C
Editorials	15A	Sports	1C
Living	1D	Stocks	5B
Local/State	1B	Television	5D

Issues of Race and Poverty at a Media Establishment That Has Largely Ignored Them.". . . The mounting problems of the urban poor, from unemployment to high infant mortality to family dysfunction, were long ago reduced to a blip on the media radar screen. . . . [P]oor people themselves were relegated to an occasional walk-on role—until the levees broke. "TV dislikes poor people," says Newsweek, because they're a "downer" and bad for ratings.[4]

Brooks and Kurtz were hardly the only people shocked by the news media's belated awareness of race and class distinctions in the country. Many asked how the media could have been ignorant of such obvious issues.

Variations of that question are asked daily by members of a wide range of groups—minorities, gays and lesbians, people with disabilities, and many others—who wonder how the media can continue to ignore or stereotype large segments of the population in a country that grows increasingly diverse.

That's a good question, but a question that unfortunately does not have an easy answer. Journalists can, however, take a major step toward making the question less frequent by becoming aware of the range of **diversity** in the population and using that awareness to strengthen their reporting and writing. That's the goal of this chapter.

The Importance of Diversity

Some people regard diversity as little more than an ill-conceived buzzword. Smart journalists know that it's far more than that. The U.S. Census Bureau projects that by the year 2050, traditional minority population (blacks, Asians and Hispanics) will make up almost half of the population.[5] In 2000, the Census was modified to reflect the growing numbers of biracial and multiracial Americans who did not know how to identify themselves using traditional categories. Those changes are noticeable in many places. As Sally Lehrman wrote in Quill:

> In Washington state, one of six people speak[s] a language other than English at home. One of eight residents in Illinois is foreign-born. Georgia is one of the fastest-growing states in the country, thanks to the African-Americans, Asian-Americans and Hispanics who have moved there from other states. . . . [In Portland, Maine] almost 1 in 12 people were born outside of the United States. More than a third of those come from Asia, with nearly as many from Europe. In Denver . . . about one-third of the population is Latino, and 11 percent is black. Almost 17 percent of the population is foreign-born. Most have journeyed from Latin America, but about 1 in 10 immigrants hail from Europe and 13 percent from Asia.[6]

Why should that matter to journalists? As Lehrman writes: "The population shift has already begun transforming U.S. cities, and it affects everyone's beat. Schools, churches, libraries, local government, even public transportation are all responding to the change."[7]

But that is not apparent from most news reports, which focus primarily on the ideas, opinions and prominence of white, upper-class males, a group to which many journalists belong. (Minorities exceeded 13 percent of all newsroom employees in 2005, the first time that ever happened. For most of the previous decade, the range had been 10.5 to 11.5 percent. Many newsrooms in smaller markets still have no minorities on staff.)[8] Rather than adapting to the new demographic realities, many journalists continue to emphasize stories centered on and appealing to people like themselves. It's long past time for journalists to stop clinging to that habit and begin covering a wider range of stories and perspectives.

Making that shift will help journalists meet the goals of thoroughness and accuracy that were discussed in Chapter 14. As Keith M. Woods of the Poynter Institute has written, "To be complete and, thus, excellent, journalists must get better at reporting and writing 'untold stories;' at bringing the fullest possible range of people and issues before viewers, listeners and readers."[9]

David Yarnold, former executive editor of The San Jose (Calif.) Mercury News, adds that diversity in reporting is "a fundamental component of accuracy." He explains:

> It comes down to a question of credibility: If readers don't see themselves and hear their voices in your pages, they will no longer view you as a credible source of information.
>
> Having diverse content is important to me because I want to be able to look a Latino leader or a lesbian activist in the eye and say, "This is your newspaper." I want our pages to mirror the ethnic, gender, sexual orientation, socioeconomic, political and religious makeup of the community we serve.[10]

Why Choose Journalism?

Journalism needs me. I holler when the only photograph a newspaper picks to go along with a story about poverty, illiteracy or crime is that of a black person; I scream when the most coverage given to Latinos/Hispanics is for Cinco de Mayo; and I moan when wire stories persist in using the term "Islamic terrorists," as if it is a collocation, while sparing other religions the same kind of injurious labels.

There's a reason for such ignorance, shameful as it is in a profession that is committed to truth, fairness and justice. If there were more minority journalists in news organizations across the United States, consumers would not be forced to read between the lines. Better representation would ensure honest and powerful stories, which, in turn, hold the capacity to transform lives. Being a minority also is an important demographic in an industry that recognizes that its readership and advertising clientele are growing more diverse and global and that the competition is expanding rapidly.

My journalism experiences in Bombay, Singapore and the United States have been deeply personal and professional growth processes. Indeed, I am not just a copy editor; I immerse myself in a newspaper. For instance, I am a member of the Des Moines Register's newsroom diversity committee, which I led for several years, taking on the responsibility of confronting dehumanizing institutionalized expressions and practices.

Journalism needs me more than ever.

LATA D'MELLO
The Des Moines (Iowa) Register

FIGURE 16.2

The U.S. population is becoming increasingly more diverse every year.

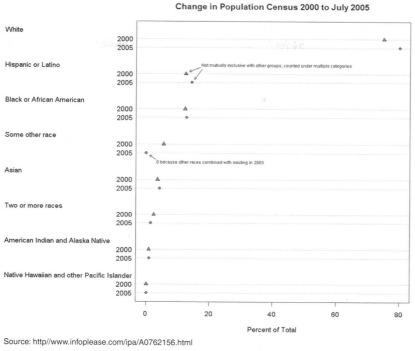

Change in Population Census 2000 to July 2005

White

Hispanic or Latino

Not mutually exclusive with other groups; counted under multiple categories

Black or African American

Some other race

0 because other races combined with existing in 2005

Asian

Two or more races

American Indian and Alaska Native

Native Hawaiian and other Pacific Islander

Percent of Total

Source: http//www.infoplease.com/ipa/A0762156.html

News coverage that reflects the changing **demographics** of a community also makes good business sense (see Figure 16.2). Readers, listeners and viewers who do not find themselves fairly represented will likely move along to other outlets that they believe serve them better. In an industry that faces ongoing financial challenges, it's senseless to lose audience members for no good reason. What the Freedom Forum's Free Press/Fair Press Project said of newspapers is true across all news media:

> There may be no other business that has a future so inextricably entwined with the changing demographics of the country. As the population becomes more diverse, only those newspapers that reflect the lives of all citizens are likely to attract them as readers. And only those newspapers that consistently attract new readers have a good chance to survive and prosper in the years ahead.[11]

The Range of Diversity

The first step toward producing news content that reflects diversity is being aware of the wide range of people in a community. A good starting point is the American Factfinder feature of the U.S. Census Bureau, online at http://factfinder.census.gov/home/saff/main.html?_lang=en. By entering a city, county, state or ZIP code, a journalist can get a detailed breakdown of population by age, education, income, race and disability status. In addition, the tool provides information on what languages people in the area speak, their ethnic backgrounds, whether they rent or own their homes, how far they drive to work, and much more. It will even let users see how population characteristics differ by neighborhood locations. This data provides a quick snapshot of a community, but it's important to bear in mind that the information will be somewhat dated (the data comes from the census, conducted only once every decade).

The census data plainly reveals that there's far more to any community than upper-class white men. In reality, any given community is likely to include a mix of people with a wide range of demographic characteristics:

Sex. In the United States overall, women now outnumber men, making up close to 51 percent of the population. In some areas (including the District of Columbia), the percentage of women is substantially higher, pushing toward 55 percent.

Age. Although the average age of the U.S. population is about 36, that hides the reality that the country is aging. About 12 percent of U.S. citizens—one in eight—is 65 or over.

Disability Status. According to the 2000 Census Bureau figures, more than 19 percent of U.S. citizens over the age of 5—nearly one person in five—has some type of long-lasting condition or disability. Their conditions range from vision and hearing loss to physical limitations to emotional and mental disabilities. That makes people with disabilities the single largest minority group in the United States. As the population continues to age, its size will likely increase.

Race. Although non-Hispanic whites still compose the majority of the population, the percentage made up of blacks, Asians, Hispanics and American Indians is growing. In some parts of the country—particularly the West and Southwest—Hispanics already make up one-fourth to three-fourths of the population.

Ethnicity and Nationality. Each racial category in turn contains people of a wide variety of ethnic and national backgrounds. For instance, the Census Bureau breaks down Asians into 16 subgroups, including the following:

- Chinese, except Taiwanese
- Filipino
- Hmong
- Japanese
- Korean
- Thai
- Vietnamese

The Census Bureau's category of Hispanic or Latino includes four subcategories:

- Mexican
- Puerto Rican
- Cuban
- Other Hispanic or Latino

If a journalist truly wants to understand his or her community, these are critical distinctions.

Sexual Orientation. Depending on whom you ask, at least 4 percent to 7 percent of U.S. residents identify themselves as gay, lesbian, bisexual or transgender, with slightly more men than women in those categories.[12] Even the lower estimate adds up to more than 11 million people. Some cities and specific communities have substantially higher gay and lesbian populations than do others, making this segment of the population an especially important part of the audience in such places.

Economic Class. Most U.S. citizens describe themselves as middle class. The National Opinion Research Center reports that fully half of U.S. families who earn between $20,000 and $40,000 annually categorize themselves as middle class, as do nearly 17 percent of families who earn over $110,000 annually. By most accepted definitions, however, the middle class includes only those who earn incomes between $25,000 and $100,000 each year; some argue that a more realistic bottom figure would be $40,000.[13] That leaves out a lot of people. In 2004, nearly 30 percent of U.S. households had incomes and benefits of less than $25,000 a year. At the other end of the spectrum, about 15 percent of U.S. households reported income of $100,000 or more. And even the meaning of middle class is under scrutiny because rising prices of food, housing and energy are pushing the middle-class lifestyle out of reach for many of those who are statistically middle class.

Religion. When most people are asked to name the major religions in the United States, they will mention three: Christianity, Judaism and Islam. The reality, however, is much more complex. One list of the largest denominational families in the United States breaks down affiliations like this:

Religion	Estimated Percent of U.S. Population, 2001
Catholic	24.5
Baptist	16.3
Methodist/Wesleyan	6.8
Lutheran	4.6
Presbyterian	2.7
Pentecostal/Charismatic	2.1
Episcopalian/Anglican	1.7
Judaism	1.3
Latter-day Saints/Mormon	1.3
Churches of Christ	1.2
Congregational/United Church of Christ	0.7
Jehovah's Witnesses	0.6
Assemblies of God	0.5

And that doesn't even include Islam and a host of smaller religions: Hinduism, Unitarian Universalism, Buddhism, Wiccanism/Paganism/Druidism, Spiritualism, Baha'i, Sikhism, Scientology, Humanism, Daoism and many others.[14] As religion comes to play a greater role in many peoples' lives, it's important for journalists to recognize the many varieties it comes in.

ASSIGNMENT
DESK **16.1**

Focusing on your current place of residence, estimate the following characteristics of the population: age, education, income and race.

Then go to the American Factfinder feature of the U.S. Census Bureau at http://factfinder. census.gov/home/saff/main.html?_lang=en, and enter the ZIP code for that area. How close did your estimates match the reality?

To get a fuller sense of the community, "Map" link next to any characteristic to see the distribution of people with that characteristic within the community. Be sure to click on the "Show More" links to access all available information.

Tapping Diverse Resources

Such a wide range of diversity at first might seem overwhelming. But the lesson is simple: The audience is not a monolithic entity, and it most assuredly is not made up wholly or predominantly of middle-class white men (see Figure 16.3).

But a list of demographic characteristics does not go far in providing insight into people. A key part of the job of journalism is to help people understand others. As the Minnesota Advisory Committee to the U.S. Commission on Civil Rights noted in a report on news media coverage of minority communities:

FIGURE 16.3

Diversity is important on both sides of the news. Both diverse journalists and diverse sources can add to the range of perspectives presented to the audience.

In this diverse nation, most Americans learn a great deal about people of different races, religions, and national origins through their exposure to media. The news media play a crucial role in educating Americans about the nation's diversity, and they have tremendous influence on the attitudes of viewers and readers regarding race relations. Likewise, with most Americans living in areas that, in reality, are segregated by race and income, it is often primarily through local news media that residents learn about the diversity of their cities and towns. News media, therefore, carry the huge burden of ensuring that all races, religions, and cultures are presented accurately.[15]

The only way a journalist can accomplish that task is by getting to know local communities: finding out what people think and care about, and learning about their cultures and traditions. To do that, a journalist must get out into the community to meet the people who do not typically show up in the news. In short, a journalist needs to plug in the holes in the news net we talked about in Chapter 3. As Keith Woods of the Poynter Institute has written: "Journalists interested in telling more of a community's 'truth' need to establish listening posts in the places that fall outside the routine of journalism. . . . Every beat reporter and photojournalist should have a range of listening posts beyond the institutions to which they've been assigned."[16]

Yanick Rice Lamb, a Howard University professor and veteran journalist, recommends several ways to do that. Among her suggestions:

- *Hit the streets.* Visit neighborhood churches, restaurants, community centers and schools. Attend meetings, games and events. You never know whom you'll meet or what you'll hear.
- *Go to groups.* Every field has a professional organization. In many cases, there is an ethnic counterpart.
- *Move beyond so-called leaders.* Ask everyday folks what they think. And don't assume that "leaders" speak for everyone or that a group is monolithic.
- *Check out the rest of the competition.* Go beyond what you normally read and watch. Turn to community papers, radio stations and Web sites.[17]

San Francisco State University professor Venise Wagner shared some additional tips with Sally Lehrman of the Society of Professional Journalists:

Go to gathering places where people linger to talk about things they care about. Try a bench in the park, a popular gym, a coffee shop or a community center. The first time you show up, listen and observe. The next time, identify yourself as a reporter and ask people broad questions. What do you care about? What are your concerns? What issues come up here? How well does media cover your community?

Take a walking tour. Notice the local enterprises, what the shops show in their windows and what the residences are like. Better yet, find someone to show you around — a well-known and respected local is best.

Get to know people. You might start at a community or recreation center and strike up some conversations. Try to figure out who knows everyone else in the community, who is the unofficial organizer, who makes sure kids have somewhere to go after school.

Find cultural brokers, people who can teach you how to introduce yourself and interact with others in a polite, nonthreatening way. Observe people's physical language, such as when it's OK to shake someone's hand.[18]

Some news organizations not only reach out to the public but also invite the public to visit them. KQED public radio in San Francisco periodically convenes "diverse advisory panels of 'citizen experts' to help us explore specific topics such as health care and education," Executive Producer Raul Ramirez reports. He believes the panels are great assets to thorough reporting:

> I have found these one- or two-hour gatherings to be productive tools to boost creativity and bust unwarranted assumptions in the crucial idea stage. They sidestep the solitary, two-way reporting trap in which reporters talk to one source, then another, then another, all along filtering and framing the story through the reporter's limited understanding....
>
> We use these sessions to kick off major projects, and they work extremely well. We bring listeners into our building and they provide us with a rich source of viewpoints and fresh ideas. While we have not turned to advisors' groups to assess past coverage, their views often come out during the conversations.[19]

Even if time and resources do not permit inviting citizens into the newsroom, there are other ways to ensure a broader perspective. For example, KRON-TV in San Francisco holds a weekly diversity group meeting to discuss how to broaden perspectives and to take an inside look at stories about racial and ethnic minority groups. "It's a more sophisticated approach," said Craig Franklin, a former producer of special news projects there.[20]

Aly Colón of the Poynter Institute offers additional suggestions for gaining cultural insights and developing story ideas:

- Search out online sites that focus on issues of diversity, race, ethnicity, sexual orientation, gender, disabilities, and other diverse specialties. Read publications, watch television/cable TV, listen to radio owned by or oriented toward diverse groups.
- Contact diversity and/or race relations specialists. Check universities, institutes, diversity consulting firms, companies known for diversity efforts. Meet with diversity committees or diverse people in your own organization.
- Contact organizations that represent diverse groups, i.e. Hispanic Chamber of Commerce, African-American Coalition, Asian-American Association, The Deaf Center. Your own company may have its own versions of these groups as well.[21]

Such work can lead to much richer stories. For example:

- The work of KRON's diversity group resulted in an award-winning series on racial profiling of Arab-Americans and a feature on Filipino veterans who had been denied government benefits.[22]
- Across the country, Albany (N.Y.) Times Union reporter Paul Grondahl and photographer Michael P. Farrell collaborated on an online series designed to give their audience insight into an oft-neglected part of the city. "Central Ave.: Broken Dreams, Second Chances" (http://timesunion.com/specialreports/centralave/) used words, pictures, audio and video to offer an in-depth look at the eclectic and culturally diverse neighborhoods sprouting up in what had for many years been seen only as a deteriorating spine of the city.
- Adam Fifield of The Philadelphia Inquirer produced the award-winning series "Echoes of the Killing Fields," focusing on the problems faced by the large

Cambodian expatriate community 30 years after they migrated to the area to escape the Pol Pot regime.

- In Daytona Beach, Fla., Ron Hurtibise and Donna Callea produced the prize-winning "Race and Punishment" report on the high rate of suspension of black schoolchildren.
- National Public Radio reporters Richard Knox, Rebecca Davis and Joe Neel won an award for "For Homeless, New Hope for Health Care" (www.npr.org/templates/story/story.php?storyId=3838065), their report on diabetes among homeless people.[23]
- Roanoke (Va.) Times writers Beth Macy and Evelio Contreras teamed up with photographer Josh Meltzer to produce "Land of Opportunity" (http://blogs.roanoke.com/immigration/), a series on the influx of Hispanic immigrants into the area.
- Reporters Greg Mellen, Felix Sanchez and Kevin Butler and photographer Stephen Carr surveyed a wide range of sources for their series on "The Working Poor: Living on the Edge" (www.presstelegram.com/poverty) published in the Long Beach (Calif.) Press-Telegram.[24]

ASSIGNMENT DESK 16.2

Now that you have compared your perception of diversity in your community with the actual statistics, it's time to look at how local news media sources measure up. Examining at least two days coverage in the local newspaper (or its online site) or television news, draw up a list of how the community would appear to an outsider. Based on the coverage you examine, what is the racial, ethnic and religious background of the community? What do most people in the area do for a living? What socioeconomic class dominates the area? Is the news media's depiction an accurate assessment of the community's residents?

Mainstreaming Diverse Sources

Doing the kind of work discussed in the previous section is both important and rewarding. But it is not the end of the road. The next step, and some would argue the most important, is including diverse sources in all stories so that every story reflects the variety of the audience. You need to think of diverse people as not just subjects but also as sources. Keith M. Woods of the Poynter Institute suggests that journalists "Show [people] in their 'ordinariness' by including them in stories and images about things other than race, class, gender, sexuality and social pathology. Use them as meaningful sources, as parents, business owners, scientists, pollsters, etc."[25] Fernando Dovalina, former assistant managing editor of the Houston Chronicle, adds: "Remember that African-Americans, Hispanics, Asian-Americans and Native Americans are business owners, professors, bankers, soldiers, students, scientists and consumers. Make sure your source list is varied enough to include them."[26]

What researcher and professor Beth Haller says of people with disabilities is true across the board: "[A]ll that people with disabilities ask [is] that they be included as news sources so they can tell their side of the story."[27] One gay man's comment in a Freedom Forum roundtable reflects the desires of most of the non-majority population: "I see some coverage of the more flamboyant gay lifestyles, but I don't see my life reflected in the paper. We go to church, plant gardens and have Thanksgiving dinner, too."[28]

Being inclusive is not a particularly difficult job. To a large degree, it requires only awareness. As Steve Buttry, director of Tailored Programs at the American Press Institute, has written:

> Seek out sources who aren't the "usual suspects" on your beat. If you always find yourself talking to white men, find some women and minorities who might bring a different perspective to your stories and steer you toward different ideas. If you find yourself always talking to the professionals and bosses, spend some time talking to the folks in the trenches. If you spend most of your time talking to liberals, seek out some conservatives. If you spend most of your time talking to people your age, seek out some younger or older sources. These people with different perspectives will point you to different stories.... Ask yourself each week whether you made meaningful contact with a new source. If you didn't, could you have?[29]

Another good way to expand your pool of sources and add more diversity to stories is by keeping a list of people who have made contact with a news organization. Maria Stuart of The Livingston County (Mich.) Daily Press & Argus explains the policy at her paper:

> What we're trying to do is what other papers already do: Keep track of some of those who've written letters to the editor or called or have been sources so we can contact them for their comments on other stories that might concern them in some way. If we know where they live, we try to track that so if a new development is pitched, or some disaster happens, we'll have folks we can get in touch with. Reporters should learn to keep databases of people who've sent them e-mails or who've called or written letters with areas of interest so that they have a batch of real people for sources at their fingertips.

Every reporter should build such a **Rainbow Rolodex,** a diverse list of sources that can be consulted for a wide range of stories.

While mainstreaming diverse sources in stories is an accomplishment, it's important that journalists not stop there. It's also important to show a wide range of people in photographs, video and illustrations, too.

ASSIGNMENT DESK 16.3

Using the local newspaper (or its online site), make a list of all the stories that deal with topics specifically oriented toward diversity issues. Make another list of the diverse sources that are used in the rest of the stories. How does the paper or site fare in this analysis?

Avoiding Stereotypes

Even the most thoughtful and thorough journalists can sometimes slip into stereotypical thinking and writing. Even when they are positive, stereotypes should be avoided because they always reduce people to clichés.

Some of the more common problems of **stereotyping** include:

- Focusing on minorities only when they are involved in crime or controversy.
- Including racial characteristics of suspects in crime stories when they are not part of a complete description that might assist the public in identifying the suspects.
- Focusing on people with disabilities only in inspirational or medical stories.
- Covering stories about diverse people with lessened respect.
- Linking "terrorists" exclusively with Muslims or people of Middle Eastern descent.
- Using words and phrases that are generally regarded as demeaning (white trash, confined to a wheelchair, jewed, gypped, and so forth).

Beyond basic stereotyping, there is one more area to watch in writing about diverse populations: how stories are framed. As Thomas C. Huang of The Dallas Morning News explains, "Framing is akin to composing a photograph." A journalist aims to capture certain things that he or she finds interesting. **Framing** is a natural part of that process. A frame helps organize and make sense of what otherwise would be a collection of unrelated observations and facts. The problem comes in, Huang says, when the same type of framing is used repeatedly, leading to monotonous, one-dimensional reporting. Huang identifies six frames commonly used in diversity stories:

1. The conflict frame: Probably the most common frame not just for diversity stories but for all of journalism. Huang cautions that "telling all of our diversity stories through the prism of conflict is not being accurate journalistically. The consequences of diversity are more complex and nuanced."
2. The bridge-building frame: This type of story focuses on diverse groups trying to understand one another, bridging the differences between races, faiths or sexual orientation, for example. Huang sees this frame as little better than the conflict frame: "[T]hese stories tend to be simplistic, surface-level and event driven. Our challenge is to chronicle true, lasting relationships that transcend differences."
3. The disorientation frame: This frame focuses on a minority group—refugees, special-needs children, transgendered people, and so on—that is out of place in mainstream culture. This frame can produce some good stories, but Huang warns that it also tends to categorize people as victims or heroes. Further, the frame rarely is used to look at how disorientation strikes the majority, too, as life changes around them.
4. The identity frame: This one focuses on how people view themselves, particularly important at a time of vast demographic shifts.

5. The creation frame: This type of story looks toward the blending of cultures and the creation of something new, whether it's in arts, politics, food or other areas.

6. The mainstreaming frame: Huang calls this "the frame that at first doesn't appear to be a frame." But it is a frame, and a good one, in that it results when "we make the commitment to populate the story with people from a wide variety of backgrounds."

Rather than forcing a story into any of these frames, Huang instead recommends that journalists be aware of them and not instinctively try to force every story into the same frame.[30]

Conclusion

Making the effort to portray a wide range of perspectives and include a diverse blend of sources in stories has become a basic principle of good journalism. Only by doing so can journalists produce work that is completely thorough and accurate. From a business standpoint, as well, diversity makes sense: The United States is moving rapidly from the model of a single dominant race, class and religion, and only by providing a range of perspectives does a news organization invite an increasingly diverse public to turn to it for the news.

KEY TERMS

demographics, 297
diversity, 295
framing, 305

Rainbow Rolodex, 304
stereotyping, 305

DISCUSSION QUESTIONS

1. Visit the Times Union project "Central Ave.: Broken Dreams, Second Chances (http://timesunion.com/specialreports/centralave/). Spend time exploring the sections of the project. How good a job does this project do in giving you a sense of the community, its promise and its challenges?

2. Check out Fernando Dovalina's "Diversity Questions" at www.ibiblio.org/copyed/diversity.html. Use this list of questions to create a list of at least 10 basic rules for ensuring diversity in a news story.

3. Do reporters have an advantage when they share the same background as those they report on?

4. Do reporters have a disadvantage when reporting on people of a different background? If so, what can they do to overcome it?

NOTES

1. Wolf Blitzer, "The Situation Room with Wolf Blitzer," CNN, 1 September 2005.

2. Jonathan Alter, "The Other America," Newsweek, 19 September 2005, p. 42.

3. Rosa Brooks, "Our Homegrown Third World," Los Angeles Times, 7 September 2005, p. B13.

4. Howard Kurtz, "Wiped Off the Map, and Belatedly Back on It," the Washington Post, 19 September 2005, pp. C1-C2.

5. U.S. Census Bureau, "U.S. Interim Projections by Age, Sex, Race, and Hispanic Origin," 26 August 2004, **http://www.census.gov/ipc/www/usinterimproj/.**

6. Sally Lehrman, "Understanding the Diversity in Your Community Is Key," Quill, September 2005, p. 39.

7. Lehrman, "Understanding the Diversity."

8. American Society of Newspaper Editors, "Minority Employment in Daily Newspapers," 12 April 2005, **www.asne.org/index.cfm?id=5646.**

9. Keith M. Woods, "A Complete Picture," PoynterOnline, 17 May 2003, **http://poynter.org/content/content_view. asp?id=25283.**

10. David Yarnold, "Why Diversity?" Society of Professional Journalists Diversity Toolbox, **www.spj.org/dtb3.asp.**

11. Robert J. Haiman, "Best Practices for Newspaper Journalists," The Freedom Forum's Free Press/Fair Press Project, p. 48, **http://www.freedomforum.org/ templates/document.asp?documentID=12828.**

12. Kevin Downey, "Targeting Gays? Look to 'South Park,'" Media Life magazine, 14 October 2005, **http:// media lifemagazine.com/artman/publish/article_676.asp.**

13. "Politics and the Economy: Who is the Middle Class?" PBS NOW, 25 June 2004, **www.pbs.org/now/politics/ middleclassoverview.html.**

14. "Largest Religious Groups in the United States of America," Adherents.com, 7 December 2005, **http://www.adherents.com/rel_USA.html#religions.**

15. "Minneapolis–St. Paul News Coverage of Minority Communities: Executive Summary," the Minnesota Advisory Committee to the U.S. Commission on Civil Rights, December 2003, **www.usccr.gov/pubs/sac/mn1203/ summ.htm.**

16. Keith M. Woods, "The Listening Post," PoynterOnline, 6 August 2002, **http://poynter.org/content/content_ view.asp?id=9524.**

17. Yanick Rice Lamb, "Tips for Better Sourcing," Society of Professional Journalists Diversity Toolbox, **http://www. spj.org/dtb6.asp.**

18. Lehrman, "Understanding the Diversity."

19. Raul Ramierz, "Call on the Community," Society of Professional Journalists Diversity Toolbox, **http://www.spj. org/dtb4.asp.**

20. Sally Lehrman, "Diversity Is Accuracy," Society of Professional Journalists Diversity Toolbox, **http://spj.org/ diversity_toolbox_accuracy.asp.**

21. Aly Colón, "The 5 W's of Journalism from a Diverse Perspective," Poynter Online, 1 July 1999, **http://poynteronline.org/content/content_view. asp?id=4604.**

22. Lehrman, "Diversity Is Accuracy."

23. Lehrman, "Understanding the Diversity."

24. Jon Marshall, "Diverse Sources Make for Best Stories," Quill, January/February 2007, p. 43.

25. Woods, "A Complete Picture."

26. Fernando Dovalina, "Diversity Questions," Institute for Midcareer Copy Editors, **http://www.ibiblio.org/copyed/ diversity.html.**

27. Beth Haller, "Covering Disability Issues," Society of Professional Journalists Diversity Toolbox, **www.spj. org/dtb5.asp.**

28. Haiman, p. 44.

29. Steve Buttry, "Developing and Cultivating Sources," American Copy Editors Society, February 2001, **http://copydesk.org/words/sources.htm.**

30. Thomas C. Huang, "Framing Stories: How we see stories and how we tell them," Poynter Online, 2 May 2005, **http://poynter.org/column.asp?id=58&aid=81884.**

Appendix **A**

Print and Online Writing Style

In the professional world, different types of work demand different styles of writing. For instance, physicians use the language of their field in discussing medical matters:

> Epidermal growth factors or their receptors have been implicated in the development of seborrheic keratoses. No difference was observed in the expression of immunoreactive growth hormone receptors in keratinocytes from normal epidermis and keratinocytes from seborrheic keratoses.[1]

Similarly, those in the field of law communicate in a language of their own:

> Satisfied that Plaintiff had sufficiently alleged the elements necessary to find the defaulting contemnors in violation of the injunction, the Court scheduled a non-jury hearing on the issue of damages for July 9, 2007.

What separates these professionals from journalists is that lawyers, doctors and other professionals write for their peers, who share their specialized knowledge and jargon. Most journalists, however, write for a wide range of the public and therefore need to make their writing understandable to the widest possible audience.

With that in mind, the most common advice given to new journalists is "Write like you talk." That is, journalists should imagine they are engaged in conversation with their audiences, just passing along the news of the day. As well intentioned as that advice may be, it has a couple of problems. First is that most people do not speak well, hemming and hawing, restarting sentences, throwing in lots of junk such as "like" and "you know." In addition, the way any individual talks is different from the way most other people talk. Researchers say there are anywhere from a few dozen to several thousand regional dialects in the United States alone. Slang pops up everywhere. New words enter the vocabulary daily. Put all that together and the result is conversational English like this example of a snowboarder being interviewed about his use of slang:

> Yeah, like I, like, what I say, like sometimes people just don't understand it. Like I, like, my terminology for certain things which is like, like whom I clique, my group, like my friends, like nobody else understands it, so if I go someplace else, or someplace new they are like, they don't know it so, like, and they are like, they are like, "What are you talking about?"[2]

Even without using any slang, this sentence is virtually impossible to follow.

The second problem is that too many journalists spend too much of their time talking only to other journalists. That can give them a warped sense of how regular people talk and lead to a language of their own. This "news speak" is apparent everywhere from newspaper headlines to TV news reports.

So the best advice is "Write like you would talk if you had a great vocabulary and perfect grammar, didn't use slang or a regional dialect, and never stammered." Although that's quite a tall order, the following tips can help a journalist move closer to achieving it, thereby ensuring that his or her news reports will be understood by the largest possible audience.

Keep Sentences Short

It's not unusual for the sentences written by researchers and other professionals to run on for what seems like days on end:

> But if casual hyperplanes often compete with chance alignments and do not always dominate the latter, then rotation algorithms whose convergence to local minima can disclose a plurality of provocative pattern configurations, even ones with overall hyperplane strength appreciably less than the global optimum, should be preferred to algorithm (were any to exist) that finds its criterions' optimizer without detecting any other axis placements that also merit interpretive consideration.[3]

Unfortunately, even some journalists are not immune from this affliction. It's not uncommon to find sentences in printed news reports that run 40, 50, 60 words or more — much longer than the generally accepted recommendation of keeping sentences to less than 30 words each. Even worse, many of these long sentences twist and turn tortuously, making it hard for the reader to find the subject, verb and object. The problem becomes even worse in broadcast news writing, which typically does not give audience members a second chance to catch what was said.

That's not to say that every sentence needs to be a snappy little "See Spot run" affair. Just as in any type of good writing, variety in sentence length and construction makes for more interesting reading. Alternating short and long sentences keeps things moving and more fully engages a reader's interest, as this Associated Press news story demonstrates:

> The creator of the world's top-selling cake pan has died.
> H. David Dalquist created the Bundt pan.
> Dalquist died of heart failure Sunday at his home in Edina, Minn. He was 86.
> After serving in the Navy in World War II, Dalquist founded the kitchen equipment company Nordic Ware.
> He designed the pan in 1950 at the request of the Minneapolis Hadassah Society. Members had old ceramic cake pans of similar designs but wanted an aluminum pan.
> Dalquist created a new shape and added regular folds to make it easier to cut the cake.
> The Hadassah members called the pans "bund pans" from the German word for a gathering. Dalquist added a "t" and trademarked the name.
> Since then, Nordic Ware has sold more than 50 million Bundt pans. (AP)

While the majority of the sentences in this story run between 14 and 17 words, five of the sentences are substantially shorter, running as little as three words. Adding those shorter sentences helps keep the story from developing a monotonous rhythm. It also helps that two of the sentences start with introductory phrases ("After serving in the Navy in World War Two" and "Since then") to vary the rhythm.

Here's what happens when the story is rewritten so that every sentence is structured the same way and runs nearly the same length. For the fullest effect, try reading this out loud:

> The creator of the world's top-selling cake pan has died at the age of 86.
> H. David Dalquist, who created the Bundt pan, died of heart failure Sunday at home in Edina, Minn.
> Dalquist founded the kitchen equipment company Nordic Ware after serving in the Navy in World War II.
> He designed the pan in 1950 at the request of the Minneapolis Hadassah Society. Members had old ceramic cake pans of similar designs but wanted an aluminum pan.
> Dalquist created a new shape and added regular folds to make it easier to cut the cake.
> The Hadassah members called the pans "bund pans" from the German word for a gathering. Dalquist added a "t" to the word and proceeded to win a trademark for the name.
> Nordic Ware has sold more than 50 million Bundt pans in the years since then.

That version tends to sound "sing-songy" and may lull listeners into a trance.

> ## Writing Tip
>
> Once you have a draft of your story, run a word count on each sentence. Highlight your sentences one at a time, and in Microsoft Word, choose "Tools" > "Word Count." That will let you check the lengths of your sentences and make sure they're not too similar. ●

Sentences, Clauses and Phrases

Although constructing a sentence doesn't take much work, news writers sometimes come up short in creating sentences and instead end up with sentence fragments, such as this: "A year like no other."

The first step in avoiding this problem is understanding the difference between independent clauses, dependent clauses and phrases. While they look similar, there's a big difference in how they should be used.

An *independent clause* can stand on its own as a sentence (that's what makes it independent). It must include a subject and a verb. Sometimes one or the other is understood, as in these two examples of the shortest sentences in the English language: "Go" and "I." In the first, the subject *you* is understood; in the second, the verb *am* is understood (as in response to the question, "Who is going?"). Most of the time, however, both subject and verb appear, as in this example: "The gunman surrendered."

A sentence typically also includes an *object*. An object is a noun or pronoun that receives the action of a verb or shows the result of the action:

Powerful rainstorms sent millions of gallons of treated and untreated wastewater into Southern California waterways. (Los Angeles Times)

The object of this sentence is *millions of gallons of treated and untreated wastewater*.

In news writing, the concept of the object of a sentence is more relaxed than what strict definitions would require. Generally speaking, an object is the word or words that finish the thought begun by the subject and the verb:

The Supreme Court ruled today that judges can raise or lower the length of prison sentences for convicted criminals.

The phrase beginning with *that* completes the main idea of the sentence.

So far, the rules could not be simpler. However, things become complicated when either the subject or the verb contains multiple elements, as in these examples:

Brad Pitt and Jennifer Aniston reportedly split after she refused his ultimatum to have children this year.

Americans should eat less and exercise at least a half hour each day, according to new government guidelines released today.

In the first sentence, the subject is *Brad Pitt and Jennifer Aniston*. In the second sentence, the verb is *should eat ... and exercise*. Despite the additional elements, these examples still qualify as simple sentences because they contain only one independent clause each.

Compound sentences consist of two or three independent clauses joined in a series:

Diets that contain high amounts of fruits and vegetables will not protect against breast cancer, but diets containing a great deal of red meat may raise the risks of other cancers.

The two clauses in this example are joined by a comma and the word *but*, which is a coordinating conjunction. Using a *coordinating conjunction* is just one way to join two or more independent clauses, as the following table shows:

Comma and coordinating conjunction	, followed by *and, but, for, or, nor, so, yet*
Semicolon	;
Semicolon followed by an independent marker word	; followed by *therefore, moreover, thus, consequently, however, also*

Joining two independent clauses together with no punctuation results in the grammatical problem known as a *fused sentence*:

> The Pentagon plans to delay construction of the new base the plan needs congressional approval.

Using only a comma to join two independent clauses together results in the grammatical problem known as a *comma splice*:

> The Pentagon plans to delay construction of the new base, the plan needs congressional approval.

In each case, solving the problem simply requires the use of one of the three options discussed previously. For example:

> The Pentagon plans to delay construction of the new base, but the plan needs congressional approval.

A *dependent clause* often closely resembles an independent clause. But although it contains a subject and a verb, it does not convey a complete thought. The difference can be as simple as one word, such as a dependent marker word. Common dependent marker words include *after, although, as, as if, because, before, even if, even though, if, in order to, since, though, unless, until, whatever, when, whenever, whether,* and *while*. Look what happens when we add one of these to two of the independent clause examples we looked at previously:

> When the gunman surrendered

> After powerful rainstorms sent millions of gallons of treated and untreated wastewater into Southern California waterways

While those clauses were able to function as sentences before the addition of the dependent marker words, adding those words makes the clauses incapable of standing alone. That's why they are called dependent clauses: They have to depend on another clause to form a sentence. Combining an independent and a dependent clause creates a complex sentence:
Combining an independent and a dependent clause creates a complex sentence:

> The U.S. trade deficit hit a record high last month as imports of oil and food reached all-time highs.

> After U.S. forces in Iraq spent more than two years looking for weapons of mass destruction in Iraq, the hunt has been abandoned so that the troops can assist in counterinsurgency efforts, officials said today.

In the first example, the sentence begins with the independent clause. No comma is used to join the dependent clause. In the second example, the dependent clause opens the sentence and requires a comma to set off the independent clause.

At the highest level of complexity is the *compound-complex sentence*. This combines at least two independent clauses and one dependent clause. This type of sentence requires careful attention to make sure it meets the rules of good grammar:

> Although the previous week had been quiet, an Israeli man was killed by a roadside bomb in the Gaza Strip today, and Israeli soldiers tracked down and killed four armed Palestinians, including those who planted the explosive.

This sentence begins with a dependent clause and then adds two independent clauses. The order will differ in other sentences.

Phrases

Many writers get tripped up not by clauses but by phrases. A *phrase* differs from a clause in that it does not contain a verb. That means a phrase can never be used on its own as a sentence. Phrases come in four different varieties:

A *prepositional phrase* starts with a preposition (such as *after, for, from, in, to* or *over*):

> After school each day, he spends three hours at the mission.

An *appositive phrase* contains a noun or pronoun that explains or identifies the subject of an independent clause. This example opens with an appositive phrase:

> A federal appeals judge and former prosecutor who played a role in drawing up the Justice Department's antiterrorism bills, Michael Chertoff was nominated today as head of Homeland Security.

Verbal phrases come in two forms. Both include a form of a verb and therefore can look like a clause. Unlike a clause, however, a verbal phrase does not include a subject. Instead, it modifies the subject of the independent clause that follows. The first type of verbal phrase is the *infinitive phrase*, which includes an infinitive (the "to" form of a verb):

> To remove the appearance of a conflict of interest, she announced she is stepping down from the board position.

The second type of verbal phrase is the *gerund phrase*. It contains the *-ing* or *-ed* form of a verb:

> Struggling to remain solvent, Delta Air Lines announced it was cutting its most expensive fares by up to half. Awarded the Nobel Peace Prize, he said he had finally accomplished his life's desire.

In all of examples of phrases so far, the phrases appeared at the beginning of the sentences. But phrases also can be tucked inside independent clauses:

> Western U.S. ski resorts, helped by a warm winter in Europe and bountiful snow at home, prepared for a record-setting season.

> ## Writing Tip
>
> Let your computer help you weed out sentence fragments. In Microsoft Word, choose "Tools > Options" > "Spelling and Grammar" > "Check Grammar with Spelling." Then when you run spell check, the program will alert you to fragments. Be careful of the other advice the grammar checker gives you, however: Some of it is good, but some is not. ●

Paragraph Length

Like the sentences they contain, paragraphs also tend to be shorter in news writing than in other forms of writing. News writers typically ignore the English class rules about formatting paragraphs:

- Begin with a topic sentence.
- Follow with several sentences that explain, develop or support that theme.
- Close with a summary sentence.

Instead, news writers think of a paragraph as a place to explore one idea or to highlight a key fact or good quote. Many paragraphs contain no more than a single sentence. The following story illustrates this use of paragraphs:

> An angry crowd beat a man to death after a vehicle he was riding in struck and injured a young girl, police said Wednesday. Police believe 2,000 to 3,000 people were in the area for a Juneteenth celebration when the attack occurred Tuesday night.

The driver had stopped to check on the little girl at the entrance to an apartment complex when a group of men attacked him, authorities said. The passenger, David Rivas Morales, 40, got out to try to help the driver, but the crowd turned on him, said police Commander Harold Piatt.

Morales was beaten to death by as many as 20 men and left lying in a parking lot, Piatt said. A preliminary autopsy listed blunt force trauma as the cause of death.

The little girl, 3 or 4 years old, was taken to a hospital with non-life threatening injuries.

The driver, who got away from the crowd, is cooperating with investigators, police said.

Piatt did not know how many witnesses had been identified, but thousands of people had been in the area for the daylong festival. He said no guns or knives appeared to have been used in the fatal attack.

Juneteenth marks the day Gen. Gordon Granger arrived in Galveston in 1865 to share news of the Emancipation Proclamation, which freed slaves two years earlier on Jan. 1, 1863. (AP)

Even the longest paragraph in this example is short by non-news writing standards. In fact, at 51 words, it isn't much longer than sentences routinely found in other types of professional writing.

> ## Writing Tip
>
> Once you have a draft of your story, run a word count on each paragraph. Highlight your paragraphs one at a time, and in Microsoft Word, choose "Tools" > "Word Count." That will let you check the lengths of your paragraphs and make sure they're not too long or too similar. ●

Voice

To hold the audience's attention, a writer needs to use active voice. Sentences written in active voice begin with the doer of an action. In contrast, passive sentences begin with the object of the action:

Rescuers found her body deep in the woods. *(active)*

Her body was found deep in the woods by rescuers. *(passive)*

Notice that the active sentence conveys a sense of movement, but the passive sentence does not. Notice also that passive sentences tend to be longer than active ones.

There are times when passive voice can be effective, such as when the doer of the action is obvious or unknown. In cases like these, using passive voice lets the writer focus on the action or what is acted on:

Rogers was taken into custody around 10 p.m. Thursday.

The store had been robbed twice in the previous year.

A writer must pay careful attention to voice in compound sentences. It can be jarring for the reader when one clause is written in active voice and the other in passive:

Scientists are counting on the spacecraft to carve out a huge hole in Comet Tempel 1, but it has not been conclusively proved capable of the task.

This revision makes it easier for readers to follow the sentence:

Scientists are counting on the spacecraft to carve out a huge hole in Comet Tempel 1, but they concede they have not conclusively proved that it is capable of doing so.

Forms of the Verb "To Be"

Just like their passive counterparts, sentences based on forms of the verb *to be* also tend to be dull. Anytime a writer notices a sentence built around *is, are, was* or *were,* chances are he or she can find a quick way to give it more zip:

> Revenue is up by about $50 a cab, to $314 a day.

> Revenue has risen about $50 a cab, to $314 a day.

> The supervisor says it is not uncommon for inmates to become angry around the holidays.

> The supervisor says inmates often become angry around the holidays.

Sentences that begin with *It is* or *There are* are perhaps the worst offenders because they not only use passive voice but also lack even a real subject. For example:

> There are rigid standards for using acronyms and abbreviations in military communication.

Look how the sentence springs to life once that opening phrase disappears:

> People writing military communications must follow rigid standards for using acronyms and abbreviations.

One caution: As long as they are part of a longer verb, *is* and *are* do not pose a problem. For example, when an action is ongoing, such verbs are perfectly appropriate:

> San Francisco is considering steps to make sure its dogs are well cared for.

> ## Writing Tip
>
> To help eliminate passive voice, run a search on your story for the words *is, are, was* and *were.* In Microsoft Word, choose "Edit" > "Find" and then enter one of those words. Check each sentence that's identified to determine if it is passive. The grammar checker can also help with this task. ●

Dangling Modifiers

Another problem to watch for is sentences in which it is unclear what a phrase is supposed to modify. These are called *dangling modifiers*:

> Seeking to secure $100 million in funding, the plan was designed to commence in July.

It's uncertain who was seeking the funding — it was not the plan, as this sentence literally says. This revision eliminates the problem:

> Seeking to secure $100 million in funding, the legislature designed the plan, which will begin in July.

Verbosity and Clarity

"Make everything as simple as possible, but not simpler." That directive from Albert Einstein may be the best advice for writers that ever came from a scientist. Unfortunately, news writers often write long, confusing sentences because they give in to two common and related problems: verbosity and lack of clarity.

Verbosity refers to excessive wordiness. News writers need to find a balance between using as few words as possible and providing all the information the audience needs. That's best accomplished by eliminating words that do not add information to the story. In some cases, it's as simple as changing *Easter Sunday* to *Easter* or *newborn infant* to *infant.* In other cases, it's a matter of finding a word to do the work of a phrase, or a short word to take the place of a longer one: *resigned* instead of *tendered his resignation, lit* instead of *illuminate, before* instead of *prior to.* The following sentences are typical in that they contain verbosity that's easy to overlook and just as easy to eliminate:

> Kestler said the delays in reopening the bridge were largely due to fiscal constraints.

> The school will be one of only two universities in Maryland, public or private, in which all residence halls are equipped with sprinklers.

In the first sentence, the phrase "largely due to fiscal constraints" means "We didn't have the money." So it could be rewritten:

> Kestler said funds had not been available earlier to repair the bridge.

In the second sentence, the phrase "public or private" adds nothing essential because the writer has already said the school is one of only two universities in the state. What other kinds of universities are there?

Clarity relates to verbosity in the sense that writing is sometimes hard to understand because it's too wordy. A national literacy survey undertaken by the U.S. Department of Education in the 1990s found that the majority of adults could not comprehend or use information of the sort commonly found in the mass media.[4] Given sentences like the following, that's no surprise:

> The findings reflect the sentiments of carpool-lane users, who have inundated state officials with complaints about increased delays and congestion over the past six months. (Washington Post)

Even though this example contains no technical information or specialized jargon, many people would find it hard to follow and understand. The problem can be corrected partly by using shorter sentences with no more than one idea per sentence and partly by using more common words. For example, the sentence might be rewritten this way:

> The findings reflect the frustrations of drivers who use carpool lanes. In the last six months, many of them have complained to state officials about increased delays and congestion.

One of the most common roadblocks to clarity occurs when the verb doesn't directly follow the subject, forcing readers to have to double back to connect the two. For example:

> The givers, encouraged by President Bush, who made a $10,000 personal donation and declared that "the most important contribution a person can make is cash," range from movie stars writing million-dollar checks to a 9-year-old California boy who gave up his birthday party and asked his mother to send $250 to Asian children instead. (Washington Post)

Twenty-three words — the number in a good-sized sentence — separate the subject (givers) from the verb (range). (Of course, that's not the only problem in this 54-word behemoth!) Although rewriting sentences to move the subject and verb closer together sometimes requires a good deal of work, in this case closing the gap is simple:

> Encouraged by President Bush, who made a $10,000 personal donation and declared that "the most important contribution a person can make is cash," the givers range from movie stars writing million-dollar checks to a 9-year-old California boy who gave up his birthday party and asked his mother to send $250 to Asian children instead.

Another problem occurs when writing can be understood in more than one way. For example:

> Police at the drowning scene said no swimming signs were prominently displayed in the area.

That sentence leaves the audience member wondering if there were no signs in the area, or if there were "No Swimming" signs in the area. If a sentence can be understood in more than one way, it should be rewritten. In this case, it could be as simple as changing the sentence to read:

> Police at the drowning scene said signs were prominently displayed warning that swimming was prohibited.

Writing Tip

Finding every instance of verbosity and lack of clarity requires careful attention to every word you write. One quick way to make headway, though, is by scanning your stories for long words and phrases, then trying to replace them with shorter alternatives. You can right-click your mouse on a single word in a Word document and choose "Synonym" to see a list of other possibilities. Keep in mind, however, that many suggested synonyms might subtly alter the meaning of your sentence — and that many words have more than one meaning, so some suggestions will make no sense. ●

News Pointers

When Is It OK to Use Specialized Jargon?

Although news writers should strive to reach the widest audiences possible, it's not unusual to find news stories containing sentences like these three:

> However, the American Viticulture Area also includes exposures (or "aspects") to the north, south and west as a result of erosion incisions carved by York Creek as well as Sulphur and Ritchie creeks (which form the appellation's southern and northern boundaries, respectively). (Washington Post)

> Rogers made a clutch jumper at the buzzer to force the overtime.

> "An 88-billion-cubic-foot draw in natural gas stocks is obviously market bearish, especially given the comfortable surplus we have in total stocks," Smith said.

Although many readers might be left scratching their heads over the meaning of such writing, specialized jargon is generally accepted in specialized news reporting (in these cases, food and wine, sports, and business). Even the same word can mean different things in different sections: A corked baseball bat has no relationship to a corked bottle of wine.

Specialized jargon is acceptable in targeted news stories because writers assume that the people interested in the specialized news will understand the terminology. While that might be generally true, it's nevertheless important to remember that at some point everyone is new to the jargon, and therefore, it should be kept to a minimum.

Subject-Verb Agreement

When a speaker says something like "We wasn't sure we was going," that utterance is taken as a sure mark of ignorance. After all, it violates one of the basic principles of writing: Subjects must agree with their verbs.

Yet subject-verb agreement problems turn up surprisingly often in news stories. Most problems occur not because writers don't understand the basic concept, but because making a subject and verb match sometimes can prove tricky. Several constructions demand special attention:

- *Prepositional phrases.* When a prepositional phrase separates the subject and verb, writers sometimes mistakenly make the verb agree with a noun in the prepositional phrase rather than with the subject of the sentence. In this example, notice how the verb *plans* agrees with the subject *group*, not *veterans*:

A group of Vietnam-era veterans plans to testify before a panel looking into possible torture by U.S. forces.

- *Compound subjects.* These come in three varieties. When the subject consists of two singular nouns or pronouns joined by the word *and*, a plural verb is required:

Bush and Blair appear to be happy with the U.N. response.

When two singular nouns or pronouns are joined by the words *or* or *nor*, however, a singular verb is appropriate:

The senator or his successor faces tough decisions on the deficit.

When one singular noun or pronoun and one plural noun or pronoun are joined by *or* or *nor*, the verb should agree with the part of the subject closest to it:

Neither the professor nor her students claim to know about the project.

- *Collective nouns.* These include *class, committee, company, family, group, staff* and *team.* Depending on the sentence, they may require a singular or a plural verb. The general rule is if the sentence makes it clear the collective noun is referring to the group as a whole, it takes a singular verb. If, however, the sentence is talking about the actions of individual members of the group, it takes a plural verb:

The family has stuck together through a wide range of tragedies and challenges.

Each summer, the family spread out across the country as they take individual vacations.

- *Inverted sentences.* As noted previously, sentences that begin with *here is/are* or *there is/are* generally should be rewritten so that they have a true subject. When time or other reasons prohibit rewriting, it's important to make sure that the verb agrees with the noun that follows it:

There are valid reasons for their concern.

Here is a list of items that need to be addressed.

- *Inclusive expressions.* Words and phrases such as *with, together with, including, accompanied by, in addition to,* or *as well as* can cause confusion when they introduce additional information after the subject. The important point to remember is that the verb must agree with the subject itself:

Thatcher, as well as his American-born wife and their two children, is free to leave South Africa at any time.

- *Plural words ending in s.* Words like *news* and *mumps* take a singular verb (e.g., *News is vital to a free society.*), but others like *trousers* and *scissors* require a plural verb (*His trousers were custom made in Hong Kong.*). To be safe, a writer should consult a stylebook or dictionary.

Antecedent Agreement

Just as the subject and verb of a sentence must agree, so must pronouns that follow and refer back to other nouns and pronouns. While few writers have problems with simple sentences, not all cases are as clear-cut. A few common problem areas:

- *Attempts to avoid sexism.* In an effort to avoid one problem, sexism, writers sometimes mistakenly create another problem, antecedent agreement. Such cases usually occur in sentences that have words like *anybody, anyone, everybody* or *everyone* (or a noun preceded by *every*) as their subjects:

Everyone who attended the hearing said they thought the proposal would benefit the neighborhood.

Because there were presumably both men and women at the hearing, the writer tried to avoid the sexism that using *he* or *she* would cause. But the problem is that the subject is singular and therefore needs a singular pronoun later on. The best result is to rewrite the sentence to make the subject plural:

All the residents who attended the hearing said they thought the proposal would benefit the neighborhood.

- *Collective nouns.* As we've seen, collective nouns can act as singular or plural words. Writers need to make sure that antecedents match the intended use:

> The group plans to take up the issue at its next meeting.

> The group promised to stay in touch after they graduate.

- *Lack of antecedent for* which. One of the most common problems is that there's no noun or pronoun for the word which to refer back to — or there is a noun or pronoun, but it does not make sense:

> The legislators refused to delete the provision, which angered the governor.

It wasn't the provision that angered the governor — which is what this sentence literally says — but the legislators' refusal to delete it. Far better is this simple rewrite, which eliminates the whole issue:

> The legislators' refusal to delete the provision angered the governor.

Problems with Series

Sentences often include series of items. The simplest pose no problems for most writers:

> The group claims that foul language, adult themes and partial nudity are becoming too prevalent in network television.

In this case, all of the items in the series are adjective/noun combinations. The problems start, however, when writers mix in infinitives and gerunds, either together or in combination with nouns:

> The governor said his priorities are teen traffic safety, tort reform and selling unnecessary state property to raise funds.

> The device can be used for viewing content from DVDs as well as to view video on the Internet.

In each case, the solution is simply to make sure all the elements are of the same type: noun, infinitive or gerund:

> The governor said his priorities are increasing teen traffic safety, undertaking tort reform and selling unnecessary state property to raise funds.

> The device can be used for viewing content from DVDs as well as for viewing video on the Internet.

Misplaced clauses sometimes pop up in series, too. They should be used only with other clauses, not with nouns, infinitives or gerunds. Here's an example of the writer ignoring that rule:

> The CEO pledged a full investigation, severe punishment for anyone found guilty and that she would accept personal responsibility for paying any expenses.

The sentence can be corrected easily:

> The CEO pledged that she would conduct a full investigation, hand out severe punishment for anyone found guilty and accept personal responsibility for paying any expenses.

Problems sometimes also creep in among items following the words *either* and *both*. Writers need to be careful that the words or phrases that follow the words *or* or *and* in those constructions contain the same type of information. These examples illustrate the common problems:

> They promised to both send cash and food.

> She will either accept the chairmanship or the directorship.

The solutions are as simple as shifting a few words:

> They promised to send both cash and food.
>
> She will accept either the chairmanship or the directorship.

One other problem area is the *false series*. In a false series, one of the items that seems to be in the series clearly does not belong there. For example:

> The students sipped sodas, bottled water and roared loudly when the singer appeared.

It takes just a little work to correct the problem:

> The students sipped sodas and bottled water and roared loudly when the singer appeared.

Notice in the corrected example that there is no comma before *and roared*. A comma is necessary only before an independent clause (for instance, if the sentence had read *and they roared loudly when the singer appeared*).

Keeping Pronouns in the Correct Case

Yet another type of agreement problem occurs when writers mix pronouns of different cases. Just as with most other issues discussed so far, few writers have problems with the basics of using case correctly.

Nominative case is called for when a pronoun is used as a subject of a sentence:

> He is the best friend a person could ask for.

Objective case is used when a pronoun functions as a direct object, indirect object, object of a preposition or object of a gerund:

> They didn't see her after the show.
>
> The company gave him a final warning in March.
>
> Coming from them, it seemed like a compliment.
>
> Failing him seemed to be the only reasonable choice.

Possessive case denotes ownership:

> Once you are vested, you are entitled to your pension.

So far, so good. Problems do lie lurking, however, but fortunately only in specific areas:

- *After* than *or as* at the end of a sentence.   Pronouns should be in nominative case when they are used in comparisons that end a sentence. That's because the verb *is* or *are* is understood in this type of construction: "No one is better with phyllo dough than he."
- *After any form of the verb* to be.   Formal rules of grammar call for nominative case when the pronoun follows *is, was* and *have been*: "It is he," "It might have been they." However, news writers regularly break this rule, using less formal constructions that sound better: "It is him," "It might have been them."
- *Before or after an infinitive.*   Any time a pronoun appears close to an infinitive, it should be in objective case: "She wanted nothing more than for him to be successful."
- *After a gerund.*   Pronouns that follow gerunds should appear in objective case: "Raising them has not been an easy task."
- *In compound structures.*   When a noun and a pronoun appear together as a compound subject or object, the noun can be dropped to determine appropriate case. For example: "Diane and she always

take a fall vacation," "The judges awarded the medals to Darnell and him." In reading the sentences with the nouns removed, it is easy to see that these are the correct cases because otherwise the sentences would read "her always take(s) a vacation" or "awarded the medals to he." For this reason, it is never correct to write "Just between you and I."

- *When* who/whoever *or* whom/whomever *is needed.*   This should not be a tricky issue, but many writers get hung up on when to use *who/whoever* and when to use *whom/whomever*. The simple answer is to remember that *who/whoever* is nominative and *whom/whomever* is objective, then follow the rules listed previously. The only time when extra care is called for is when the sentence structure makes it hard to determine whether nominative or objective case is appropriate. The best way to arrive at an answer is by substituting *he/she/they* or *him/her/them* to see which fits better: "Bonuses will be paid to whoever produces sales at least 10 percent higher than during the previous fiscal year" ("them produces sales" makes no sense); "Whom are you trying to reach?" ("you are trying to reach she" obviously doesn't work).

- *When a pronoun is followed by a gerund.*   Possessive case should be used in constructions like this: "Marvin does not appreciate your following him."

Essential Versus Nonessential Clauses and Phrases

One of the most common mistakes beginning news writers make is confusing *essential* (or *restrictive*) and *nonessential* (or *nonrestrictive*) material. The problem often involves a word or a phrase used as an appositive — that is, as an explanation of another noun or pronoun that immediately precedes it or sits next to it. Uncertainty in this area generally manifests itself in the form of unnecessary or missing commas. Fortunately, determining when commas are needed is straightforward.

An essential clause or phrase contains information that separates that noun or pronoun from others in its category. For instance:

> The chart-topping singer Eminem was the target of a video produced by Benzino, co-owner of The Source magazine.

Eminem's name here is the appositive. To determine whether his name is essential, it is necessary to ask whether the sentence would still make sense without it:

> The chart-topping singer was the target of a video produced by Benzino, co-owner of The Source magazine.

Because more than one singer has topped the charts, Eminem's name is essential to distinguish him from other "chart-topping singers." Such essential information does *not* get set off with commas. Here are a few other examples:

> A naturalized U.S. citizen *working as an Iraqi agent* pleaded guilty to federal charges that he made millions of dollars from 1992 to 2003 by secretly lobbying for the repeal of sanctions on Saddam Hussein's regime, prosecutors said. (Bloomberg.com)

> Virus experts at Sophos have discovered a mass-mailing worm *that poses as a plea for donations to help with the Indian Ocean tsunami disaster.* (Sophos.com)

> A European spacecraft *that landed on Saturn's largest moon Titan* twisted and spun as it tumbled to the muddy surface, scientists said Tuesday, revealing animated pictures of the final stage of its descent. (Los Angeles Times)

Just as in the Eminem example, the appositives in these leads answer the question "Which one?" Without the material contained in the appositives, the answer would not be clear. Therefore, the phrases are essential and require no commas. The last two examples use the word *that* rather than *which* — another difference between essential and nonessential information. Essential phrases always take *which*.

In contrast, nonessential material merely adds to the information being presented about the noun or pronoun it modifies and does not distinguish that noun or pronoun from others in its category:

> The A-380 "superjumbo" jet, which was revealed at a lavish ceremony, gives the European plane maker Airbus a new flagship. (AP)

> The president's choice for secretary of Health and Human Services, Mike Leavitt, won praise from both parties at the opening of his congressional confirmation hearings Tuesday.

> The government has approved the new vaccine to guard against bacterial meningitis, which tends to strike adolescents and young adults.

In each of these examples, there is only one item in the category under discussion: There is only one A-380 super-jumbo jet, the president had picked only one person for secretary of Health and Human Services, and there is only one disease known as bacterial meningitis. Even though in the second example a person reading or hearing the news would probably not have known who the nominee was, that does not take away from the fact that there was only one nominee, so his name adds to the preceding material and does not limit it. Because the material in all these cases is nonessential, it is offset with commas.

Regardless of whether an appositive phrase is essential or nonessential, references to people always should use *who* or *whom*, not *which* or *that*:

> Actress Ruth Warrick, who played the wife of Charles Foster Kane in Orson Welles' 1941 classic movie "Citizen Kane" and was a star of daytime soap operas later in life, died Saturday at the age of 88.

> The player whom officials had accused of using prohibited substances had the day off after winning her first-round match Monday.

Write in Third Person

A common beginning news writer's mistake is writing in first person (*I/me/mine, we/us/our*). Although some journalistic forms call for using this point of view—columns, firsthand accounts—most news is written in the third person (*he/him/his, she/her/hers, they/them/their*). Even when news writers understand that, they sometimes drift from third person to first or second person (*you/your*) within a sentence. Such shifts jar readers and make it hard for them to follow, as in this example:

> When a person becomes serious about investing, you should start by determining how much you can afford to set aside each month.

Correcting the problem takes only a few words:

> When a person becomes serious about investing, he or she should start by determining how much can be set aside each month.

NOTES

1. "Seborrheic Keratosis," 20 July 2006, **www. emedicine. com/derm/topic397.htm.**

2. Transcript of episode 3 of "Do You Speak American?" PBS, 5 January 2005, **www.pbs.org/speak/ transcripts/ 3.html.**

3. William Rozeboom, "The Glory of Suboptimal Factor Rotation: Why local minima in analytic optimization of simple structure are more blessing than curse," Multivariate Behavioral Research, 27, no. 4 (1992), p. 587.

4. Irwin S. Kirsch, Ann Jungeblut, Lynn Jenkins and Andrew Kolstad, "Executive Summary of Adult Literacy in America: A First Look at the Results of the National Adult Literacy Survey," National Center for Education Statistics, 1993, **http://nces.ed.gov/naal/resources/ execsumm.asp.**

Broadcast News Style

While broadcast news stories follow many of the same style rules as print and online stories, they also differ in many areas. In this section, we'll look at the major differences in style.

Tense

In an attempt to make the broadcast news seem as up-to-the-minute as possible, news leads *use present tense* (print and online news primarily rely on past tense). The first lead below is fine for print and online use:

> A dramatic 19-hour hostage siege on board a bus in Athens ended without bloodshed yesterday after two Albanian gunmen freed the last of their 23 hostages and surrendered. (Agence France-Presse)

For broadcast, however, the lead needs to be rewritten in present tense:

> All 23 hostages are free and the gunmen who were holding them on a bus in Athens have surrendered without bloodshed.

Writing leads in the present tense means that few leads include the time element. When broadcast leads attempt to include the time element, they can become confusing and result in what's sometimes called "false present tense," as in this example:

> Local woman dies after leap from bridge yesterday.

While that sort of awkward construction turns up frequently in television screen crawls, it does not work for a broadcast lead. Instead, the lead should read:

> A local woman is dead from injuries she suffered after leaping off a bridge.

Numbers

The first rule of using numbers in broadcast writing is to use as few numbers as possible. Numbers are hard to grasp in print or online, and they are even more difficult to comprehend in a broadcast story. The following broadcast story is an example of number overload:

> There's been a new twist in the recount of the razor-thin Washington governor's race.
>
> Republican Dino Rossi won the November second election over Democrat Christine Gregoire by 261 votes in the first count and by 42 after a machine recount. As of Wednesday he had gained 81 votes in the hand recount for a margin of 123.

> Now, election officials in King County — the Seattle area — have decided to allow signature verification on 573 newly discovered absentee ballots. Still to be decided is the fate of 22 other newly discovered ballots.
>
> The decision to move forward with assessing the validity of the 573 is a victory for Democrats, because King County is a Democratic stronghold. (AP)

It's almost impossible to get all that when reading it, let alone when listening. Therefore, the best guideline is to write around numbers, using more easily digested words and phrases such as *most, a quarter,* and so on. If those don't work, a writer can round off numbers (both 988,765 and 1,059,281 can safely be referred to as "about a million") or use comparisons (a 1,250-square-mile area can be referred to as an area "about the size of Rhode Island").

When numbers are essential to a story, they generally follow the Associated Press Stylebook guidelines for print and online news. For example, numbers from one through nine are spelled out, with figures used for 10 and above. Things diverge, however, once numbers rise above 999. For broadcast stories, at that point it's back to spelling things out (one exception: years). The reason for that difference is that the person reading the news needs to be able to understand immediately what a figure is, without having to count the number of zeros. So broadcast writers must spell out *thousand, million, billion* and *trillion,* as in the following examples:

> The deal would cover more than nine thousand workers at the company's plants in four states.
>
> The stolen goods included nearly one million pieces of jewelry.

Practices vary as to whether numbers preceding *thousand, million, billion* and *trillion* should be figures or spelled out. At some news organizations they always are spelled out; at others, figures are used for 10 and above.

Newsrooms also vary on whether all parts of a large number should be hyphenated. Many insist on a hyphen:

> Congressional analysts said ten-million people could be affected by the change in the tax code.

In some newsrooms, writers go an extra step to distinguish millions from billions:

> Within a year, more than two (m)million copies of the recording had been sold worldwide.

Fractions present another problem for broadcast. Although AP allows print writers to use constructions such as 4¾, deciphering a number like that while delivering the news could throw off a news reader. So fractions are hyphenated and spelled out:

> Both sides had said they wanted to avoid a work stoppage after the bitter,
> six-and-a-half-year stalemate.

Decimals under 1.0 should be converted to fractions so they are easier to understand. Instead of "The cost of living is up 0.9 percent," it should be "The cost of living is up nine-tenths of a percent." Decimals above one (1.0) are spelled out, with hyphens and the word *point*:

> The employees will see raises of two-point-three percent next year.

Ages should be avoided unless absolutely necessary to a story. When they are needed, ages have to be written into the copy in a conversational manner and not just inserted next to a name, as they are in print and online stories (e.g., "Kinesha Williams, 28"):

> The 69-year-old nun was an assistant principal and the disciplinarian at Holy Spirit School.

Guidelines vary on how to handle ordinal numbers (numbers that rank or order things). Some newsrooms prefer *second,* others *2nd.*

Instead of putting a dollar sign before a figure, broadcast writers use the words dollar or dollars after a figure:

> The winners will receive a utility bill reimbursement of up to 500 dollars.

Initials and Acronyms

Only the most common abbreviations and acronyms are acceptable. In most cases, the rules require that a writer use the full name on first reference, then the initials or acronym on subsequent references. Abbreviations are written with hyphens between each letter (for example, N-B-A, F-C-C, T-V, L-A). Acronyms, which are intended to be pronounced as words, do not include hyphens (for example, OPEC, NASA).

Emphasis

When the person reading a story should emphasize a certain word or phrase, the writer should underline the words or type them in capital letters:

> A new analysis shows there is <u>no</u> evidence that oral contraceptives cut the risk of heart disease.

> A new analysis shows there is NO evidence that oral contraceptives cut the risk of heart disease. (AP)

Pauses

Dashes or ellipses tell the person reading the news to pause:

> Kerri Dunn — a psychology professor at Claremont McKenna College in Pomona — was convicted of attempted insurance fraud and lying to police after spray-painting her own car with racial slurs.

Abbreviations

Although AP style requires print and online writers to abbreviate addresses, months, states and titles in a variety of circumstances, abbreviations pose a real challenge for broadcast news readers. As a rule, they are not used.

Attribution

In print and online news writing, attribution — or source of information — usually follows the information. That's because the source is not considered as important as what was said. However, in broadcast writing it's important to let listeners or viewers know the source before a statement is read, so they can judge its trustworthiness for themselves:

> Revenues were on target in nearly every state, according to the National Association of State Budget Officers. *(print/online)*

> The National Association of State Budget Officers says revenues are on target in almost all states. *(broadcast)*

Hyphenation

Words never should break between lines of copy. A news reader will likely stumble when hitting a construction such as this:

> Rescue crews are using construction equipment to find the body of a work-
> er who was trapped when rocks collapsed on him.

Personalization

Print news rarely addresses the audience directly. But such personalization is a key feature of broadcast news. In fact, one of the best ways to get the attention of audience members is by finding an aspect of a story that will directly affect them and focusing on it right from the start of the story:

> If you're thinking about taking an inexpensive road trip this summer, think again.

> You could end up paying much more for your next car if a bill in the state legislature passes.

Pronunciations

Writers should not leave anything to chance when it comes to the pronunciation of names, places and unfamiliar words. Instead, they should include a pronunciation guide immediately following any words that might trip up the person reading the news. Doing so requires paying attention to things that would not be problematic in print. For instance, rock star David Bowie's last name is pronounced BOH-ee; the similarly spelled name of a town in Maryland is pronounced BOO-ee. Such constructions are called *pronouncers*.

The Associated Press offers a list of basic sounds so that writers can standardize pronouncers:

Vowels	Consonants
a – bat, apple	g – got, beg
ah – father, arm	j – job, gem
aw – raw, board	k – keep, cap
ay – fate, ace	ch – chair, butcher
e, eh – bed	sh – shut, fashion
ee – feel, tea	zh – vision, mirage
y, eye – ice, time, guide	th – thin, math
i, ih – pin, middle	kh – guttural "k"
oh – go, oval	s – see
oo – food, two	y – yes
ow – scout, crowd	z – zoom
oy – boy, join	
u – curl, foot	
uh – puff	
yoo – fume, few	

A pronouncer should appear in parentheses after the word it is used for, and the stressed syllable should be printed in all capital letters, such as in the following example:

> The tank has been leaking a chemical called acetic (a-SEE-tic) acid for two days.

One great resource for broadcast journalists who work with foreign names and places is the Voice of America online pronunciation guide at http://names.voa. gov/. Developed primarily for VOA broadcasters, the searchable guide is available to anyone who's curious about the correct pronunciations of names in the news.

Quotations

Direct quotes rarely turn up in broadcast writing, for two reasons. First is that a broadcast news writer generally can say the same thing more clearly and with fewer words. Second is that it's hard to indicate to the audience when a quote begins and ends. If a quote proves too good to pass up, the rules for indicating it's a quote vary from newsroom to newsroom. Many newsrooms follow print and online practices, putting quote marks around the phrase so that the news reader will know it's a quote and thus be able to use voice inflection to indicate that:

> Defense attorneys said the tactic was "designed to shock and intimidate the defendant, his family and staff."

Other news operations prefer that writers avoid quote marks and instead indicate quoted material by setting it off with a pause (and *not* by adding "quote...unquote"):

> His attorney said the tactic was...designed to shock and intimidate the defendant, his family and staff.

Titles

Just as attribution should precede statements, titles should precede the names of those who hold the title. This practice is the opposite of how titles are usually handled in print and online:

> Sen. Barbara A. Mikulski, D-Md. *(print/online)*
>
> Maryland Senator Barbara A. Mikulski *(broadcast)*

As was noted previously, abbreviations used in print and online stories are not used for broadcast writing.

For longer titles, paraphrasing usually makes things easier to follow. For example, "Jordanian Secretary General of Ministry of Public Works and Housing Maan Jaradat" would typically be rewritten as "a top Jordanian public works official."

Associated Press Style

Nearly every news organization relies on The Associated Press Stylebook to make sure that copy is consistently prepared. A story that refers to 7-Eleven in one paragraph and Seven-11 in another, or one that refers to the National Organization of Women instead of the National Organization for Women makes it seem as though the news organization cannot get even the basics correct and seriously undermines the organization's credibility.

If you haven't worked with The Associated Press Stylebook before, it might seem to be quite a challenge to learn, with its more than 400 pages packed full of entries of all sorts: preferred spellings, definitions and background information. To be honest, mastering The Associated Press Stylebook does take work, especially because the editors periodically make major changes. Fortunately, a few tips and a simple "cheat sheet" of the most common stylebook rules will put you well on your way to becoming a style expert.

Let's begin with the tips:

1. *Forget what you think you know.* Although AP style is ubiquitous in the world of news (and public relations because PR practitioners have to prepare copy for news people to use), it has no clout outside that area. Advertising agencies, law firms, scholars, tech companies and many others either have their own style guides or just make things up as they go along. Just because you've seen Elvis Presley commonly referred to as "the King of Rock and Roll" does not mean that's how AP would have you write it: "the king of rock 'n' roll."
2. *Zero in on the question at hand.* The best way to waste time is by meandering through the stylebook. Instead, you should always start with the word, phrase or topic for which you need guidance. Don't know whether United Nations should be abbreviated? Flip open the stylebook (or, if you're lucky enough to have access to it, launch the electronic version) and check the *United Nations* entry and there's your answer. If you can't find an answer at the most logical place, try to think of another entry that might provide an answer; in this case, a logical next stop should be *Abbreviations and Acronyms*.
3. *Use the stylebook as your primary dictionary.* When you are unsure of the proper spelling of a word, check the stylebook first. While it generally accepts the first spelling listed in Webster's New World Dictionary, the stylebook sometimes prefers an alternate spelling.
4. *Don't jump to conclusions.* While most stylebook entries offer simple and clear guidance, in some cases they include exceptions and even exceptions to the exceptions. If you're going to go to the trouble of looking something up in the stylebook, make sure you don't miss the most important part of the entry. (And be sure to look in the separate Business and Sports sections for information not contained in the main section.)

The next step in mastering AP style is learning the rules that cover the vast majority of questions you'll have. Memorize these basic guidelines, and you'll only need to crack open your stylebook for more esoteric questions. Note that some of these rules apply only to print and online writing. Be sure to check Appendix B when writing for audio and video stories.

Abbreviations and Acronyms

- As a general rule, use only commonly recognized abbreviations. The most common, such as NASA, FBI and CIA, can be used on all references. Less well-known but still common ones such as OSHA and NATO can be used after you spell out the full name on first mention. In most cases, however, the stylebook suggests using a generic reference such as *the agency* or *the alliance* for all references after the first.
- Don't put unfamiliar abbreviations in parentheses after the first reference (for example, "The American Copy Editors Society (ACES) . . .") Instead either repeat the full name on subsequent references or use a generic reference, such as *the society.*
- Use an apostrophe and spell out academic degrees: "She holds a bachelor's degree." Use abbreviations for degrees only when you need to include a list of credentials after a name; set them off with commas: "Peter White, LL.D., Ph.D., was the keynote speaker."
- Abbreviate junior or senior directly after a name, with no a comma to set it off: *Justin Wilson Jr.*
- Spell out the names of all states when used alone: "He lives in Montana." Abbreviate state names of seven or more letters when used with a city name, with commas before and after the abbreviation: "Pittsburgh, Pa., is a great weekend getaway spot for people who live in Youngstown, Ohio." You'll find the list of acceptable abbreviations under *State Names* in the stylebook.
- Be sure to use the stylebook abbreviations and *not* the U.S. Postal Service abbreviations for states *unless* you are providing a full address including ZIP code: "Send contributions to Relief Fund, Box. 185, Pasadena, CA 91030."
- Spell out the name of a month when it is used without a specific date: "August is too hot for a visit to Florida." Abbreviate months with six or more letters if they are used with a specific date: *Sept. 28.* Always spell out those with five or fewer letters: *May 15.* See the list of preferred abbreviations under *Months* in the stylebook.
- Spell out titles used alone: "She was the first female senator from her state." Abbreviate and capitalize most titles when they are used directly before a name: "Sen. Boxer posed hard questions for Rice." To determine if a title is abbreviated, look for an entry for it in the stylebook or check the listing under *Titles.*
- Spell out titles with names used in direct quotes with the exception of Dr., Mr. and Mrs.: "Governor Pawlenty is obviously no Jesse Ventura," she said.
- Spell out all generic parts of street names (avenue, north, road) when no specific address is given: "The festival will be held on South Charles Street." When a number is used, abbreviate avenue (Ave.), boulevard (Blvd.), street (St.) and directional parts of street names: "The suspect was identified as Michael Shawn of 1512 N. Mission St."
- In writing news stories, never abbreviate:

  The days of the week.

  Percent as %.

  Cents as ¢.

  And as & unless it is an official part of a name.

  Christmas as Xmas.

Capitalization

The AP Stylebook uses what's known as downstyle; that is, words are lowercased unless a rule says to capitalize them. If you can't find a rule for capitalizing a word in the stylebook, use it in lowercase. Most of the capitalization rules should be familiar to you.

- Capitalize common nouns such as *party*, *river* and *street* when they are part of a proper name for place, person or thing: the Libertarian Party, the Ohio River. But lowercase these common nouns when they stand alone or in subsequent references: "The party did not have a candidate for president," "She nearly drowned in the river." Lowercase all plural uses of common nouns: the Libertarian and Green parties, the Monongahela and Ohio rivers.
- Lowercase the names of the seasons unless they are used in a proper name: the Summer Olympics.
- Lowercase the word *room* except when used with the number of the room or when part of the name of a specially designated room: *Room 315, the Lincoln Room.*
- Lowercase directional indicators except when they refer to specific geographic regions or popularized names for those regions: *the Northeast; the Midwest.*
- Lowercase formal titles that appear on their own or follow a name (in the latter case, they should be set off by commas). Capitalize formal titles that come directly before a name: "The students were delighted when they heard they would meet President Bush." Never capitalize job descriptions: *shortstop, police officer, attorney* and so on.

Numerals

The AP Stylebook entry for numerals is deceptively short. A close look reveals that there are plenty of rules hiding among the many cross-references. The most common rules are:

- In general, spell out numbers one through nine and use figures for numbers 10 on up. There are many cases in which figures are always used, however. Most, but not all, involve units of measurement. Common exceptions include:

  Addresses: 7 Park Place.

  Ages, even for inanimate objects: The 4-year-old car.

  Cents: 8 cents.

  Dollars: $3. Notice that AP style does not include a period and two zeroes when referring to an even dollar figure.

  Dates: March 4. Notice that dates take cardinal numbers, not ordinal numbers (don't use 4th).

  Dimensions: 5 foot 2, 5-by-9 cell.

  Highways: Route 7.

  Millions, billions: 6 billion people.

  Percentages: 1 percent. Notice that percent is one word.

  Speed: 8 mph.

  Temperatures: 2 degrees.

  Times: 4 p.m. Notice that AP style does not include a colon and two zeroes when referring to an even hour.

- Spell out numbers used at the beginning of a sentence: "Ten thousand people marched on the capital." Exception: Never spell out years: "1999 was a terrible year for technology companies."
- Use commas to set off each group of three digits in numerals higher than 999 (except for years and addresses): *12,650.*
- Use decimals (up to two places) for amounts in the millions and billions that do not require a precise figure: *$3.74 billion.*
- Add an *s* but no apostrophe to a number to make it plural: "She kept rolling 7s." The same rule applies to decades: the 1980s. Use an apostrophe on a decade only if cutting off the initial figures: the '80s.

Punctuation and Miscellaneous

For the most part, AP style follows the same rules of punctuation as you were taught in grade school. There are some important exceptions, however:

- Don't use a comma before a conjunction in a simple series. A simple series is defined as one in which no elements contain the words *and* or *or*: "The dinner choices were chicken, cod or beef." Use a comma for series that include elements containing *and* or *or*: "The menu offered a choice of bacon and eggs, pancakes, or waffles."
- Use a semicolon to clarify a series that includes a number of commas. Include a semicolon before the conjunction: *Parts for the carrier are made in Tampa, Fla.; Austin, Texas; and Baton Rouge, La.*

Other Common Stylebook Rules

- Use a person's full name on first reference. On subsequent references, use only his or her last name with no title. Second and following references to a married couple should refer to them as Mr. and Mrs.: "Mr. and Mrs. Oakes will honeymoon in Las Vegas." In stories in which two people share the last name, use full names on each reference.
- Time should be expressed as a figure followed by *a.m.* or *p.m.*: 8:33 *p.m.* You do not have to add other words (*night, morning,* and so on) to distinguish between day and night. Use *noon* or *midnight* rather than 12 p.m. or 12 a.m.
- Use hyphens to link all the words in a compound adjective: "The five-volume report called for cleaning up the area over a 10-year period." Do not use a hyphen if the construction includes *very* or an adverb ending in *–ly*: *a very big project, barely legal procedures.*
- To form a plural of a single letter, use *s* and an apostrophe: "All the B's lined up to the right." To form a plural of multiple letters, add *s* with no apostrophe: "She mastered her ABCs in little time."
- Titles of books, movies, recordings, television shows and similar works are set off in quotation marks, with all principal words capitalized: "Harry Potter and the Deathly Hallows," "Letters from Iwo Jima," "Memory Almost Full," "Grey's Anatomy." Titles of magazines, newspapers and reference works get no special treatment: Newsweek, The Boston Globe, The Associated Press Stylebook.
- According to AP, it's Web site and ZIP code.

Index

Note: Page numbers in **bold** indicate definitions.

Credits